A Socialist Review

A
Socialist
Review

*Edited by Lindsey German
and Rob Hoveman*

BOOKMARKS

London, Chicago and Sydney

A Socialist Review –Edited by Lindsey German and Rob Hoveman
First published 1998
Bookmarks Publications Ltd, c/o 1 Bloomsbury Street, London WC1B 3QE, England
Bookmarks, PO Box 16085, Chicago, Illinois 60616, USA
Bookmarks, PO Box A338, Sydney South, NSW 2000, Australia
Copyright © Bookmarks Publications Ltd

ISBN 1 898876 32 0

Printed by BPC Wheatons Ltd
Cover by Sherborne Design

Bookmarks Publications Ltd is linked to an international grouping of socialist organisations:
Australia: International Socialist Organisation, PO Box A338, Sydney South, NSW 2000
Britain: Socialist Workers Party, PO Box 82, London E3 3LH
Canada: International Socialists, PO Box 339, Station E, Toronto, Ontario M6H 4E3
Cyprus: Ergatiki Demokratia, PO Box 7280, Nicosia
Czech Republic: Socialisticka Solidarita, PO Box 42, Praha 42, 140 02
Denmark: Internationale Socialister, Postboks 642, 2200 København N
Greece: Sosialistiko Ergatiko Komma, c/o Workers Solidarity, PO Box 8161, Athens 100 10
Holland: Internationale Socialisten, PO Box 92025, 1090AA Amsterdam
Ireland: Socialist Workers Party, PO Box 1648, Dublin 8
New Zealand: Socialist Workers Organisation, PO Box 8851, Auckland
Norway: Internasjonale Socialisterr, Postboks 5370, Majorstua, 0304 Oslo 3
Poland: Solidarność Socjalistyczna, PO Box 12, 01-900 Warszawa 118
South Africa: Socialist Workers Organisation, PO Box 18530, Hillbrow 2038, Johannesburg
Spain: Socialismo Internacional, Apartado 563, 08080, Barcelona
United States: International Socialist Organization, PO Box 16085, Chicago, Illinois 60616
Zimbabwe: International Socialist Organisation, PO Box 6758, Harare

Contents

Acknowledgements

The articles collected in this book are only a small selection of those published in *Socialist Review* over the past two decades. Thanks are due to all those who have contributed to helping produce the magazine over that period. Chris Harman, Peter Morgan, Judith Orr and John Rees helped to read and select articles and in the production of the book.

Socialist Review is the monthly magazine of the Socialist Workers Party. Copies are available from PO Box 82, London E3 3LH.

Introduction

Lindsey German

The 1990s have seen widespread rejection of the 1980s slogan, 'Greed is good.' There has been a rebirth of socialist ideas especially among a new generation of working people untouched by direct experience of the defeats of the 1980s. In France huge industrial struggles rocked the government and the ruling class at the end of 1995, resulting in a further wave of industrial struggles, a growing movement against the fascist Jean-Marie Le Pen and the surprise election of a socialist government in the summer of 1997. In the US, where workers' wages have been pushed down in real terms over the past 20 years and where workers have sustained repeated attacks on union organisation and living conditions, there are signs of a turn round. The victorious strike at UPS in the summer of 1997 has given a new confidence to US workers to organise and to look to left wing ideas. In Britain the May 1997 landslide victory of Labour after 18 years of Tory rule demonstrated a move to the left in popular consciousness which many had denied could ever recur.

Everywhere in the advanced capitalist countries the picture is of workers recovering from the worst of the 1980s and beginning to develop the confidence to build independent organisation once again. However, there is nothing automatic about ideas of solidarity and collectivity leading to successful struggles or taking root among large numbers of workers. That depends on the conscious activity of socialists, organised to fight for their ideas.

For socialist ideas are opposed every step of the way. Tony Blair's government tells us repeatedly that it is not realistic to talk of full employment, decent welfare payments or the abolition of poverty. Everything, they say, must be left to the whims of the market. Only by allowing the market full rein can sufficient wealth be created to allow any of these things to happen.

So while socialist ideas have a much bigger audience today, they cannot hold their ground without a fight—an ideological fight against those who tell us there is no alternative to the market. This is the importance of *Socialist Review*. Published every month, it attempts to give a voice for socialist politics and to create a framework for helping to build a fightback. As the monthly magazine of the Socialist Workers Party, the *Review* is dedicated not just to interpreting the world but to changing it.

Socialist Review has been in existence for nearly 20 years. The ideas of socialism have taken a battering over that time. The Thatcherite ideology which so dominated the 1980s led to the worship of the market in every area of life. Everything private and individual was feted as good, everything in the public sector or which involved a degree of collectivity was bad. Even worse, social inequality became greater and the gap between rich and poor widened dramatically, so there developed ideas which blamed the poor for their misfortunes and praised the rich for their enterprise.

On an international scale, the collapse of the Berlin Wall and the demise of the former 'Communist' bloc seemed to confirm that we were experiencing, in the words of the former US State Department adviser Francis Fukuyama, the 'end of history'. The future would be one where a triumphant capitalism reigned supreme—all its contradictions having been resolved. Those left behind in this exciting new world were deemed an 'underclass' to be pitied or more likely pressured into working for low wages or living on increasingly inadequate benefits.

For it was assumed that—along with the end of socialism—the era of welfare, full employment and state intervention had also drawn to a close. No longer could future generations expect the same living conditions that their parents had come to expect since 1945. Instead their lives would have to be more like previous generations of workers: dominated by unstable or casual employment with no safety net provided by wider society for those who grew old or were sick.

Even in the worst of times, however, these ideas did not go unchallenged. Those of us organised in the Socialist Workers Party were able to put forward arguments which cut against the grain and found an audience. This was true even when the audience was very small—for example, at the time of the Falklands War in 1982. *Socialist Review* has been an invaluable banner around which the left could rally.

Today that audience is incomparably larger and more confident in its ideas. But the battles ahead will demand even greater clarity of ideas. We need to understand the past in order to change the future;

we need an analysis which explains where capitalism is going and what the limits of reformism are today.

This collection is designed to contribute to that process. We have gathered together a small selection of some of the best articles published since the *Review* first appeared in 1978. The bias of the collection is towards historical and theoretical articles rather than month by month analysis or international issues. Hopefully these articles will introduce a new generation to socialist ideas and traditions which can help influence the coming struggles.

Revolution and socialism

Chapter 1

Fifty five years a revolutionary

Interview with Tony Cliff

What made you become a revolutionary in the first place?

I became a socialist and thought of myself as a Marxist in 1932. I read two books that I remember very well. One was the *Communist Manifesto*; the other was a short edition of the three volumes of Marx's *Capital*. They made me think of myself as a communist.

But my real motivation was the fact that I was born into a Zionist family. We were a middle class family with a relatively good standard of living, especially compared to the Arab neighbours. The shock of seeing Arab kids without shoes—and my parents took it for granted that Arab kids would be without shoes—while I never had to suffer in this way, was the first thing that really led me to those ideas. I was of course a Stalinist at the time although I didn't really know it.

Shortly after that came a very important turning point: the victory of Hitler in Germany at the beginning of 1933. This affected the rest of my life. The victory of Hitler was as important historically for the counter-revolution as the victory of October in 1917 was for the revolution.

The impact was absolutely massive. Socialists today haven't a clue what it was like. Stalin led to the policy of social fascism—I didn't know this at the time, but read Trotsky on it later—and this helped lead to the victory of Hitler. Stalinism internationally was

First published July 1987

strengthened by the defeat of the German working class. After Hitler the working class internationally felt very much dependent on Stalin. It was like a religion for many workers—the heart of a heartless world, the only thing they could look to.

A friend of mine years later got a pair of boots from Russia and he kissed the boots. That summed it up. On the one hand, there was Hitler with millions of soldiers, on the other, there was Stalin with millions of soldiers. It was a massive pull.

This was the fundamental problem for Trotskyists. Whatever Trotsky's ideas—whether they were good or bad—their appeal was very, very small. I remember the shock in 1934 or 1935 when I met a German Trotskyist who was a refugee in Palestine. I asked him how many Trotskyists there were in Germany. He replied that on the eve of Hitler's victory there were 100.

Trotsky's writings on Germany are probably the best things he has ever written—they're sharp, hard and clear, magnificent—but they weren't translated into practice. If he'd had an organisation of say, 10,000 in Germany then the 10,000 would probably have been able to get a united front—not with the SPD which had eight million supporters or the Communist Party which had six million supporters—but with 60,000 Social Democrats or 20,000 Communist supporters. If you can then mobilise, say, 100,000 you can prove in practice that the idea of the united front is meaningful.

The trouble is with 100, it may be good propaganda, concrete propaganda, but you can't prove that the ideas are correct. When I became a Trotskyist it was absolutely painful because the attraction of Stalin was massive. Practically everybody supported the Moscow trials.

All this shaped my political development. There was no alternative but to accept the need to build the organisation from square one—what Trotsky called the primitive accumulation of cadres.

What was it specifically though that made you a Trotskyist and made you break from Stalinism? What made you opt for the Fourth International?

The victory of Hitler made me open my eyes to what was happening in the world. The first article I wrote on international politics was on the seventh congress of the Communist International. I denounced the popular front. I'm ready to bet that my criticism in the article was ultra-left. I'm not trying to say it was perfect—far from it. But it was a gut reaction against the idea of the popular front.

I had read Trotsky's *History of the Russian Revolution* and his autobiography. In 1934 or 1935 I also read Trotsky on Germany. I read
quite a few other things as well.

Then once I was a Trotskyist we had the problem of the primitive
accumulation of cadres. In Palestine this was even more difficult. I
was a semi-Zionist until 1936 or 1937, perhaps even later. I didn't
think of myself as a Zionist. I was for defending the Arabs, and anti-
Zionist. But I used to argue that poor Jewish refugees should be allowed
to come to Palestine, that they shouldn't be excluded. That was an un-
justified compromise, when you look back at it.

One of the difficulties is that you have to start practically on your
own. It's not like a country like Britain, which has a tradition of 100
years of the Marxist movement, whatever its faults. In Palestine there
was nothing like that. It was also much more complicated, with the
divisions between Jews and Arabs. It was further complicated because
many of the Jews who were Zionists thought of themselves as socialists. When Lenin died, Ben Gurion called for a one day strike in
honour of Lenin.

For all these reasons, building cadres meant having to build cadres
among Arabs. This was extremely difficult. In Britain whether you
are a Jew or a gentile doesn't make much difference. You live in the
same neighbourhood, speak the same language and your kids go to
the same schools. In Palestine it was incomparably more difficult. The
first time I lived in the same house as a Palestinian Arab wasn't until
I was in Dublin in 1947. The languages are different. So building
cadres was a really tough proposition.

I worked for nearly ten years to build the organisation. When I
left Palestine in 1946 we had around 30 Jews and seven Arabs. Because it was very tough you had a choice: you either gave it up or
persevered. There are no easy solutions. At the same time I learnt
a huge amount. It wasn't a question of me teaching them, but of
them teaching me.

I knew very little about the Arabs. One man, a very good intellectual called Jabra Nicola, was the editor of the Communist Party's
legal paper—the CP was illegal but they had a legal paper. He worked
nights and I spent months discussing with him during the day. We
would talk for five or six hours, on and on, until after a couple of
months I won him to Trotskyism. His living conditions were out of this
world, they were so harsh. He lived in a room—a wooden hut—with
his wife, his daughter, his sister, her eldest daughter and his mother who
was dying of cancer and in terrible pain.

Under those conditions he had to write and he was a very good worker intellectual. He shaped my attitude because it's not a question of the Marxists teaching the workers; the workers have to teach the Marxists. He taught me a lot about the Arab CP, the Syrian CP, the whole of the Middle East.

How did the conditions of repression which existed at the time in Palestine affect how you operated?

The difficulty we faced was not really the repression. A number of us were imprisoned, but that wasn't the real problem. The real difficulty was trying to get roots among workers. We were illegal, of course. I was arrested when the war broke out, for issuing a leaflet against the war. It said our enemy is not the aggressor of 1939 but the aggressor of 1917. It meant that the enemy was not the Germans, but the British who went into Palestine in 1917.

It was really a very good leaflet against the imperialist war. To my sorrow, the original in my handwriting was left in my room even though I'd asked my brother to clean it out and I was arrested.

What building a group really meant was doing a lot of research on the Middle East. We wrote some good things. In 1935 I wrote *The Agrarian Problem of Egypt* and I would be proud if I wrote it now. We really worked at trying to understand the problems. We didn't just put forward slogans or say that Trotsky could give us all the answers. We said we are Marxists, Marxism is a guide to action so we have to understand the local situation.

During the whole of that period from the victory of Hitler to the end of the war I was always convinced that Trotsky was absolutely right, that Stalinism had no future, that reformism had no future, that our cadres are stronger than the revolutionaries were at the end of the First World War.

In the middle of the war was the death of Trotsky. It was really a terrible shock. Every week I used to get the American *Militant* to read Trotsky's articles. I also got the *New International* from the US. It was absolute joy. It meant you knew there was somewhere you could get these magnificent articles.

When you read them today in volumes, I don't believe you appreciate them the same. When you are somewhere in a backward country and really isolated, you suddenly have a source of ideas. And they weren't just general ideas—they were always on the dot. Trotsky is the most concrete writer, which is why I never understood how people could describe him as fatalistic. His death was shocking. I was a grown man but I was nearly in tears. It was terrifying—one of the worst events.

What made you leave Palestine and come to Europe?

The end of the war came. The reason I decided to leave Palestine was that I came to the conclusion that revolutionary activity in the Middle East had to be from a base in Egypt. That is the centre of the Arab working class. The relation of forces between the Zionists and the Arab Palestinians means that the Arabs can never win on their own. But going to Egypt for me was simply not on physically. There was no way I could live there. I tried to go to a number of countries—the US, France—but I got admitted to Britain as a visitor.

One reason I wanted to come to Europe was to write a book on Eastern Europe. It was clear to me that somehow things weren't right with the theory. There were six extra countries under Stalinist rule. Trotsky had said that the Stalinist bureaucracy was counter-revolutionary, and the book was to prove that Trotsky was right— the theory of the degenerated workers' state as applied to Eastern Europe.

I had the shock of my life when I met Mandel in Paris and got the Fourth International documents. They characterised Russia as a degenerated workers' state, while Eastern Europe was capitalist. This just didn't fit. So I set out to prove that they were all degenerated workers' states. There were obviously similarities—the same army in control, the same extension of the economy.

I worked on the book for about six months to prove Trotsky right. My aim wasn't to produce something new. But for a month or two I was really worried. Then I came to the conclusion there was something wrong with the theory. Because if they are workers' states without a revolutionary party, without smashing the state machine, without the self activity of the working class, where does Marxism fit in? That's how I came to the theory of state capitalism.

Another thing hit me between the eyes at the time. The standard of living for workers in Britain was high. When I first visited a worker's house—just an ordinary house—I asked his job and he was an engineer. My English wasn't very good so I thought he meant an engineer with a degree. But he was a semi-skilled engineering worker. It was a complete shock. Children were better off than in the 1930s. The only time I saw children without shoes in Europe was in Dublin. Children didn't get rickets any more. This helped me to realise that the final crisis wasn't around the corner.

So how did your theories develop?

The major difficulty always for revolutionaries is not finding the solution to a problem, but asking the right question. The RCP (the Fourth International in Britain) did not do so. They wrote, for example, that anyone who believes that there will be only three million unemployed in the immediate future is suffering from reformist delusions. They also wrote, in November 1945, that the Attlee government is like the Kerensky government in Russia in 1917—except that it won't survive as long. This was really stupid.

It happened because they wouldn't look at things as they really were. Of course they said they did in the abstract. It's easy to talk about the ability to face reality, the necessity to state things as they are, or quote Lenin or Marx saying that communists never tell lies to the class. It's very different in concrete situations. I never found it too difficult because I'm not able to tell myself lies. So I couldn't say workers are suffering terribly when I could see the opposite.

People quote Lenin as saying reform is a by-product of revolutionary struggle, but it isn't always like that. Many reforms come without revolutionary struggle. Some come gradually. And the reforms after the war were absolutely massive. So we faced a problem. There were those who believed the 30s would continue—unemployment would go up. And then there were people like G D H Cole or John Strachey who thought in the 30s everything would get worse and worse. By the 50s they were saying exactly the opposite—capitalism's getting nicer and nicer, all its problems can be reformed. Capitalism is more rational.

So the choice was either to accept that analysis—and that goes against the grain of Marxism—to suggest that the system after Hiroshima and Nagasaki was suddenly more rational. The other alternative was to deny that any reforms had actually taken place. The one is dogmatic. The other is opportunist.

The basis of the theory of the permanent arms economy was to say that capitalism is basically as irrational as ever, as wasteful as ever, but at the same time it is prosperous. The boom was on the cone of a bomb. My article 'Permanent War Economy' in *Socialist Review* in 1957 wasn't a particularly good article, but it posed the question correctly. That was the important thing.

What impact did these theories have on the RCP?

I was in Britain from September 1946 to September 1947. Then I had to leave. In that year I belonged to the RCP. I used to go to the Political Bureau meetings although I didn't have a vote. They accepted there was a boom. All of us thought it was temporary because of reconstruction after the war. My article 'All that Glitters is not Gold' simply assumes this. It doesn't talk about the arms economy at all. So I worked quite well with those comrades.

But they weren't clear at all. They were playing with ideas. The tragedy was when in 1948 the Stalinists took over completely in Czechoslovakia, the *Socialist Appeal* had the headline saying that the proletariat was victorious and the bourgeoisie defeated.

When I saw the headline, I knew they were finished. The RCP leadership went all over the place. Jock Haston, who was by far the most able, moved towards Stalinism. Then he supported the Americans during the Korean War. He attacked Nye Bevan for opposing German rearmament. He finished as education officer for Frank Chapple's union. The London industrial organiser joined the CP. They went to pieces because their perspective didn't fit.

One of their real tragedies was that they didn't have a sense of reality about themselves. During the last stages of the war they were cutting with the grain. There were lots of strikes which the CP at the time opposed. The RCP supported the strikes. The RCP was very active and its name was well known. The total organisation was tiny—400 people—but its influence appeared much greater. They were accused of leading the Barrow-in-Furness strike of 20,000 engineers. This was also true of the apprentices' strike in 1944, and the miners' strike.

In 1947 things changed radically. Capitalism was expanding, so Labourism had quite a good base. And the Communist Party turned to supporting strikes. They had 40,000 members. The RCP could look influential when the CP opposed strikes. Once the CP's 40,000 were supporting strikes the RCP's 400 became totally marginalised.

Because I sat on the Political Bureau of the RCP I knew how small it was. There were seven members in Sheffield, a dozen in Liverpool. They were a tiny organisation. When they spoke about preparing for power it was nonsense. They suddenly found themselves without any wind.

We were a tiny little group inside the RCP. In 1950 when we broke we had at most 40 at our meeting when we were expelled. At the second meeting we had only eight. It was extremely tough. It was extremely difficult to build, but there was no alternative.

What was the attitude of the Trotskyists at the time to working within the Labour Party?

The RCP majority at that time was against joining the Labour Party. The minority around Gerry Healy was in favour of joining. His perspective was that there would be mass radicalisation, and polarisation within the Labour Party, which would provide opportunities for revolutionaries to work in.

We couldn't accept this because rather than a capitalist crisis there was expanding capitalism. Therefore we were against joining the Labour Party on such assumptions.

The International Secretariat of the Fourth International supported Gerry Healy, which created demoralisation in the RCP. In such circumstances the majority of people against entering decided they had no alternative but to enter.

We agreed (actually I was in Ireland at the time). I never believed that a small group of eight, ten or even 50 people could survive by talking to themselves. It was necessary to have regular political discussion with people outside the group, and the only place you could do so at that time was the Labour Party.

The real danger we faced was that of becoming a sect. The problem was, how do you establish a Marxist group in Britain that is not a sect? The most important thing was to be realistic and not have pretensions.

To give you an example, during the Hungarian Revolution of 1956 there was a meeting to which six groups sent a delegation to discuss the exciting events in Hungary.

A resolution was moved to send arms to Hungary. Five voted for— we voted against on the basis we had no arms to send them. They also moved that we should free Imre Nagy from prison. If they had said protest about his imprisonment of course we would have supported them, but how were we supposed to free him?

After Hungary the *New Left Review* was founded. Eight hundred to 1,000 people used to meet regularly. They used to talk about the working class, and they called a trade union conference. Only seven turned up, four of us and three others.

When it came to the big things like listening to Isaac Deutscher they could draw 1,000 people, but they didn't relate to workers in the real world.

How did your group relate to workers?

A tiny group like ours couldn't issue factory leaflets. We didn't even report on strikes unless we had a member involved. For instance we had a couple of articles on ENV in our monthly paper *Socialist Review* because we had a comrade in the factory. Again we had an article on a strike by the workers in the Co-op because we had a member working for them.

It would have been pretentious to have had general coverage, and wouldn't have related to the people we could talk to. You have to be concrete and ask, what exactly are the people we can talk to talking about?

In all honesty therefore we were writing about those issues that we ourselves were interested in. We wrote about the roots of reformism, the permanent arms economy, the crisis of Stalinism. We painted a much more general picture. We were not even operating at the level of concrete propaganda. All this was abstract propaganda. There is no alternative when you are speaking to a few dozen people.

At the same time, though, we tried to relate to anything that moved. So for example we went to all the meetings of the New Left Review Club. When some of them wanted to form a forum with ex Communist Party members, we were part of it. Nothing really came of it but we perhaps influenced a few individuals.

We recruited individuals either directly or indirectly from such activities. If we had sat at home they would never have heard our ideas.

Can you describe more generally what the general situation was like for the left in the 1950s? And why did you write the book on Rosa Luxemburg?

On the one hand there was the Labour Party that had the mass support of workers, and because of the Cold War there was another pole of attraction, the Communist Party.

The left of the Labour Party was very much influenced by supporters of the Communist Party. When people like Nye Bevan began to speak of a third force, what they were really talking about was a bridge. Their position was not 'Neither Washington nor Moscow'; on the contrary, it was both Washington and Moscow.

There were a massive number of strikes but they were tiny. There was no generalisation because there was no confrontation with the state. There was no confrontation through incomes policy or the Industrial Relations Act or things like that. It was simply the workers versus the employers. Most strikes ended after a day or two. So the possibility of intervention was slim. The possibility of generalisation was as well. I remember one worker said to me, 'All right, you know a lot; but how much money have you in your pocket?' That was a very good answer.

There was very little framework for our ideas. In 1956 the CP lost 10,000 members over the Russian invasion of Hungary. Their ideas fitted with the Deutscher phenomenon—the idea of reforming Russia. And they fitted with Gerry Healy's ideas that Russia was a workers' state, and that revolution was around the corner. The people who had left the CP were very impatient, and Healy built the Socialist Labour League (SLL) on their impatience. We didn't have the same sort of pull.

The Socialist Labour League rank and file conference in 1958 was astonishing. They had recruited a couple of hundred very good comrades from the CP. They were quite prominent industrially, with four rank and file papers. They also recruited some very good intellectuals.

But they called for a flying picket organised by them, so every time there was a strike they would be there. The idea was there would be a snowball effect. It led to massive substitutionism. People thought there were short cuts. The pressure at the time for short cuts was immense. In 1958 our group decided to join the SLL. Myself, Jean Tait and Chanie Rosenberg opposed it. The majority supported it. Before long luckily they changed their minds. But the reason was people were impressed by the SLL. Their conference attracted 1,000 in 1958, with Brian Behan speaking who had been on the CP executive. The pull was very great.

I used to joke that to lead the revolution in Britain we needed a party of say half a million. So we needed to recruit 499,950 members. Healy was in a much better position. He only had to get 499,700.

The more isolated you are the more you believe that the slogan does the trick—that's really the pull towards substitutionism. If you don't intend doing anything, the higher the slogan the better. That was the problem with the SLL.

Trotsky wrote in the 1930s, 'The party is the programme.' I can understand why—his back was to the wall. But the truth is the party is not the programme. The party is people with a programme.

The book on Rosa Luxemburg was written mainly against this idea of substitutionism. It tried to rescue her ideas about the self activity of the working class.

The first big breakthrough for the Socialist Review Group came with the growth of CND. Can you explain how it happened?

CND rose, and we were active in it. By that, I mean we went on CND marches. In 1958 there were only 50 of us, so there was no question of us being in the committees.

We used to march with a banner that called for industrial action against the bomb. We put the emphasis on working class struggle to get rid of the bomb.

We could not mobilise workers to do so, but maybe we could influence a couple of hundred people who'd seen our banner.

There was a lot of discussion about the bomb, and we were known as the people who were anti-bomb on principle. Others favoured the workers' bomb, the idea of workers' states having a bomb.

But we said we are not pacifists. The gun can distinguish between different people and is therefore progressive or reactionary depending who is holding it, but the bomb does not distinguish. It is a weapon of genocide. You cannot have progressive racism, and you cannot have progressive genocide.

The Labour Party Young Socialists were affected very much by CND. The Young Socialists had perhaps 40,000 members and it was very lively. The main issue inside it was the bomb.

There were three wings inside the YS: the Healy wing, which had seven members on the National Committee; we had four members on it; and the Militant who had one member from Liverpool. There must have been another couple unattached. The main debate was between us and the Healyites. Very few people among the youth supported Gaitskell. So the question of Russia was very central. The bomb was obviously central.

I would guess that we recruited a couple of hundred people at least from the Young Socialists in the years 1960 to 1963—maybe it was 300. That was very important for us. We grew from 50 or 60 to 200 between 1960 and 1964. We kept 200 including a number of very good comrades.

Then Labour came into office in 1964. All the steam of opposition left the Labour Party. Michael Foot wrote a pictorial biography of Wilson which was real hagiography. Frank Allaun described him as the greatest socialist since Keir Hardie—and meant it as praise.

From then onwards there wasn't much life in the YS. Labour was in office. Life was outside the Labour Party. The Healyites were expelled; we left—there was nothing there to fight for.

Between 1964 and 1968 the organisation was sizeable enough to continue to exist. Nothing great happened. One important thing for us was that in 1966 the Labour government introduced an incomes policy. This gave a little opportunity to generalise. Before, strikes were individual things—now the incomes policy related to all workers. Colin Barker and I published a little book entitled *Incomes Policy, Legislation and Shop Stewards*. It sold more than 10,000 copies. It had an orientation towards workers.

We were also lucky because we built a factory branch at ENV in west London in the mid-60s with 12 members in it. Their wage standards were much higher than the rest of the district. It was known as a factory which would give solidarity. So we were sinking small roots among workers.

The YS had also helped to improve our composition slightly because some of them were young workers—the Glasgow YS was mainly working class, for example, and we recruited some very good young workers.

This meant that the group was quite well placed to gain from the upsurge of 1968. How did that take place?

Things moved on two fronts in 1968. Firstly there was an explosion on the industrial front: the rebellion of the low paid in 1968-69. This was the time when women workers moved to the front; it was also the time of the Ford equal pay strike. There were the first national teachers' and nurses' strikes. These gave us opportunities to generalise, and we started issuing leaflets around these strikes. We also issued a quarter of a million leaflets to GLC tenants in London. We changed our method of work. To be a member of the International Socialists then was to be a leafleter.

The second major political issue was the rise of the movement against the Vietnam War. In October 1968, 100,000 people demonstrated in Grosvenor Square. We were not more prominent than the International Marxist Group (the Fourth International). Tariq Ali was better known than any of us.

The big difference between us and them was that they didn't know how to relate the struggle in Vietnam to what was happening in Britain. So they could speak to 100,000 people but they didn't know what to do with five people the next day. We did, so we produced a very good leaflet which argued that on Sunday we were demonstrating and on Monday we should go to the factory or the docks because that was where the power to change society lay—with the working class.

At the time I spent a month in the London School of Economics arguing and we recruited something like 40 members. We recruited anything that moved. So we grew from 400 in April 1968 to 1,000 in October.

We had two conferences that year. There were all sorts of arguments. While we were a small propaganda group there was no problem about structure. But once you have intervention, you need a structure. We had real difficulties. The new members had very little tradition.

There was a reason for all this tension inside the organisation. Vietnam, the invasion of Czechoslovakia by the Russians, strikes on a big scale in 1968-69—events were very big. The results looked poor in comparison. We were still very small, and because people were new and inexperienced they really believed it was easy to recruit. People had to find out for themselves that life was still very hard.

The early 1970s saw the highest level of class struggle in Britain for generations. How did revolutionaries relate to that and what opportunities did it present?

When Heath came to power in 1970 there was a new situation. The Tory Industrial Relations Act produced widespread generalisation. There was an incomes policy. Struggles became much broader. We had to change our tactics, and we became industrial activists. That was practically all we did. When the dockers were imprisoned in 1972, we produced the leaflets for them. We produced propaganda on a very big scale. We had a meeting in east London after the Pentonville Five were freed and three of them were on the platform. That shows the relationship we had with the struggle.

We started a rank and file paper in the docks which had a circulation of a few thousand. Again there was a strike at Perkins Diesel in Peterborough. We were able to recruit about 50 workers from the factory.

In 1972 and 1973 we built something like 50 sizeable factory branches. We must have had something like 500 members in those branches. It was quite impressive. We had branches in the car industry in Coventry, Birmingham, Linwood in Scotland, and Oxford. Our influence was quite sizeable. We had something like a dozen rank and file papers. We grew from around 1,000 in 1972 to 3,800 by the end of 1973.

However, we ran into problems from 1974. We understood the generalisation in terms of what workers didn't want. They didn't want an incomes policy; they didn't want the Industrial Relations Act; they didn't want the Tories. But we weren't at all clear what workers wanted in a positive sense. When they shouted, 'Heath out', we didn't understand that they wanted Labour in. So we weren't clear what the impact of a Labour government would be. All of us assumed that the Labour government would mean a short honeymoon period—that trade unionists would give Labour the benefit of the doubt for a short period, but then would see the reality and fight.

But the Social Contract wasn't just a honeymoon period—it had much more impact for years to come. It made scabbing respectable. The toolroom workers in Longbridge went on strike. Derek Robinson, the CP convenor, stood on the picket line and told the other workers to cross. It didn't save his job—he was victimised in 1979. Then the Port Talbot electricians struck and other workers crossed the picket lines. In 1977 over 4,000 BEA engineers went on strike—16,000 TGWU workers crossed their picket line. The worst thing was in 1977 when the unity of the miners was cracked by introducing the bonus system. This split Nottingham and Leicestershire from the rest of the country. The results of that came to fruition in the strike of 1984-85.

The Social Contract was really the beginning of the downturn. This was the experience of the Labour government of 1974-79. It took us time to understand it. Once we did, we fitted our politics and our activity to the changed political climate.

The conditions then meant that, instead of workers believing that they had to fight and vote, they just looked towards change through voting. So the downturn in industrial struggle took the form of a rise in the political struggle in the form of Bennism. It also meant the rise of tokenism. In 1968 women fought for equal pay. By the early 1980s the women's movement was fighting not to raise wages, but to raise consciousness.

What runs through everything that you've said is the need for revolutionaries constantly to adapt to fit the changing situation. Isn't that the lesson of how we came to terms with the downturn?

To be a Marxist means you have to be extremely hard in your principles but very adaptable in terms of relating to the specific situation all the time. Workers will never change society unless they change themselves. Revolutionaries will never be able to participate in changing the working class unless they change themselves.

That is the most important thing. Everyone thinks the most important thing is not to make mistakes. But making mistakes is not terrible as long as you learn from them. The worst thing is if you are so frightened of making mistakes you don't do anything.

At the same time adaptation doesn't mean opportunism. You have to stick to the principles, but then adapt to the circumstances.

In 55 years as a revolutionary I've tried to stick to that. I've made plenty of mistakes. But basically I was consistent. And if I had to do things all over again, I would do the same—but with a few less mistakes. I'm not a worse Marxist now. I'm as enthusiastic as I was when I was 16.

Chapter 2

Red Petrograd: the workers who seized power

Colin Sparks

You don't need to have been talking to SWP members for very long before the subject of the Russian Revolution of 1917 comes up. In discussion on almost anything from the miners' strike to the Lebanon we take as one of our points of reference events which took place a long time ago and in a country far away.

The reason we have this apparent obsession is that the Russian Revolution is the best example of how workers can take control of society. What happened in 1917 in Russia was, quite simply, that ordinary workers overthrew first the tsar and then their own factory bosses and ran things for themselves. That is a historical experience of the greatest possible interest to socialists.

The ruling class and its ideological supporters repeat day after day that running society is an enormously difficult business, and that only those who rule are fitted for the job. The rest of us, they imply, are too stupid to ever be able to control our own lives.

Taking power

Those arguments stick. You will meet all sorts of people, including very militant workers, who agree that capitalism is rotten and that

First published April 1984

it would be much better if the world ran on the basis of need rather than profit, and then balk at the idea that the working class has the energy and ability to run the world for itself.

From the Fabians back in 1888 to the supporters of Joseph Stalin in the 1930s through to the Ken Livingstones of today, there are those who think that the way to get socialism is to get the right people into positions of power from where they will usher in a world of peace and plenty.

The Russian Revolution is the best example of how wrong that pessimism about the working class is. It was concrete proof that workers, ordinary workers like you and me, can break with the stultifying ideas of their own inferiority and take power.

Because it is such an important example, we keep on referring back to it. And because it is such a dangerous example, the bourgeoisie and their hired intellectuals have spent almost 70 years trying to obscure the truth of the revolution.

One of their favourite ploys is to argue that what happened was not a real workers' revolution but a coup in which Lenin and the tightly organised Bolshevik Party aspired to grab power and run the whole show themselves.

S A Smith's book *Red Petrograd* is a very interesting nail in the coffin of that ruling class argument.

Smith, an academic with left wing sympathies, has studied the factory councils in Petrograd (now St Petersburg) during and after the revolution. The factory councils were directly elected bodies based on the workplace and their delegates were subject to recall. They were quite like shop stewards committees in many of their functions, although the fact that they were thrown up in the middle of a revolution meant that they had rather wider scope than we are used to. Even more than the 'soviets' or councils of delegates from all the factories in an area, these factory committees were the day to day voice of the workers.

The first myth that Smith demolishes is that the workers of Russia were in some way special and different from workers in the West. It was certainly true that industrialisation took place very late in Russia and that many workers were born into peasant families and often wished to return to the land, but there was also a hard core of workers, particularly amongst engineering workers, who had been born into proletarian families and were just as much real workers as anyone in Glasgow or Berlin.

Indeed, there were important ways in which the working class in Petrograd was much more a modern working class than its brothers and sisters in the West. Capitalism in Russia started late and almost from scratch. Very often factories had been set up, or actually run, by the most advanced technicians from the West.

The factories had therefore been planned from the start to take advantage of the most modern techniques of production. The planners had not been hampered by the need to fit advances around existing buildings or plant, and were able to design very advanced workshops.

Because the labour force was a relatively new one, it was, initially, in a much weaker position to resist than engineers elsewhere, say, with 50 or 100 years of craft tradition behind them. There was no Russian equivalent of the craftist Associated Society of Engineers defending the interests of the skilled and forcing the capitalists to compromise on new methods.

Of course, there were skilled workers in Russian factories. The literate, highly trained worker, born in the cities and without roots in the countryside, was at the core of the Petrograd working class. And there was unskilled labour, often drawn straight from the village by the promise of relatively high wages, without urban skills and used in the dirtiest jobs.

The Petrograd working class was as modern, perhaps more so, as its equivalent in the older capitalist economies, but its divisions reflected this too. There were big differentials of pay between skilled and unskilled workers, between the mostly male workers of the engineering industry and the overwhelmingly female labour force of the textile industries.

There was, however, one way in which the working class of Russia was very different from that of the West. The tsarist state had always been determined to crush any attempts at independent trade union organisation. It had never been entirely successful—the normal processes of capitalist production had meant that some very limited negotiating rights had been won by workers at favourable moments in the class struggle. But there were none of the huge bureaucratised parties and trade unions that were, and are, the norm elsewhere.

The political world that the working class had to operate in was different in other respects too. The tsarist state was an 'absolute' one, like that of Charles I or Louis XVI.

Leon Trotsky

It was this political backwardness that led many people, including the majority of socialists, to think that what would happen in Russia would be a repeat of 1642 in England or 1789 in France. These revolutions were what Marxists call 'bourgeois' revolutions because they swept away the power of the monarchy and the landed aristocracy and placed the capitalist class in power.

Almost alone amongst Russian socialists, Leon Trotsky argued that because the Russian bourgeoisie was so tied to the tsarist state, and because the working class was so developed and advanced, there could be no bourgeois revolution.

Instead the working class would, leading the peasantry who formed the vast majority of the population, sweep away the tsar. They would not then simply hand over power to their exploiters, but would go on to take power themselves. This was the famous theory of permanent revolution.

Smith shows that Trotsky was right. The tsar's regime was not held up by a few policemen. It was now based on the production which poured out of the factories. The demands of the First World War had turned Petrograd into a boom city with new factories working flat out to meet orders. That output was guaranteed by managers, experts and foremen who used every barbarous method they could think of to screw more profit out of the workers.

In February 1917 the tsar and his secret policemen went down under the onslaught of militant workers and soldiers. The confidence that had overthrown an ancient despotism also turned to the question of how the factories were run. Smith shows how workers seized the opportunity to settle scores with their immediate enemies:

> Throughout the factories of Petrograd workers clamoured for the removal of all members of the management hierarchy who had made their lives miserable under the ancien regime, who had behaved tyrannically, who had abused their authority, who had taken bribes or acted as police informers. Sometimes administrators were removed peacefully, sometimes by force. At the Putilov works, the director and his aide were killed by workers and their bodies were flung in the Obvodinyi canal; some 40 members of management were expelled during the first three 'days of freedom'.
>
> In the engine/assembly shop, Puzanov, quondam [former] chief of the factory's Black Hundreds [fascists], was tossed in a wheelbarrow, red lead was poured over his head, and he was ignominiously carted out of the factory and dumped in the street. In the brickyard of the same plant, A V Spasskii, the foreman, was deprived of his duties for (i) rude treatment of workers and (ii) forced overtime, as a result of which such incidents occurred as when the worker, S Skinder, having worked overtime, collapsed at midnight of exhaustion and had to be taken to hospital...

The removal of the worst managers and foremen was followed by struggles against the whole capitalist class, even the benevolent ones. Workers fought for the eight hour day and higher wages. The political revolution led to massive economic struggles.

The struggle increasingly involved workers through their factory committees taking decisions about the day to day running of the factories and challenging every aspect of management power. But when a capitalist was kicked out of his own factory he turned to the state to get it back for him. It soon became clear to workers that in order to settle with their own capitalists they would have to settle with all capitalists and with their state machine.

Ordinary workers

It was real workers, not some breed of supermen and women, who came to this conclusion. No one should think that Russian workers were better than workers in the rest of the world, or freer from the prejudices and shortcomings that real people everywhere else have to struggle against.

In July 1917 the government planned to evacuate plant and equipment from Petrograd, dismissing most of the workers with two weeks pay. They wanted to 'rationalise' war production and feared a German occupation. Workers saw it as an attempt to break the revolutionary movement. The following is a typical resolution from workers in the Putilov works. After denouncing the plan as a counter-revolutionary plot, they went on:

> We the workers and peasants will stay put, since we believe that...the people will have the opportunity to take power into their own hands and then no crisis need occur. We suggest that Petrograd be unloaded of its monasteries, infirmaries, asylums, alms houses, and many thousands of its idle bourgeois. We also propose to find out why there is such a great concentration of Chinese in the city.

This example shows that although workers had class hatred in ample measure and were prepared to fight for their class interests, it was not because they were less prejudiced any more than it was because they were more exploited than other workers.

The fact that an upsurge of militancy does not automatically transform the whole of the working class is a general one. It had only been in the course of a long struggle that the working class of Petrograd became conscious of the need to seize state power.

What the working class found itself engaged in was a struggle for control. It began as a struggle to control the factories but inevitably progressed to the question of the state. An economic crisis developed in the summer of 1917 and the factory committees found themselves forced more and more to keep the factories running against both the logic of profitability and the various attempts at sabotage by the owners.

What happened in the course of that struggle was that the composition of the local leadership in many factories changed. At the time of the overthrow of the tsar, for example, the pro-war Mensheviks had been strong in many of the largest factories—dominating, for example, the famous Putilov works. But as workers learned bitter lessons in the struggle for control, in the fight against closure and the battle against the reactionary military conspiracies designed to bring back the despotism, the local leadership changed. Increasingly the factory committees came to be dominated by Bolsheviks since it was only they who put forward arguments that met the needs of the hour.

The Mensheviks suffered from the problem that their leaders were in the government. The minister of labour in the Kerensky government was one Skobolev who had won his spurs three years earlier whipping up enthusiasm for the war. In those circumstances the Bolsheviks, who fought against class collaboration and put the needs of the workers at the centre of its demands, quickly gained support.

But it was their own experience of what was necessary in the struggle that convinced the mass of workers. The closer any organ of power was to rank and file workers on the shopfloor, the more quickly it moved to Bolshevik positions. Smith records workshop committees of Bolshevik sympathy clashing with factory committees of Menshevik views. Then he records factory committees of Bolshevik persuasion clashing with soviets, union leaders and government. Radicalism and the drive for workers' power began at the bottom.

The role of the struggle to end the war in all of this is not very clear from Smith's book. In his account the war and the economic demands it placed upon Russian society form a background against which the struggle for control was fought out. The simple issue of, 'Are you for war or peace?' does not seem to have dominated many factory meetings. Perhaps that is just a result of his perspective on the events but there is a deeper point at stake.

If there is one thing that comes out of his book it is that, although the revolution itself may be a simple single act of seizing power, the reasons why the mass of workers support such an act is that it is the essential step towards solving their concrete problems. Revolutionary politics is not something that is grafted onto the workers' movement nor is it a stage of consciousness which workers reach as the result of their enlightenment at the hands, or rather the tongues, of the enlightened socialist. It is something that arises out of the very logic of the struggle against capitalist society. The Russian Revolution was a workers' revolution in the fullest sense: the working class took power from the bottom up.

In this perspective the war as a direct issue was of more importance to the army. The discipline of military life and the slaughter of the front turned the backward peasants into revolutionaries too—someone who disobeyed the orders of officers and would not shoot on his fellow toilers. In that light the war made the revolution possible because it destroyed the internal cohesion of the army and thus deprived the ruling class of the chance of drowning the workers' movement in blood.

Today's lessons

So another myth about the Russian Revolution falls: it was not some aberration produced by conditions of military chaos and therefore unrepeatable in different circumstances. Yes, the war was crucial in putting enormous stress on the economic and social fabric of Russia. Yes, the war was crucial in shaking the whole of society and in exposing the rotten bloodstained incompetence of the rulers. Yes, the war was crucial in demoralising and splitting the army. But the forces which made the revolution were influenced by the war and not produced by it. The motor of the Russian Revolution was the nature of production in a capitalist society.

It is the strength of Smith's book that it shows how the revolution developed in the factories. Because of that tight focus it is not the best place to start your study of the Russian Revolution. For that read Trotsky's *History of the Russian Revolution* or Tony Cliff's second volume of *Lenin*. They have the wider sweep which puts things into better perspective without which large parts of Smith's book are difficult to follow.

With that qualification, the book is well worth your time. Get your local library to order it.

Smith shows that the Russian Revolution developed along lines that can be understood by looking at modern British society. It was long ago and far away but the essential conditions that turned a popular revolt into a working class seizure of power were ones that we can see all around us.

Chapter 3

1968: 'Everything seemed possible'

Chris Harman

Mention 1968 at any gathering of the left and you get two quite different reactions. There are those who can be expected to subside quickly into a rather sickly nostalgia, with tales of how they petrol bombed the police in the Boulevard Saint Michel or (more likely) of how they ransacked the vice-chancellor's office. And there will be others, younger, more working class, who will ask what was so special about their last year in primary school.

Yet 1968 was an important year in a way which neither the aging ex student rebel nor the younger cynic realises. For it marked a qualitative change in the whole character of the international class struggle.

There had been great struggles in the industrialised countries in the decade prior to 1968. But they had been isolated and their impact soon dashed. People rapidly forgot the mass movement that overthrew the Kishi government in Japan in 1960 or the general strike in Belgium in December of the same year.

These were little more than hiccups which the system could take in its stride. As Tony Cliff remarked of the Belgian general strike, capitalism was 'still expanding, even if in an uneven way. Society as a whole was not at an impasse. Hence neither of the contending classes felt it necessary to change the balance of forces fundamentally' (*International Socialism* 4, Spring 1961).

The picture in the decade after 1968 has been quite different. Eruption has followed eruption—a general strike in one country, an

First published May 1978

insurrection in another, a military coup somewhere else. Whole countries have been stuck in seemingly permanent political crisis. The old Comintern phrase about 'an epoch of wars and revolutions' has once more rung true.

Only in a narrow belt of northern Europe have the ruling classes been able to keep their heads completely above water; only in the United States has the old order been able to neutralise and reabsorb the forces that rocked it in the 1960s.

1968 was not just one wave of student insurgency or one general strike (even if the biggest in history). It marked the watershed between two eras. It was preceded by the longest boom in capitalist history, with 20 years of permanent economic expansion and social peace: it was followed by a new period of never-ending economic and political crisis.

The pattern to the series of political upheavals that began in 1968 only makes sense when you see how various forces that had grown up in the first period reacted when faced with the second.

The most important effect of the long boom was a massive growth in the working class throughout the world. Tens of millions of workers were sucked into new centres of industry: French, Algerian, Tunisian, Spanish and Yugoslav peasants into the car plants of Paris; Turks, East German refugees, Yugoslavs and Italians into Düsseldorf and Cologne; the toilers of southern Italy into Turin and Milan; the radical agricultural labourers of south Portugal into the factories of Lisbon and Setubal; the children of the Navarre peasants who had fought enthusiastically for Franco into the new factories of Pamplona.

Although in northern Europe and the US the boom was accompanied by a steady rise in living standards, in many other countries it was financed by a deliberate pushing down of working class living standards. France under de Gaulle, Portugal under Salazar and Caetano, Spain under Franco, Argentina under a military regime, Chile under Allende and Frei, Pakistan under Ayub Khan, Poland under Gomulka—all could have high rates of capital accumulation because of varying degrees of repression directed against the most elementary workers' struggles.

Many of the old peasant prejudices exploited by the ruling classes to maintain their political control began to wilt in the industrial concentrations. This process affected both the Catholic church in the Latin countries and the Stalinist apparatuses in Eastern Europe.

The traditional left within the workers' movement was incapable, at first, of taking advantage of this break up of the traditional right.

Social democracy was too closely bound to the CIA and its image of the 'free world' to take the initiative: in Spain and Portugal its underground organisations were more or less dead; in Italy participation in Christian Democrat governments lost it voters to the left; in France its backing of the war in Algeria and its support for the advent of de Gaulle so devastated it that at its low point (in the 1969 presidential election) it received only about 4 percent of the popular vote.

Paralysed by their desire

The Communist Parties were often much stronger. But they were paralysed by their desire to prove their respectability to the ruling classes long before anyone thought of the term 'Eurocommunism'. In France they restricted the workers' movement to occasional one day token strikes; in Spain they preached 'national reconciliation' and a peaceful general strike as the alternative to fascism; in Portugal they refused any attempt to turn huge street demonstrations against the dictator Salazar in the early 1960s into a general insurrection.

The result globally was what we in the International Socialists (now the Socialist Workers Party) in Britain called a 'vacuum on the left'. There was immense and growing resentment among workers that the traditional institutions of capitalist society could not hold down for ever. But working class organisations capable of unifying and directing those resentments did not exist.

Transformed by the boom

It was this that gave the student movement immense, if transient, importance in many countries. The universities themselves had been transformed as a result of the boom. Big business had felt that the old cloistered playgrounds for the youth of the privileged classes were no longer adequate for supplying its technological needs. In every country it opened university education up to hundreds of thousands of youngsters from the lower middle class and even the working class, in the expectation that these would learn to man its technological apparatuses and its bureaucracies.

Growing numbers of young people flocked into the system of higher education, expecting the old lifestyle and the old privileges, only to be bitterly disappointed. They were faced with the exam system where they had expected enlightenment, with authoritarianism where they had expected liberalism, with repression where they had expected tolerance. Their disillusion rapidly took political forms. Their youth made them willing to turn to new, radical ideas; the fact that they were not bound to the daily grind of productive work gave them a freedom to argue and demonstrate that workers rarely have. The general ideological crisis of society found its easiest expression in their ranks. And so, whether in Paris or Milan, in Berlin or Berkeley, Warsaw or Prague, they poured by their tens of thousands onto the streets, providing a focus for everyone else who was fed up with the old order.

One other product of the 1960s was of particular importance for many of the movements of 1967-69. This was the American attempt to assert their dominating position as the world power at the expense of the people of Vietnam; 1968 was the year when the attempt came apart, as the Tet offensive of the National Liberation Front inflicted the first major defeat on the Americans. The 'war came home' as GIs began using fragmentation bombs against their officers and joined in peace rallies, as the American campuses erupted, as President Johnson was forced to abandon his plans to run for re-election, as armed police beat demonstrators to a pulp outside the Democratic Party convention in Chicago. To all sorts of people, throughout the world, the message of Vietnam was, 'Everything is possible'.

All these different factors came together to cause the explosion that shook France in May and June 1968. A student movement, stimulated by the Vietnamese struggle, clashed with the university authorities, provoking massive police repression and, in its wake, massive, spontaneous solidarity action by a working class rebelling against ten years of right wing rule and depressed living standards.

The French May was followed a little over a year later by the Italian 'hot autumn', the 'May in slow motion'. Spontaneous walkouts from Italy's big factories were followed by street demonstrations and clashes with the police, in which the workers of Turin and Milan took up the slogans of the left wing students.

In 1969 Argentina experienced the Cordobaza—a virtual uprising as the workers of the car plants of Cordoba fought against the military forces. In Prague too the spring of that year saw a brief alliance between the student organisations and the renovated trade unions.

New, confident and unfettered

Many of the same elements were still at work six years later, when student-worker demonstrations overthrew the empire of Haile Selassie in Ethiopia and when a group of middle ranking army officers finally brought down the fascist dictatorship in Portugal. The byproducts of the world boom—especially a new, confident, powerful and ideologically unfettered working class—were once again tearing asunder the shell of the old society. But by this time there was a full blown international economic crisis, leaving much less room to manoeuvre for the defenders of the old order than in France or Italy in 1968-69.

Everything seemed possible in 1968. Yet ten years later, after a decade of 'wars and revolutions', there is still not one example of a successful bid for power by the working class.

In the May events there was one great weakness—and it has stymied every movement since. There did not exist an organised and centralised network of militants inside the factories—a party—prepared to lead the movement forward. Workers were not prepared to follow the students when it came to the question of political power—they looked to their traditional organisations, especially the Communist Party, and on their advice returned to work.

When it came to the Italian hot autumn, once again a militant revolutionary minority succeeded in 'igniting' massive conflicts; but likewise, the reformist trade union organisations eventually succeeded in absorbing much of the new energy.

In Chile the revolutionary left (especially the MIR) showed that on occasions it could speed up the radicalisation of the masses; but it could not prevent the reformists of the Socialist and Communist parties channelling the radical impulses in a disastrous direction.

In Portugal the revolutionary groups and the extreme left within the armed forces were able to push things to the point where the capitalist power structure had virtually disintegrated; but they did not have the influence within the workplaces to get the workers to build an alternative. Nor did they attempt to do so: as a result, on 25 November 1975, a few hundred right wing soldiers were able to reassemble the fragments of the bourgeois state structure while the reformists held the working class back from action .

The revolutionary left in 1967-69 could grow in the vacuum. But it could not fill the vacuum. It was just too small in the first place.

The fingers of two hands

People today often have no conception of how weak the revolutionary left internationally was before 1968. In France at the beginning of the May events the three main revolutionary groups had at most 600 members each. In Britain the left was even smaller. We in the International Socialists were already the biggest revolutionary group but we had at most 400 members and about half of those were concentrated in London. In major industrial centres like Glasgow, Liverpool, Birmingham, our membership could be counted on the fingers of two hands.

There was no way in which such small organisations could provide practical leadership even in quite small industrial disputes affecting one industry, let alone in the huge spontaneous upsurges of 1967-69.

But the organisations themselves could grow, with the perspective of developing the roots necessary to provide leadership in the next great round of struggles.

But, in fulfilling this task, the revolutionary left was held back not merely by its size, but also by its social composition and its politics. And, in many cases, the three different sorts of weakness reinforced one another.

The smallness of the revolutionary organisations meant that only those who were very highly motivated politically and who had plenty of spare time were likely to join. That usually meant those from a student intellectual background. But this then created an atmosphere inside the organisations which made manual workers feel out of place. Discussions were dominated by highly articulate ex-students with little knowledge of what was happening in the real world. The very language they employed reeked of academic 'Marxism'.

The small size of the organisations and the social composition of the membership led in turn to an attitude which discouraged any attempt to take the everyday struggles of workers seriously.

In Britain, for instance, the International Socialists were attacked on all sides for 'economism' and 'workerism'. Even within the IS there were minority tendencies which denounced any recruitment campaign directed at workers as a 'dilution' of the organisation. Meanwhile in the broader revolutionary milieu, sociologists and would-be Marxists enjoined us to create 'red bases' within the universities, which would be 'sociologically inaccessible' and from which we could bounce socialist ideas 'like billiard balls' into the working class. Their efforts went into producing papers and journals for the radicalised student and ex-student milieu (*Black Dwarf*, *Ink*, *Red Mole*, and, in its own way, *New Left Review*) instead of attempting to build in the class of which these papers sometimes spoke.

The initial success of the French students in 'igniting' a general strike led to futile attempts at imitation, with groups of revolutionaries taking to the streets and fighting it out with the police in complete isolation from the working class: the failure of these efforts led in the worst cases merely to more refined forms of militarism (bombs and revolvers). In

South America a whole generation of revolutionaries committed political (and all too often physical) suicide by turning to guerrilla actions as a substitute for working within the class to develop its self confidence and organisation.

Even where the lesson was learnt about the need to build inside the working class there was not always an escape from the easy illusions of 1968-69. In Italy for example the most successful and rapidly growing of the groups in the early 1970s, Avanguardia Operaia, began life by denying the need to work inside the unions. In Spain the whole left exaggerated the revolutionary consciousness of the workers, talking year after year about an 'incipient pre-revolutionary situation'.

Politics abhors a vacuum. Once millions of men and women have been thrust by their own spontaneous actions into political life, they will attempt to define politically what they are doing. If they do not find a revolutionary definition, they will adopt a reformist one.

This is particularly the case in periods of economic crisis. Every spontaneous economic struggle is then portrayed by the ruling class and the media as pushing society to the edge of 'chaos'. People either develop a total view of the system, or they end up trying to fit their own actions into it.

The vacuum of the late 1960s was not filled by the revolutionary left; therefore a new reformism had to fill it—especially after the onset of the world economic crisis in the mid-1970s.

Outlets for their anger

There was a new growth of the existing reformism, which usually meant the Communist Parties and the unions they controlled. Young workers who had been on the barricades in 1968-69 now looked for an outlet for their anger in terms of the day to day fight in the factories. The older workers most able to advise them on this were the established Communist Party militants, intent on capturing the militancy for their parties' project of reforming capitalism from within. They could offer the young workers 'practicality', short term goals, advice, apparent results. The revolutionary left, waving its red flags outside the factory, screaming of 'red bases', denouncing activity inside the unions, could not.

A second form of reformism developed in many countries through a rejuvenation of the old social democratic parties. With a little help from their friends in the CIA and the north European governments they developed a new image and put a lot of money into building up new apparatuses. They did not usually succeed in building a new workers' cadre: but in France, Spain and Portugal they did manage to capture a lot of working class votes.

This revival of social democracy in turn stimulated the Communist Parties to make new efforts to appear respectable: the Stalinist ugly duckling was miraculously transformed into the liberal Eurocommunist swan.

Regardless of the form taken by the growth of the new reformism, it posed deep problems for the revolutionary left—especially for the impatient street fighters of a couple of years earlier.

They suddenly found they were isolated. The young workers who had marched alongside them and helped them raise the barricades had suddenly opted for surer, more concrete, if illusory, aims. In France they chose to wait for apparently guaranteed success, first from the 1974 presidential elections and then from the 1978 assembly elections; in Italy they argued that the new Communist-tolerated government should at least be given a chance to halt the drift towards 'chaos'; in Spain they flocked to vote for the Communists and Social Democrats in parliamentary and union elections.

All too often the former 'ultra-lefts' reacted by replacing a new form of impatience for the old. In the past they had believed that an activist revolutionary minority could by its own radical action transform society for the working class; now they believed manoeuvres with reformist parties could transform society for the working class. In neither case did the class itself have to develop a revolutionary consciousness and a revolutionary party.

A fairly typical example is that of the former 'ultra-lefts' of Democracia Proletaria (previously Avanguardia Operaia) who now call for import controls and give the impression that a 'left government' of the Communist Party, the Socialist Party and themselves could 'open up the revolutionary road' in Italy. The result has been a drastic decline in the cohesion and influence of what was once the strongest far left in Europe.

In France the growth of illusions in electoral possibilities among workers found its reflection among the revolutionary left in an obsession with electoral activity and with demands for various governmental combinations of reformist parties. Of course revolutionaries should use elections to make propaganda, and should welcome the advent of the reformists to office as a way of showing that reformism cannot work. But with much of the European left you cannot help feeling that once ultra-impatient revolutionaries are now themselves in danger of behaving like the left wing of reformism.

The practical tendency to move to the right to meet the new

reformism has its theoretical expression in certain allegedly 'new' Marxist thinking.

The Eurocommunists, of course, write off the dreams of 1968 as 'unrealistic utopianism'. Using bowdlerised versions of Gramsci they suggest that any assault on state power is impossible in the 'West'. The tendency today is for much of the far left to succumb to a slightly more radical version of this thesis. An assault on state power, they suggest, can only come via a 'left' or 'workers'' government, by replacing the stress on building the revolutionary party by a stress on 'blocs' with other social forces, and by adopting an uncritical attitude to the bourgeois democratic illusions of most workers.

For these people, the failure of the last ten years is a failure of revolutionaries to dilute their ideas in the direction of the various reformist currents, not a failure to fight reformism in the factories through the building of a revolutionary party. Typically, those who treated the 'student vanguard' or the 'red bases' as a substitute for the party in 1968-69 now once again displace the task of building the party into the distant future by arguing that it cannot occur until electoral manoeuvres have split the reformist organisations.

It seems that they will never learn that reformism will recover from any crisis unless there already exist at least the beginnings of a party, with members capable of carrying the revolutionary argument and giving practical leadership in every factory.

The media have already started their celebration of 1968. It consists chiefly in portraying it almost exclusively as a student movement and then claiming that students have calmed down a lot since. In that way what actually occurred can be made to seem distant and irrelevant.

But the claim is not even true when applied to students. In this country the wave of student struggles in 1970-71 was much bigger than that in 1967-69, and the wave in 1976-77 was even bigger than that in 1970-71. When it comes to workers, the claim becomes a joke. There may not have been a general strike in France in the last two years, but there have been massive explosions of anger in Tunisia, Poland, Argentina, Colombia, Peru, Egypt, Spain, South Africa—to name but a few.

The wave of insurgency that began in 1967-69 is still continuing, flaring up first in one part of the world, then in another, and only in one place has the working class yet suffered a decisive defeat—in Chile.

What is true, however, is that much more is at stake in the battles today than ten years ago. The continuing economic crisis allows capitalism very little room for making concessions. It therefore tries to contain the militancy by using the reformist parties and unions to get workers to identify with the competing national capitalist units of the world system. Massive, spontaneous struggles erupt. But they are followed by new governmental combinations (or sometimes just by talk of new governmental combinations), by longer or shorter lulls which prepare the ground for fresh spontaneous outbreaks.

The employing class everywhere uses these lulls to its own advantage, moving quickly from concessions designed to make the tasks of the reformists easier, to new offensives against the working class. Real wages are cut, 'rationalisation' destroys hundreds of thousands of jobs permanently, social services become increasingly inadequate, various forms of racism and nationalism grow, efforts are made to create a 'new right' to gain from disillusion with the new reformism, and the state's repressive forces are strengthened.

Yet hardly anywhere does the employing class feel confident enough yet to put all its eggs in the far right basket: in France, in Britain, in Italy, in Spain the 'new right' has to fight it out within the institutions of the ruling class with those who know the social democrats and 'Eurocommunists' are still vital. For the ruling class itself cannot fully forget how repression and depressed living standards proved a dangerously explosive mixture in France and Italy and Argentina and Portugal and Spain and even, in 1972, in Britain.

Just as there have been many 'Mays' in the last ten years, there will be many more, much more bitter than before, in the next ten years. The revolutionary left has to remember this. But it also has to remember that the worse the general crisis of society the greater the need for an active, intransigent but cool headed revolutionary party.

Growing bitterness is going to be accompanied by growing despair—especially of those forced to live on the margins of society as jobs are destroyed. The bitterness of unemployed youth can feed into the working class movement via a party, giving added power to the revolutionary forces. But there is another alternative: the despair can be utilised by capitalism, whether to encourage insane acts designed to discredit revolutionaries, as with the Red Brigades in Italy today, or to build up extra-parliamentary forces of the far right, as in Italy and Germany before the Second World War.

Bourgeois journalists rarely see things in a context wider than a couple of months: they are paid to titillate readers with the clever phrases which carry a sensation of immediacy, however misleading this might be. Revolutionary socialists have to be much more perceptive. The death throes of an old social order can drag on for decades, rather than for days. That is why we have to insist that the game begun in 1968 is still continuing, but the stakes are getting much higher.

Chapter 4

Earthquake in the East

Tony Cliff

We are witnessing the most massive earthquake of the social and political order in Eastern Europe. It is on a scale reminiscent of 1848 and 1917.

In 1848 there was revolution in France, Germany, Austria and Hungary, and a massive impact elsewhere. The 1917 Russian Revolution was followed by revolution in Germany, Austria and Hungary and had an international impact on an even greater scale.

To understand an earthquake you have to look at the pressure inside the system. It is summed up with Marx's statement that when the social system becomes a brake on the development of the productive forces, the epoch of the social revolution starts.

Marx put the emphasis on the word 'epoch'. It is not a question of one day or one year—it is a long process of tens of years, for as long as the social system is a brake on the productive forces.

Why do the state capitalist regimes act as a brake? In the USSR itself the annual rate of growth of the gross national product between 1950 and 1959 was 5.8 percent. In the period 1970-78 it was down to 3.7 percent. In 1980-82 it was down to 1.5 percent. My guess is that over the last three or four years there was a negative rate of growth.

The manufacturing working class in the USSR is nearly a third larger than that of the US. The number of technicians in Russian manufacturing industry is twice that of the US. Yet the output is half that of the US.

First published December 1989

Thirty percent of the population of the USSR are in agriculture compared with 4 percent in the US. But the 4 percent produce enough food for the US, plus exports. Russia, by comparison, is a net importer of food, even though the level of consumption is much lower.

The downturn and stagnation of the last two decades seem to be in complete contradiction to the experience of the Russian economy under Stalin, when the rate of growth was absolutely massive.

Stalin achieved such massive growth rates by putting the emphasis on heavy industry, on capital goods. Capital accumulation is the heart of the system—machinery to produce machinery to produce machinery.

The problem is that, despite the success, it also makes the system very rigid, because the emphasis is on volume of production.

Look at the steel industry in Britain. Enterprises are near to the sea because it saves on the cost of transport of coal and iron ore which are very heavy raw materials.

By contrast, the centre of diamond production is South Africa, while the centre of diamond distribution is Amsterdam. The fact that they are thousands of miles apart doesn't make any difference as a small volume has a high value. The steel industry is different.

The biggest steel enterprise in the world is in the Urals, at Magnitogorsk. There is no coal there, therefore they bring the coal from thousands of miles away over land. The second biggest steel enterprise in Russia is in the Donbass, in the Ukraine. There is a lot of coal but no iron, so they bring the iron thousands of miles.

The cost of transport must be 30, 40 or 50 times higher than the value of the final product. This is a fantastic waste. Steel is kept artificially cheap. The massive subsidy to these industries has become a formidable burden on the whole economy

Another example of irrationality is that two plants in Russia produce a bolt 12mm by 60mm in size. One charges 10 kopeks for it. The other produces exactly the same bolt and charges 140 roubles, 14 times dearer.

In Britain the difference between the price of Daz and Persil is perhaps 5 percent. If there was a difference of 1,300 percent, one of them would go bankrupt.

The problem in the USSR is that, as long as there was expansion of resources, growth could be maintained by employing more people, using more raw materials and building more factories.

However, once you need to increase the intensity of production, or productivity—to increase output per worker or per unit of capital, in other words to shift from extensive to intensive growth—then the picture is completely different. The extensive method simply doesn't work.

Look what has happened in agriculture. Total agricultural output never rose under Stalin. When he died in 1953 the total agricultural output of Russia was a little lower than it was in 1928, before collectivisation. However, collectivisation still worked for Stalin as it transferred millions of people, and with them food, from the countryside to the town.

In order to syphon off the food from the countryside he had to organise the peasants into collective farms. There was no way of controlling 26 million peasant families, forcing them to deliver the grain, because they would have simply hidden it.

It is much easier to control 200,000 collective farms. But Stalin was worried that even the 200,000 couldn't be controlled. The 500 families on each farm could agree among themselves to hide the grain to pretend they hadn't produced 1,000 tons but only 600 tons.

He therefore organised to control the collective farms by setting up Machine Tractor Stations. Each of these state institutions looks after 20 or 30 collective farms. They did the ploughing and the harvesting.

It's much easier to control 10,000 Machine Tractor Stations than 200,000 collective farms.

The problem is that the tractor driver can decide whether to plough a shallow or a deep furrow. If he ploughs a shallow one he can work much quicker and therefore get a bigger bonus. Nobody is going to be able to go and measure what he has done. If the yield is bad five months later no one can prove it was his fault. It could have been the weather.

The net result of the system is that Stalin's attempt to control agriculture failed to improve output.

In 1959 the private plots of the collective farm members accounted for less than 1 percent of cultivated land. On these plots there is no machinery, not even a plough. There are no young workers, therefore they are very primitive. Yet in 1959 these plots produced 46.6 percent of all meat, 49.2 percent of all milk and 82.1 percent of the eggs produced in the country.

If Gorbachev could cut the labour force in agriculture from 30 percent of the population to, say, 10 percent, there would be a massive opportunity for increased production in industry. As he can't do this, his emphasis must be on increasing industrial productivity and here is where the trouble starts.

Perestroika is about rationalising, making the economy lean and strong. Thatcher carried out a perestroika in Britain in 1979-81. She cut the labour force in manufacturing by over a fifth. Every capitalist country has perestroika. In Japan the capitalists closed factories, they opened new factories and they changed machinery. But because the Japanese economy is much more modern than the British economy, the restructuring can be much less traumatic. The Russian economy needs even more radical perestroika than that carried out by Thatcher.

When Boris Kagarlitsky was in London he spoke about the three main groups in the bureaucracy.

One of them says we need rationalisation, we need the market and we have to follow Swedish social democracy.

A second group argue for a much more radical restructuring—they are called Thatcherite marketeers.

However, according to Kagarlitsky, the biggest group, called the Pinochet Marketeers, says Thatcher is too soft. They want to introduce measures as radical as those carried out by General Pinochet in Chile.

A recent Channel 4 programme on the Polish economy featured the manager of the steel plant at Katowice. He said, 'We have to learn from Ian McGregor.' He argued for a radical cut in the labour force and said he'll only be happy when there are two workers looking for each job.

This is the logic of what Gorbachev has to do. In Britain they closed 20 to 25 percent of manufacturing capacity. In Russia they will have to do more. The estimate of 16 million unemployed as the result of perestroika is probably an underestimate.

The first opposition will come from the bureaucrats in the factories. Secondly, in order to overcome the resistance Gorbachev needs greater openness, glasnost. The trouble with glasnost is it gets out of control. Rulers rule by force and persuasion, with a whip and a carrot. They run into trouble when the whip is not strong enough and the carrot is not big enough.

When Stalin died Russia was still a graveyard in terms of political upheaval. Then in February 1956 Khrushchev denounced Stalin and started some measure of democratisation. The Hungarian uprising took place eight months later. Workers took the factories. They set up workers' councils. They smashed the Hungarian police and army. Khrushchev gave them a finger and they took a hand. After that, of course, Khrushchev sent the tanks in.

This effect is nothing new. Alexander II came to the Russian throne in 1855 and promised freedom to the serfs, local government and freedom for women to go to universities. Alexander Herzen, the leading revolutionary democrat at the time, called Alexander II the 'Tsar Liberator'.

The only trouble is he gave freedom to the serfs but he did not give them the land. He gave local government but he didn't allow the Poles national autonomy. Instead he sent the troops against them.

The result was that the Narodniks formed a large and active movement and Alexander II became the first tsar in the history of Russia to be murdered by revolutionaries, in 1881.

The problem with glasnost today for Russia's rulers is that it is opening the door to fantastic demands. Look at the workers in Vorkuta who have gone on strike against the law.

Glasnost opens the way for a flood of opposition and anger, both in Russia and the rest of Eastern Europe.

The explosion of the crisis is extremely fast. But the solution to the crisis is a long term matter. This is because here again the past lives with us.

Stalin pushed history forward on a massive scale by creating a huge working class. The working class of Russia today is incomparably stronger in terms of size, concentration and power than the working class of 1917. At the same time there has been a massive regression in terms of ideas, workers' organisation and living traditions.

This is why workers are extremely strong, yet are fighting for very elementary things that were raised as long ago as 1848: democratic rights, the right of assembly, the right of elections and the right of trade unions.

Even more important than this retrogression is the lack of a physical continuation of ideas. When Trotsky writes that the revolutionary party is the memory of the class he stresses the memory is not simply something hanging in the air—it is carried by human beings. They transfer their experience, tell one another about the books they read and so on.

One example of regression was the shocking picture of people carrying the banners of the tsar on the 7 November demonstrations in Moscow and Yaroslav. Even worse than that, in Lvov in the Western Ukraine during the summer they carried the blue and white banners of Petlura, a Ukrainian nationalist who killed 150,000 Jews in 1919.

The problem is that genuine communism, planning, and the red flag are all identified with an oppressive regime.

There is another problem for the revolutionaries, such as Boris Kagarlitsky and the thousands of others like him all over Eastern Europe. They find it extremely difficult to find their way in terms of ideas. They have to start practically from square one—there is no tradition.

The process of clarification will take time. There needs to be a process of political differentiation. Within Kagarlitsky's group there are anarchists and people with a whole number of other political ideas.

It took Marx years to break from the anarchist Bakunin. In the West today I don't know of any organisation with both Marxists and anarchists in it. But in Russia they are together as there hasn't yet been a process of differentiation.

In one way, the development of the workers' movement is very speedy and in another way it is extremely slow, because there is a 60 year desert to overcome. Socialists have to win ideas that were taken naturally in 1917 by masses of workers.

There is also an imbalance between the way in which workers can learn about some aspects of struggle extremely fast, but take much longer to generalise. The contradiction in people's brains is the result of a contradiction in their experience.

Russian workers have massive experience of solidarity in the factories. Basic democratic demands could therefore grow out of the situation. Everybody wants democratic and trade union rights.

The problems are that when the issue goes beyond the immediate factory to be more general, then a whole number of things are missing. Here it is important to understand the attraction of the market.

When Russian workers compare their living standards with those abroad, they compare them with those in West Germany.

If they compared the housing situation in Moscow with Calcutta, where there are hundreds of thousands of people sleeping in the streets, they would say the market doesn't work in Calcutta. But when the comparison is made with West Germany, the market seems very attractive.

When Lenin said revolutionary ideas must come to workers from outside, he meant from outside their immediate experience. In other words, to be a worker and fight for higher wages is natural. To fight against racism is not natural—it doesn't come automatically. You must go beyond the immediate experience.

On 9 January 1905 in Russia the march to the Winter Palace was led by Father Gapon, a priest and a police agent. People didn't know he was a police agent, but they knew he was a priest and a prison priest at that. The demonstrators carried icons, not red flags. Instead of shouting, 'Down with the tsar,' they cried, 'We love you, our little father.'

The revolutionaries were a tiny minority, a couple of hundred at the most. When the army shot 500 people dead the mass of people began to change.

It was a very quick jump from 9 January to the slogan of the soviet later that year: 'Eight hours a day and a gun.' The fact that people have to go through transition doesn't mean the transition must take

500 years. As Lenin said, in one day of revolution workers change more than in a century.

There are massive problems for socialists in Eastern Europe to overcome. Even those we call revolutionaries will be mixed with centrists moving leftwards. There will not be a clear line of demarcation. We can expect to see centrists moving leftwards and then differentiation.

The experience of Poland shows that every time force is used the force is weakened. In 1980-81 the ruling class was not as confident as in 1956. The Russian army did not intervene. There is no question that they are terrified of using the 380,000 Russian troops in East Germany in the present situation.

Therefore they have to use both reform and repression. The miners went on strike so they rushed through a law which said strikes are illegal in the mines, on the railways, in the power industry. Then the miners broke the law, but they didn't break it completely because only 18 pits in Vorkuta went on strike.

There will be ups and downs in the struggle. It is not a simple one way process. The miners' strike committee in Kusbass in Siberia was against the strike. It was the workers who decided to go on strike. There is already a differentiation there among the militants.

The events in Eastern Europe are also having a massive impact in the West.

People say Thatcher and Kinnock are right to support the market, that planning doesn't work and that socialism is old hat.

One Polish economist defined communism as a transition stage between capitalism and capitalism. From the West it looks as if socialism has no future as the regimes are falling to pieces. This is a massive boost to the right wing.

This is especially important because of the illusions much of the left has had in the Eastern regimes.

But this situation can also change radically if the workers' strikes in Eastern Europe come to the fore. Then it will be clear that the class struggle is still the dominant factor in the whole situation.

State capitalism is vitally important as a theory. Anybody who thinks there is any form of socialism in Russia is in trouble. Even Ernest Mandel argued in 1956:

> The Soviet Union maintains a more or less even rhythm of economic growth, plan after plan, decade after decade, without the progress of the past weighing on the possibilities of the future...all the laws of development of the capitalist economy which provoke a slowdown in the speed of economic growth are eliminated.

Isaac Deutscher said in the same year that Russia's standard of living would surpass that of Western Europe in the space of ten years. Anybody who believed these things is now completely demoralised. The assumption that Russia is more progressive than what everybody accepts as capitalism has fallen to pieces.

The importance of the theory of state capitalism is that it explains why the economy works the way it does. The emphasis on capital accumulation explains both the massive rate of growth and the impediments to future growth. As I wrote in 1963:

> If by the term planned economy we understand an economy in which all component elements are adjusted and regulated into a single rhythm in which frictions are at a minimum and above all in which foresight prevails in the making of economic decisions, then the Russian economy is anything but planned. Instead of a real plan, strict methods of government dictation are involved in filling the gaps in the economy made by the decisions and activities of this very government. Therefore instead of speaking about a soviet planned economy, it would be much more exact to speak of a bureaucratically directed economy.

This explains the dynamic of the system, the capital accumulation, the creation of a working class. This is the strength of state capitalism. At the same time it becomes an impediment to the development of the productive forces, the most important productive force being the workers themselves.

Secondly, the theory prevents us being too impressionistic one way or another.

With all the break that Stalin brought in the Marxist tradition, these traditions are still alive. It is very interesting to hear Boris Kagarlitsky talk of the continuation in Vorkuta between the old Trotskyists, who were sent there to the biggest gulag, and their grandchildren who are miners.

Ideas cannot be smashed by tanks, by force alone. The ideas of Trotsky can be very much like a stream. The stream disappears from sight and then reappears miles later. The stream hadn't dried up—it was just obscured from our sight below the surface.

The same applies to ideas. As Trotsky wrote in 1939, 'The vengeance of history is much more terrible than the vengeance of the most powerful general secretary.' He has been proved right. Trotsky is smiling and Stalin is dead.

Chapter 5

Socialism since the 1970s

Lindsey German

The first issue of *Socialist Review* appeared in April 1978. It was an important time to launch a new socialist monthly. We were four years into a Labour government which had been elected on the back of a wave of class struggle, but which had failed to live up to any of its promises.

Those were years of crisis, of a Social Contract between government and unions, of falling real wages and the first substantial cuts in public spending for decades. They were also years when the fascist National Front grew to frightening proportions, threatening to replace the Liberals as the third party electorally in parts of London, the Midlands and Lancashire. Those who tried to confront the Nazi threat on the streets also found themselves up against the police who defended the fascists' 'right to march' and Labour leaders such as Michael Foot who denounced the left as no different from the Nazis.

It was a testing time for socialists. The left had been reborn internationally through the great struggles of the late 1960s and early 1970s. In country after country the old values and ways of doing things had been challenged and a new mood of change had arisen. It seemed, as one of the slogans of the time put it, that everything was possible.

But the promises of the first half of the decade were not fulfilled in its later years. The mood of revolutionary or radical change was replaced by attempts at compromise between the capitalist class and the representatives of the working class—the trade union and labour

First published September 1996

leaders saw no alternative but to accept what little was on offer from a crisis ridden capitalism. This led to a change in the working class movement. In Britain the confidence and strength which had marked the early 1970s were being dissipated. The trade union leaders moved to the right, to the extent of even sanctioning scabbing on strikes in certain situations. Strikes became much more defensive rather than offensive, and shop stewards' organisation—which had formed the backbone of the upturn in the struggle of the early 1970s—was seriously eroded.

So *Socialist Review* was launched against a background of crisis, the crisis of reformism internationally. As Tony Cliff argued in our first issue:

> If the job of trade unionists is to get benefits within the framework of capitalism, then the sicker the capitalist system the more concessions the workers must make to the system. This is the reason why left reformists, who were ready to fight when capitalism was doing well, will not fight when capitalism is doing badly. (April 1978)

The reformists had grown as a result of the struggles of the previous decade. When those struggles subsided, they found themselves and their organisations well placed and established to give a lead to young militant workers in a way that the revolutionaries still could not. They tended to channel the aspirations of these workers into electoral politics, arguing that electoral changes would bring the sorts of reforms that were wanted.

But the crisis of reformism also became a crisis of the revolutionary left, as those who had looked to street fighting and student vanguards in the late 1960s looked to manoeuvres with the electoral parties to make advances. Chris Harman debating with Tariq Ali in the *Review* in 1978 argued that revolutionaries were too influenced by the Eurocommunists, as the new 'democratic' Communist Parties called themselves, and that 'for these people the *failure* of the last ten years is a failure of revolutionaries to dilute their ideas in the direction of various reformist currents, not a failure to *fight* reformism in the factories through the building of a revolutionary party' (May 1978).

Yet diluting their ideas in the direction of various reformist currents was precisely the course which many revolutionaries and former revolutionaries were taking. The idea that the *only* advance in a period of working class retreat could be made through electoral change became more dominant. This was coupled with increasing criticisms of those who attempted to build revolutionary organisation. Such criticism came from some who had always criticised this strategy—the Communist Parties, for instance, whose own recent history had been rigidly Stalinist but who now claimed revolutionary organisation was 'dogmatic', 'rigid' or 'sectarian'.

It also came from the 'movements', especially members of the women's movement who counterposed their own 'autonomous' organisation to socialist organisation. A group of Hackney socialist feminists claimed to:

> ...have been grappling with questions relating to organisation, within or without the left groups. Many of us have been, at some time in our lives, in left groups for years and some of us were socialists before we were feminists! We are now *feeling* towards a balance between the spontaneism of the women's movement...and the old *bourgeois* centralist hierarchies we've experienced and have witnessed in left groups. (November 1978)

This splintering of the left and the inward looking approach which developed took acute forms in some countries—especially in Italy where the once flourishing revolutionary left collapsed. In Britain the process was accelerated by the election of a Tory government under Margaret Thatcher in 1979.

The bitterness and sense of betrayal felt by many workers at the disastrous policies of the Callaghan government were reflected in the move to the left inside the Labour Party. The Labour Coordinating Committee, set up in the dog days of Callaghan's administration, was an umbrella grouping of the left around Tony Benn, the most prominent left figure. The left called for an alternative economic strategy—of more public ownership, state intervention, industrial democracy and import controls—plus a democratisation of the Labour Party to make its leadership more accountable to the members.

Winning constitutional changes inside Labour became of paramount importance for the left over the next two years. Those who argued that the real struggle lay elsewhere were regarded as irrelevant. And because of the defeats inside the workers' movement (for example that of the steel strike in 1980) the activities and campaigns which did take place tended to reinforce the argument about joining Labour and winning electoral change, rather than generating rank and file organisation from below. So the huge demonstrations in various cities against unemployment and the movement against the missiles which grew up in response to the new Cold War in 1980 tended to strengthen the Labour left.

The feminists too were moving towards the Labour Party. *Beyond the Fragments,* an influential book by three socialist feminists which came out in 1979, argued that there needed to be an alternative to traditional left wing organisation—one based on pulling together the various local groupings and fragments in the 'community'. However, the main point of the book, as Sue Cockerill pointed out at the time, was to polemicise against Leninist and other socialist forms of organisation. 'The politics of its authors are defined negatively in the main, as a reaction against the revolutionary left rather than a positive political strategy' (May-June 1980).

The truth of this statement was borne out as the local community campaigns became subsumed into a rush towards the Labour Party—encompassing eventually at least two of the authors of the book itself.

So the left which was large and varied in the 1970s came under increasing pressure to abandon any independent existence and become part of a Labour Party whose left was promising good times just around the corner in the form of constitutional reforms and electoral success: a left government. The Labour left and their enthusiastic new recruits knew that Labour's manifesto on which it fought the 1974 election had been as left wing as anything it had produced; the problem then was that Healey and Callaghan were not accountable. This time it would be different.

It is difficult now to remember the mood of euphoria which swept so many on the left, and the difficulty that revolutionary socialists had in maintaining their argument that elections changed little and that it was struggle from below that really mattered.

The sense of unreality which gripped the Labour left was most dramatically illustrated in its response to the special Labour conference at Wembley in January 1981, when left constitutional changes won. Virtually all the left was jubilant, despite the warning of Chris Mullin in *Tribune* that the final outcome of the vote combined 'brilliant tactics on the part of the Rank and File Mobilising Committee, pigheadedness on the part of some right wing union leaders and a fair dose of good luck' (*Tribune,* 30 January 1981). *Militant* described it as a 'great victory. The block vote will become a vital transmission belt for the demands of an aroused and mobilised working class' (*Militant,* 30 January 1981). 'Wembley was a famous victory for the labour movement' wrote *Socialist Challenge* (29 January 1981), paper of the Fourth International.

Our lead article was entitled 'An Illusory Victory' and made the point that little had changed. It went further: the centre and right of the party would regroup to defeat the left. Already the defection of the 'Gang of Four' to form the SDP was being used as a means of enforcing discipline on the left and moving the party to the right.

This was an argument which few wanted to hear. Years of frustration, of defensive struggles and of a right wing Labour government followed by an aggressive Tory one led most of the left towards seeing electoral change as the option most open and most 'realistic' for them. Building independent socialist organisation had been hard and was likely to get harder; surely it was better to join a ready made Labour Party where the left had been revitalised and was growing?

The Labour left was also boosted by the election of François Mitterrand as president of France in May 1981. *Tribune* described his election as the 'first salvo in the attack to drive back the madness of monetarism which has affected so much of the Western industrial world' (*Tribune*, 15 May 1981).

Looking back to the legacy of Mitterrand—mass unemployment, austerity, corruption, attacks on immigrants, the growth of the fascist Le Pen—it seems almost incredible that the French revolutionary paper *Rouge* could write:

> An immense hope is born. The French workers have just won a substantial victory. It needed the general strike of 1968, then years of struggles and battles, often fought under difficult conditions, to lead to the defeat of the bourgeois parties and the opening of a new period. The victory of François Mitterrand is not only evidence of the rejection by a majority of the policies carried out for seven years by Giscard and the employers, it is also the expression of a victory, of a will for radical change, a will to get rid of a society which exploits and oppresses the workers.

Such talk was characteristic of much of the left in the early 1980s, and created dangerous illusions in what could be achieved through electing 'left' governments. It gave the impression that the logical conclusion of the big struggles of the late 1960s and early 1970s was the election of such a government and suggested that the most important thing revolutionaries could do was help elect such a government.

In Britain this fervour reached its peak in the 'Benn for deputy' campaign, where Benn stood for the post of deputy leader of the Labour Party against right winger Denis Healey. Huge enthusiasm greeted his candidacy, and he attracted very big audiences of Labour supporters all round Britain.

Such was the attraction of Labour that our summer issue of 1981 had as its lead article 'The Case for Keeping out of the Labour Party'. In it we described that what characterised the early years of the 1980s was a political upturn—growth in the Labour Party, the creation of new Broad Lefts in the unions, the movement of Bennism itself—coupled with an industrial downturn. Unless at some point the working class struggle began to recover to match the political upturn, then the political upturn would itself decline towards the level of industrial struggle.

Again this was very much a minority view. Many of those most identified with revolutionary politics flocked to join Labour, seeing Bennism as one of the biggest threats to the capitalist system. So Tariq Ali, writing in the *Review* in December 1981 on 'Why I'm joining the Labour Party', stated that 'Benn's programme of reforms will meet fierce resistance from the capitalist class and its state bureaucracy' and that it could 'throw the bourgeoisie on the defensive'.

Even when Benn lost the deputy leadership by the narrowest fraction, many on the left considered this only as a temporary setback. They believed that one final push could win. But the final push never came. The autumn of 1981 in reality represented a turning point and from then on they were increasingly on the defensive in what was to be a long retreat from the heyday of Bennism.

The leadership offensive inside the Labour Party was reinforced by the electoral success of the SDP. The gap between the political upturn—2,000 turned up to hear Michael Foot in Glasgow's Hillhead by election in early 1982, another 2,000 to hear Benn—and the reality of the general level of passivity and demoralisation inside the working class was dramatic, as Labour lost ground from its 1979 election showing and came third with the SDP victorious.

Michael Foot and the Labour leadership blamed the defeat on the left and by the autumn—the left further weakened by Labour's jingoism during the Falklands War—the Labour conference showed how far the party had shifted within a year. The right wing won a majority on the party NEC, courtesy of the trade union block vote, and launched a witch hunt against Militant. Benn had agreed earlier in the year under the 'peace of Bishop's Stortford' engineered by union leaders including Jack Dromey (today a Blairite) of the TGWU not to stand for the leadership election. As the next election loomed so the humiliation of the left got worse, culminating in the defeat of left candidate Peter Tatchell in a by-election in solidly working class Bermondsey at the hands of the Liberal candidate.

We argued that there was no short cut around the fact that the emancipation of the working class was the act of the working class. 'Especially there is not the short cut of the tiny minority of those of us who are socialists now trying to cover up our weakness by simply trying to capture an electoral machine' (March 1983).

Labour's vote in the 1983 election was disastrous. Labour lost working class strongholds such as Medway, Swindon, Southampton and Slough. The general debacle led to the resignation of Michael Foot and his replacement by Neil Kinnock who accelerated the move to the right and continued the witch hunt against left wingers in the Labour Party. The response of the left was twofold: some argued that the election result was the sign of an all triumphant Thatcherism, whose right wing individualist politics fitted with a society where the working class was in decline and where workers saw themselves as consumers above all else. This view was most identified with those around the Communist Party magazine, *Marxism Today*. Others adopted a spurious optimism, claimed that there was no real problem, that the witch hunt could not destroy socialist ideas and that the left would rise again. This view was identified with Benn himself and with Militant.

While this view was preferable to the super-pessimism which increasingly came to dominate the left during the 1980s, both tended to ignore the real balance of class forces and therefore drew quite wrong conclusions about what could be done to build socialist ideas. In June 1983 we wrote, 'The outcome of Thatcher's second term of office depends, as did the first, on how much the working class is prepared to put up with and how far it can fight back.'

Very soon after the election it became clear that despite the industrial and political defeats of recent years militancy was growing again. A rash of strikes had taken place in 1983 among car workers, dockers and engineering workers. After the election the employers, backed by the government, went on the offensive. This led to a wave of struggle first by the NGA print union against Eddie Shah's union busting in Warrington. Then in early 1984 the ban on unions at the GCHQ in Cheltenham led to widespread strike action and in March that year the 12 month miners' strike began.

The strike and its outcome were to dominate the left for years to come. In the short term it revitalised the left, with a movement developing in its support, a polarisation of 'official' politics and a climb in the polls for the Labour Party. But the strike was increasingly defensive—faced as it was by a hostile Labour leadership, a TUC which did little to build solidarity, and an NUM leadership which failed to build on the support which existed among millions of trade unionists. Colin Sparks wrote at the beginning of the strike that support had to be concrete:

> Intervening in the class struggle at present means organising the minority of the class who want a real fight against the government so as to enable them to begin to lead the passive majority. Collections for the miners play an absolutely vital role in that. Such collections begin to pull together the active minority and to draw behind them some of the more

passive majority to [lay the ground for] more active forms of solidarity. (April 1984)

The argument of Militant supporting MP Terry Fields at the time was quite different: 'When people say take collections for people on strike, we put an alternative. We say take the wealth of the City of London and give it to the working people.'

But such abstract calls for socialism only left people more isolated as the strike went down, precisely because of the failure to build solidarity to a sufficient level. However, the strike became a rallying point for the left, with collections and support groups springing up. But once the strike was defeated, right wing Labour ideas became more dominant again. It was accepted that the strike failed because there had not been a ballot, or because workers were in a minority, or because Thatcherism was all powerful.

An article in the May 1985 Labour Party magazine *New Socialist* entitled 'Bennism without Benn' pointed to a left realignment, where much of the left who once supported Benn were moving to embrace Kinnock to 'try to detach him from the embrace of the parliamentary right'. In practice this meant abandoning Benn himself (who stuck to his politics of the early 1980s), accepting the witch hunt against Militant and compromising with Kinnock.

Alongside this went an abandonment of the jewel in the Labour left's crown: the use of local government as a platform against Thatcher and Labour's right. The GLC leader Ken Livingstone led the capitulation by nearly all Labour authorities to the Tory policy of ratecapping. Even Militant dominated Liverpool followed suit the following year. This was the end of the GLC as the left's practical alternative—now all they could argue was to wait for a Kinnock government in 1987 or 1988.

Paradoxically, the supposedly invincible Thatcherism was undergoing its own crisis. The victory over the miners had been bought at tremendous cost both economically and politically and now the government found itself with problems. Labour shot ahead in the opinion polls (despite the received wisdom that strikes were unpopular). The Tories were beset by crises such as Westland and seemed to have run out of steam. They had won many of the battles against groups of workers but they had not won the war. It was much more the weakness of the left and its own capitulation to right wing ideas—not the invincibility of Thatcher—that rendered it powerless. Events in the next few years were to bear this out.

The move to the right inside the Labour Party, the capitulation of the left over ratecapping, were all part of a developing political outlook which accepted that nothing could be as it had been in the past. The working class was now dead. A notorious *New Statesman* article in 1987 identified the *Sun* page three model Samantha Fox with the aspiring working class and declared that this section of workers was leaving the poor and dispossessed far behind. Thatcher's third election win in 1987 reinforced this view.

In a different way, so did the changes taking place in Russia and Eastern Europe. The left developed tremendous illusions in the reforms of Mikhail Gorbachev. For example, Fred Halliday wrote in *Marxism Today* (November 1987), 'Who would have guessed that in 1987 the best thing happening for the left would be in Moscow?' Tariq Ali even claimed that Gorbachev's reforms were at last addressing the problems of the regime which Trotsky had pointed to in the 1930s! This was the political revolution awaited by him and his co-thinkers for so long.

When Gorbachev's supposed revolution failed, when the various Eastern bloc regimes collapsed, this further fed the view among those who had equated the Eastern European regimes with socialism that socialism itself was dead. And their substitutionist politics, seeing left governments or various spontaneous movements as the alternative to working class self activity, meant that they were unable to take advantage of what was a new mood among workers in the early 1990s. By the late 1980s the dominant view on the left was that socialism had failed and there was no alternative to the market, that liberal democracy was the natural form of government, and that the Cold War was over.

Much of *Socialist Review* was dedicated to arguing against all these propositions. We said that the market could not deliver; that only a democratic, planned economy could achieve equality and better living standards; that liberal democracy was far from representing the mass of people and that it would be hard to achieve in areas such as Eastern Europe; and that the world was becoming more unstable following the collapse of the USSR and we were entering a new and more dangerous period.

The 1990s have proved us right. The crisis which began in 1989 revealed the misery of the market and the depth of bitterness and unhappiness among workers around the world. The Gulf War, the collapse of former Yugoslavia, the horror afflicting huge parts of Africa, all point to greater instability. And the supposed strength of rulers such as Margaret Thatcher was exposed by the revolt against the poll tax which led to her departure.

How has the left responded to these changes? The contrast between deep pessimism and facile optimism which we pointed to throughout much of the 1980s is still there. Dominant among the Labour leadership, the former *Marxism Today* crowd and the right wing inside the unions is an acceptance that the market has won, that all the left can do is ameliorate some of the worst excesses of capitalism. What were firm tenets of even right wing Labourism a decade ago—full employment, a welfare state, decent pensions—are now abandoned. Those who oppose this view too often fall into the trap of simply stating that socialism will triumph without spelling out how.

The crisis of recent years has seen huge struggles, most notably in France at the end of 1995, where workers' anger has been evident enough, but where the passive and electoralist approach has left the left disarmed. This has allowed the growth of the far right, especially in France.

However, there is another approach which we have argued consistently in the pages of *Socialist Review*: that the market creates the problems we have, rather than solves them; that the only answer to these problems—of poverty, war, famine and inequality—is socialism based on workers' control and production for need; that now is not the time to abandon socialist ideas and join the retreat of so much of the left.

The illusions in Labourism and Stalinism have led a whole generation of revolutionaries throughout the world away from such an understanding and towards looking for substitutes for working class self activity. The women's movement, for example, moved in the 1980s through the mystical politics around Greenham Common to trying to change the Labour Party, to virtually total inactivity. When these substitutes failed, they abandoned the whole project. It doesn't have to be like that. In recent years hundreds of thousands have demonstrated against the poll tax, fought against the Nazis, opposed pit closures and the logic of capitalist 'rationalisation'. There has been a growth of working class anger. Those who run our society have no answers to the problems that they have created.

That is why after 200 issues *Socialist Review* is more successful and widely read than ever—and is able to make a small contribution to building the socialist organisation which is so desperately needed as an alternative to Blairism.

Theory

Chapter 6

Marx's real tradition

Paul Foot

The tumultuous revolts in Eastern Europe have divided socialists into two camps. In one camp there is gloom and introspection. In the other there is excitement and delight.

The two camps represent two different traditions, both calling themselves socialist. For much of the last hundred years or so these two traditions have become entangled with one another. We had better disentangle them fast, for one tradition is now dead; the other lives. Unless they can free themselves fast, the living will be dragged down by the dead.

'Ever since the beginning of time', says a disembodied voice over a spinning globe at the start of Cecil B de Mille's *Samson and Delilah*, 'man has striven to achieve a democratic state on earth.' That was probably putting it a little high (especially as the voice went on to assert, 'Such a man was Samson'), but there is something in it.

In all human history, which is the history of exploitation, there have been people who pined or fought for a day when exploitation would cease. Such people wrote utopias in which men and women lived side by side in freedom, prosperity and peace.

Some of these utopias were in heaven, some on earth. Their instigators were benevolent men and women who saw themselves as parents leading bemused and discomforted children to a promised land. They were, therefore, all of them elitists, none more so than the French utopian 'socialists' of the early 19th century. They believed their own

First published March 1990

education, feeling and compassion would usher in the new society.

In England the word 'socialism' was first popularised by such a man: Robert Owen. Owen detested the exploitation he saw all around him during the Industrial Revolution. He urged benevolent employers to set up dream factories in which the workers would get clothed, fed, educated and introduced to the fine arts.

He didn't just say it; he did it. If you happen to be near Lanark in Scotland you can go and see the carefully kept result: Owen's model mill in which most of his ideals were put into effect, without the slightest impact on exploitation in the West of Scotland or anywhere else.

New Lanark and all similar utopias and charities were greeted by the young Karl Marx with the ferocious contempt for which he had a peculiar genius. Marx reckoned that for the first time in history it was possible to end exploitation once and for all. Up to that time so little was produced that there wasn't enough to share with everyone. If there was to be any progress, therefore, a surplus had to be creamed off by a ruling class.

After the advances of production in the Industrial Revolution there was enough to go round. It was possible to talk (as they started to do in Germany only from 1842, when Marx was 24) of 'socialism', a society where things are produced and distributed socially, to fit everyone's needs, and in which it is considered a crime for one person to grow rich from the labour of another.

How could such a society come about? Was it inevitable because it was so obviously fair and decent? Were industrialists, landlords and bankers suddenly to be struck, as St Paul pretended he was on the road to Damascus, by a blinding light which would show them how monstrous their riches were in the midst of so much poverty?

From a very early age Marx recognised the ruthlessness of class rule. He observed how the ruling class behaved like vampires. They sucked blood, which led them to be thirsty for more of it. They were as impervious as vampires to pleas for mercy. They would relinquish their surplus, he concluded, only when it was seized from them by the very class they robbed. So the first reason why Marx reviled all collaborators with the capitalist system was that they made the abolition of that system and the creation of a socialist society more distant and difficult.

There was, however, a second reason, which was even more important to Marx and to his friend and collaborator, Frederick Engels. They were faced by an argument which we hear on all sides today. 'The working class', they were told, 'are backward, ill educated, racist, dirty, mean. How can such a class create a new society free from exploitation and fear?'

Marx reacted angrily to such abuse. His descriptions, for instance, of the meetings of workers in Paris, when he was first exiled there in the mid-1840s, are full of admiration. But he knew that exploiting society makes wretches of the exploited just as it makes monsters of the exploiters.

He knew that centuries of exploitation had left the masses full of, not to put too fine a point on it, shit. And this was the best reason of all for the revolution:

> This revolution is necessary, therefore, not only because the ruling class cannot be overthrown in any other way, but also because the class overturning it can only in a revolution succeed in ridding itself of all the muck of ages and become fitted to found society anew.

That was in *The German Ideology*, written in 1847, when Marx was 29; and the theme—the importance of the self emancipation of the working class—goes on and on throughout all his writing. It is the very linchpin of Marxism.

When in 1864 he wrote the principles of the First International Working Men's Association his very first clause said, 'Considering that the emancipation of the working classes must be conquered by the working classes themselves...'

This clause was written into the membership cards of every member of the International. Seven years after the formation of the International the workers of Paris rose, threw off the muck of ages, and set up their own administration entirely free from exploitation. Marx, in a fever of excitement and enthusiasm, wrote perhaps the most powerful political pamphlet in all history, insisting that the Commune's greatest achievement was the self emancipation of the working class:

> They have taken the actual management of the revolution into their own hands and found at the same time, in the case of success, the means to hold it in the hands of the people itself; displacing the state machinery of the ruling class by a governmental machinery of their own. This is their ineffable crime!

The most consistent theme of all Marx's writing is this zest for the potential of the working class in struggle. It goes back to the very earliest of Marx's ideas, when as a young journalist he called himself an 'extreme democrat'.

Vulgar Marxists of the bureaucratic school ('Marxists' whom Marx and Engels came to despise while they were alive) detect a 'great shift' from Marx's early idealistic journalism to his later scientific work. It is not a shift which Marx recognised. Rather he noticed that he developed logically from a passionate belief in democracy to a passionate belief in communism.

Communism, brought about by a working class in motion, was the most democratic society conceivable, since it came about through democratic action and it removed the most undemocratic aspect of all: economic exploitation of the many by the few. By as early as 1845 Frederick Engels was spelling this out in simple language:

> Democracy nowadays is communism... Democracy has become the proletarian principle, the principle of the masses... The proletarian parties are entirely right in inscribing the word 'democracy' on their banners.

The democratic inspiration and the belief in self emancipation (which are part of the same thing) are the essentials of Marxism. Without them, all the carefully constructed economics, all the earnest philosophy, wither on the vine.

The spirit of a revolt, the need for a class battle against exploitation— these are the antidotes to the determinism of which Marx was so often accused.

The famous statement that people make their own history but they do not make it as they choose is usually quoted by Marxists with the accent on everything after 'but'. In fact, the emphasis in the sentence is that men and women determine what happens to them. The point that they have to work within historical circumstances laid down for them is made only to ensure that they fight more effectively.

Not long after Marx died (in 1883) a new threat arose to the fight which he believed would soon be won. Men calling themselves Marxists found themselves at the head of 'great labour movements', vast trade unions, socialist newspapers, socialist sporting societies.

Such men started to wonder whether all this talk of revolution wasn't going over the top. They felt they might get to positions of power and influence through the newly granted franchise, and that when they did so they could legislate for socialism without having to go through messy and probably bloody revolution.

Thus at the end of the 1890s Edward Bernstein, like countless others after him, proposed to the masses that their world could be improved gradually and peacefully. All they needed to do was vote in a secret ballot. For Bernstein (and for Karl Kautsky, though few noticed his backsliding at this stage) the idea of millions of workers emancipating themselves in the streets and factories was faintly distasteful, if not downright dangerous.

The works of these men (except on the fringes: Bernstein, perhaps, on Cromwell; Kautsky on Christianity) do not survive with any relevance today. What does survive is the furious reply delivered to Bernstein and company by the Polish born revolutionary, Rosa Luxemburg.

Her reply came in two parts: *Social Reform or Revolution* (1900) and *The Mass Strike* (1906). The common theme of both pamphlets, the element which lifts them above all other contemporary political writing and makes them so important today, is the 'living political school', 'the pulsating flesh and blood', the 'foaming wave' of the working class in struggle.

Luxemburg fought like a tiger for Karl Marx's central principle: that the workers can only be emancipated if they themselves overthrow capitalist society. She exulted in the 1905 Russian Revolution which in a few weeks knocked out an absolutism which had reigned unchecked (in spite of all sorts of benevolent reformers who tried to make it better) for centuries. She rejoiced from her prison cell at the Russian Revolution of 1917.

The Russian revolutionary socialists more than anyone else in all history understood Marx's insistence on self emancipation. Where Marx had called for it and encouraged it, they carried it out.

Reactionary historians and commentators tell us that the tight discipline of the Bolshevik Party made it an undemocratic organisation dedicated to commanding the workers, not representing them. The truth is exactly the opposite.

The Bolshevik Party won its soviet majorities in the spring and summer of 1917 precisely because it took its stand on the strength, confidence and potential of the Russian workers. In *State and Revolution* and *The Proletarian Revolution and the Renegade Kautsky*, Lenin fulminated against parliamentary democracy because it was not democratic enough. It left the capitalist machine intact. It removed working class representatives from the cooperative atmosphere of everyday life in factories, mills, mines and offices.

Lenin, in *State and Revolution*, restated his belief in the 'elective principle' as the cornerstone of any new socialist society. He repeated again and again in the months and years after October that the working class which had emancipated itself was the only hope for the revolution. 'I calculated', he said:

> solely and exclusively on the workers, soldiers and peasants being able to tackle better than the officials, better than the police, the practical and difficult problems of increasing the production of foodstuffs and their better distribution, the better provision of soldiers, etc, etc.

He told the First All-Russian Congress of Soviets in January 1918:

> In introducing workers' control we knew it would take some time before it spread to the whole of Russia, but we wanted to show that we recognised only one road—changes from below: we wanted the workers themselves to draw up, from below, the new principles of economic conditions.

Lenin's inspiration, if less flamboyant, was exactly the same as Marx's and Luxemburg's. Their socialism depended on the exploitative society being overthrown in struggle by the workers. Lenin realised, therefore, that without the revolutionary class of self emancipated workers, the revolution would, in his own words, 'perish'.

Perish it did, for precisely that reason. The self emancipators, the small Russian working class, were annihilated in war and famine. By 1921 all that was left of them was the top layer, the bureaucracy of revolutionaries without the class which put it there.

The self emancipators were replaced by workers from the countryside who had not emancipated themselves or anyone else. The revolution in Germany was defeated. In Britain it never started. Russia was isolated, its revolutionary inspiration snuffed out. The revolution was lost. Soviet democracy was replaced by state capitalist tyranny.

Sad to say, most socialists and communists throughout the world did not notice that it was lost at all. Almost imperceptibly, communists who had been brought up to believe that the emancipation of the working class must be the act of the working class became idol worshippers in the old utopian tradition, falling at the feet of Stalin as the benevolent Father of Socialism.

In the name of Marxism, the very essence of Marxism, its democratic and self emancipatory spirit, was at first forgotten, later ridiculed and condemned. Dictatorship over the proletariat was hailed as dictatorship of the proletariat. Murdering opponents was hailed as democratic discipline. Communism and democracy, synonymous for Engels, became exact opposites for Stalinists.

More predictably anti-communists made the same mistake. They said there was a direct line from Lenin to Stalin, that all revolutions somehow end in tyranny. The answer to them is a simple one.

For all his myriad fetishes, racism and pettiness, Stalin bent his dictatorship to one central purpose: to squeeze out of Russia every single surviving breath of the revolution. He killed all his former Bolshevik colleagues—save Lenin, who died early enough to be turned (against everything he had ever believed) into another icon. Revolutionary decrees were repealed and replaced with their opposites.

Factory control was replaced by one man management; educational reform by educational reaction; internationalism by nationalism and racism; free abortions by rigid abortion controls. The death penalty for serious crimes, abolished by the revolution, was reimposed. Privileges, domestic servants and all the paraphernalia of ruling class 'superiority' were the order of the day.

All this was heralded throughout the world as socialism—though the essence of socialism, Lenin's control from below, had been turned into its very opposite, control from above.

After the Second World War, the tragedy repeated itself, as Marx would have said, this time as farce. In the carve up of the victorious powers, Russia swiped six countries in Eastern Europe. In none of these had the working class emancipated itself. Their emancipation, instead, was imposed by Russian bayonets.

Replicas of Stalin's state capitalist tyranny were set up in Hungary, Czechoslovakia, Romania, Bulgaria, Poland and East Germany. The workers played no part in any of these governments. They did not even have the right to vote them out, as their fellow workers had in much of the West. Resistance of any kind, especially resistance in the workplaces, was met with the most horrific repression. Uprisings in Hungary, Czechoslovakia, Poland and East Germany were put down by tanks.

The economies were bent and corrupted to the sustenance of Great Russian imperialism. Ruling class bureaucracies set themselves up in Stalin's image.

The countries came to be known as 'socialist countries'. Either their relationship with Russia, or their centralised 'planned' economies or their stuffed shirted socialist rhetoric convinced hundreds of thousands of socialists in other countries that at root they were socialist. The word caught on in the Eastern European countries themselves, but with a different result.

In those countries, where the workers knew that they were being dragooned and terrorised, socialism became a synonym for brutal dictatorship and exploitation. Socialism, the great emancipation, became the word for slavery. And the revolt against that tyranny, when it came, and when it was led, as it inevitably had to be, by the working class, turned first and most viciously against anything which called itself 'socialist'.

Now large numbers of socialists, who spent much of their lives in some posture of obeisance to these 'socialist countries', are fleeing the field.

Some of them are giving up all political commitment. Some, very few, place their faith in the 'revolution from above' which they imagine has been set in motion, singlehandedly, by Mikhail Gorbachev. Others, probably the majority, have abandoned any talk of revolution, and now work for 'reform from above' in the Labour Party and its equivalents.

The world in which we live is not in its essentials any different from the world which Marx described. It is still run on exploitative lines. A degenerate and cancerous capitalism still gnaws away at the lives of most of the world's people. There is no sign that 'reform from above' worries it even for a moment. It flicks aside the reformers with the same casual cynicism which Marx exposed.

The chief difference is that the working class, which still carries the hopes of change, is much bigger now than it was in Marx's day. While sophisticated commentators insist that the working class is vanishing, it is growing by hundreds of thousands every year and by millions every decade. Russia itself now has 60 million exploited industrial workers: China over 100 million and among the teeming, hungry masses of what was until recently known as the Third World, new robust organisations are arising, as Rosa Luxemburg predicted 'like Venus from the foam'.

The events in Eastern Europe have proved, like nothing else in the last 50 years, that sudden volcanic social change does not happen when stockbrokers forecast it or academics work it out. It comes when the masses move, seek to emancipate themselves and in the process, in Marx's famous phrase, 'educate themselves, the educators'.

Dictators and bureaucracies can call themselves socialist for so long. In the end the actions of the masses will sort them out, and start once more to reveal things as they are. An industrial economy which is 'planned' in the interests of a militaristic and parasitic minority is not socialist. It is its opposite: state capitalist.

If state capitalism is being 'conquered' by the masses emancipating themselves, then those same masses have blazed a path towards the conquering of all capitalism.

The urgent need for socialists is to kick the rotten corpse of state capitalism away from Rosa's 'living school' of self emancipatory socialism; to assert as aggressively as ever the socialist tradition which started with Marx and Engels, and was taken on by Luxemburg, Lenin, Trotsky and the Russian revolutionaries, and by a small band of socialists who knew all along that socialism and democracy are synonymous, that neither can ever exist without the other, and that both can only be achieved when the exploited masses use their irresistible power.

Chapter 7

Times that try men's souls

Gareth Jenkins

Two hundred years ago, in 1791, Tom Paine published *The Rights of Man*. It was a brilliant defence of the French Revolution, written in a language everyone could understand. Over 200,000 were sold within two years.

The ruling class hated Paine's book. They persecuted both it and the growing numbers of artisans and workers who read and were inspired by its message. They tried Paine for sedition in one of the great show trials of the 1790s. Luckily, he had already left England, to take up his seat as the elected member for Calais in the French National Convention.

The publication of *The Rights of Man* marked the summit of Paine's career as a revolutionary propagandist. It set the seal on the reputation he had forged during the American war of independence, a fight to free the former colonies from British rule.

He had emigrated to America in 1774 at the age of 37, abandoning the corset making trade his father had taught him and his father's Quaker religion.

As radical editor of a Philadelphia newspaper he was not content just to champion American grievances against Britain. If equality was desirable, then women should be equal with men and the black slaves should be freed. Very few American reformers were prepared to go that far.

The same uncompromising stance marked his contribution to the struggle against Britain. His pamphlet *Common Sense*, published in

First published June 1991

early 1776, was an instant best seller. The aim of the struggle, Paine argued, should not be some compromise with the old country.

Only an independent democratic republic could bring real change. But this would require all out mass struggle—which was precisely what the compromisers, many of them wealthy merchants, feared would threaten their power and prestige.

Paine's other journalism during the war was brilliant propaganda aimed at overcoming demoralisation in the face of a physically superior enemy. George Washington ordered these famous words to be read to his retreating troops:

> These are the times that try men's souls. The summer soldier and the sunshine patriot will, in this crisis, shrink from the service of their country—but he that stands it now, deserves the love and thanks of man and woman.

Paine's message was stunningly simple. Ordinary people had the right not to be managed by their betters but to elect their own representatives. They could reject any authority—kings, priests or judges—which was not accountable to them.

Paine's book was a reply to the attacks made on the French Revolution and its British supporters (and particularly, the 'swinish multitude') by a former defender of American rights, Edmund Burke.

Burke claimed that the British constitution could not be overthrown. We had inherited it from our forefathers and it was our duty to transmit it to our successors.

Paine was repelled by this grotesque notion that the past should govern the future, the dead control the living.

'Every age and generation', Paine declared:

> must be free to act for itself. The vanity and presumption of governing beyond the grave is the most insolent of all tyrannies. Man has no property in man; neither has any generation a property in the generations which are to follow. It is the living, and not the dead, that are to be accommodated.

Burke's appeal to tradition was a way of dressing up the whole rotten system of patronage, corruption and wealth that went with hereditary monarchy—what Paine called 'a continual system of war and extortion'.

Burke tried, as conservatives from his day to ours always do, to whip up emotion over 'mob violence'. In a passage of flowery rhetoric Burke bemoaned the fact that no one had been chivalrous enough to raise a sword to defend the French queen against insult. Paine's answer stripped away the poetry to look at the daily violence inflicted not on Marie Antoinette ('let them eat cake') but on her long suffering subjects. Burke, he wrote:

> ...is not affected by the reality of distress touching the heart, but by the showy resemblage of it striking his imagination. He pities the plumage, but forgets the dying bird.

Paine was just as plain in his ridicule about the mystique surrounding the British royal family:

> It requires some talents to be a common mechanic; but to be a king requires only the animal figure of man—a sort of breathing automaton.

Paine wanted the monarchy and the lords abolished—not just for political reasons. Abolition would have economic benefits. It would mean the enormous amounts of money consumed by these drones and their hangers on could be redistributed.

Paine also wanted a progressive income tax, out of which the sick, the old and the needy could be helped, and which would provide education, public jobs and unemployment relief.

This was what was dynamite about Paine's *The Rights of Man*. It made political reform not the business of a well disposed elite but of the mass of the population. As one of these respectable reformers, the Reverend Christopher Wyvill, put it:

> It was unfortunate for the public cause, that Mr Paine took such unconstitutional ground, and has formed a party for a Republic among the lower classes of the people, by holding out to them the prospect of plundering the rich.

But Paine had confidence in the lower classes and the talents that would blossom through activity. As if to answer the good vicar's fears, Paine wrote in *The Rights of Man*:

> It appears to general observation that revolutions create genius and talents, but that these events do no more than bring them forward. There is existing in man a mass of sense, lying in a dormant state, and which, unless something excites to action, will descend with him in that condition to the grave.

It was among these lower classes of the people that a party for a republic spread in the 1790s. Groups sprang up all over the country, the best known being the London Corresponding Society, which attracted at first small tradesmen and shopkeepers, masters and their journeymen, but then, later, porters, dockside labourers and even gentlemen's servants.

Paine was the toast of radical artisans. In Sheffield they even produced a parody of the national anthem, 'God save great Thomas Paine'.

But if Paine had a genius for expressing the egalitarian ideals of the revolution, he never really understood the class struggle that began to emerge within the new republics. This was a tragic failing in the French Revolution.

Paine's ideal was the small producer. His attack on the powerful and wealthy was not in order to do away with private property. It was rather to fight for a political state of affairs (the democratic republic) in which everybody would be able to enjoy the fruits of their labour.

'Labour' could include both the right to decent wages and the right to make a living out of small scale property, such as a farmer owning a few acres, a tradesman operating with a small amount of capital or an artisan possessing a few tools might enjoy.

Democracy, he believed, would prevent large scale property from creating poverty and misery, such as he had experienced in undemocratic societies.

The idea that there these two forms of 'labour', one working class, the other petty bourgeois, could have antagonistic interests would not have occurred to Paine.

In the struggle for American independence Paine could stand on the extreme left of the revolution, because that antagonism was minimal. This was not the case in the struggle against the old order in the French Revolution.

Paine's identification with the French Revolution did not go beyond siding with the Girondins, the moderate republicans. He voted against the King's execution and found himself thrown into jail by the Jacobins in 1793.

Paine was disillusioned. He could not understand why the republican constitution he had helped draw up was not the solution to all the inequalities of the old feudal order.

What he did not grasp was that the revolution could only be secured by the extreme dictatorial methods of the Jacobins, relying on the struggles of the Parisian sans culottes against small producers for the necessities of life. The intensity of economic class struggle put him out of his depth.

Yet Paine did not renounce his radicalism. While in prison he started writing The Age of Reason, his great attack on religion. Just as he had alienated moderate reformers with The Rights of Man's appeal to the masses, so now his ridicule of Christian myth put him beyond the pale.

What was particularly offensive was his appeal to a mass audience.

'Were any girl that is now with child to say, and even to swear to it, that she was gotten with child by a ghost, and that an angel told her so, would she be believed?' was Paine's way of effectively debunking the Virgin Birth.

Paine narrowly escaped execution while in prison. But even after the fall of the Jacobins in 1794 it took some time for him to be released. Not even the American government was very prompt to secure his freedom—an indication of how far the new republic had travelled from its revolutionary birth.

Paine briefly returned to the National Convention of which he was still a deputy. It is to his credit that in the face of Thermidorian reaction he continued to champion universal suffrage which the Directorate were attempting to limit.

After completing *The Age of Reason* Paine wrote one last major pamphlet, *Agrarian Justice*. It shows the strengths and limits of his radicalism. Though he denounced Babeuf's communist conspiracy of 1796 because it went against his belief in private property, which he defended as inseparable from the right to individual liberty, he was vehement in his attacks on the growing gulf between rich and poor.

Paine still hankered after a form of political democracy in which different interests could be reconciled. But he could not square the circle despite his proposal to bring about justice through fundamental agrarian reform.

Paine died back in America in 1809, an isolated figure. His historical greatness lay behind him and a new kind of radicalism, communism based on the working class, was yet to stir.

The core of his beliefs are rooted in the ideals of the world of the rising bourgeoisie. His commitment to equality and democracy went hand in hand with an Adam Smith belief in individual economic freedom.

But it took revolution to overthrow the old world. For his part in that Paine was hounded by kings and neglected by those who rode to power on the backs of the masses.

Without his fight against physical and mental oppression there would be no subsequent fight against the world he helped bring to birth. But since he refused to be tied to the past he undoubtedly would have appreciated this irony of history.

Chapter 8

Gramsci's real legacy

Sam Ashman

January 1991 marks the hundredth anniversary of the birth of the great Italian revolutionary Marxist Antonio Gramsci. Unfortunately the occasion will, no doubt, involve a good dose of the reinterpretation and misinterpretation of his thought by many who claim to stand in his tradition.

The Italian Communist Party (PCI) used him in the 1970s to justify the 'historic compromise'—the search for a parliamentary coalition with the Italian Christian Democrats which involved the PCI supporting Italy's membership of NATO and voting for various pieces of repressive legislation.

In Britain *Marxism Today* [the monthly magazine of the Eurocommunist wing of the British Communist Party, now ceased publication] claims the intellectual heritage of Gramsci. Martin Jacques, editor of the magazine, wrote a few years back, 'Gramsci has been the single most important theoretical influence on *Marxism Today* over the last decade.'

Gramsci has been systematically presented as an adherent of parliamentary gradualism, of the development of a new 'non-economistic' Marxism which replaces the crude demand for insurrection with a more gradual struggle for ideological dominance through broad cross-class alliances.

He has even been cited as the inspiration for the Bad Godesburg programme of 1959 which transformed the German Social Democratic Party and abandoned its last pretence at any commitment to Marxism.

First published January 1991

But Gramsci's life was dedicated to the interests of the international working class movement. A committed revolutionary, he was a witness to, and an active participant in, some of the major upheavals in Europe this century.

He was an active member of the left of the Italian Socialist Party (PSI) until he left and became one of the founders of the Communist Party of Italy (PCI) in 1921.

He died in 1937 as a result of 11 years of imprisonment in one of Mussolini's jails. The prosecutor at his trial summed up the aims of his imprisonment. 'For 20 years', he said, 'we must stop this brain from working.' Thankfully they did not succeed.

Above all Gramsci was a revolutionary, not a reformist. He had nothing but bitter contempt for reformists who are 'like a swarm of coachman flies on hunt for a bowl of blancmange in which they get stuck and perish ingloriously'.

He first came to prominence during the *biennio rosso*—the red years of 1918-20 when workers in Italy engaged in massive confrontations with the employers and the state that culminated in a wave of factory occupations in 1920.

From this experience he emphasised the need to build factory councils because he saw that only through building new non-parliamentary institutions could workers make a successful revolution:

> The socialists [reformists] have simply accepted the historical reality produced by capitalist intitiative.
>
> They believe in the perpetuity of the institutions of the democratic state. In their view the form of these democratic institutions can be corrected, touched up here and there, but in fundamentals must be respected.
>
> We on the other hand remain convinced that the socialist state cannot be embodied in the institutions of the capitalist state but must be a fundamentally new creation.

In the *Lyons Theses*, presented to the party's 1926 Congress shortly before his imprisonment, Gramsci draws out the lessons of the factory occupations and their eventual defeat:

> The defeat of the revolutionary proletariat in this decisive period was due to political, organisational, tactical and strategic deficiencies of the workers' party.
>
> As a consequence of these deficiencies, the proletariat did not succeed in placing itself at the head of the insurrection of the great majority of the population and channelling it towards the creation of a workers'

state. Instead it was influenced by other social classes which paralysed its activity.

Hence Gramsci spelt out the need for a Communist Party whose 'fundamental task' was to 'place before the proletariat and its allies the problem of insurrection against the bourgeois state and of the struggle for proletarian dictatorship'.

But Gramsci was more than simply aware of the need for socialism to be the self emancipation of the working class.

Most importantly he was clear about the need to fight to develop a revolutionary working class consciousness, and how this could only be developed through struggle, as a product of workers' own practical experience.

In 1919 he set up and became editor of the weekly paper *L'Ordine Nuovo* (*The New Order*) which was used to intervene in the factory occupations. He wrote later:

> The workers loved *L'Ordine Nuovo* and why did they love it? Because in its articles they discovered part, the best part of themselves. Because they felt its articles were pervaded by the same spirit of inner searching that they experienced: 'How can we become free? How can we become ourselves?' Its articles were not cold, intellectual structures but sprang from our discussions with the best workers, they elaborated the goals and the passions of the Turin working class.

So how have such seemingly clear ideas been distorted to the degree that they have?

The answer lies in some of the peculiarities of Gramsci's life. His imprisonment in 1926 placed him in a unique position. He was removed from the fight against Stalinism and not forced to take sides in the way he would have been if active.

As such it was later possible for both erstwhile Stalinists and Eurocommunists to present him as a loyal communist free from the taints of Stalinism and use him as justification for their twists and turns.

Second is the nature of his writings while in prison. The *Prison Notebooks* were written in a highly abstract style because Gramsci was mindful of the watchful eye of his fascist censors.

His language is deliberately obscure. For example he refers to Marxism throughout as the 'philosophy of praxis'. In this way the *Notebooks* lend themselves very well to an abstract, academic interpretation.

But the sort of distortions made by the Eurocommunists are only possible on the basis of a highly selective reading of the *Notebooks*, and the detachment of these from the rest of his work and life activity.

The central area of the distortion of Gramsci's thought is also the key to understanding his specific contribution to Marxism—and that is on the question of the possibilities of revolution in Western advanced capitalist societies.

The basic argument of the followers of *Marxism Today* is that Gramsci's work shows that Western capitalist societies are quite different from backward economies like tsarist Russia.

In Russia in 1917 the power of the bourgeoisie was much less developed than in the West. However, the economic development of the West allowed the power of Western ruling classes to be based less upon force and repression and more upon the control of workers' ideas—fraud. As Marx wrote, 'The ideas of the ruling class are in every epoch the ruling ideas.' This ideological domination is exercised through a network of voluntary organisations and institutions that pervade everyday life—what Gramsci calls civil society.

Political parties, trade unions, the mass media, the church, state education, the welfare state, mass entertainment and so on are all institutions of civil society. Repressive institutions are thus only one among the many defences of capitalist society. These other institutions buttress the capitalist state and make it less fragile.

Therefore, reformists have concluded, it follows that the key struggle for revolutionaries is not the direct assault on state power, but the struggle to achieve ideological dominance—what Gramsci called hegemony. Hegemony, they claim, can only be won through a long and drawn out battle over a number of years to make the working class 'counter-hegemonic'.

This involves winning over the main sections of intellectuals and the classes that they claim to represent because of the crucial role they play in manning the apparatuses of ideological domination.

The working class has to be prepared to sacrifice its own short term interests in order to do this, but the sacrifice is worth making, because until the working class is the hegemonic class in society, its attempts to seize state power will be doomed to failure.

The Eurocommunists' justification for this interpretation of Gramsci comes from a military analogy Gramsci makes in the *Prison Notebooks* in which he draws a distinction between two types of war.

The first is what he calls a 'war of manoeuvre' which involves rapid movement by both rival armies with thrusts forwards and backwards as each tries to outflank the other.

The second is a 'war of position' which involves a long drawn out struggle in which the two armies are deadlocked, each unable to move forward—something like the trench warfare of the First World War.

Gramsci says that the latter method is generally the most applicable method of struggle for revolutionaries in the West.

The last successful example of a war of manoeuvre was the Bolsheviks' seizure of power in the Russian Revolution of October 1917. A switch in strategy was necessary in the West, based on the fact that tsarist Russia and Western Europe have different social structures. Gramsci thus writes in the *Notebooks*:

> It seems to me that Ilich [Lenin] understood that change was necessary from the war of manoeuvre applied victoriously in the East in 1917, to a war of position that was the only form possible in the West.
>
> The most advanced states, where civil society has become a very complex structure, [are] resistant to the catastrophic incursions of the immediate economic elements (crises, depressions, etc).
>
> In Russia the state was everything, civil society was primordial and gelatinous; in the West...when the state trembled a sturdy structure of civil society was at once revealed. The state was only an outer ditch, behind which there stood a powerful system of fortresses and earthworks.

Gramsci's formulations here should not be accepted uncritically. At times he uses the metaphor in a contradictory and confusing way.

But there are a number of points which need to be made to rescue him from his latter day adherents.

Firstly, the war of position is still precisely that—a war, a class war, and not the politics of class collaboration pursued by reformists and Stalinists to this day.

Secondly it is not exactly new to say that revolutionary politics for much of the time is devoted to the war of position. Simply charging at the forces of the state without spending time building up support and respect inside the working class through the day-in-day-out battles against the employers would not get revolutionaries very far.

Moreover, Gramsci was engaged in an argument with one of the leaders of the PCI, Amadeo Bordiga, who had an ultra-left disdain for parliament, trade unions and the mass of workers who had not yet been won to revolutionary ideas.

Lenin and Trotsky argued for a united front with reformist parties to expose their inactivity and inability to fight consistently and to therefore win the majority of workers away from them.

Trotsky won Gramsci away from the influence of Bordiga so that in the *Notebooks* Gramsci explicitly identifies the war of position with the united front. He states it is designed to 'unmask so-called proletarian and revolutionary parties which have a mass base'.

Crucially though, Gramsci's notion of the battle for hegemony is not simply an ideological battle. His development of the concept of civil society was an important step forward and he correctly identifies these institutions as areas of struggle. But Gramsci never saw it as a battle of books and articles, or for that matter the struggle to achieve directorships of Channel 4. The revolutionary war of position is waged from below, primarily by the workers in those institutions— students, teachers, civil servants and so on.

Gramsci stressed, and understood brilliantly, the way that Marxist theory and spontaneous working class struggles can come together. He argued that implicit in workers' everyday struggle is a revolutionary understanding of the world.

But in the 'normal' conditions of capitalist society workers' consciousness is contradictory, with revolutionary and reactionary ideas coexisting uneasily.

Workers' struggles create the conditions under which the revolutionary elements can triumph over the reactionary ones.

But for this to happen a revolutionary party is needed to draw out the class consciousness implicit in workers' struggles and render it coherent and systematic.

Reflecting on the experience of the Turin workers' movement, he writes:

> Spontaneity was not neglected...it was educated, directed, the aim was to bring it in line with modern theory [Marxism] but in a living and historically effective manner.
>
> It gave the masses a 'theoretical' consciousness of being creators of historical and institutional values, of being founders of a state. The unity between 'spontaneity', a 'conscious leadership', of 'discipline', is precisely the real political action of the subaltern classes.

The struggle to win over other oppressed classes to the side of the proletariat never, for Gramsci, meant the abandonment of working class interests or the fight for those interests, nor was it an alternative to economic struggles.

The idea that the working class can establish ideological hegemony within capitalism is an impossibility. Only when workers are the ruling class—the dictatorship of the proletariat—can workers achieve ideological hegemony, just as only with the overthrow of capitalism can workers control production.

Similarly take Gramsci's conception of the 'historical bloc'. This was a strategic response to the 'southern question'—a long problem and major stumbling block for Italian socialists. The development of capitalist industrialisation in Italy had taken place primarily in the north, and to a lesser degree in the centre of the country. Southern Italy remained in abject poverty.

The socialist movement was based in, and focused on, northern industrial workers and tended to neglect the question of the south.

Trade union leaders followed what he called an 'economic-corporate' strategy, accepting higher wages in return for not challenging the ruling bloc of industrialists and landowners. This narrow sectional approach proved a disaster when, in 1920, peasant conscript soldiers were used against the factory occupations.

If the Italian revolution was to be successful, Gramsci considered it central for this to be overcome. The peasantry had to be detached from the influence of the ruling class and a 'historical bloc' formed between them and industrial workers.

For this to be possible, a workers' party must make clear its support for the struggles of southern peasants. The working class must seek to be 'hegemonic'—that is to build alliances with other groups but under its own leadership.

A hegemonic strategy by the working class in the context of Italy in the 1920s and 1930s meant that the working class had to offer the peasantry the prospect of land and the intelligentsia the prospect of a better society, but without ever compromising working class interests to these other groups.

For the followers of *Marxism Today*, on the other hand, the historic bloc has come to signify not an alliance between workers and peasants but an alliance between the working class and the middle class and even some supposedly 'progressive' sections of capital. From an alliance of the exploited, it has become an alliance of the exploited with their exploiters.

Gramsci talks of the need to win intellectuals, but only as an ally, never as a substitute for or equal to the working class. They must be won to following the lead of the working class. He stresses the need to group together 'organic intellectuals', workers with a grasp of the class struggle and their role within it.

Finally, nowhere in the *Notebooks* does Gramsci suggest that the struggle for ideological hegemony can, by itself, resolve the question of state power. Even when a 'war of position' plays the predominant part there are still what he calls 'partial' elements of movement, moments of violent confrontation when one side tries to break through the other's lines. For Gramsci, armed insurrection was the 'decisive moment of struggle' and his 'modern prince'—the revolutionary party—the central, co-ordinating and generalising body.

This is not to say that Gramsci's work is without its faults. The *Notebooks* in particular, accepting the difficult circumstances under which they were written, do remain at a high level of abstraction. Gramsci found it difficult at times to link ideological phenomena with their material basis.

So for example, he discusses the possibilities of the 'corporate integration' of workers— being bought off—but does not discuss the material roots that make this possible.

It is also possible to exaggerate Gramsci's greatness. To claim that he was not 'economistic' is partly to accept that economism went before him in the work of Marx, Engels, Lenin and Trotsky. Earlier Marxists were also clear about the ruling class's use of fraud as well as of force as a method of maintaining their rule.

Gramsci expanded our understanding of the model of revolution developed by Lenin and Trotsky, crucial to which is the united front.

Concepts like civil society and hegemony enhance our understanding of the world, but the united front provides the crucial ingredient for breaking workers from the ideas that accept the system or simply seek to reform it.

Nonetheless, there are aspects of Gramsci's thought that are a real contribution to the advance of Marxism that we can still learn from and use today.

The idea of workers having a contradictory consciousness is central to an understanding of reformism, of how workers look to organisations that accept capitalism whilst at the same time partially rejecting it.

The need to shift between a war of position and a war of manoeuvre is a distinction every socialist should have in their armoury. Gramsci's philosophical writings also contain great insight and clarity.

But Gramsci is at his best when he writes about workers as an active force capable of creating a completely new society and the role revolutionaries play in that.

His whole political life was given over to that struggle. It cost him his freedom and eventually his life.

It is from this we can learn today, and not from the designer socialists of *Marxism Today*.

Chapter 9

The end of history?

Francis Fukuyama and Alex Callinicos

Francis Fukuyama

I want to lay out briefly some of the arguments in the book [*The End of History*] because many reviews have caricatured them. You get the idea I'm arguing there's an inevitable and inexorable drive everywhere to turn towards American shopping centres. I can assure you that is certainly not the objective of my book.

The starting point is what has happened in world politics in the past generation. There has been a lot of new democracy in the world, and a global crisis of authoritarianism, which has been the chief characteristic of our generation in politics.

This doesn't particularly refer to the collapse of Communism, which was unexpected by everybody, but to the events in Southern Europe which began in the mid-1970s when Spain, Portugal and Greece all made transitions to stable democracies.

In Latin America in the 1980s there was a series of transitions to democracy in the major states—Peru, Argentina, Brazil, Uruguay, and finally, by the end of the decade, the Sandinistas in Nicaragua held an election and Pinochet's Chile elected a democratic president.

There was a similar set of transitions in Asia: the downfall of dictatorships in South Korea and the Philippines, and an aborted revolution in Burma. Taiwan has been moving towards greater democratisation of its political system.

Finally there was the collapse of Communism and the totalitarian system. It's quite clear watching the experiences of the Soviet Union and China that the totalitarian experiment completely failed. There

First published April 1992

are virtually no totalitarian regimes left in the world.

Is all of this simply a historical accident or part of a cyclical pattern? Whether there is actually a pattern underlying it, a universal history that explains the social evolution of all human societies was first proposed by Kant in 1784. There have been a number of attempts to write such universal histories. The first was really by Hegel but the most famous by far was that of Karl Marx: that history has a certain dialectical progressive direction and it also has an end—that is to say, a certain end state in which human society finally conforms to the underlying striving and desires of human nature.

The failure of real world Marxist societies compels us to go back to that question and ask whether in fact Marx is right about the directionality of history and its progressive nature, which has a terminal point.

That is the fundamental question of the book. It makes sense at the end of the 20th century to raise the question, is there such a thing as universal history, does it have a direction and where is that direction going?

I make two attempts to answer this question: one based on the logic of modern science, and the other on what I call the struggle for recognition.

Of all the human, social activities we see around us, modern natural science is the only one that is by common consensus cumulative. We don't ever return to the same state of ignorance in science—as certain things are known about the natural world. Natural science has all of us in its grip, most obviously through economics.

The process of industrialisation is based on the unfolding of natural science and it produces a certain kind of homogenisation of all the societies that go through it, regardless of their cultural starting point. So Western Europe, North America and Japan today look in many ways more similar to each other than they did 50 years ago and certainly 100 years ago.

The unfolding of natural science leads us at this stage of our development to capitalism. This is not a conclusion that would have been accepted readily by anyone a generation ago. Then one would have pointed to Stalin's Russia as an example of a country that could reach the most modern levels of industrial development in less than a generation without either political or economic freedom.

But the experience of the Soviet Union and China in the last generation has been quite decisive. Central planning was sufficient to get economies up to the level of industrialisation represented by Europe in the 1950s. But the post-industrial society, in which information and technological innovation become vastly more important, in which the complexity of modern economies becomes vastly greater, seems to demand a certain kind of decentralised economic decision making which is the essence of capitalism.

The next question is whether the upholding of science also makes democracy necessary. Here it is less clear. It is possible to have a technologically modern civilisation without having political liberty. An essentially economic account of history is insufficient.

And this is where I move to the second explanation of the book, based on the struggle for recognition, which ultimately comes out of Hegel, as interpreted by his great 20th century French interpreter, Alexandre Kojève. Recognition in Hegel is not a terribly complicated concept: it simply refers to the fact that man, in addition to being a biological animal with certain biological needs, is also a being that demands or desires the acknowledgement or respect of a certain human dignity or autonomy from other human beings.

In Hegel's account all the major phenomena of history are not driven by economic forces but by the struggle for recognition.

Many political phenomena are much more readily understandable to us in terms of recognition than in terms of economics. Religion is essentially an activity of people who want to have their particular gods and idols recognised by other people, and they get very angry if that recognition is not forthcoming. Nationalists are not motivated by any particular economic motive. They are in fact willing to forego all sorts of economic benefits in the short run. It is simply an act of human consciousness which is the driving force in much of the politics of Eastern Europe today.

Democracy has to be understood in terms of a desire for recognition rather than any economic motive. According to Hegel, the French Revolution solved the basic human problem by abolishing the earlier relationship of lordship and bondage, master and slave. The former slaves became their own masters in a system of universal recognition.

You can interpret the right of individual liberties that we have in a liberal democracy as essentially ends in themselves. They are an act of recognition by which we all recognise each other—so that we have the right to free speech, for example, because we are adults capable of forming our own opinion. We have the right to freedom of religion because we can make decisions regarding the most important questions of right and wrong. Above all we have the right to participation in our own governments.

The revolutions in Eastern Europe are impossible to explain in economic terms. There was clearly an economic basis for them—the workers wanted a higher living standard. But you can't really explain the totality of those events unless you look at the other part of the human personality that seeks recognition. People did not go into the streets of Leipzig, Moscow or Timisoara or Beijing simply demanding a post-industrial economy. They wanted a system of rights, a rule of law, that would recognise them as human beings, that would not lie to them, or keep them as children or not permit them to participate in their own political process. This is essentially the meaning of democracy today.

The question about the end of history really revolves around the adequacy of universal recognition in satisfying human beings in their most profound and deepest characteristics. Essentially two critiques that have been made of universal recognition leave this question open.

The first is the critique to the left, which says that the problem with universal recognition is that it recognises inherently equal people unequally. The division of labour in modern industrial society, the winners and losers created by the capitalist market place, inevitably create differences with which people are recognised. A garbage collector will never be recognised as an equal of a theoretical physicist or the chair of a corporation.

The other major critique is that from the right. By the right, I don't mean merely anyone in contemporary democratic politics—I mean that represented by the German philosopher Nietzsche. Essentially that critique is the very image of the one to the left—the problem with universal recognition is that it recognises inherently unequal people equally. According to Nietzsche all men are not created equal. But, more importantly, he would argue that if men were created equal there could be no form of human achievement, no human excellence, no aspiration, no struggle for anything higher if all people wanted was to be recognised as the equals of other people, that any society that aspires to any type of human creativity has to be based on a form of unequal recognition. The central problem of liberal democracy was not that it failed to deliver on its promises of peace and prosperity but precisely that *if* it delivered that peace and prosperity then a whole horizon of human aspiration would be eliminated. We would then have a society of what he called 'last men' that were essentially satisfied by endless consumerism, by a whole series of petty private wants that had no public spiritedness, no concern for the community around them, no ideals, no sense of struggle or sacrifice.

This is ultimately the contradiction that liberal democracy cannot solve. It cannot satisfy that side of man—the desire for struggle and sacrifice. Therefore we'll always be subject to a certain kind of instability for this satisfaction. If we are unwilling to become the contemptible last man, simply filling our lives with consumerism, then in a certain sense we will long to live for ideals or to struggle against the society which created such a flat horizon. In a way, we start history by becoming first men who are engaged in bloody besieged battles to simply prove we are human beings and can involve ourselves.

Alex Callinicos

Francis Fukuyama has pushed back onto the political agenda the idea that we should try to make sense of the overall pattern of historical development through which all human societies are going. In many ways some of the most important political questions we have to resolve are precisely to do with the nature and pattern of historical development. In that respect, if in no other, it seems to me that his intervention has been a worthwhile one and takes us on to a terrain infinitely better than a lot of the futile and stupid intellectual debates that go on in universities these days about postmodernism. So there is at least one point of agreement between us.

But I think I should move on to my disagreements. Fukuyama believes that there is an end of history ahead of us or perhaps already on us. What are his reasons?

The first and most obvious reason was the collapse of the Stalinist regimes. And although Fukuyama seeks to distance himself from contemporary events, I think it would make no sense not to address the immediate political and historical context in which his writings have had such an impact.

The collapse of the Stalinist regimes has apparently settled the question of whether there is a socialist or a communist form of society superior to capitalism. And Fukuyama has repeated the claim that no single critique in the debate his original article provoked put forward the vision of a society fundamentally different and better than contemporary liberal democracy.

There is at least one critic who is willing to defend the ideas of a society fundamentally different and better than liberal democracy. I want to defend Marx's original conception of socialism as a society qualitatively superior to capitalism and moving beyond the kind of economic and social inequalities and competitive anarchy endemic to capitalism. In doing so I want to resist one of the unargued assumptions of Fukuyama's book, that we can equate any conceivable socialist society with what used to be called 'really existing socialism'.

There's a fundamental difference between Marx's conception of socialism, an idea carried on in the classical Marxist tradition by people like Lenin and Trotsky, and 'really existing socialism', or no longer really existing socialism. The Stalinist societies were societies run from the top by an extremely narrow privileged social group, the nomenklatura, the top party state officials.

Marx's conception of socialism and the reality of the Russian Revolution of 1917 involved socialism from below, in which the mass of working people began to assume direct and democratic control over their lives. The Stalinist regimes represented a particular form of capitalism—state capitalism—in which the working class were collectively exploited by the nomenklatura. One crucial flaw of *The End of History* is that it assumes that the Marxist tradition and its conception of socialism are definitively defunct.

This then brings us on to the theory of history just summarised, which also underlies the idea that history is coming to an end. The idea that it is a struggle for recognition that moves history on, I think, owes far more to Nietzsche than it does to Hegel. It is amazingly reductive— every significant phenomenon of political, social and even economic life is reduced to some aspect of the struggle for recognition. Recognition, Fukuyama says, is the origin for tyranny, imperialism and the desire to dominate. Elsewhere he says the source of war is to be rooted in the struggle for recognition between different people, groups and nations.

What is often *falsely* claimed of Marxism as a theory of history is actually true of Fukuyama's theory of history. It is immensely reductive, but at the same time is designed to be immune from any falsification by empirical facts or by evidence.

We can see this in the preface to the book, where he says, 'And yet what I had suggested had come to an end was not the occurrence of events, even large and grave events, but History: that is history understood as a single, coherent, evolutionary process.' He's saying: don't tell me about the Gulf War, don't tell me about the war in Nagorno-Karabakh, don't tell me about the barricades which have gone up in Sarajevo. They are events, simply things that are happening. They are not part of History with a capital 'H'. At most they are what he calls 'setbacks of discontinuity', things that don't fit into the main line of historical development and that can simply be explained away as slightly inconvenient interruptions to the grand march of history with a capital 'H'.

The result of this conception of history is an immensely complacent and apologetic view of the contemporary world. So in an article that he wrote almost a year ago he drew a contrast between what he calls Ruritania—which is the general name he gave to the societies of the Third World which he said were still mired in history because they haven't reached the culminating phase of liberal capitalism—and on the other hand the societies which have gone beyond history, the developed liberal capitalisms of the West. He said:

> A large part of the world will be populated by Iraqs and Ruritanias and will continue to be subject to bloody wars and revolutions. But, with the exception of the Gulf, few regions will have an impact on the growing part of the world that is democratic and capitalist.

This is quite a revealing indication of the underpinnings of Fukuyama's conception of history. Essentially what he is saying is that Ruritania—incidentally this is a rather offensive term because it's the name given in comic novels to Balkan states in which nothing really serious happens—this 'not very serious' part of the world does not really matter and doesn't really directly affect the societies which have gone beyond history.

The majority of the world's inhabitants happen to live in these Third World societies going through bloody revolutions and wars. It is not so easy for us in the Western liberal capitalist societies to wash our hands. Fukuyama clearly has in mind Iraq in his article, but the more we learn about what happened in the Gulf War and before it, the more we discover the extent to which Saddam Hussein is someone who the Western corporations and governments did everything they could to arm.

There are a multitude of causal connections binding the so called post-historical societies of the West with Ruritania, and in many respects all the worst aspects of these countries were actually sustained and created by the developed societies of the West. The end of the Cold War means that the big arms companies are running out of their usual protected markets and so are rushing out to sell equipment in the Third World.

Finally it's not possible, even if it were desirable, for the post-historical societies to insulate themselves from the rest of the world where no one can argue that the major social and political problems have been resolved. Look at the situation of Germany. As a result of the East German revolution, reunification and the collapse of the Soviet Union, suddenly on its borders it is faced with an immense zone of political and economic instability that stretches from the Elbe to the Pacific.

There is a similarly apologetic stance adopted by Fukuyama when it comes to the developed capitalist societies themselves. In his original article he said that the United States had approximated to Marx's idea of a classless and communist society—an idea which makes me laugh. Clearly, when Marx was writing about communism it was very much part of his view of a classless egalitarian society that there should be large parts of the major cities given over to wars between rival drug gangs in the midst of poverty and suffering!

Fukuyama retreats from this direct claim which originally comes from Kojève, but not that much. He doesn't deny that Western societies are, as he puts it, highly inegalitarian, but he says the sources of inequality can increasingly be attributed to the natural inequality of talents and to the economically necessary division of labour and of culture. There's no really polite way to respond to this sentiment. I think it's just balderdash! But don't just take my word for it, take the word, for example, of Kevin Phillips, a very experienced political adviser to the Republican Party in the US, who in 1990 published a book entitled *The Politics of Rich and Poor*. In it he describes how in the United States in the 1980s social and economic inequalities grew. As a result of state intervention, in particular by the federal government, there was a massive transfer of wealth and income from the poor to the rich. And the most speculative forms of capitalism, focused on the stock market, were given official encouragement. What has this got to do with natural talents?

One of the great ironies of the end of history is that it should have appeared at a time when we are in the depths of world economic recession—what we old fashioned Marxists tend to call a global crisis of capitalism. It affects not just the societies that went in for speculative capitalism—the new right, laissez faire capitalism—in a great way like the United States or Britain. But it's even gripping the more sober developed capitalisms like Japan and Germany. Sony, for example, is losing $1.7 billion a day, making losses for the first time in its history as a corporation. There seem to be a few more problems with Western capitalism as a functioning economic and social system than Fukuyama would suggest.

This is a world in which Marx's original critical analysis of capitalism is still fundamentally relevant. This is a world in which it is still necessary to struggle for a form of society that is more advanced than capitalism, that builds on its productive achievements but does away with inequality and competition, which are the endemic features of capitalism. History hasn't yet come to a full stop. In fact the party's just begun.

Chapter 10

Jean-Paul Sartre: he missed the boat but he kept on swimming

Ian Birchall

From the flood of obituaries of Sartre a clear bourgeois party line emerges. Sartre was on the wrong side politically being 'soft on communism', an uncritical supporter of Russian labour camps, terrorism, etc, etc; his influence has waned and he is virtually unknown to the younger generation; yet somehow, despite all that, he was a 'great man'. Much of what has been written is marked by a combination of patronising smugness and pig ignorance. Thus the *Sunday Times* (20 April) quotes Mary Warnock as having consigned existentialism 'to the intellectual dustbin'. Ms Warnock's main claim to fame is a book on Sartre's evolution to Marxism in which she quotes Marx's 'fourteenth thesis on Feuerbach'. (NB for new readers—there are only 11).

In the *Observer* (20 April) John Weightman laments that Sartre did not agree with Voltaire's statement: 'I may not agree with what you say, but I will defend to the death your right to say it.' (Actually Voltaire never said any such thing.) But precisely one of the things Sartre always insisted on was that words were a form of action. Sartre never took refuge in 'theoretical praxis', 'relative autonomy' or any of the other mystifications whereby a whole generation of would-be Marxist intellectuals have sought to disconnect what they said from

First published May 1980

what they did—or more likely didn't do. For Sartre the unity of theory and practice was paramount, and it is nothing less than an insult to him to suggest that one can acclaim his 'philosophy' while dismissing the practice it led to. The only obituary Sartre deserves is one that defends him against the smears and lies of his would-be friends, while at the same time rigorously criticising his political practice.

Contrary to received opinion Sartre was never a Stalinist and never a Maoist. Nor, contrary to the wishful thinking of some, was he ever a consistent revolutionary socialist. Sartre's work is a long dialogue with the revolutionary left: a dialogue full of hesitations and misunderstandings. From the failures of this dialogue we can learn something of the weakness of the left in our age.

Clive James (*Observer*, 20 April) thinks Sartre supported Stalin and Mao because 'he was taking revenge for his bad eye'. (I don't know if Mr James has any physical disability to blame his inanity on.) A more fruitful approach to tracing Sartre's development would be to start with a story he tells in his autobiography, *Words*. As the child of a rich bourgeois family he had for a while a governess called Marie-Louise who used to lament to her pupil that she couldn't find a husband. For the young Sartre her unhappiness called into question the values which his family had tried to instil into him:

> I thought wages were proportionate to merit: so why did they pay her so badly? If you had a job, you were proud and dignified, happy to work: since she had the good fortune to work eight hours a day, why did she speak of her life as being an incurable ill? When I reported her grievances, my grandfather burst out laughing: she was much too ugly for any man to want her. I didn't laugh: so you could be born condemned? In that case they had lied to me: the order of the world concealed a state of intolerable disorder.

It is this gulf between theory and practice, between ideology and reality that led Sartre to break irreconcilably with his own class. His whole work is devoted to the quest for values which can be taken seriously, which can be implemented in practice. If god does not exist, if human beings have freedom of choice, then we must follow through the logic of those propositions, accept all the consequences they entail.

Sartre and socialism

The only solution was socialism. But for Sartre the road to socialism was far from easy. Too young to participate in the great social upheavals which followed the First World War, Sartre came of age politically as Stalin was consolidating his power over the Comintern, and fascism was rising throughout Europe.

He was never in much doubt that he was an anti-fascist, but the question of positive political alignment was a much more difficult one. In the 1930s his circle of friends included at least one Trotskyist, Colette Audry, and Sartre was certainly familiar with the debates of the period; but the revolutionary left was too peripheral to political reality to exert any real influence on him.

The major Marxist influence on him at the time was Paul Nizan, Communist, novelist and journalist. Nizan was a loyal Stalinist up to the Stalin-Hitler pact, after which he left the party; shortly after that he was killed. After the war a number of Communist Party intellectuals—notably Aragon and Henri Lefebvre—spread the totally unfounded story that Nizan had been a police informer. From this whole affair Sartre retained a distrust of the French Communist Party, which survived whatever tactical alliances he might make.

The German occupation was a crucial period for consolidating Sartre's political commitment. Not that he was in any sense a resistance hero; but the experience made clear to him the nature of writing as a political act. In 1943 his play *The Flies* was performed in Paris; Sartre's choice of a theme from Greek mythology had concealed from the German censor the fact that the play was a clear encouragement to resistance.

Sam White (*Evening Standard*, 18 April) dredged up the tired old slander that Sartre was somehow 'collaborating' with the Germans by cheating the censorship this way. This slander was first launched by André Malraux in 1959 when he was a minister in de Gaulle's government. Sartre was able to reply that the performance had been approved by the main resistance organisation for writers, the CP controlled National Writers' Committee.

Up to the end of the German occupation, then, Sartre was a man of the mainstream left: against fascism, for socialism, agnostic about Marxism. It was in 1944-45, when revolution was on the agenda for France, that Sartre faced a real choice as to whether to take the reformist or the revolutionary road.

Many years later, in 1961, Sartre described the choice he faced at the time of the Liberation:

> It was possible, in 1945, to choose between two positions. Two and only two. The first, and better, one, was to address the Marxists and them alone, to denounce the aborted revolution, the slaughtered Resistance, and the disintegration of the left. Some journals adopted this position

courageously, and disappeared unheard: it was the happy time when people had ears not to hear and eyes not to see. I am far from believing that these failures condemned their attempts, and I claim we could have imitated them without sinking... But to denounce the revolution betrayed, it would first have been necessary to be a revolutionary: Merleau [Merleau-Ponty, his collaborator—I B] wasn't one, and nor was I yet. We didn't even have the right to declare ourselves Marxists, despite our sympathies for Marx. Now revolution is not a state of mind: it's a day-by-day practice illuminated by a theory. And if reading Marx isn't enough to make you a revolutionary, you converge with him sooner or later if you are fighting for revolution. The result is clear: only men formed by this discipline could effectively criticise the left; so, at that time, they had to be more or less closely linked to Trotskyist circles; but straightaway this affiliation disqualified them, without it being their fault: in this mystified left dreaming of unity, they appeared as splitters.

So Sartre turned his back on the revolutionary road; instead he adopted a reformist line; unwilling to join the Communist Party, which he saw as manipulative and dogmatic, he sought, through his journal *Les Temps Modernes*, and later through his own political group the RDR (Revolutionary Democratic Assembly), to put pressure on the Communist Party from outside, though without any clear critique of the Communist Party's non-revolutionary nature.

Ironically, it was just at this time that the revolutionary left had some chance of breaking through. With the Communist Party deeply buried in a coalition government, following a no-strike line, the Trotskyist left offered the only militant alternative.

There were modest electoral successes, and gains in the Socialist Party Youth; in 1947 Trotskyists took the lead in the strike at the Renault car plant. But it was too little and too late; with the Cold War and the consequent turn by the Communist Party, there was setback and demoralisation for the whole working class movement.

The French Trotskyist movement dissolved into factionalism and unprincipled blocs. Instead of Trotskyism being a force of attraction to Sartre, it was the other way round. Many Trotskyists entered the RDR, seeing it as a short cut to building a mass organisation. But the RDR, with its woolly programme, was bound to disintegrate. For some, like David Rousset, briefly a close associate of Sartre, the RDR was nothing more than an easy bridge from Trotskyism to Gaullism.

Dirty hands?

Yet the ghost of revolutionary politics still walked in the corridors of Sartre's mind. In his play *Dirty Hands* the young Communist Hugo denounces the old party leader Hoederer as follows:

> The party has a programme: the achievement of a socialist economy, and one means to achieve it: the use of the class struggle. You're going to use it to carry out a policy of class collaboration in the framework of a capitalist economy. For years you're going to lie, cheat and manoeuvre; you'll go from one compromise to another; you'll defend to our comrades reactionary measures taken by a government that you are part of. No one will understand: the hard ones will leave us, the others will lose the political education they've just acquired. We shall be contaminated, softened, disoriented; we shall become reformists and nationalists; to end up with, the bourgeois parties will only have to make the necessary effort in order to liquidate us.

For Sartre, Hoederer, not Hugo, is the hero of the play; yet it would be hard to find a more acute, and indeed prophetic, indictment of the policy of the French CP in 1944 to 1947, and the sorry price it paid for it in the following decade.

But as French Trotskyism collapsed into factionalised irrelevance in the early 1950s, Sartre was more and more pulled towards the Communist Party. At a time when many representatives of the bourgeoisie were calling for the banning of the CP, Sartre argued that, whatever the weakness of the CP, to liquidate the main organisation of the working class could only bring disaster for French workers. Moreover, he claimed, those thinkers of the extreme left who denounced the CP were in effect allying with those who wanted to see it banned.

Sartre's position was sadly wrong. In the 1950s there was no short cut available, no alternative to the slow patient task of rebuilding the revolutionary current from scratch. But Sartre was never an uncritical pro-Stalinist. In 1952 he published a long article called 'The Communists and Peace', the aim of which was 'to declare my agreement with the Communists on precise limited subjects, arguing on the basis of *my* principles and not *theirs*'.

George Steiner (*Sunday Times*, 20 April) tells us that Sartre was 'damnably wrong—on the Soviet camps for example'. In 1952, however, when the CP were still denying the very existence of labour camps, Sartre wrote in a polemic against his former friend Camus:

> Yes, Camus, like you I find these camps unacceptable; but just as

unacceptable is the use that the 'so-called bourgeois press' makes of them every day. I don't say: the Madagascan before the Turkoman; what I say is that you mustn't use the suffering inflicted on the Turkoman to justify the suffering *we* impose on the Madagascan. I have seen the anti-communists rejoicing at the existence of these prisons, I've seen them use them to give themselves a clean conscience; and I had the impression that they were not bringing help to the Turkoman, but rather exploiting his misfortune just as the USSR exploits his labour.

One can only assume that George Steiner thinks it was 'damnably wrong' not to applaud the camps. But even in this period Sartre's dialogue with the revolutionary left continues. 'The Communists and Peace' contains long passages of polemic directed both against 'Germain' (Ernest Mandel) and against an ex-Trotskyist, non-Leninist grouping called Socialisme ou Barbarie (political ancestors of the Solidarity group in Britain).

The right choice

Sartre's honeymoon with the CP ended with the Hungarian Revolution and thereafter his main commitment was to anti-imperialism. Sartre had close links with those groups in France which gave active material support to the Algerian liberation struggle. François Jeanson, an old friend of Sartre's, organised one of the best known of the pro-Algerian networks; he tells how, when he visited Sartre in 1959, 'within two hours, I had an interview from him for our clandestine paper, as well as some addresses which were going to be very precious to us.' Sartre's giving of a signed interview to an illegal paper was a deliberate challenge to the state.

Apart from the Jeanson network, one of the main groups involved in giving aid to the Algerians were the French Trotskyists. Slowly, through the Algerian struggle and subsequently the Russell Tribunal on war crimes in Vietnam, Sartre rebuilt his links with the revolutionary left, and saw the increasing passivity of the CP, caught in the logic of its parliamentary aspirations.

The year 1968 was the first time since 1945 when revolutionary politics came out of the wilderness. This time Sartre made the right choice; there was no ambiguity as to his support for the students, no doubt that this could be the beginning of a revolutionary process had not the CP diverted it back into safe channels.

From then until his death Sartre was always on the side of the revolutionaries. Yet he could not escape the decline and crisis which afflicted the French left in the 1970s. His main alignment was with the Maoists, though that never meant an uncritical support for Maoist politics, let alone for the Chinese regime. When Michele Manceaux published in 1972 her book *The Maoists in France*, Sartre contributed a preface which began with the words, 'I am not a Maoist.' Sartre admired the Maoists for their activism and their total break with bourgeois legality: he rather naively hoped that Maoist students taking jobs in factories would come to be a new type of intellectual.

Sartre's determination and his continuing activism inspire respect even where his political judgement requires the most thorough criticism. If Sartre was a failure, his failure was a part of our collective failure; the corpse is ours to dissect: not a drop of blood must go to the smug ignoramuses of the bourgeois press.

Chapter 11

In a class of their own?

Hazel Croft

The decimation of key sectors of manufacturing industry through the 1980s led many on the left to believe that the possibility of united working class struggle had been wiped off the agenda.

Recent months have shown the fallacy of such arguments. The levels of poverty, job insecurity and mortgage repossessions which have hit *all* workers in the current recession have undermined the idea that workers in banking, insurance and other 'white collar' jobs have been materially bought off by the system.

But the argument still has a resonance. After all, the big battalions of the working class movement—the dockers and the miners—who led the struggles of the early 1970s have become a much weaker force. Who is there left, the argument goes, to lead a concerted surge of working class struggle? Even if suffering materially at present, isn't it true that ideologically white collar workers see themselves as middle class?

'White collar worker' is a catch-all term. It is used to refer to all those earning a salary but not engaged in traditional skilled or unskilled manual work. It can be used equally to refer to the most highly paid and highly rewarded salaried members of the ruling class or to a clerical worker stuck in a low grade doing routine office work. For Marxists it is therefore a rather meaningless category.

But the 'white collar' label does play an important ideological function: it distinguishes the mass of low paid office workers from their

First published January 1993

counterparts in the factories and lumps them together with those who are directly managing operations for the capitalist class. It therefore helps to mask the real structure of class society.

The distinction between white collar and blue collar work is a false one. Class position doesn't depend on the type of work people do—manual or non-manual—or on their own personal feelings about it but on their objective position in the productive process, crucially on whether they own or have any control over the means and methods of production.

The huge growth of white collar work this century has been accompanied by a growing polarisation between a small group of well paid executives on the one hand and the immense mass of low paid wage workers on the other.

This process has accompanied what the American Marxist Harry Braverman, in his study *Labour and Monopoly Capital*, called the 'industrialisation' of office work. Clerical work, until the end of the 19th century, was characterised by its small scale and personalised nature. Although many clerks worked in grim surroundings, the very nature of their work—in small offices with close personal contact with their employer—and the level of education needed to obtain such work marked them apart from the bulk of the working class.

This small scale mainly male occupation was overhauled in the first half of the 20th century. The expansion of commerce and finance, the development of larger and more complex distribution networks, the enlargement of capitalist enterprises and the growth of government bureaucracy, were all part of this transformation. Accounting and record keeping operations became industries in themselves, recording and duplicating the finances of individual firms.

The new offices swallowed up new labour, pulling large numbers of women into the labour market for the first time and, at the same time, downgrading the pay and conditions of work. Offices became what Braverman calls 'huge production machines' where a stream of paper was 'processed in a continuous flow like that of the cannery, the meat-packing line, the car assembly conveyor, by workers organised in much the same way'.

The same scientific management methods which had been applied to the factories were introduced to the office. All office activities were monitored, timed and checked to find ways to speed up output. Every activity—from the time it took to strike the key of a typewriter to the time it took a worker to go to the loo or get a glass of water—was studied. Each job was subdivided into smaller repetitive tasks. The worker lost any sense of the purpose of the overall process as office work became an endless round of the routine, standardised and regimented processing of meaningless data.

The office itself in the process has become just as much a site of manual labour for the office worker as is the factory floor:

> The mental processes are rendered repetitious and routine or they are reduced to so small a factor in the work process that the speed and dexterity with which the manual portion of the operation can be performed dominates the labour process as a whole.

The typical routine of an office worker today—whether they are working for local government, in a bank, or for some private firm— will typically involve clocking in and clocking off, repetitive and boring work (for example word processing, operating a complex photocopier, or just answering the phone or opening the mail) in a large impersonal office. And not only does the job itself resemble that of someone in a car plant or other factory but it is likely that members of the same family will be involved in both types of jobs.

In *Capital* Marx showed how the productive process in capitalist society was constantly transformed under the impetus of its driving force—the accumulation of capital. This involved both a change in the productive methods of each particular branch of industry and a redistribution of labour among different occupations and industries. New productive techniques mean that some workers will no longer be useful to the capitalists while other groups in different areas become vital to them.

The long term decline of manufacturing and the increase in service industries is an example of this process. Of course, some service workers have always been seen as part of the working class—for example transport workers provide a service and not a product and yet no one would consider these groups of workers as marginal. Similarly workers in the newer service industries—such as bank and insurance workers, telecommunications workers, workers in supermarkets and chain stores—have become integral to the capitalist economy.

At the same time with the development of capitalism—one of whose features is that the economy is dominated by larger and larger firms—the market encroaches on more and more areas of life. Commodity production extends not only into producing food, clothing and household items to meet our daily requirements, but into all aspects of social life.

Braverman highlights the processes that have led to the dependence of all social life on 'one gigantic marketplace' as capitalist production methods become dominant throughout the world. Workers increasingly converge to live in the vast urban conurbations when their livelihoods on the land are destroyed. In the process social life itself becomes more atomised and individual family needs are increasingly subordinated to the market. The status of a family's well-being in society becomes judged on the ability of workers to buy the new clothes and household items manufactured for the market.

Sheila Lewanhak describes the way this worked to draw women into new jobs in food manufacture and the electrical industries in the 1930s:

> Women became part of the cycle of production in which they themselves manufactured the canned and frozen goods, the labour-saving machines for homes, in which they provided the services that in turn eased their own domestic workload and enabled others to go out and make luxury articles.

This process extends into all areas of life. As Braverman explains:

> The social structure built upon the market is such that relations between individuals and social groups do not take place directly as cooperative human encounters but through the market as relations of purchase and sale.

Recreation amusements, the care of the old, the young and the sick, all become dependent on the market. Labour saving devices, television, cinema and other entertainment, the provisions of institutionalised care, are produced for sale and provide new branches of production which employ new groups of workers. The massive rise in the numbers of women at work—90 percent of the overall increase of 3.1 million jobs between 1971 and 1990 were taken up by women workers—is into these jobs.

These workers become key members of the working class. Far from working in areas which are peripheral to capitalism, their jobs in the service sector are essential to and intermeshed in its whole operation. It is impossible to conceive of the workings of huge multinational companies without the banking, finance and insurance institutions which service them. Service industries are thus crucial not just to capitalism in general, but to the survival and competitiveness of manufacturing industry itself.

The restructuring of capitalism has heralded not the decline of the working class, but its transformation to suit the needs of capital accumulation. And in absolute numbers it represents an expansion of the working class.

In 1990 one half of men and two thirds of women were employed in non-manual occupations—the vast majority as wage workers with no control over their working day. Manufacturing employment has now fallen below five million workers—out of a total employed workforce of 25 million. The service sector accounts for over 67 percent of the current workforce. These workers are employed in the post office, transport, hospitals, education, banking and finance, and telecommunications. A massive 6.1 million were employed in the public sector in 1989.

It is these groups of workers who have increasingly been pulled into struggle as their conditions have been attacked in the last decade. According to *Labour Research* (June 1992):

> Administration, health and banking, which employed 34 percent of the UK's workforce in the 1970s compared with 43 percent today, accounted for nearly a third of all stoppages in the 1980s (28 percent) compared to a sixth (17 percent) in the 1970s. Half of all workers taking strike action in the 1980s were employed in one of these growth sectors compared to a third in the 1970s. And a staggering quarter of all days lost in the 1980s were in these sectors, compared to just 9 percent in the 1970s.

These figures give an indication of how new workers can be pulled to the forefront of struggle as their jobs, conditions and pay—particularly in the public sector—are in the frontline of Tory attacks. These workers are crucial both in the mass working class opposition to the Tories' decimation of the pits and in the confidence such a wave of revolt can inspire for mounting a fight in defence of their own pay, jobs and conditions. It is in such a struggle that working class organisation can be built and arguments for socialism won.

When the miners fought and toppled Heath's Tory government in the 1970s it was the first time they had taken national strike action since 1926. This time round it is workers in the councils, banks and hospitals who can not only haul down Major and his cronies but take the struggle even further.

Chapter 12

This year's model

Alex Callinicos

Postmodernism, the *New York Times* recently observed, is 'the intellectual fad of the 1980s and, so far, the 1990s'. It's hard to find any aspect of contemporary cultural life which doesn't get called 'postmodern'.

The word is applied to so many contradictory things that it seems to lack any definite meaning. In fact postmodernism can be seen as the convergence of three distinct elements.

The first is the reaction which has developed in the past 20 years to modernism, the great revolution in the arts which took place at the beginning of the century.

The 'postmodern' reaction is most obvious in a rejection of the 'International Style'—the elongated slabs which came to dominate city centres after the Second World War. 'Postmodern' architecture represented a flight from austerity to decoration, from innovation to tradition, from rationality to humour—as in the case of office blocks decorated with classical pillars.

Postmodernism involves, secondly, a specific philosophical current—what came to be known as poststructuralism, around the group of French philosophers who came to prominence in the 1960s, notably Gilles Deleuze, Jacques Derrida and Michel Foucault.

They developed certain themes, the first and most fundamental of which was a rejection of the Enlightenment. This was the project formulated by a number of French and Scottish thinkers in the 18th century based on the idea that human reason could both understand and control the natural and social world, a project which Marx sought, critically, to continue.

First published September 1990

Reason and truth, the poststructuralists argue, are in fact illusions. Scientific theories are perspectives reflecting particular social interests. The will to know, as Foucault put it, is merely one form of the will to power.

Reality itself is indeed merely a chaotic collection of fragments dominated by an endless struggle for power shaping nature and society alike. And human beings, as part of this reality, lack any coherence or control over themselves. Thus Foucault saw the individual human subject as a mass of drives and desires brought together by the prevailing power relations within society.

The third ingredient of postmodernism is the theory of post-industrial society developed by sociologists such as Daniel Bell in the early 1970s. Bell argued that the world was entering a new historical epoch in which material production would become less and less important and knowledge the main driving force of economic development.

The French philosopher Jean François Lyotard took this idea, and argued that, in the 'postmodern condition' knowledge takes on an increasingly fragmentary form, abandoning all claims to truth or rationality.

This shift reflects what Lyotard calls 'the collapse of grand narratives'. The Enlightenment project—as continued by Hegel and Marx, who sought to offer interpretations of the whole course of historical development as a way of showing the conditions under which human emancipation could be achieved—is no longer credible, Lyotard claims, after the disasters of Nazism and Stalinism.

Central to postmodernism then is the idea of a systematic, comprehensive and very recent change. The world has entered a new social and economic epoch, accompanied by a cultural transformation—postmodern art, and a philosophical revolution—poststructuralism. Hence *Marxism Today*'s claim that we live in 'New Times'.

None of this stands up to serious examination. But the idea that we live in a new epoch is best exposed by looking at the claim that there is a distinctively postmodern art.

Probably the best known definition of postmodern art is offered by the architectural historian Christopher Jencks. Postmodernism, he says, consists in 'double-coding', that is, the combination of different styles in the same artwork—of, say, classicism and the International Style in the same building.

This is a strange claim, since what Jencks calls 'double-coding' is such an obvious feature of modernism. Thus James Joyce in *Ulysses* mingles together different voices, styles and languages—an effect captured in poetry by T S Eliot in *The Waste Land*. The idea of a distinctive postmodern art rests on a caricature of modernism.

The best definition of modernism is offered by Eugene Lunn in *Marxism and Modernism*. He isolates four features. First, 'aesthetic self consciousness': modern art tends to be about the process of artistic creation itself—thus Marcel Proust's *Remembrance of Things Past* reconstructs the experiences which led to the decision to write the novel. Secondly, 'simultaneity, juxtaposition, or montage': modern art breaks up the world of everyday experience and then reassembles it in new and unexpected combinations.

Thirdly, 'paradox, ambiguity, and uncertainty': modern art presents a world which no longer has clear signposts or a visible structure. Finally, 'dehumanisation': the individual in modern art is no longer in control of his or her own motives, let alone of the world itself.

Now the odd thing is that all these features of modernism are frequently claimed to be distinctive of postmodern art. The novels of Salman Rushdie, for example, are described as postmodern when they are in fact typical of modernism as defined by Lunn.

It's often argued that the difference lies in the fact that modernism was elitist and crassly optimistic while postmodernism is populist and pessimistic in its approach. But this involves a complete misunderstanding of modernism as a historical phenomenon.

Modernism emerged in the late 19th century especially in those countries experiencing the rapid and uneven impact of the development of industrial capitalism—Russia, Germany, Italy, Austria-Hungary. It can be seen as a response to the penetration of all aspects of social life by commodity relations. The general fragmentation this involved led to the isolation of art as a distinct, apparently autonomous, social practice.

The result was a tendency for artists, alienated from the rest of social life, to focus on art itself—for the process of artistic creation to become the object of art. This usually involved an ironic and detached attitude to reality. Art became a refuge from a social world dominated by commodity fetishism.

This attitude was compatible with all sorts of political commitments, from the Marxism of Bertolt Brecht to the fascism of Ezra Pound. The prevailing mood was, however, the pessimism summed up by T S Eliot when he wrote in 1923 of 'the immense panorama of futility and anarchy that is contemporary history'.

Modernism nevertheless contained a radical potential. Its key technical innovation was montage, the combination of distinct and apparently incompatible elements in the same work.

The cubist collages took this to the extent of incorporating bits of the real world—fragments of wood or newspaper—in their paintings.

Art ceased to be a window on the world and became, potentially at least, part of the world. The implication was to break down the separation of art and social life which had given rise to modernism in the first place.

This potential became self conscious in the avant garde movements which emerged at the end of the First World War—Dada, surrealism, constructivism. Their aim was to subvert art as an autonomous institution, as part of the more general struggle to revolutionise society.

'Dada is German Bolshevism,' said Richard Huelsenbeck. Or, as André Breton, surrealist poet and philosopher, put it in 1935: '"Transform the world", Marx said; "Change life", Rimbaud [the French poet] said. These two watchwords are for us one and the same.'

This linking together of social and artistic revolution was made possible by specific historical circumstances. It was in the period of the Russian Revolution of 1917 and the German Revolution of 1918-23 that the avant garde movements flourished. The Russian constructivists in particular— Mayakovsky, Eisenstein, Rodchenko, Tatlin and many others—put their art at the service not just of revolutionary propaganda, but of the transformation of everyday life.

The defeat of first the German and then the Russian revolutions therefore undercut the base of the avant garde. Fascism and Stalinism destroyed them, not merely through repression, but through removing the hopes of social revolution on which the realisation of the avant garde project depended.

The conditions for the incorporation of modernism by capitalism since the Second World War was thus created. The International Style which came to fill the urban skyline after 1945 was developed by architects such as Mies van der Rohe, last director of the Bauhaus, which was set up after the 1918 German Revolution to build 'cathedrals of socialism'.

The developments in various arts over the past 20 years which have come to be known as postmodernism have little in common beyond a reaction to the incorporated 'late modernism' which became the dominant cultural style after the Second World War.

They are better seen as variants of modernism than a break with it. There is, for example, nothing in David Lynch's brilliant film *Blue Velvet*, with its powerful sense of an irrational world of violence and desire lurking beneath the banal surface of everyday life, which would have come as a surprise to the surrealists.

Not only is there no distinctively postmodern art, neither are we living in a new historical epoch. The most serious attempts to make out the latter claim tend to focus on the internationalisation of capital.

But while capital has undoubtedly become much more globally integrated over the past 20 years, the nation state continues to play a vital economic role. Witness, for example, the American government's rescues first of the banking system and now the savings and loans industry. Moreover, the internationalisation of capital does not signal a new, stable phase of capitalist expansion; it has rather been a major factor in making the world economy more *unstable* since the late 1960s.

Granted that the claims of postmodernism are false, where does it come from? Why has the widespread belief emerged that we live in a fundamentally new economic and cultural epoch?

The recovery of the advanced capitalist economies from the world recession of 1979-82, involved an expansion of demand, based on easy credit and higher government spending, which began in the US in the early 1980s and spread to Europe.

Among the main beneficiaries of this recovery were the 'new middle class' of highly paid managers and professionals. The 1980s were the decade when the 'yuppie' flourished.

Secondly, however, many of the new middle class which did so well out of the recovery were part of the generation of 1968.

They had participated in the huge radicalisation of young intellectuals throughout the western world during the great upturn in class struggle of the late 1960s and early 1970s. And they had also shared in the collapse of revolutionary hopes which took place in the mid and late 1970s as workers were pushed back onto the defensive and much of the far left disintegrated.

The result was the emergence of a substantial social layer that is both economically prosperous and politically disillusioned. They don't believe in revolution any more (if they ever did), but they don't have an unqualified faith in capitalism either.

This attitude is well summed up by Lyotard's declaration of the bankruptcy of all 'grand narratives': we can no longer believe in any comprehensive theory which will allow us both to interpret and to change the world.

More than that, postmodernism involves a 'routinisation of irony'. The ironic, detached attitude towards reality which was the property of a small number of highly sophisticated intellectuals when modernism emerged at the end of the 19th century now becomes generally available, mass produced as a way of coping with a world which, postmodernists believe, can be neither transformed nor uncritically endorsed.

This is connected to the self conscious adoption of an aesthetic attitude to life. Nietzsche argued that the only appropriate response to a chaotic reality was to make a work of art of one's own life, to seek to integrate all one's experiences into a meaningful whole.

This was an idea taken up by Foucault in his last writings, where he often talks of an 'aesthetics of existence'. This too became a routine part of middle class life in the 1980s, in particular in the effort through diet, dress and exercise to transform the body into a sign of youth, health and mobility.

The politics of postmodernism is best brought out by the fashionable American philosopher Richard Rorty. Rorty welcomes the emergence of an 'increasingly ironist culture' dominated by 'the pursuit of private perfection'.

We should stop worrying about knowing and changing the world and concentrate on cultivating personal relationships.

Central to postmodernism is the denial that it is desirable or even possible any more to engage collectively to transform the world.

How on earth Rorty and Lyotard can explain how the peoples of Eastern Europe got it together to overthrow their rulers is anybody's guess.

These revolutions and events of recent months suggest that a new chapter in the 'grand narrative' of human emancipation has just been opened. As this story unfolds, postmodernism will become more obviously irrelevant. In the meantime revolutionary socialists must denounce it as the abomination that it is.

British history

Chapter 13

Revolution denied

John Rees

For a generation the history of the English Revolution was written from a standpoint that was Marxist or strongly influenced by Marxism. R H Tawney, A L Morton, Maurice Dobb, H N Brailsford and Christopher Hill argued that the revolution was a class conflict. This is Hill's classic statement of the case:

> The English Revolution of 1640-60 was a great social movement like the French Revolution of 1789. The state power protecting an old order was overthrown, power passed into the hands of a new class, and so the freer development of capitalism was made possible.
>
> The Civil War was a class war, in which the despotism of Charles I was defended by reactionary forces of the established Church and conservative landlords. Parliament beat the King because it could appeal to the enthusiastic support of the trading and industrial classes, to the yeomen and progressive gentry, to the wider masses of the population whenever they were able by free discussion to understand what the struggle was really about.

This view of the English Revolution was buttressed by the work of other Marxist historians. The work of Rodney Hilton on the medieval peasantry and the transition from feudalism to capitalism gave a materialist reading of the period preceding the revolution.

The work of E P Thompson and Eric Hobsbawm, to mention the best known, presented English history in the centuries that followed from a class viewpoint.

Right wing historians are now challenging the linchpin of this account—a Marxist analysis of the English Revolution.

First published November 1987

They do not subscribe to any one interpretation of the English Revolution, but they are 'united in an attempt to demolish Marxist interpretations of the period', says historian Brian Manning.

Even in the polite language of academia they are called, and happy to be called, 'revisionists'. Barely a month passes without a new book being added to the growing cannon.

The revisionist arguments

Common revisionist themes are:
• A stress on the accidental nature of events.

No one consciously sought revolution. Charles I and parliament's slide into conflict was due to Charles's shortcomings as a politician. Defending this theory in his book *Rebellion or Revolution?* G E Aylmer concludes:

> To enumerate the sufficient causes of almost any significant and complex event in human history is perhaps so difficult as to be beyond our capacity. The historian is not God, and should not try to be.

• An emphasis on local studies which deny any society-wide or underlying economic causes of the revolution.

John Morrill, although now repenting under criticism, was a leading 'localist'. He described the importance of this strand of revisionism:

> For several years in the 1960s and 1970s local studies were all the rage. These lay stress on purely local factors and rivalries in explaining the pattern of allegiance in each shire and borough, and played down the importance of major ideological divisions determining the pattern of events.

• An insistence that 'it was the religious issue which stood out as the decisive one' (Morrill) and that religious issues did not mask deeper social causes.

As Morrill says:

> The civil war was not a clash of social groups: it was the result of incompetent kingship which allowed religious militants to settle their disputes.

• A denial that the revolution was a class struggle.

In *The World We Have Lost*, an influential book first published in 1965 but now reissued to an appreciative audience, Peter Laslett argued:

> Once it is recognised that the rise-of-the-capitalist interpretation can be misleading as well as informative…then the idea of a social revolution…becomes an embarrassment.

• The contention that ordinary people played little role in the revolution.

Morrill claimed only 'minorities in most counties felt there was a cause worth fighting for'. Laslett claimed:

> Workers did not form a million outs facing a handful of ins... They could not be what we should call a class. [This was a] one class society [which] enabled a minority to live for all the rest.

• The role of the lords and the crown in determining political events is exaggerated by denigrating the importance of the Commons and its leaders, Hampden and Pym.

In a recent attempt to summarise the often contradictory revisionist case, J C D Clark's *Revolution and Rebellion* argued there was no decisive break in English history in the 17th century. Change only came between 1828 and 1832 and this was no revolution. Before hierarchy and deference to authority were the dominant political ideas and religion the moving force. Parliament remained weak, the crown strong and changes in government meant one layer of the ruling class replacing another. And so, the argument runs, there was no bourgeois revolution at all.

Revisionism refuted

For all their implausibility and self contradictions, we should not underestimate the importance of these ideas. As one reviewer of Clark's books says, 'If this picture becomes the new orthodoxy, then most school and some university courses are going to be in trouble.' In truth, important elements of this picture are already the orthodoxy.

Neither should we underestimate the contemporary political motivation that underlies these attacks on Marxist views of the revolution. Laslett is once again fashionable for claiming:

> In the self proclaimed socialist states of the late 20th century, from the USSR to Romania, from China to many of the new African states and to Cuba, the dogma that the English Civil War and the English Revolution represent the first national victory of the bourgeoisie is part of political belief, or of its historical legitimation.

Leaving aside the truth of these statements, it reveals that Laslett's method is to start with the Cold War and rewrite history in that light. Clark's political motivation is equally obvious. He quotes approvingly a letter to the *Times Higher Educational Supplement* which argued:

British political science was particularly torpid until the electoral shock of 1979. Too many existing political scientists belong to the generation of 1968—a provenance that almost disqualifies them from comment on late 20th century politics.

Clark clearly feels that this disqualifies them from any comment on mid-17th century politics as well.

But the revisionist attack has not gone unanswered.

David Underdown's *Revel, Riot and Rebellion*, a study of the Revolution in the counties of Wiltshire, Somerset and Dorset, provides ammunition enough to demolish a number of the revisionist theses.

Underdown has proved that local studies do not necessarily have to draw right wing conclusions. Neither do they have to show that the issues that brought people to arms in 1642 were purely local, having no connection with national politics.

He has also traced an intimate connection between the material conditions of the areas he studies and the political and cultural patterns which arose on this foundation.

In the most important passages in the book Underdown argues in close detail how the pasture lands and cloth making areas tended to produce parliamentarian sympathies, where the less economically advanced arable farming areas produced royalist allegiance.

On this basis he undermines the picture drawn by some historians of a local population who simply mimicked the views of the local magnates.

Underdown also lends weight to the Marxist analysis of the role of religion, clearly showing how the different religious factions reflected differing economic interests.

Marxists argue that religion, although a vital factor on both sides of the revolution (how could it fail to be when to control the Church was to control much of society's cultural apparatus?), could not alone explain why the civil war was fought. That explanation had to be sought in the economic and social structure of society.

It is not even true that secular economic interests never became consciously expressed. Witness this atheistic Ranter Christmas carol:

> They prate of God, believe it fellow creatures,
> There's no such bugbear; all was made by Nature.
> We know all came of nothing, and shall pass
> Into the same condition once it was,
> By nature's power; and that they grossly lie
> That say there's hope of immortality.
> Let them but tell us what a soul is, then
> We will adhere to these mad brain-sick men.

But these ideas could only be shaped by years of upheaval and struggle.

This brings us to another fatal flaw in the revisionist case. Many of them, like Anthony Fletcher in *The Outbreak of the English Civil War*, prefer to concentrate on the early years of the conflict.

This avoids having to analyse how the consciousness of the classes was transformed during the years of war and revolution.

Revisionists often argue that the common people had no idea what was at stake and that the lesser gentry and the merchants didn't make the revolution, citing the fact that many of them recoiled from what they had set in train.

This shows a simple inability to understand that every revolution involves a sharpening of consciousness during the course of the revolution. This necessarily results in new divisions and new leadership among the revolutionaries.

Although at the outset the king and his court were opposed by a broad cross-section of society, the war sharpened the class divisions. Many nobles who initially supported parliament deserted and those who stayed and urged caution were marginalised by Cromwell and the Independents.

To win the war, and to win the battle within the parliamentary side, it was necessary to mobilise huge sections of the peasantry, the artisans and day labourers. Brian Manning's work, particularly *The English People and the English Revolution*, demonstrates how mistaken is the view that the mass of the people were politically ignorant and passive during the revolution.

Manning's study shows that the London crowd and the East Anglian fenlanders defended and pushed the parliamentary leaders on, even when they were eager to compromise. This is especially important since Manning deals with the period 1640 to 1642, before the civil war broke out, before the New Model Army was formed and therefore prior to the masses being drawn in and politicised by the struggle.

With mobilisation came radicalisation. With radicalisation came organisation—army Agitators and Levellers. These groups posed a radical thoroughgoing bourgeois parliamentary solution to the impasse that had been reached between the rising bourgeoisie and the feudal court.

They were defeated, at Cromwell's hands, because the parliamentary 'grandees' had gained ascendancy and would tolerate no further movement from below that might threaten their property. The stage was set for a settlement with the old order.

Concentrating on the years 1640 to 1642 also absolves the revisionists from having to explain the revolution as the highpoint of a process which reached back a century before the 1640s and forward more than a century afterwards.

Any bourgeois revolution, and particularly the first, involves a long process of change as well as short, sharp settling of accounts between the classes.

The bourgeoisie, unlike the proletariat, gathers its strength slowly within the 'womb of the old society', as Marx put it.

The revolution grew during the 100 years that preceded 1640 when the merchants in the towns and a rising class of yeomen farmers, in alliance with the sections of the lesser gentry, became sufficiently powerful that they could resist the demands of a monarchy and aristocracy with whose economic and political interests they were parting company.

The reformation was one turning point. The dissolution of the monasteries in the 1530s and the consequent parcelling out of church land made a vital minority of the lesser gentry independent enough to provide some of parliament's ablest leaders, most notably Oliver Cromwell.

The English monarchy's alliance with Spain was another watershed. Under the Tudors the merchant class bankrolled the monarchy. In return the trade war with Spain was prosecuted with the monarchy's blessing.

But when James VI of Scotland became James I of England he came from an industrially backward country with little understanding of trade. Admiring the absolute monarchies of Europe he was not inclined to undermine the Spanish monarchy for the sake of English trade.

The beheading of privateer Sir Walter Raleigh in 1616 at the request of the Spanish ambassador is symbolic of the rift between commercial interest and kingly policy. The trading classes looked on Raleigh's exploits as natural and profitable.

Alliance with Catholic Spain, and later Charles I's marriage to a French Catholic put the Puritans, the trading classes, in sharp opposition to the monarchy for the first time since Henry VIII's day.

All this prepared the revolution which decisively changed the balance of power from king and court to trade and town. By concentrating on the immediate pre-war crisis the revisionists avoid the context of the revolution and therefore its real importance.

Even the restoration of the monarchy in 1660 could not bring the wheel full circle. The aristocracy might have regained limited entrance to the corridors of power, but they were there on sufferance.

The fundamental gains of the revolution remained. A path was cleared down which agricultural enclosure and agricultural revolution, commercial freedom, empire and industrial revolution would march.

Even for the mass of the population who had fought hardest and won least there were important gains. In the 100 years before 1640 wages for labourers in industry and agriculture fell by more than half. In the 100 years after 1640 they more than doubled. The fact that the bourgeoisie enrolled other classes to do their fighting does not disqualify it from the title 'bourgeois' revolution.

As Engels noted:

> Curiously enough in all three bourgeois risings the peasantry furnishes the army that has to do the fighting, and the peasantry is just the class that, victory once gained, is most surely ruined by the economic consequence of victory.
>
> A hundred years after Cromwell the yeomanry had almost disappeared...had it not been for that yeomanry...the bourgeoisie alone would never have fought the matter out to the bitter end.

All revolutions, prior to the socialist revolution, are necessarily movements of minorities or in the interests of minorities, as Marx explains in *The Communist Manifesto*.

Other oppressed classes might glimpse progress, some might be the minor beneficiaries of the revolution, but their full hopes were bound to be disappointed. The productive base of society was not yet great enough to support a classless society. Society could move forward, but only under the rule of a new ruling class. The bourgeoisie was the only possible candidate.

The revisionists' success clearly cannot be explained by the force of their arguments. They are just one symptom of a growing conservatism among academics. What needs to be examined are the weaknesses in the analysis of the English Revolution developed by the left. These weaknesses, while not the decisive reason for the right's success, cannot help but have made it easier.

Much Marxist analysis rests on the work of Christopher Hill, and it is with him that we begin. Hill's formative political experience was the Communist Party Historians' Group, which he helped to form in 1946.

The group became the intellectual powerhouse which enabled Marxist history to become immensely popular and to achieve a position of academic prestige from which it has still not been completely dislodged.

Just to name those who joined Hill in the group is sufficient to establish its importance—E P Thompson, Eric Hobsbawm, Maurice Dobb, Rodney Hilton, John Saville, A L Morton, Dorothy Thompson, George Rudé and a young Raphael Samuel.

Naturally they imbibed the version of Marxism current in the Stalinist tradition, tempered by a certain freedom of interpretation allowed them if they obeyed the party's injunction to avoid 20th century history.

They did. The group was, Hobsbawm remembers:

> As loyal, active and committed a group of Communists as any, if only because we felt that Marxism implied membership of the party. To criticise Marxism was to criticise the party, and the other way around.

This naive faith in Stalinism received a rude shock when, in 1956, Russia crushed the Hungarian Revolution.

Ten years after they founded the Communist Party Historians' Group nearly all its leading figures, including Hill, left the party. Hobsbawm and Dobb were the only remaining luminaries.

Thompson and Saville organised a magazine called the *Reasoner*. After they left the CP this became, eventually, *New Left Review*.

Socialist humanism was the name given to the interpretation of Marxism that the rebels began to develop.

Socialist humanism is best known for its philosophical dimension. The return to Marx's early works in search of a more activist Marxism as a challenge to the dead hand of Stalinist fatalism was its hallmark.

There was much to admire in this effort, but its fatal weakness was that in rejecting the determinism associated with Stalin's vulgar Marxism, it often fell into the trap of rejecting any form of determination, flipping over from economic reductionism to idealism.

There were similar developments in the historical field.

Here 'History from below' became the battle cry. Again there is much to praise—an insistence that ordinary people make their own history and a commitment to ensuring that their struggles will no longer be hidden from history.

But again in rejecting Stalinism something vital to Marxism was lost. The objective economic and social confines within which working people make their own history has, partially at least, been neglected.

Perry Anderson opposed Thompson's views and ousted him from *New Left Review*. The nature of the English Revolution was debated by Anderson and Thompson as part of the ensuing debate on the future of socialism in Britain.

Anderson, ever the intellectual butterfly, has since moved through Althusserianism to an academic form of orthodox Trotskyism [by 1987].

But in 1965 he argued that the historical weakness of the entire working class movement dated back to the English Revolution.

In his famous essay 'The Origins of the Present Crisis' Anderson contended that the English Revolution was 'primarily fought within classes and not between classes'. Further, 'no social group was evicted or displaced by the revolution.'

Rehearsing arguments now usually deployed in the revisionist cause, Anderson claimed that the revolution 'was a bourgeois revolution only by proxy' and that the ideological rot of the British left set in in the 1600s because 'the ideological terms in which the struggle was conducted were largely religious'.

Thompson's reply, 'The Peculiarities of the English', demolished Anderson's case with characteristic elan. But it wasn't enough to stem the tide.

The separation of subjective and objective analysis was set in stone by the way in which Stalinism tried to regroup its intellectual forces throughout the 1960s.

Anderson later argued that the intellectual weaknesses of the British left that he had identified in 'The Origins of the Present Crisis' could be remedied by a hefty dose of French structuralism.

Louis Althusser, the in-house philosopher of the French Communist Party, developed a structuralist Marxism whose purpose was to beat off the challenge of the socialist humanists and the New Left.

The most striking features of Althusser's system directly contradicted the version of historical materialism being developed by Thompson and Hill.

Consciousness and activity were written out of history. Men, far from making history, were merely the 'bearers of the structure', human goods wagons in which 'the structure' rode.

This refurbished determinism had only one thing going for it—it played on the weakness in the 'history from below' school's argument, the neglect of structural factors.

Between the two interpretations of Marxism the struggle was ferocious. Anderson now turned *New Left Review* into the import agency for structuralism. In every sphere structuralism mounted a powerful challenge. In many it came to dominate.

In all this the same contours became apparent.

The structuralists argued a radical idealism. In reply the 'history from below' school defended a Marxism with very real strengths and one vital weakness—neglect of determination and a desire to get away from the base/superstructure model of Marxism because they thought that it inevitably meant a return to vulgar Marxism.

Hill became Master of Balliol in 1965. Aloof from the political in-fighting he did not have to react to the structuralists as sharply as Thompson.

The result was that, of all the Communist Party Historians' Group, Hill probably retained the greatest emphasis on the objective limits of the class struggle.

Nevertheless, there were changes. Gradually after the crisis of 1956 Hill moved away from the concerns of his classic *The English Revolution* and of the *Century of Revolution* with a total account of the revolution. These books integrated the class struggle and its economic context. He then moved towards fascinating and detailed accounts of partial, often cultural, aspects of the revolution. There is some truth therefore in this statement by a right winger: 'The left long ago aban-doned the revolution in favour of the revolutionaries.'

In Hill's magnificent *The World Turned Upside Down* the historical context and possibilities beg to be stated but go unheard. Could the Levellers have seized power? Could they have played the role later played by the Jacobins? If not, why not? What were the economic and social limits to change?

Sometimes in Hill's work we are offered opinions on these questions, but rarely is a total analysis integrated into his major work.

In recent years Hill has been obliged to conduct a more theoretical defence of his work by the onslaught of the revisionists. But there are problems here too.

Hill now argues that the revolution was bourgeois not because of the bourgeoisie's conscious aims, but because of the objective result of the events.

Sometimes Hill has claimed too much for the consciousness of the bourgeoisie—now he claims too little. This is an unnecessary confu-sion, which aids the revisionists.

The working class is the only class capable of completely clear class consciousness. All previous revolutionary classes were minorities des-tined to become new ruling classes, but in order to do so they needed to enlist the support of all the oppressed classes.

They had to present their aims as the universal aims of the ex-ploited. This was only partly true. So the bourgeoisie's consciousness was always riddled with contradiction.

At least Hill has tried to defend Marxism, but his tradition has given birth to children far weaker than their parents. A whole generation of historians based at Ruskin College and around the journal *History Workshop* now think it sufficient to merely report what working people do and say. The link with the Communist Party Historians' Group is explicit. Raphael Samuel presides aided by Sheila Rowbotham among others.

The predilection for local and oral histories is defended in the name of uncovering the history of working people. But the effect is a failure to distinguish the vital from the trivial.

Marxism has never been simply a history of the working class. It is a total history from the standpoint of the working class.

Not every folk ritual or tavern song is historically significant. What is significant can only be decided by reference to a social and economic structure wider than immediate events.

In forgetting this many socialist historians have opened the door to the localist wing of the revisionists.

The problem is present even in the best of recent writing on the English Revolution. David Underdown's book, cited above, is useful in many respects but in drawing general conclusions from a local analysis it fails to even consider the two places where the revolution reached its highest peak, the City of London and the New Model Army.

Worse, to reduce Marxism to an empirical account of what working people said and did, even if they are radical working people, is to disarm us theoretically just at the moment when the revisionists have picked up theoretical weapons of their own.

Our best model for writing history is Trotsky's *History of the Russian Revolution*. Here we find global analysis of Russia's place in the world economy, a brilliant account of the specific class structure of tsarist Russia, and a vivid history of the events of the revolution straight from the mouths of the participants.

Not everyone is Trotsky, but that is not the point. It is the method, which combines base and superstructure, consciousness and determination, which have been lost and must be recovered.

It may not be the worst of its crimes, but Stalinism and its subsequent decay has left its stain on the writing of history.

Even those who broke from Stalinism were marked by the experience.

Those who came after, or who were never part of, the Communist Party tradition were usually weaker for not experiencing a forum which, in a distorted manner, linked theory and practice. They missed therefore an outline of the relationship between subjective and objective factors.

We stand in debt to Hill and the others but we cannot even defend the ground they have taken, let alone go forward, by exaggerating their weakest aspect as many socialist historians have done.

Chapter 14

National peculiarity in British history

John Rees

When did Britain become a capitalist society? Is the aristocracy still a power in the land? Does the City dictate economic policy? These are some of the questions that are central to a debate that has been raging among Marxists for nearly 30 years.

The work of Perry Anderson in *New Left Review* has been the focus for this argument. Anderson first provoked the discussion in the 1964 *New Left Review* article, 'The Origins of the Present Crisis'. Then, in 1987, he returned to the debate in a piece called 'The Figures of Descent'.

Both pieces concern crucial turning points in British history, principally the English Revolution and the political after effects of the Industrial Revolution—the 1832 Reform Act and the repeal of the Corn Laws. The analysis draws conclusions about the nature of British class structure and the strategy socialists should pursue.

Although there are many contradictions between the two articles there a number of important similarities. Two are most significant. The first is that the industrial bourgeoisie is a subordinate class in British society. In 'The Origins of the Present Crisis' it is portrayed as subordinate to the aristocracy. In 'The Figures of Descent' it is seen as subordinate to a nexus of the Treasury and the City—to a separate class fraction of finance capital.

The second thing which unites the two essays is that they both believe the task of the labour movement, and Anderson talks especially

First published February 1990

about the Labour Party, is to overcome the historic backwardness of British society, to regenerate capitalism, not overthrow it.

In 'The Origins of the Present Crisis', Anderson argues the turning point is the English Revolution.

He argues that it is impossible to view the English Revolution as a conflict between two classes, a rising bourgeoisie and a declining aristocracy, that the English Revolution was 'the least pure bourgeois revolution of any major European country'. Instead it was a fight between 'two segments of a land owning class'. Both segments were rural, not urban.

For Anderson the effect of the revolution was that 'no social group was evicted or displaced…it left almost the entire social structure intact.' Nevertheless, he concludes, its outcome aided the development of capitalism, even if the actual classes involved in the fighting had very little to do with it. Ever since, he argues, the industrial bourgeoisie has remained subordinate to the governing class, the aristocracy.

As Anderson suggests, it is an over-simplification to see the English Revolution simply as a combat between the aristocracy and the bourgeoisie. But then this is not what Marx argued or what Trotsky argued in his *Writings on Britain*.

In fact, Marx's observation that capitalism developed in the womb of feudal society should act as a warning against reading back into history the structure of a proletarian revolution—where two clearly defined economic classes, one of which is entirely lacking control over the means of production, clash and the result is a cataclysmic change in the structure of society. This wasn't Marx's image of the bourgeois revolution.

Precisely because the bourgeoisie was a property owning class, it could emerge within the structure of the old order, and it could coexist, albeit in a subordinate position, with older property owning classes. However, as the balance of wealth and power shifted in favour of the new exploiters they increasingly found their erstwhile allies to be a fetter on further development. Then the desire, not always successfully realised, to alter the situation more radically began to grow.

This is why a clear understanding of the absolutist state is so important, as Anderson's own book, *Lineages of the Absolutist State*, shows. The monarchy had for a long period before the English Revolution become more centralised, more disconnected from its original base among the feudal aristocracy and more financially dependent on the emerging bourgeoisie.

The aristocracy, weakened by feuding, notably in the Wars of the

Roses, was unable to prevent the growth of a more centralised state. Yet the monarchy sold off monastery and church lands during the Reformation, thus depriving itself of a vital source of revenue. This, in turn, made the crown financially dependent on the wealthy new merchant class and on those agricultural and manufacturing layers which were producing for the market. In this way the monarchy attempted to balance between the old backward looking aristocratic orders from which it had sprung and the new emerging classes on which it increasingly depended.

The absolutist state was obliged to gather more powers in order to try and maintain this position. But it could only perpetuate the old feudal structures while being financed by the new emerging classes for a limited period. Eventually it was forced to try to regain control over society by attempting to vanquish the new classes, becoming a brake on any further development. It became obvious that this point had been reached in England by the beginning of the 17th century.

The way in which production was being organised in the 100 years after the sale of church lands—the Reformation—clearly shows the class forces that emerged to fight the revolution of the 1640s.

Although England was still predominantly an agrarian society during this period the nature of production on the land had changed. Increasingly, as one contemporary source put it, the small men, those who were engaged in careful bookkeeping and with an eye to trade, were the people becoming more powerful on the land. It was no longer the case that the old feudal magnates were the most powerful people.

Christopher Hill quotes one contemporary source saying, 'Gentlemen disdaining traffic and living in idleness do in this course daily sell their patrimonies, the buyers are for the most part citizens and vulgar men.' It was the careful bookkeepers to whom the aristocrats daily sold their estates.

Those who continued to produce predominantly in a way inherited from high feudalism were the ones who were losing out. Those who were beginning to produce for the market, beginning to manage the farms, became tenant farmers and in many cases employed wage labour were the ones who benefited.

The second thing about the rural nature of this society is that rural didn't necessarily mean agricultural. Often it meant the putting out system, where the merchants supplied raw materials and tools to a number of workers in their own cottages, collected the product and took it to the ports, to the towns or to London for sale. There was an increasing intersection of production of commodities for the market and the employment of wage labour on the land in the same agricultural areas. In fact those agricultural areas that were richest were those where the cloth trade grew, or where the putting out system took firmest hold.

J T Swain's study of Lancashire between 1500 and 1640, *Industry before the Industrial Revolution*, says:

> We cannot make a clear cut distinction between early modern and industrial Lancashire in terms of the proportion of people involved in industry. The chief difference, however, between 16th and 19th century Lancashire is that very many inhabitants of Tudor Lancashire pursued an agricultural livelihood in conjunction with industry, whereas the Industrial Revolution largely destroyed this combination.

So the picture of agrarian capitalism is not simply of an overwhelmingly agricultural society. It is a picture of agriculture and forms of industry in intimate connection with the merchants, the major trading ports and, predominantly, London.

It wasn't only goods for market that travelled down these trade routes to the cities and ports or along the lines of the putting out system. With that trade went ideas. This was obvious to contemporary thought. One commentator said of the handloom weavers in Kidderminster, 'Their constant converse and traffic with London doth much promote civility and piety amongst the tradesmen.' Piety and civility were codewords for Puritan values, the ideological counterpart of the way in which the world was changing economically.

Cloth may have been the major industry but it wasn't the only one. In the 100 years before the outbreak of the civil war coal production increased from 20,000 tonnes per year to 1.5 million tonnes per year. The Keswick smelter employed around 4,000 workers before the revolution. Although this was atypical, it does begin to show that the common picture of agrarian capitalism is false.

Unlike the cloth trade, where small amounts of capital were enough to get you started, heavy industry like mining needed much greater investment. Often the aristocrats were the only ones who had amassed enough wealth to invest in the new industry. So this increase in the orientation to the market and trade was burrowing all the way through the existing class structure.

Nowhere was this more true than in London. In the 17th century London was incomparably more important to the rest of the country than it is now. It was ten times the size of the next biggest city, Bristol. Seven eighths of the entire country's trade passed through London. In the 40 years before the revolution exports from London had grown five times over. Cloth from Wales and Yorkshire, nails, leather and weapons from the Midlands and dairy products from the Home Counties and the south of England all came through London.

This economic background to the English Revolution makes the class divisions that occurred when the revolution began much more understandable. It explains why the ports, the tenant farmers, traders, artisans and most of the merchants—although not some of the very richest—were for parliament, why the most advanced agricultural areas and those in which the cloth industry was developing alongside agriculture also generally declared for parliament.

Meanwhile the most backward agricultural areas were frequently those which declared for the king. Yorkshire, which was fiercely contested all the way through the civil war, saw the cloth towns siding with parliament and the surrounding rural area with the king.

Some of the rich merchants—those who were granted royal charters and monopolies to trade—did side with the king. But, as historian Brian Manning has said, they raised no money or arms and were, in effect, neutral.

The gentry, the land owners without noble title, split. A third sided with parliament, while two thirds sided with the king. As Norah Carlin has pointed out, since 'the gentry' are not a separate class with their own distinct relationship to the means of production there is no particular reason why they should behave in a homogeneous manner. Those sections of the gentry excluded from power by the traditional local oligarchies, those most associated with trade, particularly overseas trade in the new colonies, and with new methods of farming, were those most likely to side with parliament.

The economic skeleton pushes through the flesh of the civil war at every decisive phase. For example, when the king was on the verge of crushing London at the outset of the war it was the trained bands from the City of London who defeated him at the battle of Turnham Green.

And the king's pincer movement on London in the middle of the war was foiled by the merchant classes in Plymouth and Hull, who rose against the town elders, deposed them, put a new order at the head of the town and so blocked the king's intentions.

Until 1644 only the City of London financed the parliamentary side. There were no national taxes or other funds. After that, in the areas they commanded parliament implemented a taxation system to help finance their efforts. But the king depended for the duration of the war on individual donations from supporters.

Whatever disagreements there are about the nature of the classes that fought the civil war, there is a large measure of agreement about its outcome. The final settlement in 1688 was a bourgeois settlement involving the establishment of a stock exchange, the Bank of England and navigation acts which guaranteed trade to British ships. Parliament was established as dominant inside the state.

Anderson's dismissal of the English Revolution as impure can only survive if the revolution is judged against some ideal model of what a bourgeois revolution should be, as E P Thompson pointed out in his famous 1960s rejoinder to Anderson, 'The Peculiarities of the English'. But judged by its causes, its moving forces and its effects, the revolution was bourgeois in the fullest sense.

Far from having no effect on the social structure, it removed the power of the last relic of feudalism, the absolutist state transforming some of its institutions, abolishing others and creating new ones. Many of those who led the revolution and nearly all the resources which made their victory possible came precisely from those classes and fractions of classes most closely connected with the new forms of producing and selling.

In Anderson's 1987 essay, 'The Figures of Descent', the civil war, previously considered to be the key event, virtually disappears from the text. Now he argues that, far from the aristocracy being the dominant force which blocked the development of the industrial bourgeoisie, the aristocracy was an integral part of the capitalist plutocracy. The aristocracy has the 'longest consecutive history as a capitalist strata proper'. So instead of the continuity which Anderson claims for his two articles there is the largest possible gulf on the issue of the aristocracy.

Anderson now argues that the aristocracy is such a powerful capitalist stratum that it is elevated above most manufacturers. The explanation for the industrial bourgeoisie's lack of nerve is that it was predated by a commercial bourgeoisie that controlled the state machine and developed foreign trade. According to Anderson, it had in fact been a capitalist class for so long before the Industrial Revolution that it managed to hold the state machine against the rise of the manufacturers.

But the agrarian and manufacturing elements of the bourgeoisie were integrated at a very early stage in the development of capitalist relations in England. Anderson, like American historian Robert Brenner, sees the development of the English Revolution as stemming from agrarian developments and therefore counterposes the agrarian, commercially oriented stratum of the capitalist class to the later development of the industrial bourgeoisie.

Anderson repeats the argument that he used in 'The Origins of the Present Crisis' that the industrial bourgeoisie had its chance to achieve a 'second revolution' but its conservative reaction to the French Revolution pushed it back into the arms of the older commercial and financial strata.

As a result the industrial bourgeoisie merely scored some 'modest' political victories in the 1832 Reform Act and the 1845 repeal of the Corn Laws, before it was brushed aside and became a junior partner which accepted the status quo.

There is another way of interpreting the period between the final settlement of the English Revolution in 1688 and the 1832 Reform Act. The integration of agrarian and industrial development meant that the settlement of 1688 suited the rising manufacturing class very well—up to a point. It was, after all, a settlement in which its voice had been recognised, if only as a junior partner. It was also a settlement after which the interpenetration of merchant and manufacturing capital proceeded apace, wage labour became even more widespread and remaining guild restrictions were put aside. The banking system developed. Taxes were used both to fight colonial wars and as a way of directing trade, limiting imports and encouraging exports. The manufacturing bourgeoisie clearly benefited from these developments.

In the period from 1688 to the Napoleonic Wars there *were* significant changes inside the ruling class. The Industrial Revolution, the rise of factory production and the growth of the cities all brought changes in the composition of the ruling class. The movement for reform which was developing before the French Revolution was delayed by the need to keep social order.

However, when in 1832 the question of widening the franchise arose, allowing part of the industrial bourgeoisie to directly represent itself politically, there is no doubt that it was a turning point. A barrage of new legislation deliberately directed against the working class followed the Reform Act. The reform of local government in 1835 and the passing of the new Poor Laws show that the industrial bourgeoisie was moving into the first rank of rulership.

This is even more obvious if we look at the political ramifications of the repeal of the Corn Laws. This legislation protected the agrarian section of the bourgeoisie by keeping the price of corn high. It was directly inimical to the industrial bourgeoisie which wanted cheap corn, even if it was imported, in order to suppress wages.

The repeal of the Corn Laws absolutely broke the old Tory Party, the political representatives of agrarian capital. Peel, a Tory, took the decision to back the repeal and so sent his own party into the political wilderness for 20 years. Gladstone, himself a Tory who followed Peel's lead on the Corn Laws, later became the leader of the Liberals and was responsible for reorganising the army, the civil service and the education system to meet the needs of this reformed ruling class. Twenty years later Disraeli was able to rebuild the Tory party only by placing it wholly on the ground of the manufacturing bourgeoisie.

The depth of Anderson's error becomes obvious when he argues that the free trade policy was something which commercial and City interests foisted on an unwilling industrial bourgeoisie, thereby damaging the country's manufacturing base. Yet it should be obvious that Britain adopted free trade because of its industrial strength, not because of the industrial bourgeoisie's weakness. In 1870 the British state controlled a third of world manufacturing. Under those circumstances, it would obviously seek to break open all the old protective barriers, using free trade as its flag of convenience just as US capital did after the Second World War.

Many of the ideas aired in Anderson's articles can be found among sections of the Labour left, including the idea that the City holds honest northern industrialists to ransom.

This has been used over the years by the Communist Party to justify an alliance between workers and sections of the bourgeoisie against 'international monopoly capital'. Today, as a reaction to the 'Big Bang' and the supposed rise of the City, this argument has gained renewed currency.

Finance capital is seen as free to move internationally in a way industrial capital cannot. But both finance and industrial capital have partly broken free of national constraints. Manufacturing corporations like ICI can be every bit as multinational as banking houses. Britain is second only to the US in the development of multinational corporations.

As the international nature of capitalism has developed, the connections between finance and industrial capital have become much stronger. The constant pressure to increase the size of productive plant has meant that finance capital has become the way in which mergers are achieved and capital enlarged. Many industrial companies have developed their own financial operations.

The solution Anderson proposes to the weaknesses of the British economy is national reconstruction. His attitude to the labour movement is shaped by this approach. He condemns 'the complete failure of Labour's attempt to reconstruct industrial capital by state action'. Anderson bemoans the labour movement's inability to behave like its Swedish and Austrian counterparts:

> There, stable social democratic hegemony in the political order, based on mass trade union and party organisation, has been translated into sustained economic steerage towards competitive industrial branches...the key to this is a...disciplined labour movement...willing to respect the rules of capital accumulation.

The economism for which Anderson berates the British trade union movement is that it stubbornly refuses to sacrifice itself on the altar of national reconstruction.

Anderson's approach is wrong because it attempts to read back into history a particular contemporary moment. In 1964 he saw in Lord Home, then leader of the Tory party, the historic dominance of the aristocracy over the bourgeoisie since the 1640s. The unstated conclusion of this analysis was that socialists should place themselves on the left wing of Harold Wilson's technological revolution.

Today Anderson shares the common attitude, which sees the Thatcher era as a period in which the financial institutions of the City dominate the economy. He has now read this mistaken view back into the entire development of British capitalism. Were we to accept this view, we might find ourselves holding Neil Kinnock's left hand as he prepares to attack workers' living standards in the name of defending our industrial base.

That is no position for a socialist.

Some of the articles and books mentioned in the text:
Perry Anderson, *New Left Review* 23 and 161.
E P Thompson, *The Poverty of Theory*, contains his 'The Peculiarities of the English'.
Christopher Hill, *Century of Revolution*.
John T Swain, *Industry before the Industrial Revolution*.
S R Gardiner, *History of the Great Civil War*.
Leon Trotsky, *Writings on Britain*.
Norah Carlin, 'The English Civil War' (*International Socialism* 10).
Colin Barker and David Nichol (eds), *The Development of British Capitalist Society*.
Alex Callinicos, 'British Exceptionalism?' *New Left Review* 169.
Peter Earle, *The Making of the English Middle Class*.
Paul Langford, *A Polite and Commercial People*.

Chapter 15

Partners in crime

Chris Bambery

Scotland was a very poor, backward and turbulent country... As one of
their historians said, it was ruled by an aristocracy which was 'the poor-
est, the proudest, the most unscrupulous and the most mercenary in
Europe'. Consequently power in England meant domination of Scotland. Scotland was easy—it did not require thoroughgoing transformation. Money was sufficient and the Scottish aristocracy was bribed.
(Duncan Hallas, *Socialist Review*, October 1988.)

Along with Ireland, Scotland had remained outside the Roman
conquest. It was subject to Irish, Germanic and Scandinavian
immigration in the Dark Ages and it emerged as a country composed
of clannish regional authorities on both sides of the Highland line.

By the 11th century a central royal authority based on the Lothi-
ans, Fife and the north east had emerged (though it had no control over
the Highlands). Scotland was now subject to that remarkable Norman
expansion which stretched from Ireland to Sicily. But in Scotland's case
this did not involve conquest. The native Canmore dynasty (which
climbed to power against Macbeth with English aid) imported a
Norman aristocracy and institutions. The native Scottish nobility was
encouraged to integrate with these new arrivals.

The result was a late but thorough feudalisation of Lowland Scotland complete with manors, fiefs, castles, sheriffs, chamberlains and the
imposition of vicious serfdom. Lowland Scotland now became delin-
eated from the Highlands. South of the Highland line, English was now
spoken, or at least Lallans, the Scottish proto-language used by Robert
Burns and Hugh MacDiarmid.

First published April 1989

North of it remained a Gaelic speaking society which in its own mountain fastness began to see its clan system evolving in a feudal direction.

But the Scottish monarchy never succeeded in imposing its central authority. Constant frontier war with its southern neighbour buffeted the kingdom. In the anarchic conditions of the 14th and 15th centuries, feudal grandees succeeded in establishing total control of various regions: large noble houses, of a type unknown in England, emerged. The houses of Hamilton, Huntly, Angus and Argyll operated on semi-legal lines, with their own courts, vassals and military retinues.

One sign of Scotland's backwardness in comparison with its southern neighbour was that while castle building ceased in England with the Wars of the Roses it continued in Scotland well into the 17th century.

The House of Stuart, which ruled from the 15th century on, made little headway, weakened in turn by civil war, early and often bloody deaths of the monarch, and a series of royal regencies fought over by the nobility.

It promoted diplomatic and military links with France, the 'Auld Alliance', as a buffer against England. In the 16th century the reigns of both James IV and James V ended in military disaster at the hands of Tudor England. The succession fell to the infant Mary Queen of Scots. Her mother, part of the French royal house, determined to maintain the crown's power by making herself regent, importing a French army and, to secure the alliance, marrying her daughter to the Dauphin.

Tudor England was incapable of fully conquering both Ireland and Scotland. Its rivalry with France and Spain made both countries weak flanks. That was made more serious by England's commercial expansion into the Atlantic.

The attempt to impose royal power in Scotland at French hands sparked an aristocratic revolt that had popular support, funded and aided by Elizabeth I in London.

This rebellion succeeded in not only defeating the French Stuart axis, after the English fleet cut Scottish links with France, but it also brought about the most crucial development in the creation of modern Scotland, the Reformation of 1559-60.

Calvinist ideas had been introduced by Scottish students studying in Geneva and Holland, the best known being John Knox. They took root among the burghers of Edinburgh, St Andrews and Aberdeen. They also appealed to the lairds, the poor equivalent of the English gentry. In reality whatever the noble standing of these people they were evolving to become commercial farmers. But neither group had the power to accomplish a thorough Reformation. Instead they relied on the nobility.

Calvinism had a number of attractive features for the nobility. The most attractive was the excuse to seize for themselves church lands and rents! But Calvinism also stood for ideas which could strengthen the nobility's hands. While formally separating church and state it was clear that the kirk was in the dominant position. If the nobility could secure control of the kirk it would block any ambitions of the Stuart house.

The Calvinist religion was based on predestination, which meant the existence of an elect who alone would get to heaven. This in turn rested on a formalised distinction between 'superiors' and 'inferiors' defined by personal wealth. Thus Calvinism presented the nobility with a potentially ideal vehicle.

The new Church of Scotland united noble grandees, the lairds, and the tiny urban middle class. The kirk's General Assembly became the key institution in Scottish life for much of the late 16th century and the 17th century.

But Calvinism was also attractive to the peasantry. Their material conditions worsened in the 16th and 17th centuries as the nobility imposed tenurial conditions which either gave no security over their plot of land or often a lease of just one year. That tightening of the knot reflected the development of market orientated agriculture.

Writing in the 1640s one observer said that most Scots were 'by continual custom, born slaves and bondsmen, their ordinary food pease and beans'. Farming a rocky plot with starvation an ever present reality meant Calvinism offered some hope.

Scotland virtually alone in Europe had no tradition of peasant revolt. Yet amongst its backward peasantry there developed an intense religious faith in a society where the kirk dominated everyday life. It operated its own courts and controlled education and poor relief.

It was from this society that James VI rode forth to claim the crown of England and unite the two monarchies in 1603. James had been educated under kirk control following the defeat of his mother, Mary Queen of Scots. While he was a child the regency was fought over by the nobility. As late as 1600 he had been kidnapped during an unsuccessful aristocratic coup.

Yet by an astute mixture of coercion, flattery and conciliation James had strengthened the monarchy's hand. He played off the great magnates against each other, developed a strong Privy Council in Edinburgh and began to attempt to control the powers of the kirk—that 'mother of confusion' as he termed it—by appointing bishops responsible to the crown and insisting on his right to convene the kirk's ruling body, the General Assembly.

England offered a real power base. James carefully moved to construct an absolute monarchy on continental lines. In Scotland that centred on strengthening Privy Council rule and anglicising the kirk by imposing the control of bishops over the clergy.

But after James's death in 1625 his son Charles I began to move more recklessly. The cost of war with Spain had to be met by ways which got round parliament in Westminster. Scotland contributed just £11,000 to the crown.

Events in Scotland were about to detonate Britain's bourgeois revolution. Charles appointed his own men from London to run the Scottish Privy Council (James had previously relied on allies from within the Scottish elite). They now hit on a scheme to raise funds by repossessing former church lands so they could then sell them off.

This threatened the Scottish nobility where it mattered. The Earl of Mar declared 'no subject in Scotland in effect has any securities of his land'.

It was a reckless move. As Bishop Burnett complained:

> The most unaccountable part of the king's proceedings was that all the while when he was so endeavouring to recover so great a part of the property of Scotland as the church lands and tithes were, from men who were not going to part from them willingly, and was going to change the whole constitution of that church and kingdom, he raised no force to maintain what he was about to do, but trusted the whole management to the civil execution. By this means all the people saw the weakness of the government at the same time that they complained of its rigour.

Charles had no army with which to impose *both* direct control and the removal of land from the aristocracy. In addition, the forcing of Anglican practice on the kirk led to a riot in Edinburgh's High Church of St Giles.

Charles had created a formidable opposition. In 1638 Scotland's elite met in the kirk of Greyfriars in Edinburgh to set their seal on the Covenant. It was a remarkably conservative document which upheld the rights of the kirk and the nobility against the bishops and the crown. A General Assembly was convened which was opened to lay delegates again.

In terms of rebellion it had more in common with the aristocratic reaction in France prior to 1789 or the successful attempt by the Polish nobility to destroy royal power altogether.

But it had at its disposal one powerful weapon—an outside force which could break the deadlock in England between king and parliament. The archaic social structures of Scotland and its internal anarchy meant it was still a militarised society. The Covenant could field an army unmatched in Britain until Cromwell's New Model Army. Nobles rallied their tenants, burghs provided funds and Scots mercenaries fresh from the Thirty Years War provided leadership in the field.

In 1640 this army marched unchecked into northern England. A fuse was lit. Charles was seen to be powerless. He was forced to convene parliament and confronted a crisis over whether it or he would control the army needed to check the Scots. It was a crisis which erupted into civil war two years later.

The Scottish nobles now hoped to be the crucial players in this civil war. Their price for entering the conflict on parliament's side was an agreement that Calvinist rule would be imposed on England. But already these hopes were coming unstuck.

Even as they signed the Covenant in Greyfriars kirkyard many nobles could see that by weakening the king's powers they would in the long run weaken the position of the nobility. One grandee, the Duke of Montrose, broke away to field a royalist army in 1644. He raised it among the Highland clans who still lay outside the control of Edinburgh or London, clans which would provide a consistent reservoir of support for the Stuarts until 1746.

In the words of the Scottish socialist historian Victor Kiernan, 'In the civil war they [the Scots] floundered from side to side, becoming more and more deeply divided in the process.'

The rise of Cromwell and republicanism terrified the aristocratic rebels north of the border. They wanted a crown they could control, not its abolition. Increasingly they began to look for a compromise with Charles—which is why their allies in England, the Presbyterian Party, became identified as the moderates in parliament.

In 1648 they entered into alliance with Charles and invaded England only to be defeated at Preston. Two years later they crowned his son King of Scotland on condition he signed the Covenant and agreed to Calvinise England. This time defeat followed at Worcester. Cromwell invaded Scotland. The ministers had already purged the army of ideologically impure commanders. Now at the battle of Dunbar they overruled its commander in chief and threw away territorial advantage so guaranteeing defeat.

The Cromwellian conquest of Scotland pointed to the shape of future Britain. It weakened feudal power by establishing formal bourgeois property relations. Power equalled personal property, not feudal supremacy. The power of a unified British state was deployed to conquer the royalist Highland clans. Roads and forts were established as a check on them. Above all commerce underwent real growth based on its structural assimilation into the English market with the Commonwealth establishing internal free trade.

Yet Cromwellian rule was opposed by the mass of the population. A vague nationalism, identified with Calvinism, dominated the population as the Protector recognised. But the kirk itself was now split into various factions which had taken differing positions in the course of the civil war.

The restoration of Charles II in 1660 was followed by the convening of a Scottish parliament (which was tightly controlled by the crown), the reintroduction of bishops and a purge of dissident ministers. Four hundred ministers were expelled from their parishes in 1662 after they refused to bow to royal control of the kirk.

These dissidents, soon termed Covenanters, organised their own illegal open air services. Repression followed. In turn the Covenanters fought back.

But in social terms they represented neither a peasant jacquerie nor a forward looking movement like the English Levellers. Instead they simply wanted the restoration of the old kirk.

Under Charles II restrictions had also been reimposed on Scots trade with England and its colonies. The Scottish economy had undergone profound change. The old nobility had been defeated and bankrupted in war. Increasingly, led by the key grandee the Duke of Argyll, the nobles consciously moved to 'improve' their lands by agricultural commercialisation. In addition they profited from controlling the coal, woollen and salt trade with England and the Continent.

Glasgow had begun to muscle in on the Atlantic trade, particularly in tobacco. Scotland now had a growing merchant class coupled with an agricultural system dependent on a British market.

The Glorious Revolution of 1688 gave the Scottish parliament full powers and removed bishopric control of the kirk. But Scotland's exclusion from England's markets coupled with the growth of mercantilism on the Continent which blocked off these markets was creating a crisis.

As the historian Rosalind Mitchinson puts it, 'The economy of Scotland was passing from a position of narrowly making ends meet into conspicuous failure to do so.'

In 1696 and 1698 there were poor harvests which raised the spectre of famine. In 1704 there was a sharp trade slump. In the years between 1688 and the Act of Union in 1707 the population fell by between 5 and 15 percent. In 1704 the English parliament went further in declaring Scots to be aliens, threatening an even greater commercial rupture.

The one great attempt to break out of this morass was the Darien scheme—a plan to create a trading metropolis in Panama. Blocked from raising capital in the City of London, the money for the scheme was scraped together in Scotland. Yet despite the ruinous costs, the attempt at direct Scottish colonialism died in the swamps of Central America as both Spain and England combined to ensure it was stillborn.

Yet Scotland was still of major concern to Westminster. It still remained a weak flank—the centre of Jacobite and French intrigues. And the Scots still had control of their own legislation. In 1704 they passed the Successor Act under which the successor to the English throne could not succeed to the Scottish throne unless there was complete freedom of trade and navigation between the kingdoms. With the Hanoverian succession in doubt it was an effective sanction.

There can be no doubting the element of bribery used to procure the Scottish parliament's acceptance of the Act of Union in 1707. Daniel Defoe, one of the English agents active in Edinburgh, was appalled at the mercenary nature of the Scots nobility:

> The great men are posting to London for places and honours, every man full of his own merit and afraid of everyone near him: I never saw so much trick, sham, pride, jealousy and cutting of friend's throats as there is among the nobleman.

But even the one noble who opposed the Union on some sort of principled basis admitted in the debate:

> We are an obscure, poor people, though formerly of better account, removed to a remote corner of the world, without name and without alliances, our ports mean and precarious so that I profess I do not think any one port of the kingdom worth the bringing after.

The Scots historian Christopher Harvie summed up the basis for Union:

> Aristocrat and merchant alike looked south, the first attracted by political power and patronage, the second by an expanding English market and the possibility of liquidating his Darien losses. 'The motives will be, trade with the most, Hanover with some, ease and security with others,' wrote the Earl of Roxburghe in 1705.

Was Scotland in any way oppressed as a result of Union? Harvie rightly declares 18th century, post-Union Scotland to have been 'semi-independent'. The Act of Union—apart from paying £400,000 compensation for Darien—gave complete independence to the kirk as the established church, plus control over local government, the education and legal system. Administration of Scotland was left under the control of the Dukes of Argyll.

In addition, ruling class Scots were not barred from access to office in the British state. Indeed John Wilkes could incite the London mob over the alleged control of George III by the Earl of Bute and his Scottish cronies.

It was Scots capitalists who pioneered that most spectacular of industrial revolutions, seizing on the tobacco trade prior to the American Revolution, cotton following it, iron in the 1820s, shipbuilding in the 1860s and steel in the 1880s.

These developments were reflected in the remarkable Enlightenment which raised Edinburgh to an intellectual centre on a par with London, Paris or Vienna in the eyes of those like Voltaire. Reading David Hume or Adam Smith one can see why Thomas Jefferson declared in 1789 that in science 'no place in the world can pretend to a competition with Edinburgh'.

Scots too were scarcely barred from Britain's colonial expansion. Indeed the ruling classes of Canada, Australia and Hong Kong pay witness to the enthusiasm for imperialism north of the border. Scots soldiers were crucial to British might from Cork to Calcutta.

In a very real sense Scotland was the junior partner of British imperialism. Far from being oppressed, it was rewarded for Union with what in retrospect were extraordinarily generous terms.

And if one were to search for victims of Union one would have to identify the sufferings of the Highland clanfolk at the hands of not the English but largely Lowlands Scots.

More Scots fought at Culloden for Cumberland than for Charles Edward Stuart. More Scots soldiers than English wasted the glens thereafter. It was Scots landlords and factors who forced the Highlanders onto immigrant ships or to the slums of Glasgow to make way for the Great Cheviot sheep.

The Scottish ruling class used the power of the newly unified British state to finally complete the conquest of the Highlands for their own benefit.

Until 1914 Scotland was marching forward arm in arm with England, experiencing the benefits of industrial expansion and imperialism. You would have to search hard for signs of any real nationalist sentiment during those years.

But as Scotland emerged from the slaughter of the trenches, things were to change. British capitalism was now firmly in decline. Within a decade Clydeside giants like Beardsmores, Fairfields, Colvilles and the Steel Company of Scotland were ruined. If, prior to 1914, London had more unemployment than Glasgow, the balance was now reversed.

That opened the road to the birth of modern Scottish nationalism.

Chapter 16

The horrible history of the house of Windsor

Colin Sparks

An undistinguished military man in his early thirties is to be married in front of vast crowds and the world's press. How does this come about? What is there about the man which makes his person and doings so fascinating to millions of people? It can hardly be his personal qualities. Despite acres of newsprint, there seems to be nothing very special about him which would distinguish him from thousands of other upper class twits who merit much more modest treatment. The only possible explanation is the family he was born into. But what's so special about the Windsor family?

All families have long histories and they are usually littered with rather sordid events about which it would be better to say nothing. It is in the nature of the institution that it makes people behave in very strange ways. But since this particular family is held up as a model to us all, and rests its wealth and power purely and simply on its history, it is well worth looking hard at that history.

If Charles is going to be king because, and only because, of his descent, it must be admitted that his family's record is so spectacularly sordid, and so riddled with malice and accident, that he would do better to change his name and try to lead a normal life.

Without delving too far into the murky and bloody history of the

First published July 1981

English crown, with its murders, imprisonments, usurpations, massacres and general bloodiness, we can conveniently begin with one James II. His subjects suspected him, quite rightly, of secretly preparing tyranny and of being a crypto-Catholic (about the worst thing you could be at the time). He was consequently deposed in the 'Glorious Revolution' of 1688. This was a bloodless coup, largely because the commander of the royal forces, a certain John Churchill, later Duke of Marlborough and ancestor of the current warmonger Winston Churchill, was bribed to change sides just before the decisive battle. This noble act founded the young officer's future fortune but left the old king with no army and no choice: he had to run away.

He was replaced by his daughter Mary. Her claim to fame was that she was a Protestant and was married to the equally Protestant William of Orange—King Billy himself. So the origins of the modern monarchy are based upon a military coup and surrounded by bribery, treachery and foreign mercenaries.

After a few years, the direct line of descent ran out. The descendants of James II were disqualified for their obstinate persistence in Catholicism. So parliament had to look around for someone else. There were two qualifications: some sort of distant claim and Protestantism—the second of which was much more important. They lighted on an obscure German prince, the Elector of Hanover, and duly shipped him over to be George I. There was not much wrong with him as a king, apart from the fact that he could not speak English.

Despite having locked his wife up in a castle for 32 years, George I somehow managed to produce offspring, and he was duly succeeded by his son George II, who managed to learn English. His main claim to fame was that, despite having fought in many battles, he eventually died by falling off a lavatory seat in Kensington Palace, striking his head against a chest and expiring from the wound thus gloriously received. His son, Frederick, was already dead, having been hit by a tennis ball nine years earlier, so he was succeeded by his 22 year old grandson, George III.

If Georges mark one and mark two had been harmless if rather expensive, George III was not at all harmless. He was simply the most prominent of a pretty bad lot.

His sister, Caroline Matilda, for example, was married off at the age of 15 to the King of Denmark, whose major activity was, as the chronicles quaintly put it, pursuing 'low amours'. To recompense herself she took as a lover the prime minister, Struensee. This being discovered, he was hanged for his temerity and she was locked up in a castle for the rest of her life.

George's youngest brother, the Duke of Cumberland, seduced Lady Grosvenor, was sued by her husband for 'criminal conversation' (ie adultery) and had his love letters read out in open court. Another brother lived with a woman who had the triple handicap of being a widow, illegitimate and the daughter of a tradeswoman.

George III, who was a bit of a snob and a lot of a puritan, decided that these goings on were getting the family a bad name, and he determined to clean things up a bit. One of his main instruments was the Royal Marriages Act, which he forced through parliament in 1772. This piece of despotism, which is still in force, states that any marriage of a descendant of George II is null and void if contracted without royal consent. This caused an awful lot of trouble because, while George III had a lot of children, they were, in the main, a very much worse lot even than his brothers and sisters.

All of his morality had an unfortunate effect on poor George, and he became a little crazy. On one occasion, driving through the Royal Park at Windsor, he stopped his coach, got out and tried to shake hands with an oak, being under the impression that it was Frederick the Great, King of Prussia. This state of mind came and went with George until, opening the 1811 session of parliament, he began his address, 'My lords and peacocks...' This was going too far: he was declared unfit to rule, locked away in Windsor Castle, and his eldest son was made Prince Regent.

Now, if George III was mad, his son was positively bad. He had, for example, committed the greatest crime that any future king of England is capable of: he had married a Catholic. Besides this, his extravagance, his reaction, his general uselessness, were nothing. His marriage, to a Mrs Fitzherbert, in 1785, he kept a secret, but it presented him with problems. It made it difficult to marry legally and beget an heir, and without that assurance of future monarchy parliament would not agree to pay off his enormous debts. Fortunately, Mrs Fitzherbert was a reasonable woman, and for a bribe of £3,000 a year agreed to keep quiet about the whole thing.

This noble gesture freed the Prince of Wales to marry his cousin, Caroline of Brunswick, who had been located on the prince's instructions that 'one damned German frau is as good as another.' The couple met for the first time three days before the wedding, and hated each other on sight. The Prince was drunk during the wedding and had to be supported by the Duke of Bedford. The bride nearly fell down under the weight of her wedding dress. Despite these ill omens, the marriage produced a daughter, the succession was secured, and Princess Caroline was given her marching orders in the shape of a formal letter of separation. The Prince of Wales resumed his life with Mrs Fitzherbert.

So far, things have been simple if unpleasant, but at this point it starts to get complicated. In 1817 the successor, Princess Charlotte, died giving birth to a stillborn child, and the whole business was back in the melting pot.

The Prince Regent was in a mess. He was married to Mrs Fitzherbert but she was a Roman Catholic, and if this was discovered he would forfeit his title and be convicted of bigamy to boot. He could shelter behind the Royal Marriages Act but his second regal wife was completely estranged from him. One recourse was to divorce Caroline and find a third wife. This could only be done on grounds of adultery, which was quite drastic since the adultery of the wife of the heir to the throne is high treason and, if convicted, Princess Caroline would have to be beheaded.

(Incidentally, this piece of barbarism is still law, so Lady Di had better keep her vows if she wants to keep her head.)

There were plenty of children floating around from his various brothers, but they were all illegitimate—due once again to the aforesaid Royal Marriages Act—and none of them would do. The prince started proceedings to divorce his wife, which turned up a good deal of extremely unsavoury evidence as to her activities with her brother Bergami, but she died before she could be tried. The royal brothers also took matters in hand. They left their long standing mistresses in the lurch and hurried off to find eligible princesses.

The situation was pretty desperate. The unemployed regularly took pot shots at the Prince Regent with live ammunition, and if one of them were to aim straight, the first 17 candidates for the throne had no children who could legally inherit. And the first 11 candidates were all themselves over 40. Unless one of them could get legally married and produce a legal heir, then it was a fair bet that the crown would pass from ageing hand to ageing hand quicker than the ball at Cardiff Arms Park. This, it was felt, would be bad publicity for an already detested monarchy and might give occasion for seditious activity tending in a distinctly Jacobin direction.

There was an additional incentive: legal marriage and legal heirs were the only things that would persuade parliament to raise the salaries of these extravagant drones and pay off their vast debts.

Fortunately for all concerned, numerous royal houses of Germany had numerous offspring whose parents were quite happy to overlook the moral and personal shortcomings of future spouses who might be expected to sit on the throne of England. Consequently a ready supply of royal brides and bridegrooms were on hand. Thus a Princess Adelaide of Saxe-Meiningen had no qualms in marrying the foul mouthed and disgustingly reactionary Duke of Clarence, despite the fact that he had only just left the actress Mrs Jordan, with whom he had lived happily for years. And at the same ceremony Princess Victoria of Saxe-Coburg took on the relatively progressive Duke of Kent, who had just left Madame de St Laurent, with whom he had lived for 27 years.

There were a flurry of other royal weddings, but the succession was soon secured: the Duke of Kent and Princess Victoria produced a daughter named Victoria. Thus, when George III, described by Shelley as 'an old, mad, blind, despised and dying king' finally snuffed it in 1820, the Prince Regent duly became George IV. He was succeeded by his brother, the Duke of Clarence, as William IV, and he by Victoria.

With her, things settled down a bit. She reigned for an awfully long time and was pretty respectable. Around her, the myth of the modern monarchy was built. Some idea of the breadth of her comprehension can be judged from the fact that female homosexuality has never been illegal in Britain, since she refused to believe that women did that sort of thing and consequently it was exempted from legislation.

She married yet another royal German stud, Prince Albert, and produced an enormous brood. Her successor, Edward VII, was rather less respectable, gambling prodigiously and allegedly cheating at cards, but his personal scandals were confined to illicit liaisons with actresses and married women rather than horrendous crimes like secret marriages to Catholics. His successor, George V, was again very respectable. On being told that a famous man was a homosexual, he replied, 'But I thought that chaps like that shot themselves.'

So far the vagaries of the succession had depended on the bizarre accidents of dynastic matrimony, and with George V's marriage to Princess Mary of Teck, great grandaughter of George III, it looked as though things were nicely sewn up among the petty German princes. Almost without exception, these people had been political reactionaries of the deepest hue, but they had never been too far out of step with the ruling classes. At this point there comes about a filthy coincidence of reactionary politics and the absurd regulations of royal marriage which once again shifted the line of succession drastically.

The successor to George V was Edward VIII. He wanted to marry a Mrs Simpson, who was a commoner, an American and a divorcee. About the only thing going for her was that she was not a Catholic. In addition, young Edward was an enthusiastic admirer of Adolf Hitler. The British ruling class did not much mind fascism as long as it kept the workers in check, but some of them saw a war coming with Germany over the spoils of the world, and thought that they needed to watch their backs. Consequently, Edward was forced to abdicate.

He immediately shuttled off to Berchtesgaden to have an audience with Hitler, who went on record as considering him 'an ideal fascist monarch'. He continued his contacts with the Nazis during the war. In 1940 the Spanish foreign minister, one of the intermediaries, reported that 'The duke is a firm supporter of a peaceful arrangement with Germany. The duke definitely believes that continued severe bombing would make England ready for peace.' A later dispatch said, 'The duke was considering making a public statement...disavowing present English policy and breaking with his brother (ie the king).' Even when shipped off to the West Indies, he continued contact with Nazi agents and, after the war, settled down next door to Oswald Mosley outside Paris.

His brother and successor, George VI, broke with tradition by marrying a commoner, Elizabeth Bowes-Lyon, the current Queen Mother and an enthusiastic admirer of Ian Smith (the racist prime minister of Rhodesia who declared independence unilaterally to preserve white rule). Their eldest daughter is now queen, married to a Greek of German royal origin, and mother of the splendidly undistinguished Charles. It is on that illustrious history that his claim to our attention and respect lies.

Nothing sums up the tacky nature of the British royal house so much as its name. We have traced a welter of Guelphs, Saxe-Coburgs, Saxe-Meiningens, and god knows what else, none of which seem to bear much relation to homely old Windsor. The fact is it was changed to Windsor for 'patriotic' reasons during the wave of anti-German feeling at the start of the First World War. They are a family whose record proves time and time again that they will do literally anything to hang on to their wealth and power.

None of this would count for much, or even be worth telling, if it were not for the ideological importance of the House of Windsor. They are projected as a central image of our society. They buttress the idea of the family. They prove that some are born to rule and others to be ruled. They embody the notion that merit is of no importance and inheritance is everything. They are the focus of every attempt to paper over the stinking, decaying reality of British society with pretty pictures of an ideal dream of the past. Like the reality they conceal, they are a festering sore, and the great lie that they are fitted by breeding to reign over us is the apex of a system of lies which drowns the truth every day.

Chapter 17

A criminal system

Duncan Blackie

Punishment—from body to soul

His cell was thirteen and a half feet from barred window to bolted door, seven and a half feet from wall to wall, and nine feet from floor to ceiling. Its contents were spare: a table, a chair, a cobbler's bench, hammock, broom, bucket, and a corner shelf. On the shelf stood a pewter mug dish, a bar of soap, a towel, and a Bible. Except for exercise and chapel, every minute of his day was spent in this space among these objects.

Familiar? This is not Strangeways or Dartmoor in 1990 but an account of Pentonville Prison soon after it opened in 1842. The regime shocked contemporaries even then.

The fact that many of today's prisoners are incarcerated in jails built during Victorian times and earlier—Dartmoor was started in 1806—is well known.

But why should it be that after nearly two centuries, when virtually all other conditions in society have changed so radically, the penal system is still essentially just as barbaric?

The underlying reason is simple. Prisoners are at the sharp end of state repression, denied their freedom and dignity according to 'Her Majesty's Pleasure'.

Various means are used to protect capitalism and private property. Police break picket lines to defend the bosses' profits. But, just as importantly, they also work to defend the private property of the rich from poorer individuals.

And when all else fails, then the state is prepared to use the most

First published May 1990

authoritarian means to defend itself—today that means incarcerating at least some of those who step outside of their laws. Thus the vast majority of prison inmates are sent down for crimes against property, not against individual people.

The penal system is part and parcel of class rule, and the evolution of the present system shows how it is designed to fit the needs of capitalism.

Prior to the development of industrial capitalism imprisonment was a very rare occurrence. Exceptional 'enemies of the state' might be locked up in the Tower of London and political and religious dissenters were put in local jails, but virtually no 'common criminals' were incarcerated. Between 1770 and 1774 only 2.3 percent of sentences handed down at the Old Bailey were for imprisonment.

The vast bulk of punishments involved direct damage to the body—hanging was the most extreme, but whippings, brandings and a spell in the stocks were also widely used for even the most petty offences.

The steady entrenchment of the new bourgeoisie led to the development of a set of criminal laws, popularly known as the 'Bloody Codes', and to a steady increase in the number of punitive sentences handed down by judges. The number of capital offences increased from about 50 in 1688 to around 160 in 1765 and then to over 200 by the end of the Napoleonic Wars. Most of these had a political purpose—to help secure all social power in the hands of the bourgeoisie.

The Black Act, for example, made new offences of any activity deemed likely to slow up the expansion of capitalist farming, then ruthlessly taking over rural livelihoods. Two thirds of those convicted of forgery were executed as it was reckoned this crime was a mortal danger to the development of commerce. Other capital offences included stealing goods to the value of more than 40 shillings and impersonating an Egyptian.

The start of the Industrial Revolution threw this system into crisis. The rise of the factory system meant that workers could not be ruled by naked repression alone. In addition, growing urbanisation led to large collections of potentially unruly people. It also made forms of punishment based on humiliation by the offender's own community, like the pillory for example, less effective.

Spells in the pillory were supposed to be occasions for the population to join in vilifying a criminal, but in the towns they could just as easily become rallying points for mass defiance against the authorities. When radical printer Daniel Isaac Eaton went into the stocks outside Newgate in 1813 a garland was put around his head and the crowd abused the attendant magistrates instead.

The huge numbers that turned out for public hangings are today usually explained by a blood lust on the crowds' part. In fact, as often as not, they would turn up in the hope of having a go at the authorities.

Open air hangings outside Newgate had to be suspended in 1783, because, according to the sheriffs:

> It has long been a subject of complaint that our processions to Tyburn are a mockery upon the aweful sentence of law and that the final scene itself has lost its terror and is so far from giving a lesson in morality to the beholders that it tends to the encouragement of vice… Numbers soon thicken into a crowd of followers and then an indecent levity is heard, the crowd gathers as it goes, and their levity increases till on their approach to the fatal tree, the ground becomes a riotous mass, and their wantonness of speech breaks forth in profane jokes, swearing and blasphemy.

Another factor which sharpened the crisis was the suspension of transportation to the American colonies in 1775. This had been a crucial weapon in the armoury of the British state.

Many were transported for political offences, such as the Captain Swing rioters, Luddites, Chartists, trade unionists and Irish rebels. But in the mid-18th century the most petty theft could also result in transportation. A more serious crime, however, if committed by someone of immediate use to the ruling class, such as a servant or an apprentice, would be more likely to attract a whipping.

When transportation resumed in the late 1780s, this time to Australia, it never regained its former importance, partly because it was felt to be ineffective. 'Tho' a transported convict may suffer under his sentence, his sufferings are unseen,' it was said.

The authorities initially compensated for the lack of effect of the old forms of punishment with short term methods. Prison hulks were pressed into service as a 'temporary expedient', although they lasted for decades. More convicts were disposed of by simply increasing the number of hangings—by 50 percent between the early 1770s and the early 1780s.

Still the jails quickly overcrowded. The population increased by 73 percent between 1776 and 1786, taking the system to breaking point. In 1784 a riot at Wood Street Compter, led by a prisoner described as 'ferocious as Beelzebub', was only put down with the help of a private military club, the London Military Foot Association.

The jails that existed were simply not up to the task. Newgate was regarded by the reformers as being the best argument for prison reform, as its day to day operations were virtually independent of the rest of the state. Power in the jail was distributed between the keeper and a hierarchy of inmates.

Conditions were appalling. In 1750 two prisoners with typhus were called to the Old Bailey, where the 'putrid streams from the bail dock' took out over 50 people, including the judge, the jury and the lawyers.

Reform

Against this background of dissent, chaos and disease the arguments of 'penal reformers' for a new system of punishment which would both terrorise the population and neatly fit the needs of the new industrial capital, started to get a hearing.

John Howard's *The State of the Prisons*, published in 1777, called for 'fixed hours of rising, of reading a chapter in the Bible, of praying, of meals, of work etc'.

The arguments had an enlightened ring to them: 'The notion that convicts are ungovernable is certainly erroneous. There is a mode of managing some of the most desperate with ease to yourself and advantage to them. Shew them that you have humanity and that you aim to make them useful members of society,' argued Howard.

Others, such as John Brewster, tried to capture the new scientific spirit of the times and take any element of randomness out of beatings by devising a whipping machine with flails of cane and whalebone.

But behind all these efforts was an attempt to restore the legitimacy of a legal system thoroughly discredited by the Bloody Codes.

Fundamental to all the reform proposals was the idea that prisons could fulfil two functions. Firstly, they could assist in destroying all means of livelihood outside of the control of the bourgeoisie. A particular target was a section of the urban poor which scraped by through petty crime.

Secondly, the prisons could be used to imbue these people with the new work ethic of the times. This was to be achieved, in a new network of 'hard labour houses', according to the Penitentiary Act of 1779:

> By sobriety, cleanliness and medical assistance, by a regular series of labour, by solitary confinement during the intervals of work and by due religious instruction…to inure them to habits of industry, to guard them from pernicious company, to accustom them to serious reflection and to teach them with the principles and practice of every Christian and moral duty.

Many of the most notable reformers were Quakers, who combined a concern for punishment with an interest in establishing a rational foundation for the expansion of capital. They drew up schemes for 'panopticans'—buildings in which an overseer could view everything going on from one vantage point—which could serve either as prisons or as factories. Many mills were laid out on the same basic design as the prisons.

Some of them also sought to combine industry and punishment more directly, by building new jails which would also be dedicated to industrial production.

As one of the most famous reformers, Jeremy Bentham, proposed:

> What hold can another manufacturer have upon his workmen, equal to what my manufacturer would have upon his? What other master is there that can reduce his workmen, if idle, to a situation next to starving, without suffering them to go elsewhere? What other master is there whose men can never get drunk unless he chooses they should do so? And who, so far from being able to raise their wages by combination, are obliged to take whatever pittance he thinks it most his interest will allow?

As it turned out, 'free labour' could be just as ruthlessly and more efficiently exploited than prison labour, but many of the disciplinary techniques proposed by Bentham and others were adopted when the huge new establishments required to deal with urban dissent were built.

Opposition to the new penitentiaries was not long in coming. Jacobins produced a pamphlet called *Gloucester Bastille*, attacking the, 'pathetic particulars of a poor boy sentenced to suffer seven years solitary confinement in Gloucester jail'. 'Jail delivery riots' became commonplace in the 1780s. And by the 1790s many of the penitentiaries had returned to the same level of disorder as the earlier jails.

Further crises followed after 1815, with the demobilisation after the Napoleonic Wars when the inmate population more than trebled. By 1818 accommodation intended for 8,545 housed 13,057 people.

In 1818 there was a mutiny over the bread ration at the first national penitentiary, at Millbank in London. So bad had this become that prisoners rioted to be returned to the prison hulks, to get away from the stifling disciplines of jail!

More reform was clearly needed to hone the machines of repression into tools of modern class rule.

This same period saw the creation of the first of the modern police forces. The rationale for the new forces, which were to replace the army in the day to day control of working class communities, was similar to that for the new prisons. Naked terror alone was not enough to quell working class revolt. Indeed the appearance of troops often served to increase the level of dissent.

On the other hand, the ruling class could not leave its property unguarded, so they required a more subtle force—the police to patrol the richer areas of the towns. However, the police were also forced to extend their operations in the working class districts, not in order to protect the poor, but to develop a knowledge of and access to the working class communities from where the threat to property sprang.

Similar efforts were made to turn the prisons into effective weapons to deal with working class dissent.

The new jails would attempt to isolate offenders from the outside world as opposed to the older custom of having the prisons semi-open to the public. This would serve to atomise the prisoners themselves and to create an image of the prisoner as an unseen alien enemy. The rest of society were encouraged to regard prisoners as quite separate from the mass of the population.

Prisoners were further isolated within the jails through the introduction of the cell system.

Pentonville was the new 'model' when it opened in 1842, with absolute isolation for prisoners for the first 18 months. Even the chapel was divided into separate compartments. Each cell had a separate exercise area, but even then masks had to be worn to prevent recognition. Ten more similar ones were built by 1850. A Pentonville guard said in 1856, to the question of whether the loss of the thumbscrews gave them less control:

> I think we have greater power over them, sir. For at present, you see, we cut off the right of receiving and sending letters, as well as stop the visits of their friends, and a man feels these things more than any torture that he could be put to.

The Victorians, like those who followed, attempted to use the prison system to isolate the most unruly and alienated sections of the working class. A 'dangerous' class was codified as a supposedly limited and definable enemy which could be isolated from the working class as a whole.

In certain periods, like the long economic expansion of the mid- to late 19th century and again during the 1950s and 1960s, it proved possible to drive a wedge between the poor and the skilled sections of the working class. But in the late 19th century economic crisis, the building of mass unions and eventually the Great Unrest in the early part of this century put paid to that.

The attempts to portray the prison system as a necessary defence for the population from a minority of 'criminal elements' still persist today. The reality of the jails—as instruments of repression overwhelmingly targeted at the most vulnerable sections of the population—continues too.

The modern jail

Victorian jails still brood over the centre of virtually every city in Britain. Hangings no longer take place within their walls and prisoners no longer have to walk treadmills, but the tortures of modern prison life are just as bad as they were a century ago.

Thousands are locked up, three to a cell for twenty three and a half hours a day. Prisoners are kept in jail for much longer than the original prison builders would ever have thought endurable.

The 'local prisons' such as Strangeways, which have the worst conditions, were originally meant to hold people for a maximum of two years. In 1837 Lord John Russell estimated that a ten year sentence would be 'a punishment worse than death'.

Even in 1904, of the 190,000 offenders sent to prison, more than two thirds went in for two weeks or less. Only 1 percent got a sentence of over 12 months.

As late as 1971 Justice Chapman made legal history by being the first judge ever to recommend that someone be kept in jail for the rest of their life. Today such a statement would not raise an eyebrow.

Britain now has the highest per capita prison population in Western Europe, greater even than Turkey. Almost one person in 1,000 is in jail at any one moment—that's nearly 70 percent more than in Italy and two and a half times the rate for Holland.

And the vast bulk of this population are put away for offences which do not involve violence. Only 13 percent of prisoners have been sent down for violent crime, and 3 percent for sexual offences.

Much of the recent rise in the prison population is due to specific policy decisions, such as only allowing remission on half of the sentence rather than two thirds, and the setting of minimum terms for a whole range of crimes.

In addition judges increasingly hand out longer sentences The average sentence in 1983 was 10.9 months. By 1987 it was 15.1 months.

The rise in the prison population has been inexorable. In 1987 there were 54,400 people in jail. This figure has since nosed down by a marginal amount, but is enormous by historical standards. The prison population in 1961 for example was 31,500.

In 1976, 16 percent of convicted men were sent to jail. That figure rose to 21 percent in 1986. The rates for women are 3 and 8 percent. The percentage of the prison population on remand has doubled to 23 percent between 1980 and 1988. The average length of time on remand has also doubled since 1976—40 percent of those on remand end up not going to prison after their trial. A study of the Risley remand centre found that 85 percent of the inmates should have been given bail.

It is not an 'underclass' which goes to jail but it is, by and large, the less fortunate sections of the working class. A study in the early 1970s found that three quarters of prisoners were manual workers. A third were homeless at the time of sentencing and 15 percent illiterate. Some 21 percent of prisoners come from ethnic minorities. And 300 are seriously mentally ill at any given time.

And it is the most trivial offences that most of them are put away for. In 1988 nearly a fifth of the total, 22,000, were sent down for defaulting on fines.

The situation in Britain today is particularly bad, and could be alleviated by simple measures such as not locking people up for petty offences.

Yet it has also long been known that prisons don't work to stop crime at all. If anything, a prison term only serves to increase the economic and social disadvantage that leads to 'offences' being committed in the first place.

The increase in punishment in Britain can only be punitive, as even the Home Office admits that longer sentences don't discourage crime.

Table 1
NUMBERS SERVING LONG SENTENCES
(England and Wales, over 21s only)

Length of sentence	1971	1987
4 years (excluding life)	3,320	6,590
Life	770	2,170
All	24,870	27,680

The 1986 Home Office handbook for courts states:

Evidence suggests that imposing particular sentences, or particularly severe sentences, has a very limited effect on crime levels. Longer periods in custody do not produce better results than shorter ones. No increase in prison terms would make a substantial impact on crime rates.

Around 55 percent of men and 34 percent of women are reconvicted within two years of release.

An American study found in 1965 that 91 percent of adults 'admitted they had committed acts for which they might have received jail or prison sentences'. American studies also show that the more often someone has been in jail, the more likely they are to commit a crime. More than 80 percent of serious crime, according to the 1965 President's Clark Commission, is committed by people who have already been in jail.

If prisons don't work, and every bit of evidence shows they don't, what are their functions?

Firstly, they fix the blame for the failings of society upon individuals themselves. Secondly, the system defines the prisoner as a dangerous non-person, with no rights. Society, therefore, has no obligations to them. Thirdly, the system can be used to neutralise dissent. Lastly prisons, along with other agencies, provide a means for socially neutralising the most alienated sections of the population.

They do not target the most persistent lawbreakers, such as the bosses and city financiers who ignore the law as a business practice. Rather they concentrate on the weakest in society and blow their misdemeanours up out of all proportion.

These factors have been left out of the debate sparked by the recent riots. Even liberal commentators have been loathe to go beyond looking at various horrific aspects of the system to condemning the prison system as a whole.

But such things as the hierarchy of violence, 'privileges' and the scapegoating of sexual offenders held under Category 43 are component parts of a wider system. They are safety valves which operate most of the time to make it possible for the state to subject over 50,000 people to the most barbaric treatment.

When conditions become so intolerable that even the safety valves fail to save the system, then the resulting explosion gives us a glimpse of what the prisons are really like.

The prisons have been thrown into immediate crisis by the increase in bitterness, alienation and desperation caused by economic deprivation during the Tory years. To that extent the prison riots are a component part of the wider revolt against everything the Tories have stood for over the last decade.

But at all times, both prosperous and lean, the prison system stands as a gruesome monument to the way that industrial capitalism today, just as at its birth, needs to use terror to mop up the social casualties left in its wake.

Chapter 18

Their finest hour?

Geoff Ellen

No Labour government evokes more nostalgia within the Labour Party than Attlee's. Between 1945 and 1951 major industries were nationalised and a welfare state was established: it was what one writer called 'the climax of Labourism'. It was also, a Tory MP reflected soon after, a time when it was 'easier to make higher profits without being really efficient than probably at any period in my lifetime'.

In the country, its troops lit bonfires and dreamed aloud: in the Commons, its lieutenants, to Tory consternation, struck up the Red Flag; and in the cabinet, its generals pinched each other. Labour had—massively, euphorically and, for some, astonishingly—won its first majority government, and in that 'blissful dawn of July 1945' its 393 MPs tingled, as one of them put it, with 'joy and hope, determination and confidence'. Ahead lay 'a new society to be built; and we had power to build it.'

What sort of society? For those to whom the result of the general election meant 'the revolution without a single cracked skull', there now seemed 'nothing to stand in the way of laying the socialist foundation of the new social order'. It was not an entirely unrealistic hope.

The electoral beneficiary of an outburst of popular radicalism unknown since the days of the Chartists, Labour had been swept into office by a landslide: and awaiting it there, intact from the Second World War, lay an unprecedented range of state controls over the economy. In short, the new cabinet had both the mandate and the means to carry through major change.

It also had leaders aware of the implications. The prime minister,

First published November 1982

Clement Attlee, and the President of the Board of Trade and future chancellor, Sir Stafford Cripps, had warned a decade earlier that 'the ruling class will go to almost any length to defeat parliamentary action if the issue is…the continuance of their financial and political control.' Therefore 'the moment to strike at capitalism' was when the government was 'freshly elected and assured of its support. The blow struck must be a fatal one…' In other words, wrote Cripps, an Emergency Powers Bill limiting the movement of capital and abolishing the House of Lords would have to be passed on the first day of the new parliament. Nothing less than a constitutional revolution was required:

> Continuity of policy, even in fundamentals, can find no place in a so-cialist programme. It is this complete severance with all traditional theories of government, this determination to seize power from the ruling class and transfer it to the people as a whole, that differentiates the present political struggle from all those that have gone before.

In the summer of 1945, with Labour 'fresh elected and assured of its support', with Cripps and all the other 'brilliant prophets of the in-evitability of violence'—Aneurin Bevan, Ellen Wilkinson, Emanuel Shinwell and John Strachey—in office, with the Tories reeling from their biggest electoral defeat in half a century and with the armed forces radical enough to discourage any would-be British Franco, Attlee was uniquely placed to strike his 'fatal blow' at capitalism.

By then, however, he and his colleagues were talking the language not of class but of 'nation'. Attlee's socialist rhetoric had already become muted when, in May 1940, he led Labour into a coalition government dominated by Tories and headed by a man seen by many with memories of the general strike and Tonypandy as the labour movement's most bitter enemy—Winston Churchill. Having briefly shaken his fist at the ruling class, Attlee now offered it his hand: five years of governing with Tories would provide him with 'very pleasant' memories. The Labour leaders not only learned, said one of them, 'a great deal from the Conservatives in how to govern': they invariably found themselves in agreement with them. Party conflict arose only 'very seldom', Attlee recalled.

Consensus reigned. Capitalism would be preserved, but with the 'socialism' of state supervision. A Tory, Butler, reshaped education and a Liberal, Beveridge, outlined what became the welfare state: there were even Tories, Churchill among them, willing to counte-nance a degree of nationalisation. When the bluster of the general election finally disturbed this harmony, it was still difficult, said one observer, to find in the parties' official literature 'any basic conflicts separating the left from the right'.

Behind the consensus lurked a fear. After two decades of mass unemployment, means testing and sacrifice, millions were insisting 'Never Again'; to ignore them was to risk a resurgence of the class conflict which had unnerved Lloyd George's cabinet at the end of the First World War. 'If you don't give the people social reform', Quintin Hogg, then a young Tory MP, warned in 1944, 'they will give you social revolution'. The pressure from below could not be evaded: could it then be diverted? The answer was that it could—and Labour would show how.

It was to prove a sobering experience for those of its supporters intoxicated by the promise of a new society. A Gallup poll discovered that for all those who wanted to see Labour govern 'along existing lines only more efficiently', there were twice as many who were demanding 'sweeping changes such as nationalisation'. Such expectations could be seen on election night in crowded Labour halls and celebration bonfires up and down the country, and they could be heard in the cheers of his supporters when Attlee told a victory rally that 'the principles of our policy are based on the brotherhood of man'.

Five days later troops were sent into London's Surrey Docks to break industrial action by dockers seeking a basic 25 shillings a day.

It was a curious beginning for ministers who had devoted much of their electioneering to exposing the scandal of working class living standards, and a curious beginning, too, for the new era of the 'brotherhood of man' when, within a fortnight and with Attlee's support, a different sort of bonfire was lit in the streets of Hiroshima. For Labour, the 'responsibilities of office' came easy.

Conventionally bourgeois

In retrospect, of course, there had to be something faintly ludicrous in the idea of Attlee—a man so conventionally bourgeois that, it was said, he shuddered if the port was passed round the wrong way— storming the citadels of capitalist power. At best, notably with the creation of the National Health Service, his government merely humanised inequality: at worst they promoted it. In education, largely under the guidance of 'Red Ellen' Wilkinson, party policy on comprehensive schooling was shunned in favour of Butler's inegalitarian system of selection, with the result that—in the words of one of the party's present educationalists—'possibly the greatest opportunity in the century to implement radical educational and social change' was lost. In foreign policy, such was Labour's 'disregard for all traditional socialist values' that one backbench MP was prompted to jibe at foreign secretary Ernest Bevin, 'Hasn't Anthony Eden grown fat!'

This was 'continuity' with a vengeance, and nowhere more so than in industry. Twenty years earlier George Bernard Shaw had disdainfully remarked that nationalisation need not affect the workers in the slightest: to them it 'would only be a change of masters'. And so it proved. By 1951, it has been reckoned, only nine of the 47 full time members and seven of the 40 part time members of the boards of the nationalised industries were trade unionists, and five of the boards had no trade unionists amongst their full time members at all. Most directors were drawn from 'the existing managerial hierarchies'. Nor was it any different outside the boardrooms: in mines, for example, 'the same old faces' remained in charge at every level.

Workers' control for Attlee in the 1930s, 'an essential part of the new order', was now dismissed by Herbert Morrison as failing to 'demonstrate good socialisation in its methods of administration and management'. The scale of this shift became apparent when, in 1946, a leading minister let slip his belief that there was:

> not as yet a very large number of workers in Britain capable of taking over large enterprises... Until there has been more experience by the workers of the managerial side of industry, I think it would be impossible to have worker-controlled industry in Britain, even if it were on the whole desirable.

The speaker was Sir Stafford Cripps.

Nationalisation may have given little to the workers, but it was far from a disappointment for their former bosses. Extraordinarily generous compensation was paid to the owners of what were, for the most part, crippled industries. As a result, Attlee wrote later, 'there was not much real opposition to our nationalisation proposals, only iron and steel roused much feeling': and, he might have added, they were left to last, before being carried through in such a way as to make denationalisation easy when the Tories returned to power in 1951.

From all of this, the ruling class had little to fear. 'Leading businessmen', Harold Wilson, President of the Board of Trade, boasted in 1949, 'admit that, had it not been for the improved output since nationalisation, there would have been no basis for private enterprise to work on.'

For those who worked in the nationalised industries, however, there was a sense of disorientation. Many miners, for example, had long treasured the hope of nationalisation and, if now they felt a certain disenchantment, it was less easy to express it through the traditional method of industrial action. This did not prevent such action but the argument—plausible to many and repeated ad nauseam from on high—that they were striking against their government and their industry was bound to weaken it, especially when voiced by a miners' union leadership opposed to any stoppages. One of the union's area organisations, Durham, even suggested that miners' lodges should reimburse the Coal Board for losses resulting from unofficial strikes. It was hardly surprising that astute Tories such as Iain Macleod should come to see in nationalisation a means of strengthening the power of the trade union bureaucracy against the rank and file.

The claims to working class loyalty of the Labour government were crucial in creating industrial peace in years when high employment gave workers formidable bargaining potential. Strike days between 1945 and 1951 totalled 14,260,000, compared with 192,230,000 in the seven years after the First World War.

Nevertheless, Labour often acted ferociously against the few strikes there were. One MP:

> ...noticed year by year in the House of Commons, with interested
> horror, that all the innumerable answers to questions in parliament re-
> lating to strikes made by the late George Isaacs as Minister of Labour
> were based on the standpoint that the strikers and not the employers
> were to blame for the strikes.

Not only were almost all strikes unofficial, so solid was the union leaders' support for the government, most were also technically illegal, since Labour took care to maintain in peace time the draconian laws which Bevin had introduced during the war. Nor was this all. Troops were sent in by Labour to break strikes of dockers in September 1945, July 1946, June 1948, May to July 1949 and March 1950, of lorry drivers and meat porters in April 1946, January 1947 and June 1950, of power workers in September and December 1949, of gas workers in September 1950 and, in a touching act of concern for the royal family's comfort, of Buckingham Palace boiler stokers in March 1948. By 1948, it has been said, 'strike breaking had become almost second nature to the cabinet'.

Behind the scenes, as the recently released cabinet papers reveal, there were other interesting developments. Within a month of taking power, Attlee and home secretary James Chuter Ede discussed the possibility of reviving the Supply and Transport Organisation which a Tory prime minister, Stanley Baldwin, had used in 1926 to help defeat the general strike. In March 1946 Ede presented the cabinet with his proposals, which had been drafted in great secrecy lest they were leaked at a time when the government was repealing the Trades Disputes Act, the Tories' legislative reprisal for the general strike. The plans were put into effect during a strike of London lorry drivers in 1947.

By 1950 the cabinet was considering secret proposals to outlaw 'subversive propaganda', to ban strikes in essential industries and to enforce secret ballots on strikes. Much of this was aimed against the Communist Party, whose 'disruptive' activities in industry became the target for mounting Cold War propaganda which Labour, conveniently overlooking the fact that until 1948 the CP had opposed strikes, was only too willing to orchestrate.

Twice in its six years in office Labour declared states of emergency to deal with dock strikes, using in the process the Emergency Powers Act which a Tory dominated parliament had passed in 1920 to crack down on working class discontent. It also, in the autumn of 1950, had ten striking gas workers sentenced to imprisonment (though fines were substituted on appeal) and dragged seven dockers before an Old Bailey judge in February 1951 for daring to lead another strike.

No orderly revolution

And so the indictment could go on and on. Labour took Britain into Nato, secretly funded an atomic energy programme, helped to put down revolution in Greece, exiled an African chief for presuming to marry a white woman, toyed with the idea of racist immigration controls (at a time when immigration was negligible) and pushed through a wage freeze.

Yet it lost office in 1951 with the comfort of a working class vote the size of which it has never bettered. It helped to see British capitalism through a sticky patch, but it also, uniquely for a Labour government, carried out its manifesto promises. By the end of the 1940s workers were immeasurably better off than they had been at the end of the 1930s. Full employment and an expanding, resurgent capitalism gave moderate reformism its chance.

It was done in the name of socialism, when really it was at the expense of socialism. And it is here that the impotence of the Labour left is most starkly revealed. In theory, this should have been their finest hour. In practice, they were irrelevant. Their figurehead, Aneurin Bevan—so much more of a fighter than today's messiah, Tony Benn—proved, nonetheless, willing enough to maintain cabinet secrecy on plans to break strikes or prop up reaction in Greece or even, when the government ignored party conference demands or censures, to defend the leadership against the rank and file.

If 1945 showed anything, it was that 'socialism' from above—the prescription of the Labour left, then as now—is a contradiction in terms. As one bewildered MP said at the time, 'What is the use of having an orderly revolution if it turns out not to be a revolution at all?'

Chapter 19

Striking from below

Duncan Blackie

The starting point of the militancy in South Yorkshire was the overtime ban. As a tactic for winning the wage claim it was a total disaster. It led to passivity for the militants. Every miner was losing money, and some were losing much more than others. At a time when the NCB wanted to cut output, Scargill was boasting that the ban was effective and costing the NCB money. The seven month coal stocks were hardly affected at all.

But the ban did lead to a large number of niggling little local problems. A rash of strikes broke out over South Yorkshire when managers and deputies went in to do extra maintenance work. The ban also meant layoffs when essential safety work had not been done. These too often provoked small local strikes in response.

On 5 March Yorkshire Main colliery was threatened with closure after pickets refused to allow managers to do safety work to deal with a gas build up. The same day at Goldthorpe near Doncaster pickets were threatened with disciplinary action after allegedly venting their anger on management cars.

At Manners Main 1,400 miners were out over meal breaks and the dispute looked like spreading to several other local pits.

Miners at the Frickley/South Elmsall colliery walked out when energy secretary Giles Shaw visited the pit on 29 February.

Thus there took place a number of small disputes with not much direction or coordination overall. But it did mean that a significant

First published April 1984

number of rank and file miners were involved in fights with the NCB.

The local NUM officials spent the few weeks before the strike dashing from pit to pit arguing with miners to allow management into the pits. In one case they had to persuade miners to allow management *out*. When pickets were accused of violence, Yorkshire president Jack Taylor said, 'We do not condone violence at all. We are in a very serious situation. We expect our members to act in an orderly fashion and in a disciplined way.'

Despite the officials, 5 March saw 23,500 Yorkshire miners away from work, 9,000 of them on strike. Seven of the 15 South Yorkshire pits had responded to the strike over the meals dispute at Manners Main.

On 2 March the NCB announced that it wanted to close two Yorkshire pits: Bullcliffe Wood and Cortonwood. These were the first threats of closure of Yorkshire pits on economic grounds since the current wave of NCB attacks began. Unlike South Wales and Scotland, Yorkshire miners do not have a long experience of seeing battle after battle against closure fizzle out. They were ready to fight.

On Monday 5 March a meeting of the Yorkshire NUM executive took place. It was originally called over the meals dispute but the closure question soon dominated proceedings. A lobby of 400 miners pushed for a county wide strike starting the following Friday night. By 6 March the whole of the South Yorkshire area was closed down. By Friday 21 Yorkshire pits were out on unofficial strike. Taylor was still running around trying to stitch up a deal.

The national executive meeting in Sheffield on 8 March, lobbied by 500 miners from Yorkshire and Scotland, had little alternative but to try to keep up with events. Scargill and McGahey were both very careful to avoid calling for spreading the strike and, even when Yorkshire was all out, Taylor was pleading with miners not to go out and picket in other areas. 'Let them make their own arrangements,' he said.

His own attitude towards the strike was revealed when a picket at South Kirkby was hit by a director's car:

> At a time when we are exercising such restraint, we deplore both the unnecessary violence and the impossible attitude of the board towards our members and the future of our pits.

Fortunately the strike was not in his hands. The real motor of the dispute was now rank and file militants who were pushing the strike forward against the wishes of both the Yorkshire and national executives.

On the night of Sunday 11 March there was a mass meeting of 1,000 miners at Armthorpe colliery near Doncaster. The question was what to do next. A rank and file miner and SWP member spoke for spreading the strike.

He argued about what the Tories were up to at GCHQ and the strength of response which the day of action had shown could be mobilised. He talked about the seriousness of the situation and about the need to fight both the closures and the anti-union laws that could be used to cripple any fightback.

With 1,000 miners already out on strike, he argued, it was stupid not to draw these people into further activity by sending out flying pickets to Nottinghamshire and other areas. That was the most important argument: the strike would only be spread by rank and file miners going out and arguing for solidarity action. The executive would simply postpone matters and wait for a national ballot to take the heat out of the situation. That would only benefit the right wing.

When the vote came, only eight miners were opposed to the flying pickets. The meeting then immediately moved to organise on their decision. Names were taken of those willing to go out the next day. On the Monday morning the Harworth pits were closed by pickets from Armthorpe.

The very same day the Yorkshire and Notts executives did a deal to try to stop the flying pickets. Ray Chadburn, the Notts president, claimed to have instructed his members not to cross picket lines, but the officials at Harworth were encouraging miners to cross.

The Yorkshire side of the bargain was to send area vice-president Sammy Thompson to a special meeting at Armthorpe to try to stop the pickets going out.

Thompson, like so many others in the NUM bureaucracy, had once been a very good militant. It was he who had organised the flying pickets in the Rescue Brigade dispute in the 1970s. But away from the rank and file and sitting in a cosy office he started to change. Now he spent most of his time with managers and other union officials and his response was to try to contain any action as quickly as possible.

At the meeting around 300 miners from various pits, including Armthorpe, Hatfield and Yorkshire Main, heard Thompson argue for calling off the pickets. He got a hostile response and the meeting voted to continue picketing. The very next morning a mass picket at Bevercoats in North Notts closed the pit down. The militants had been able to beat the bureaucracy not just with resolutions but in action.

By the afternoon of that Tuesday the Yorkshire executive had met and changed their line to one of endorsing the picketing. It has to be strongly emphasised that the pickets were the dynamic of the strike. In some disputes picketing is one facet of the strike, a useful or even essential activity for maintaining the struggle, but not the driving force of the thing. In the case of the mines, the picketing was so bound up with the progress of the strike that as soon as it stopped and the more active strikers started to take it easy, the bureaucracy regained control and the management could take the offensive.

Building for the flying pickets meant arguing from the basics. Since 1974 some 80,000 miners, nearly half the total, have joined the industry and have never been through a national dispute before, let alone learnt in practice about the nature of picketing.

Flying pickets

The most basic argument of all took South Wales as its focus. Yorkshire militants argued that the history of resistance in South Wales was an admirable one, but that the tactics had not been too effective. The Welsh miners had relied too heavily on appealing to the union leaders for support, and had not got it. The Yorkshire militants argued that the only way to make sure of support was to go out and win it by picketing.

The success of the flying pickets, who by Thursday had succeeded in closing the whole of the Notts coalfield, was based on the enthusiasm of the younger miners and the experience of the older militants. It was these older militants who won the arguments for the mass picket, but once the decision was made, it was the younger militants who played the decisive organising role.

Again on the picket line itself the elements of enthusiasm and experience were combined. At times in the North Notts coalfield it was possible for the younger miner to get trapped into thinking every Notts was a dyed-in-the-wool scab who needed the same sort of treatment as a manager. The more experienced miners were able to take up the arguments with the Notts men.

The closure of the Notts pits was not achieved just by determined picketing but by argument as well. That was proved by the fact that once the Yorkshire miners had closed a place down they were able to move on and leave the picketing to local miners won over to the need to spread the strike.

The closure of the Notts pits depended partly upon solidarity and the tradition of respect for a picket line and partly because of the convincing argument that if fellow miners would not respect a miners' picket line it would be that much harder to argue with workers at power stations and coal depots about the need for solidarity.

The key to turning the dispute from a purely local one into something of national importance lay in a local leadership emerging on the Monday morning which could see that the situation was ripe and would initiate the pickets. It was militants at Armthorpe who provided that edge and pulled a large number of pits behind them.

This was not an accident. Armthorpe has a long tradition of solidarity—Grunwick's, the Anti Nazi League and numerous other campaigns. This is a record shared by Hatfield and one or two other collieries in the Doncaster area. When one of these pits moves, there is a well established tendency for the others to follow very quickly, so the strike was built from a firm local base.

The pickets organised themselves very well using telephones and CB radios to move from pit to pit as the situation demanded. Particularly in the early stages the police were totally outmanoeuvred.

At the area level things were less impressive. For example, the Yorkshire area produced no literature or leaflets for the pickets to use. SWP members who turned up at the picket lines with party leaflets had the pleasant experience of miners taking over handing out the only material available that put the arguments for strike action.

In fact the whole development of the strike was one that produced a very rapid political generalisation. Not only were large numbers of miners actively involved in the strike but the police tactics and the NCB use of the courts helped to drive the lessons home. Any socialist at Thursby colliery on the morning of the first Thursday of mass picketing would have seen a pleasant sight: a *Sun* reporter was thrown over a fence by miners. Some of those critical of the press were *Sun* readers themselves a few days before.

In some cases involvement in the strike has been very impressive. For example at Armthorpe there was a core of around 200 people in the first week who were regularly involved in picketing. Unfortunately, that was not repeated throughout the coalfield. In many pits the strike has meant that miners simply sat at home and listened to the news.

The difficulty in bringing out the Notts coalfield has been an important element both in the strike itself and even more in the ruling class propaganda against the strike, so it is worth looking at the situation more closely.

Nottinghamshire is historically a less militant area and the vote of 26.5 percent for strike action was considerably better than previous results in the coalfield. Their reluctance to fight is partly explained by the fact that the coalfield is productive and many of the miners, some of whom have been relocated from other wrecked areas, feel very confident in their own future. It is also the case that they have been getting more bonus payments than workers in other coalfields.

In fact in the first week the attitude of most Notts miners to the pickets was very far from shameless scabbing. Most wanted to work, it is true, but when it came to crossing a picket line most were prepared to respect union traditions. The real violence was caused by the police. Where they did manage to smash through a picket line there were usually only a dozen or so deputies prepared to follow them in.

Police violence sometimes assisted the work of the pickets. At Ollerton colliery a picket was killed and the pit stopped. The Yorkshire pickets moved on to Thursby. About 200 pickets massed at the gate and while they and the Notts miners turning up for work observed two minutes silence for their fallen brother, the police launched a charge on the pickets. Two Yorkshire miners were hospitalised, but the Notts miners were so sickened by the police tactics that only a handful of deputies were prepared to follow the police into the colliery.

Thursby had voted just four days earlier not to strike, by 800 votes to 17. After the picket and the police attack the colliery closed down and it was kept closed by *local* miners mounting a picket.

The whole of the first week of the strike was an object lesson in the politics of rank and filism. It was not a case of the rank and file having to organise independently because the officials are all right wing scumbags. The Yorkshire leadership of the NUM is made up of people who are on the left of the trade union bureaucracy and have good records of militancy behind them. Scargill and Taylor, for example, are the men who organised the flying pickets in 1972.

Even before the strike Scargill was the major bogeyman of the bourgeois press but there has been a growing gap between his rhetoric and what has actually happened on the ground. Scargill and Taylor have been among the most effective proponents of the Broad Left strategy in the unions. They have seen their job as winning things for the members and only calling on the rank and file to act as an occasional stage army. In fact in this dispute the rank and file have had to bypass the machine in order to get anything done at all.

This is not a question of personal failings on the part of Scargill and Taylor. A whole layer of the militants who came to prominence in the battles of 1972 have moved into the comfort of a union office. Only a few of the people who learned their politics in those mass struggles have remained in the rank and file. This time round, however, the struggle has thrown up another layer of young militants.

It is this layer that shows what is meant by rebuilding a network of workplace militants. This is not an abstract proposition for the distant future. In the coalfields the embryo of such an organisation already exists.

Whatever the final outcome, the first week of the miners' strike showed us a taste of things to come. The upturn of the 1980s will not be the same as the early 1970s. Disputes will be much more bitter and much more nasty. In comparison with the 1972 strike, 1984 is very weak, with sharp divisions inside the mining workforce very obvious today. In 1972 the mass picketing was directed outside the NUM: this time it is a part of an attempt to forge unity.

Future battles will be fought with the legacy of the downturn to contend with. The lack of confidence and sharp unevenness in the class will not disappear overnight. The police have wasted little time in raising the stakes and this will occur more and more frequently as the ruling class is forced to take workers head on. The miners' strike gives us a picture of the future.

Chapter 20

That sinking feeling

Lindsey German

The Tories have never been so isolated in the last 11 years as they are today [April 1990].

Their hammering in the Mid-Staffordshire by-election was the worst Tory defeat for over half a century. Thatcher's third term is turning into nothing short of a disaster.

The balance of payments deficit is at a record high. The inflation rate is among the highest in Western Europe and rising. Growth has slowed dramatically—forecast at just 1 percent this year. Finding a strategy to deal with such problems lay behind the row between Thatcher and her former chancellor Nigel Lawson last autumn.

Thatcher has faced one political crisis after another. By far the largest of these is over the poll tax which is proving an unmitigated disaster. Coming on top of the ambulance workers' dispute, disquiet about the NHS and the hikes in interest rates and hence mortgages, it has dealt a body blow to Thatcher.

All this flies in the face of accepted wisdom over recent years. On the right, it has long been assumed that Labour was unelectable and that Thatcher had permanently won over the majority of workers to 'popular capitalism' by increasing share and home ownership. The working class in the old sense was said to have disappeared into a contented, greatly expanded middle class.

Similar ideas have dominated the left. Thatcherism is regarded as a unique and dangerous phenomenon, characterised by a free economy,

First published April 1990

strong state and an 'authoritarian populist' ideology. Most of the left have also assumed her reforms run very deep and are unlikely to be reversed.

According to these readings of events there will probably be a fourth Thatcher term after the present crisis. All that is required is for the economy to stabilise, interest rates to fall a couple of points and a pre-election subsidy for the poll tax. Working class voters, who supposedly only care about their material conditions, will then return to the Tory fold.

But this scenario has become increasingly unlikely. It's much more probable that Thatcher will go or be voted out and that Labour will win the next election. The main reason for this is the poll tax itself.

The poll tax has always been unpopular. Some Tory MPs protested and tried to stop it or minimise the damage right from the start. These were minor revolts led even by some right wingers such as Rhodes Boyson. They resulted in only minor concessions. The tax became law despite the massive opposition and despite the experience of Scotland where a large minority refused to pay.

Few in the Tory party predicted the scale of revolt against the tax which has now broken out, especially among former Tory supporters. The Tories now trail Labour by up to 28 points, as opposed to only 2 points in September, mainly due to the poll tax. Loss of Tory support has been greatest among skilled working class voters.

Thatcher's personal rating has plummeted. Lifelong Tory voters are saying they will never vote for the party again. And responsibility for the tax is firmly pinned on the government and on Thatcher in particular. A recent *Financial Times* editorial opened:

> What is the difference between Mrs Thatcher and the captain of the *Titanic*? The captain of the *Titanic* did not see the iceberg.

Government ministers are still arguing for full steam ahead. But things are likely to get worse for them before they get better. The poll tax bills have just started going out. No one yet knows the level of non-payment and the May local elections look grim for the Tories. Are these just mid-term blues, from which they can recover, or do they go much deeper? Again most commentators, having spent years asserting that Labour can never win, are loathe to say the Tories can lose. Some see the poll tax problems as little more than an unfortunate blip for the government.

The primary explanation for the resurgence of Labour, or rather loss of support for the government, is a crude economic one. The idea is that, as soon as the poll tax is subsidised slightly, workers will once again abandon Labour.

This is not only insulting to most people's intelligence. It also seriously underestimates the Tories' problems. Of course their *root* is economic. Workers have been hit by an inflation rate pushing 8 percent, by massive rises in housing costs, by higher water and electricity prices and now by the poll tax. No wonder John Major's exhortations to save mean very little. Wages are only just keeping up with inflation, and in some areas are falling behind. But there is also a deeper resentment against Thatcher's most recent attacks on working class welfare, which have been both generalised and obviously unfair.

The poll tax is the starkest example. According to Peter Kellner in the *Independent*:

> The 10 percent of households with the highest rates bills pay around 25 percent of all domestic rates. Under the community charge, that figure is likely to fall to around 13 percent.
>
> This year domestic rates are raising £9.7bn; next year's poll tax will raise £13bn. But the contribution from those householders who pay the highest rates will fall from £2.4bn to £1.7bn.
>
> When we remove that slice of gainers from the poll tax sums, the effect on the remaining 90 percent is dramatic. Their total rate bill this year is £7.3bn. Their total poll tax payments next year will be £11.3bn. That is an increase of 55 percent.

Anger at this gross inequality has been fuelled by the high level of the tax, which many Tory MPs thought would be around £150 a head apart from in inner city Labour areas. The fact that the figures are two and three times that level has to do with one of Thatcher's major dilemmas, how to cut public spending without eating into traditional Tory support.

The aim of the poll tax, at least for Tory ideologues, was always to force local government to cut spending on pain of being voted out for 'profligacy'. So Nicholas Ridley introduced the tax all in one go, rather than phasing it in gradually as was originally intended.

This alone would have caused enough pain to millions of people. But Thatcher also tried to use the opportunity to cut existing levels of local government spending through underfunding implementation of the tax itself and not allowing for the real rate of inflation.

The level of funding has highlighted Thatcher's basic economic problems. In a sense there are two separate problems which have come together. The first is the underlying weakness of the British economy in relation to its competitors. The second is the political and economic difficulty the Tories have in cutting public spending.

Thatcher has aimed to progressively reduce public spending as a proportion of gross domestic product (GDP). Cuts, privatisation and council house sales have all helped. The sorry state of hospitals, schools, transport and the general environment are all signs of the cuts which have been made by Thatcher (and by Callaghan before her).

Even in less visible areas of life—colleges, the arts, museums—the dogma of the market now rules. Every public enterprise is run according to the profit motive, usually on a completely arbitrary basis.

The Tories' reasoning is that everything from inflation to 'dependency' could be cured by ending reliance on public spending. To this end it has progressively reduced the public sector borrowing requirement.

This, of course, ignores private sector borrowing. Private debt is at a record high as credit has expanded at three times the rate of growth of the economy.

The Tories have ended up with the worst of both worlds from their point of view. They have caused deep resentment and a feeling that cuts have been savage. At the same time, public spending has in fact been reduced by very little. Today it is around 39 percent of GDP, a slight decline since the mid-1980s.

But during Thatcher's early years spending as a proportion of GDP went up, largely due to massively increased unemployment. The last Labour government did much more damage to public spending than the Tories have.

Even today the Tories are finding it hard to keep levels below 40 percent. They are unlikely to do so in the next couple of years, given the contraction of the economy and the increasing number of promises the Tories are having to make to buy themselves out of trouble.

In certain areas spending is rising much faster than the government would like. The only major cuts in real terms have been in housing and nationalised industries (in this case largely due to privatisation), and to a lesser extent state intervention in industry.

Real spending has increased in most other areas. Some of these are predictable. Law and order costs 67 percent more than in 1979. Spending on motorways and trunk roads has risen by 39 percent in the same period. But health spending has also increased by 35 percent, social security by 33 percent and even education by 10 percent since 1979.

Services have got worse despite these real increases, because running costs—especially wages—remain much higher than the government would like, in spite of attacks on the unions in recent years. So the major cuts have come in capital spending, new schools and hospitals are not being built and vital repairs are not being done.

In addition, high unemployment and increased longevity mean more people depend on various sorts of state benefits.

Further cuts, therefore, have proved very hard for the government. Attacks on the welfare state are rightly seen as a generalised attack on working class living standards and are resisted. Since the last election the NHS has become a rallying point for opposition to the Tories—first over nurses' pay, then over general conditions and most recently in support of the ambulance workers.

Attacks on housing, schools, student grants, transport, have all provoked angry responses. The poll tax is only the final straw. Public opinion polls have shown large numbers of people prepared to pay more taxes rather than see further cuts in the infrastructure and welfare.

The net result of the past three years has been a sea change in attitudes against the Tories. They have embittered working class people but haven't inflicted a defeat on them through fundamentally shifting state spending onto the shoulders of the private individual. This is a very dangerous situation for the Tories.

Therefore Thatcher's crisis cannot be explained simply by mid-term blues. Even in purely electoral terms, no government so far behind another single party in the mid-term has been able to fully recover. More importantly, the scale of anger shown in recent weeks will not easily disappear.

In reality, the 'Thatcher revolution' was never much of a revolution. It never represented a fundamental shift in loyalties or ideas for working class people. Those ideas have remained remarkably social democratic and collectivist, as surveys such as *British Social Attitudes* have demonstrated in recent years. Any commitment to 'people's capitalism' has been skin deep.

It is true that many workers have adopted *some* Tory ideas over the past decade. Rising living standards led them to believe that things would continue to improve. The recession of the early 1980s was deeply unpopular, but as the economy recovered many workers reluctantly accepted its consequences (a third of manufacturing industry destroyed, unemployment at over three million) as the price for solving the problem of stagnation.

It is precisely these problems which have returned to haunt the Tories, and which now aid the scepticism which many workers feel towards them.

But the demoralisation and defeats suffered by workers for much of the 1980s did not mean *wholesale* acceptance of Thatcherite values. Even during the 1987 election there was growing disquiet over the

Tories' future plans in areas like the NHS. But the boom engineered by Lawson meant low mortgages, rising house values, reasonable wages and falling unemployment. Consumer goods had never been easier to obtain. Even then only 43 percent voted for the Tories.

The boom itself, however, began to exacerbate Tory problems. The infrastructure couldn't cope and workers' confidence increased as a tight labour market led to a number of wage disputes in 1988 and 1989.

And soon after the election the boom began to falter. Now there are fears of a full blown recession. The pound remains weak internationally, sustained only by high interest rates which in turn feed government unpopularity and higher inflation.

Forecasters are uncertain whether growth and therefore rises in real incomes can continue, or whether the economy will contract further. The government is banking all its hopes on the former but has little room for manoeuvre. Inflation will certainly go over 8 percent, government policies alone will see to that, and may move even further.

The Tories are increasingly paralysed in directing the economy. They are trying to hold the line on public sector wages, hence the millions spent on trying to break the ambulance workers. In the private sector they are much less successful, with employers regularly paying over the rate of inflation. Internationally they have even less control.

The rise in Japanese interest rates, the expected rise in German rates to counter the inflationary pressures of unification and the perceived weakness internationally of the British economy are all fuelling the Tories' problems. Hence the distinctly unenthusiastic response to John Major's budget from most of the City and big business.

Underlying all this is the weak state of British industry. Manufacturing output has barely recovered to 1973 levels. Exports vastly undermatch imports, and there are whole areas of manufacturing where British industry no longer even competes. Indeed most of its success stories are where it does not have to compete internationally.

Thatcher's original aim of making labour costs more internationally competitive has also failed. Since 1979 wages have risen more in real terms than in virtually any other competing country. There have, it is true, been major productivity gains in manufacturing at the expense of workers. But these are from a relatively narrow base. Recent figures show that, because of the overall increase in employment, government estimates put productivity gains higher than they actually are.

With the end of the boom there are all the signs of the economy returning to the familiar stop-go cycle of the post-war years and there is also a danger of stagnation, a stagnant economy with high inflation.

Where does this leave the Thatcher revolution? She has neither succeeded in fundamentally changing attitudes in her favour nor has she solved the long term decline of the British economy. In fact she has created further problems for herself. The most unpopular policies today are those which Thatcher has most heralded as radical and far reaching.

As far back as the 'Ridley Plan' of the late 1970s the Tories were warned that they should not take on too many opponents at once and that they should be careful about attacking the NHS too strongly. Their strategy up to 1987 was cautious. During the miners' strike for example they were careful to buy off other groups of workers.

Now their generalised attacks have provoked a generalised response. Maybe the Tories have been victims of their own propaganda and self delusion, or maybe they felt they had to go for everything in their third term. Either way, they are now suffering the consequences.

Even their erstwhile supporters are abandoning them. The ruling class in general prefers Tory governments, but some of them are beginning to wonder whether this one isn't becoming counterproductive.

The major question now being asked is not can the Thatcher revolution succeed, but can she survive? The optimistic predictions about the economy are probably whistling in the dark. But many socialists will be wondering whether the Tories can buy themselves out of trouble with another pre-election boom.

The answer is that they will certainly try, but they have many constraints—far more than before the 1987 election. Firstly the state of the economy is not good. As we have already seen, the government has only limited control over interest rates and may not be able to engineer a drop.

There is a spending surplus which could finance all sorts of sweeteners before 1992. But it is already going down fairly fast. It would be difficult for the Tories to let it go down much farther without increasing taxation. Anyway, the £7 billion in the coffers is not that high when judged against what the Tories intend to do.

They are already talking about subsidising the poll tax to the tune of £3 billion to £4 billion in the next financial year. The NHS and education need massive amounts to maintain standards. One new tube line in London alone costs over £1 billion. Such is the neglect of the infrastructure over the past 15 years that the vast sums needed will not be forthcoming from the weak and feeble British economy.

The Tories therefore probably can't sort themselves out politically or economically. They may try to ditch Thatcher for a more acceptable leader, or they may decide to hang on. Either way they are in for the roughest ride they have had in 11 years.

The major beneficiary of all this will be Neil Kinnock. Labour's fortunes have improved massively, culminating in the Mid-Staffs by-election victory.

But Labour's policies remain relentlessly right wing, from condemnations of poll tax violence to loving up to City businessmen. They have committed a future Labour government to very little in terms of reversing Thatcher's policies.

The Labour revival has come on the back of struggles like that of the ambulance workers and against the poll tax, but it has not led or directed those struggles.

The danger with this is that if Labour refuses to capitalise on the anger that is around, by giving it maximum support and thus the best chance of success, it increases the likelihood of defeat and therefore demoralisation. This, in turn, would again damage Labour's position.

And, if Thatcher does go, Kinnock will be under enormous pressure to accept many of her policies. That is why the idea of just waiting for a Labour government is such a disaster. The character of a future Labour government, and indeed its chances of election, will be determined by the level of struggle outside parliament.

Workers are beginning to realise that Thatcher's policies have to be fought actively in order to stop them. They will come to learn that under a Labour government their only guarantee of retaining and improving living standards will be their own activity. But ensuring we are in the best state to fight those battles means making the maximum efforts now to get rid of the poll tax and the Tories.

Chapter 21

Monumental folly

David Widgery

I wrote the book [*Some Lives*] in ten weeks flat in the late 1980s when Thatcher was still in command, the poll tax in place and the economy said to be booming forever. It seems like a very long time ago.

Going to work each day in Limehouse, the silver phallus of Canary Wharf rose up like some mysterious UFO (Unidentified Fiscal Object). Although it had no purpose except to make money for the developers (Richard Rogers called it 'a monument to human greed'), it became the object of cult worship.

Motorways were built underground to it. Tube extensions were tunnelled. Money became mysteriously available to buy off the locals whose homes were demolished. Neighbourhoods were destroyed to make way for it.

I wanted to argue that the creation of things like Canary Wharf was part of the same process which was shrinking the NHS, creating homelessness and increasing poverty only a few hundred yards away. And the ripping asunder of Limehouse by the LDDC [the London Docklands Development Corporation] was part of the same system that created Cardboard City and emptied County Hall, and was destroying that sense of neighbourhood, community and mutual solidarity which had given proletarian London its special character.

The publishers who first read it were scathing. The general attitude was that you lefties may not like it but it's progress. Yet exactly the same people say to me three years later that the book's a classic and that Canary Wharf is a symbol of everything that went wrong in the 1980s. So much for liberals.

First published June 1992

But the collapse of Olympia and York [the developers of Canary Wharf] does represent the completion of a cycle which began with Heseltine's invention of UDCs [Urban Development Corporations] as vast government funded estate agents to give away inner city land to speculators. It is a microcosm, a rather large one, of the follies of the Thatcher years.

Canary Wharf was, after all, where Mrs T started her most suc-cessful election campaign and it's virtually in the hands of receivers. Even if Heseltine can persuade his minions in the Department of the Environment to go and work there, the impression will be of neo-colonial government rather than economic regeneration.

Extracts from *Some Lives*

I pass a council flat where I was called out one Easter as an emergency. It was the first contact with his doctor for 14 years, made by an ex-docker who lived on his own. 'Fags help unclog me a bit, Doc. You will have to speak up. I'm a bit mutton.' On examination he was grossly emaciated, had a collapsed lung, a knobbly enlarged liver and about three weeks to live. His apologetic face will always stick in my mind. 'Don't want to be a nuisance, Doc,' he insisted. 'Don't want to be a trouble.' (Chapter 1, 'On Yer Bus', p9)

What is remarkable is how well East End mothers do themselves in conditions which would tax better off and better educated mothers. And how much better things would be if they and their children were allowed to flourish without the incessant erosion of economic and social deprivation. We have progressed in absolute terms but those advances have not been made available equitably across the board. 'When one knows of the conditions of life,' wrote John Scurr [a working class socialist and campaigner for women's rights] in 1924, 'one stands in admiration of the struggle which is put up against their environment by thousands of men and women... What chance have they or their children?... Our society passes them by and abuses them for [what] our social system has thrust upon them.' (Chapter 5, 'Growing up Tough', p89)

London has undergone a dramatic change in both its physical appearance and its economic character. Now enduring its inevitable downside of economic recession and property slump, we are only slowly realising the social costs and consequences of Thatcher's sado-monetarism. The 1980s, a decade of free market 'liberalism', privatisation and remorselessly rising property prices, generated a commercial building boom to house the Big Bang of deregulated dealing and screen based trading. 'Si monumentum requiris' look round from the monumental folly of Canary Wharf and see the humiliation of ordinary Londoners by the triumphal obelisks of commerce.

And with the decline of existing council housing and the virtual halt on new public housing starts, traditional working class residential areas like Fulham, Battersea, Islington and parts of the East End were recolonised by the middle classes. This process is highly unpopular but has proved impossible to resist. The abolition of the Greater London Council and the underfinancing and undermining of inner London councils, together with the general decline in the NHS, education and welfare services, makes it very difficult for working class London effectively to oppose the process. Halting London's loss of manufacture or reversing land ownership patterns is a tall order when you are struggling to stump up the poll tax, waiting in pain for an elusive hospital bed, or looking after the children at short notice because there are not enough teachers that day.

So the reshaping of our metropolis is experienced passively in odd disjointed glimpses: the grimness of a once excellent public transport service stuck in semi-permanent traffic jams, the thundering skip lorries, helmets, grit and strange shantytown feeling of ubiquitous rebuilding, being begged from by fit young people in theatre doorways, the sudden flash of riot among Nelson's lions. But in a way it's not surprising that the price of a recreation of 'Victorian values' to our most Victorian of cities should be a dirty, lawless, polluted capital where the very rich spend much of their time protecting their wealth from an increasingly disaffected and disenfranchised working class. And the respectable middle class despair of both and concentrate on the struggle to keep the aspidistra flying by paying up their credit cards promptly. This sort of polarisation has after all happened before and led, in London, to the upsurges in the mid-19th century which brought about the Reform Bill, to the post First World War agitation (known as 'Poplarism') which led to the richer boroughs assisting the poor in housing and welfare, and to the work of the interwar LCC [London County Council] and the postwar Labour government's 'welfare state'.

But late 20th century restructuring of inner London means something more fundamental than a lot of Lego-like office blocks and the return of the braying classes to Soho dining rooms. It requires the ejection of the urban proletariat and tradespeople from the city centre. The traditional London pattern of flat residential villages arranged on centuries old road and river networks, a topography retained in this century by the emplacements and groynes of low rent council housing which shielded the human heart of the city, is changing rapidly. Canary Wharf and the LDDC are only the most ostentatious example of a process by which multinational commercial developers, largely financed and controlled from outside Britain, will have been allowed to create a new 'free market' metropolis.

'The inner cities next,' announced Mrs Thatcher in her paroxysm of third term triumph in 1987: what she meant was the recolonisation of the old proletarian-Bohemian, artisanal-shopkeeping, Labour voting areas of the city centre by the values and the personnel of the Home Counties. In that process the proletarians, especially those among them who are poor, socially unattractive, sick or mentally ill, are debarred from both production and consumption. There are jobs, minus tiresome old fashioned things like unions, closing times and safety regulations, as cooks and nannies, waiters and drivers, cleaners and guards, entertainers and prostitutes: jobs Londoners have always done by choice but are now expected, like cheerful imbeciles, to delight in or else. But very little production in the great manufacturing districts which once shaped London's industrial physiognomy: the light engineering of north west London, the newspaper printing of Fleet Street, the docks- and river-related industries of the East End, the furniture and shoe workplaces of Hackney and Shoreditch. Ordinary Londoners, whose parents and grandparents built the capital and created its wealth, are increasingly in the way. Expensively in the way, consumers of the wrong things: not high price leisure products but hospitals, schools and social services.

Bernard Shaw, who was turned into a socialist by the social and economic chaos and cruelty of late 19th century London, wrote over 100 years ago that what the city needed was 'the development of individual greed into civic spirit; of the extension of the laissez-faire principle to public as well as private enterprise; of bringing all the citizens to a common date in civilisation.' Architectural facelifts would be of no value 'until London belongs to, and is governed by, the people who use it.' (Chapter 13, 'Unhappy City', pp229-233)

Chapter 22

Why Labour lost

Paul Foot

After the gloom, the reckoning. Just how many sacrifices have been made for this miserable election result? When the votes for Mid-Staffs came in at about 3am, I noticed that Sylvia Heal had lost the seat for Labour. She had triumphed there only two years earlier in one of the most amazing by-elections this century. A safe Tory seat seemed to have been turned into a safe Labour one. Sylvia's triumph then seemed to vindicate her remarkable speech at the 1988 Labour Party conference in which she confessed that she was dropping her lifelong commitment to unilateral nuclear disarmament.

The reason, she explained, was simple. Someone had calculated that Labour could not win with a policy of unilateral disarmament, which apparently lost it the elections of 1983 and 1987. Drop the commitment, then, she argued, and the chances of a Labour government would immeasurably increase. Thus Labour was left with a policy of support for nuclear weapons at precisely the time when the 'enemy', whom those nuclear weapons were meant to deter, had disappeared.

Lots of other radical policies were chucked into the bin on the same basis. Commitments to get rid of most of the Tory trade union laws were watered down. So were the promises to take back into public ownership all those utilities and public services which the Tories had privatised. In a Gadarene stampede to appease floating voters in the middle of the road, anything which smacked of socialist anger against the stock exchange or any other citadel of modern capitalism was wiped out of Labour's language.

Bryan Gould declared in 1987 how he loved to see workers buying and selling shares. John Smith, Margaret Beckett and Co entered a long

First published May 1992

dialogue with charming hosts in the City of London, in a ceaseless effort to persuade them that Labour's policies were good for business. In one sense, they succeeded. On polling day the *Financial Times* agreed with Labour that it was 'time for a change'. How many of its readers agreed can be measured by the fantastic celebrations which went on throughout election night and the whole of the following day across the length and breadth of the City of London.

We lost socialist policies by the score. We also lost countless opportunities to organise and fight even for the policies which were left. The miners' great struggle in 1984-85 was left high and dry by the Labour and trade union leaders. Why? Because, it was argued, 'this was not the way to get Labour returned.' Exactly the same argument was used when hospital workers exploded in rage in early 1988, or when the ambulance workers went on strike soon afterwards, or indeed in every dispute since the last general election. 'Don't rock the boat', was the cry. 'Labour will make things better for everyone.' How does that argument look now? We went to bed in those early hours of 10 April reflecting that the boat had hardly been rocked at all. There'd been hardly a strike or major demonstration for more than a year. Yet the unrocked boat was lying in ruins at the bottom of the sea.

Some have taken comfort from Labour's 40 gains, and pretended that the new Tory government, with a much smaller majority than its predecessor, will be comparatively tame. Nothing could be more ridiculous. Major and Co never expected anything like the luxury of an overall majority of 21. Their supporters among the wealthy are beside themselves with joy. They are confident they can hang on to the enormous gains made under Thatcher, the booming private hospitals and private schools, the whole disgusting paraphernalia of a greedy and confident ruling class.

For all his tinny rhetoric about a nation at ease with itself, Major's new cabinet shows exactly where he is going. Peter Lilley, a man who has devoted his whole life to picking the pockets of the poor and the disadvantaged, is in charge of social security. Poll Tax Portillo, who hates all government spending, is Chief Secretary at the Treasury in charge of public spending. The only Orangeman to sit for an English seat in the House of Commons is the new Secretary of State for Northern Ireland, and the new Solicitor General is a neanderthal from Brighton who can't contain his enthusiasm for the hangman's rope. These men are completely at ease with themselves about another five years of squeezing still more wealth from the working people and passing it across to their friends and paymasters.

What is to be done? At once, in the wake of defeat, a great howl of misery goes up on all sides of the official left. The argument is that, because all this surrender has achieved precisely nothing, we should surrender more. Trade unions (who were completely silent through the entire election campaign) are told that they are to blame and that they must cut links with the Labour Party. The very name 'Labour', apparently, is a hindrance. The Liberal Party, a deeply right wing organisation which fought more than half its campaign against Labour's central proposals for taxing the rich and restoring some freedom to trade unions, is named as the saviour of the future.

Like a Greek chorus renting their clothes, the psephologists and former Social Democrats, the *New Statesman* and the *Guardian*, almost anyone who can be found who was once a member of the Communist Party, shout for constitutional reform, electoral reform, Lib-Lab election pacts, and, if such a person can possibly be found, an even more right wing leader for the Labour Party than Neil Kinnock. Forget for a moment that none of these things (except a new leader who is being catapulted into office before anyone can catch their breath) can be achieved while the Tories have a majority in parliament. The point about all of them is that they seek to shift Labour still further down the road which has taken it so inexorably to its fourth defeat in a row.

There is another common feature to all these demands—passivity. People are told that the priority is to change the voting system or to rely on backroom deals between the leaders of the trade unions, the Labour Party and the Liberal Party. No one outside these back rooms, the argument concludes, can do anything much except, as before, wait and see how well their leaders perform. The prospect held out by these 'new realist' reformers is one of utter despondency, amounting to total surrender to the Tories.

It is time to rescue a few simple facts about the world we live in. Its fundamental characteristic is that it is divided by class. The means whereby the people at the top of society grow rich and powerful by exploiting the majority is much more obvious now than it was a decade ago. The contradictions and horrors of such a society—unemployment, mass starvation, disease for thousands of millions of people while a small group wallow in unimaginable luxury—are more striking and more devastating. The cry for change is as loud and anguished as it has ever been.

So where does change come from? The central point about a society dominated by the struggle between the exploiters and the exploited is that it relies for its success on passivity from below. The engine of change is the activity and confidence of the people who are being exploited, most effectively where they are exploited directly, at the point of production. These sound like slogans. But they explain the changes which have taken place in modern Britain.

Looking back over the last quarter of a century I pick out three decisive changes to the left which profoundly improved the living standards of working people and decisively changed the balance of confidence in the struggle between the classes. The first was in 1969, when the Labour government proposed drastic new laws to control the trade unions. A few months later the proposals were withdrawn—not because the government had changed its mind or because civil servants at the Department of Employment were suddenly sympathetic to trade unions—but because of a short, sharp campaign in the trade union movement which included unofficial strikes.

Much more remarkable was the change which came over the Tory government in 1972. At the beginning of that year it looked rather like the Tory government now: confident, aggressive, privatising, anti-union, anti-poor. At the end of the year it was pumping public money into industry and building up the public services more energetically than any government before or since. Its whole strategy and philosophy had changed. There had been no general election, no constitutional reform, no Lib-Lab pacts, pretty well no change in parliament. But there had been a victorious miners' strike, a building workers' strike, a hospital workers' strike, a dockers' strike and even a threatened general strike which not only smashed the Tories' anti-union laws but also changed the whole face of politics.

Thirdly, in 1987 the Tories were re-elected on a manifesto based on their flagship—the poll tax. Four years later the same government, which made no new pacts and still had a parliamentary majority of nearly 100, withdrew the poll tax. Had they been terrified by the parliamentary opposition? Not at all—they were contemptuous of it. What changed their minds and abolished the poll tax was a mass campaign of civil disobedience, whose climax was probably the biggest demonstration since the war, which turned into a full scale riot. These huge political shifts in our direction were all set in motion from below. They were almost unaffected by what was going on in parliament or even by which government was in office. The pace of events was determined by the ebb and flow of the struggle between the classes—when they win, we lose, and vice versa.

The same test—who is winning between the classes—can be applied to elections. Elections are the most passive of all political activities, but they do concentrate people's minds on politics. A common cliche from pundits and pollsters after the election was that Labour should have won because Britain was in recession. In fact, Labour has never won an election in a recession. Even in 1929, when Labour was elected as the largest party, the real depth of recession did not come for two years (and parliamentary Labour was reduced to a rump). The big Labour victories of 1945 and 1966 were won when the unions were strong, when nobody was out of work and when the workers were full of confidence and hope. The same point comes from a comparison of the recent election with that of February 1974. In 1974 a Tory government seeking re-election was buoyed throughout the campaign by polls which gave it big leads. Then, as the crunch came, floating voters were suddenly worried that a Tory government would lead to instability and chaos. So the Tories lost the election. In 1992 the polls showed people veering to Labour. But when it came to the crunch, the floaters shied away. This time it was Labour which seemed to hold out the prospect of chaos.

What was the real difference? In 1974 the miners were on strike, less than a million people were out of work, and the unions still felt strong and confident from their victories in 1972. In 1992 no one was on strike, nor had been for years. The balance of class confidence favoured Labour in 1974 and the Tories in 1992.

Marx argued that the prevailing ideas will always be those of the ruling class. Labour has to challenge these ideas to win elections, and is far more likely to do so when its supporters are strong, confident, acting together, than weak, uncertain, fragmented and left to think things out on their own, at the mercy of these prevailing ideas.

But this is not a hard and fast rule, an 'objective circumstance' which condemns us to Tory victories whenever they can engineer a recession. People make their own history, and their anger and discontent can be reflected in elections. However, especially in times of recession, that anger needs to be awakened, prodded, inflamed in ceaseless agitation. After the election, though not before it, the former heroes of the SDP (RIP) Peter Jenkins (*Independent*) and Malcolm Dean (*Guardian*) suddenly discovered that Labour was 'unelectable'. There was not a word of this before polling day when all the signs pointed in the opposite direction. Opinion polls are not conspiracies. They are measurements. The near unanimity of all the polls before the election that Labour was in the lead, often handsomely, was probably accurate. The tide of hatred against the government was so strong that it looked as though it would carry the floaters with it.

The crucial task for Labour was to sustain the anger against the government until the last moment. Class anger had played a large part in the early stages of the campaign. Even John Smith, one of the least angry men ever to grace a front bench, introduced his alternative budget with the claim that the '1 percent at the top has had its way for 12 years—now it's the turn of the rest of us.' The broadcast about Jennifer's ear operation struck a chord of rage. This was not just moaning about a bad health service. It was comparing the bad (for the poor and the workers) with the good (for those who can pay). There wasn't a street in the land where some such story had not been told. And people were indignant about it. Kinnock's speech at Sheffield comparing Major's soapbox with the cardboard boxes of the homeless touched an angry nerve.

But then suddenly the campaign faltered. The second NHS broadcast was cancelled. Suddenly the talk was not of private healthcare and snob schools, but of consensual and responsible government. Major clung on to his soapbox, but Kinnock was always in limousines, or on battleships releasing balloons. Edwina Currie said that Kinnock looked more like a prime minister than Major, and that was suddenly a problem. The Tories organised their fear and hate campaign to coincide with polling day. On the eve of poll the *Sun* had nine pages on 'The Nightmare on Kinnock Street'. The City staged a run on the pound and announced that Labour would bring higher interest rates. The Labour leaders, as though worn down by endless City lunches, did not respond. There was no attack on the undemocratic power of financial barons seeking to influence the election.

Labour was not unelectable. The results themselves prove it. It required only two or three extra people in every hundred to vote Labour (as they were probably intending to do until the last moment) for the Tories to have been kicked out. It was these vital floaters who, at the last moment, as the Tories pounced and Labour dithered, swung round from their anger to their fear.

Like all the guesses about why the election was lost, this may just be speculation. What is not speculation is that the Labour leadership now has absolutely nothing to offer us. Before we have time to catch our breath, the Tory government will be on the attack again, hacking away at the schools and hospitals they promised were safe, raising the taxes they promised to cut. Labour can do nothing to stop them. Schools, hospitals and jobs can only be protected by action outside parliament, by demonstrations, petitions and strikes. All these will be a thousand times more successful if they are sustained and led by socialists, people who make no concessions to capitalist society because they want to replace it, root and branch, with an entirely different society: a socialist society which can plan its production to fit people's needs, and distribute its wealth on the principle that human beings, whatever their different abilities, have the same right to benefit from what is commonly produced.

Tens of thousands of socialists have held their breath and bitten their lips rather than speak out in protest as the Labour leaders continued on their promised march to parliamentary power. After Black Friday, 10 April, every one of them is disappointed and indignant. Their disappointment is useless. But their indignation can still stop the Tories—if it is channelled into real resista e, and into a socialist organisation which bases itself on that resistance, and can therefore hold out the prospect of real change.

Chapter 23

The return of the working class

John Rees

Politics will not be the same again. Twice in one week in October demonstrations bigger and more working class in composition than any since the early 1970s have shown that the working class movement, so long proclaimed dead by commentators on both the left and the right, is still a force.

The crisis in ruling class circles—over devolution, the recession and Europe—has become a general crisis of society, pulling even the most apathetic and demoralised sections of the working class into political life.

The ferocity of the storm has taken everyone by surprise, but the fact that there was a storm gathering has been clear for a long time. Indeed a mood of resistance to the Tories from some workers has been perceptible since the late 1980s.

Nevertheless, it is now essential to understand that a *qualitative* shift in the situation has taken place. After even the greatest of struggles in the recent past a period of relative calm set in during which it was not uncommon, even among socialists, to hear the argument that nothing had really changed, that the mass of workers remained passive and that the Tories still held the aces.

The current struggle cannot simply be registered as another peak on the same scale. It represents the beginning of a period when politics will have to be calibrated on an entirely different scale, judged according to entirely different criteria.

First published November 1992

This is partly because even the biggest of previous recent struggles, like the poll tax, involved minorities. As the boom of the 1980s broke up, these minorities became larger. As recession has turned to slump the anger has accumulated until finally the damn burst and the attitudes and bitterness felt by the minority have now swept across the flood plain of the whole working class. Of course there will still be periods of greater and lesser activity, still be defeats as well as victories, but they will take place at a higher level of struggle.

But the change in the period is also partly a result of the fact that the decline in the confidence of the government has been even steeper than the rise in the confidence of the working class. It is scarcely believable that Major's ramshackle regiment won an election just a few months ago. Their vacillation between half baked monetarism and half hearted Keynesianism has lost them the support of many of their natural supporters in industry. And Europe (raising the same issues in a different form) continues to cause huge rows.

But the rise in confidence of the workers and the crisis of the government is not fully reflected in the political consciousness of the majority of workers. Still less is it reflected in the consciousness of the leaders of the Labour Party and the TUC. Here old bad habits are ingrained. This is the primary reason why the Tories are still in power. Had the TUC matched the undoubted mood for a general strike among a very wide layer of workers the government would have been forced out of office.

If it proves to be the case that the TUC's failure has given the government a breathing space, then previous experience tells us what the government will try to do with the time it has bought. As in 1981, when Thatcher retreated from her original pit closure programme, or as in 1925 when the government was forced to appoint a royal commission to investigate miners' wages, the government will go away, lick its wounds and attempt to force the closures through at a later date—as it did by defeating the miners' strike of 1984-85 and the General Strike of 1926.

But we do not know whether this turning point in the class struggle will even last long enough for the government to recover its balance over the coal crisis. At the longest it will last until the government's pit review reports after Christmas. But the decisive confrontation over economic strategy as a whole will probably come before then.

Neither can we be sure which issue will spark renewed action. It could be a central issue like the ratification of Maastricht or a public sector pay freeze or the round of cuts due in November, or some apparently secondary issue like the announcement of the expected £600 average council tax. Or it could simply be that a group of workers, for instance the tube workers who have taken heart from recent events, refuses to take any more.

Whether or not workers can win this round of struggle as well as the battle over the pits depends on whether the now dominant strategy of the TUC and Labour leaders can be challenged.

This strategy is easily stated and easily recognised because, in spite of new realities, it does not differ significantly from the TUC's disastrous public opinion oriented new realism during the Wapping dispute, the attitude of the TUC to the miners' strike itself or the attack on the dockers. All the hallmarks of those defeats are there: the refusal to countenance strike action, the obsequious bending of the knee to Tory anti trade union law, the ridiculous courting of 'rebel' Tory MPs and the blind fear that any demonstration may 'get out of hand'.

The Labour leaders are not alone in carrying this argument. Some of the capitalist class proper and their closest supporters—industrialists, high civil servants, a few Tory MPs, the leaders of the Liberal Democrats—have sympathy with this strategy, at least for the time being. Many among the middle classes support them. Some lesser trade union bureaucrats and the Kinnock generation of new realists in the Labour Party will provide a supporting chorus. Finally, the majority of workers still support such a strategy.

This should not surprise socialists. Every great social movement, indeed every great revolution, begins with broad unity among those who oppose an isolated government. The English Revolution of 1640 began with a united aristocracy and bourgeoisie confronting an isolated crown. So did the French Revolution. The Russian Revolution of 1905 began with the mass of workers petitioning the tsar under the leadership of a priest, Father Gapon. In 1917 the Bolsheviks were initially a tiny minority dissenting from the unity of all other workers' parties behind the provisional government.

In each case the movement polarised, not just once—from the moderate parliamentarians to Cromwell, from the supporters of limited reform to the Girondists, from the Cadets to the Mensheviks, but twice—from Cromwell to the Levellers, from the Gironde to the Jacobins, from the Mensheviks to the Bolsheviks.

Even movements which don't end in revolution follow the same pattern. The Chartists of the 19th century, the suffragettes of the early years of this century, the CND and Vietnam solidarity campaigns in the 1960s all divided between those who supported reformist methods directed at winning 'respectable opinion' and those who wished to maximise the striking power of the movement by linking its fate with working class aspirations and by adopting the most militant forms of struggle.

Such divisions are inevitable in the current struggle because the class divisions submerged in today's broad front will inevitably erupt as the movement develops. Why?

Firstly, the government's decision to close the pits is not, at least from the capitalists' point of view, some totally irrational miscalculation which every right minded citizen, be they managing director or shop assistant, will want to oppose. The power companies are following the logic of the market and trying to secure the largest possible short term profits and the most secure form of supply (the costs of which they can always pass on to the consumer anyway). Some sections of the ruling class, whose view is reflected in the attitude of the *Financial Times*, think that the government has simply done too much, too soon. A review that makes a few minor concessions will be enough to see them happy so long as it also demobilises the mass movement.

Other sections of the ruling class criticise the government because they aren't looking after the interests of all the capitalist class equally— many sections of manufacturing industry, for instance, are bitterly critical of the way in which the Lawson boom favoured finance and service industries. Major's 'stumble for growth' may be enough to quiet them. But, in any event, no capitalist class will want to push such an internal dispute to the point where it may encourage a movement that could threaten the stability of the system. This is not to say that such ruling class criticism of the government will stop short of getting rid of Major and perhaps his entire government. Ruling class disenchantment may well be sufficiently deep that it prefers a coalition or even a Labour government. In fact the more powerful the mass movement becomes the more attractive such an alternative will look, precisely because it has a greater chance of containing protest within acceptable bounds.

But ultimately, whichever poor compromise emerges as the economic strategy that a working majority of the capitalist class is happy with, and whichever form of government is cobbled together to see it through, it will involve an enormous attack on working class living standards.

The aims of most workers involved in this struggle are diametrically opposed to such an outcome. For them the sacking of the miners was the occasion for a much wider protest. Of course they want, immediately, the whole pit closure programme abandoned. But they have not come onto the streets just for this, and especially if the movement's immediate aims are realised, they will not stop at this. Many already want rid of the government and an end to the cuts, unemployment, poor housing, high mortgages and low pay that are blighting their lives. It is already, in embryo, a revolt against the system.

None of the likely outcomes of the current crisis, including the fall of the Tories and the return of a Labour government, is going to meet even the most elementary of these needs. The expectation must be, therefore, that irrespective of the outcome of the immediate crisis we are destined for a longer period of sharpening struggles between the two major classes. The continuing high level of struggle in Greece over recent years and the intensifying struggle in Italy are important examples.

In these struggles, as in the current dispute, it is important to understand the place of two groups who both, in their different ways, stand between the major classes: the middle class and the trade union bureaucracy.

The middle class is by nature a divided class. Its consciousness is schizophrenic. But the degree and the nature of such divisions depend on the state of the struggle between the two main classes. At the moment, it is clear that many sections of the middle classes, the professionals and middle managers have added their voice of protest to the howl of rage directed at the government.

What does this extraordinary sight—the once loyal supporters of privatisation share offers and English Heritage speaking up for the miners—mean?

It is the squeal of the once confident acolytes of Thatcherism turned belly up by the crisis. Long ago, during the Lawson boom, the middle class patronised the working class with the idea that all workers were, or wanted to be, 'one of us': all workers were £400 a week *Sun* reading dockers clamouring to be yuppies. The emphasis was on *shared* values, while of course never losing sight of the fact that there was, ideology aside, an unbridgeable gap between 'them' and 'us'.

Now that even the middle classes are threatened by bankruptcy and house price collapse there has been a polarisation among them. Some, possibly the majority, are concerned that the recession is so deep that, if it has not already touched them, it will do soon. The ideological icons of the Thatcher age have been tarnished almost as much in their eyes as in the eyes of many workers: the British bobby turned corrupt and brutal liar, British justice no longer quite 'the best in the world', the royals exposed as just another dysfunctional family unit and Arthur Scargill more truthful than 'honest' John Major.

But their worries are nowhere near as great as the bitterness and anger which haunt wide layers of the working class. The concerned middle classes have some loose sense of how great this resentment is among workers. But they have no real gauge of its depth because no political party, media outlet or even trade union ever really expresses this anger. So this section of the middle class suffers from an inchoate fear, a fear that has increased gradually since the late 1980s and the revolt against the poll tax, that the 'social fabric' (ie you and I) is 'coming under strain'.

But a sizeable proportion of the middle class has *not* been converted to the 'caring nineties'. Their reaction to the worsening recession is to hanker nostalgically for the high summer of Thatcherism. Their voice is still all too audible and it would be quite wrong to forget how much they *hate* working class people. A recent edition of the *Observer* brings it home. The paper ran a selection of the late poet Philip Larkin's letters. Here's one from the last winter of discontent in 1979:

> Up to a century ago, if you wanted more money you just worked harder or longer or more cleverly; now you stop work altogether... In fact the lower class bastards can no more stop going on strike now than a laboratory rat with an electrode in its brain can stop jumping on a switch to give itself an orgasm.

Larkin then recalls 'my dreary little hymn' which he 'sings quite a lot these days.' It goes like this:

> I want to see them starving,
> The so-called working class,
> Their wages yearly halving,
> Their women stewing grass...

But perhaps Larkin is a lone, eccentric reactionary? Afraid not. In the same week that the people who edit the *Observer* thought that it was worth reprinting this cretinous diatribe, Peter Lilley was impersonating Gilbert and Sullivan's Lord High Executioner and claimed that 'no one would miss' the benefit claimants and pregnant women he was about to cut out of the classless society. At the same Tory party conference John Major tried to rescue his declining fortunes with a speech that punched the buttons of every petty bourgeois prejudice in the book (bar hanging). Trendy teachers, bureaucratic civil servants, the disappearance of family values, the lack of motorway service stations, student union lefties and the threat to private property posed by new age travellers were all denounced in an inspiring monotone that brought the union jack bedecked delegates staggering to their feet.

The political stream is running firmly against these people for now.

But to keep the middle class polarised on terms favourable to workers will mean that the movement has to show the strength capable of keeping the ruling class proper on the defensive. If we are defeated, if the ruling class sense they can get away with making us even more fully the victims of their crisis, then the journalists and lawyers, social worker supervisors and literati will start roaring in support of Peter Lilley just as surely as the hard core blue rinsers did at the Tory party conference. The 'sympathy' for the miners will vanish just as suddenly as it has appeared and the antique shop owners of Kensington will follow the political lead of their customers, not the people who march past their doors. Paddy Ashdown will no longer tell us that 'the real heroes and heroines' are those who march for the miners.

Thus the TUC's strategy of undermining independent working class politics and activity in the name of a broad alliance will achieve the very opposite of what it sets out to accomplish.

The trade union leaders are not a different class, but a *separate* layer within the working class. They are separated from the rank and file of the unions not only by higher pay, comfortable lifestyles and not having to share the working conditions of their members but, as importantly, by their function. They are there to represent their members to the capitalists, not to challenge capitalism. They fear any movement that threatens this balance as much as, if not more than, they fear capitalism itself. The balance of fear, however, is not constant.

At the moment the trade union bureaucracy feels that it has been weakened and snubbed over 13 long years of Tory rule. This makes it timorous, but it also makes it worried that if it does not capitalise on the current mood it will be seen as even more of an irrelevance, both by the ruling class and by its members. Hence its strategy of *wanting a movement*—but *only* so long as it stops at the point where TUC leaders are invited back into the 'counsels of the nation'. Or, as Bill Jordan of the AEEU put it, 'of course there will be demonstrations, but the most important thing is that the TUC and the CBI sit down together face to face.' The left of the TUC, and especially Arthur Scargill, will not share this cretinous attitude—but the scars of the 1980s make them worry that without the new and unexpected unity they will fail, especially given the weakness of their own base.

But support for such ideas will not stop there. Although many new to the movement will feel more angry and more militant than their leaders, there will also be many who treasure the unity of the first days of the struggle and who see it as the greatest asset we have. They will cherish the support of the press, note the banners hung from the well to do shops of Kensington, feel encouraged by the priests and businessmen who castigate the government.

But more than any of this, they want to win. And it is the contradiction between the strategy of the Labour leaders and what people know (most recently from the experience of the poll tax) is necessary to win that will enable those arguing for a distinctive working class strategy to gain influence.

Two events have already opened up such opportunities. The much touted Tory revolt has already proved a hopelessly weak reed. Likewise the NUM's route for the national demo proved a desperate disappointment to many, especially those new to the movement. They assumed we would march on parliament. They assumed that the anti poll tax methods were the effective methods. They thus received a sharp lesson in the real meaning of the TUC's politics when they were led around Hyde Park for several hours without a chance to really show how they felt even to passers by, never mind MPs.

Each failure to meet the mood of anger opens the possibility of socialists winning a hearing for a very different strategy—and the tempo of politics means that such failures are likely to come sooner rather than later. These are lessons that are not just good for this struggle. Popular frontism—subordinating working class struggle to what is acceptable to middle class and ruling class opinion—is not a 'mistake' on the part of the TUC and Labour Party leaders. It is a way of life determined by their basic commitment to working within the system.

The only effective antidote is for those already committed to challenging the system to work alongside those who follow the Labour leaders and prove, at every turn of the road, that independent working class politics and organisation are the most effective way of pulling sections of the middle class behind workers' demands and of gaining victory in the struggles of today. These politics, the politics of the united front, can keep the ruling class divided, the government isolated, and begin the process of winning the mass of workers to the belief that they have the power to break the system and build a socialist society.

The rise of resistance

We need to remind ourselves how the current explosion arose if we are to be clear about the future.

The horrible litany of defeats—steel workers, miners, print workers, dockers—was first interrupted by the opposition to health cuts in 1988. The outcome was not a complete victory, but the battle did more damage to the Tories than to the working class. Most importantly, and

coming so soon after the stock market crash of 1987, it broke the suf-
focating ideological deference to free market ideology that seemed to
dominate the majority of the workers' movement for much of the mid-
1980s.

Then came the poll tax movement of 1989-90 and the Nalgo, rail
and tube strikes of 1989, rising against the background of the East European revolutions—interpreted by the ruling class as the triumph of
the market but seen by many in the working class as a triumph of popular power over authoritarianism—and culminating in the fall of
Thatcher. Perhaps inevitably, given the battering that the unions and
the idea of strike action had taken in the 1980s, this rebirth of workers' self confidence was more marked among a, albeit large, minority
in the communities and on the streets than it was among the majority that would be needed for action in the workplace.

But even though the resistance to the poll tax was not based on the
workplace, victory had an effect on industrial relations. The days
when the Ridley Plan reigned supreme were gone. The strategy of
picking on one union after another, isolating it from solidarity and provoking battle on terms favourable to the government always cost the
Tories more than either they or many on the left were willing to admit.
But it was finally abandoned in Thatcher's third term when the Tories
realised that they needed to move from isolated battles with particular groups of workers to wholesale confrontation with the working
class—hence the poll tax. It was an escalation of the struggle which
backfired so badly that the Tories have never even returned to the
old Ridley Plan methods. They simply have not dared to confront a
major national union in a national strike since the poll tax. When they
looked as if they might be staggering into such a battle over wages
with Nalgo and the rail unions, they backed off.

After the defeat of Thatcher the anger did not disappear but it
did run underground for a period, only breaking surface briefly among
the sizeable minority who opposed the Gulf War. Now, under the
whip of domestic and world recession, it has re-emerged more powerfully than in any of its previous eruptions. Unlike the poll tax, the
movement is now one of the organised working class even if, as yet,
the level of industrial action remains low.

Chapter 24

Shutting the door on the poor

Peter Morgan

The Tories have fought every election since 1979 with a manifesto which promises tougher immigration and asylum legislation. They did it in 1979 and brought in the 1981 Nationality Act. They did it in 1987 and brought in the 1988 Immigration Act. They did it in 1992 and brought in one of the most vicious pieces of legislation, the 1993 Asylum and Immigration Appeals Act. This makes it virtually impossible for all except the most desperate (or indeed the luckiest) to enter this country—those fleeing persecution, imprisonment or possibly death in their 'own' country.

Now Michael Howard is repeating the familiar cry about the dangers of 'bogus' asylum seekers taking advantage of Britain. The *Guardian* (6 October 1995) reported him as saying:

> We are seen as a very attractive destination because of the ease with which people can gain access to jobs and benefits. While the number of asylum seekers for the rest of Europe is falling, in this country it is increasing. Only a tiny proportion of them are genuine refugees.

Kenneth Baker used the same language in 1991. The result in the few years since the 1993 act has been a further tightening up on immigration and asylum. The new proposals introduced by Howard include forcing employers to check someone's residential status before they are employed. It is estimated that two million people a year will have to prove their identities with a passport or birth certificate before

First published December 1995

they can gain work.

Howard's use of the term 'bogus' is misleading—what may be a legitimate refugee one year becomes a 'bogus' applicant the next, as the law is changed and the screws are tightened—even though the persecution in the applicant's 'own' country may be just as severe. The British Refugee Council, in its monthly newsletter *Exile* (April 1995), puts it like this:

> Fewer ELR [Exceptional Leave to Remain] grants and more refusals do not represent more bogus refugees. They simply reflect a less generous policy framework. In arguing that refused asylum seekers are 'bogus', the government has committed the fallacy of adducing the effect of their policies as a validation of them.

The term also implies that immigrants and refugees are 'a burden on the system' that is already stretched to the limit, unable to cope with the problems of massive 'domestic' unemployment, and the demands on the welfare state. So next January about 40,000 people who have claimed asylum after entering Britain as ordinary visitors, or who have had their claims rejected but are appealing, will have their rights to benefits removed, while Home Office regulations prevent them working until they have spent six months in Britain. Yet although Howard's new proposals have been heralded as a cost cutting exercise for the government, benefits paid to asylum seekers account for less than a tenth of 1 percent of the total social security budget.

Far from being a drain on resources and welfare, the history of immigration and refugees is that they enrich and improve a country's economy as they contribute more to general taxation and the welfare state than they receive.

Moreover, domestic sources have added greater numbers to the labour force than immigration ever has. Increases in the number of women available for work between 1960 and 1980 in the US added 8.5 million workers to the labour force, a number well in excess of the number of immigrants over the same period, without women being blamed for unemployment. And the postwar baby boom in the US created four million extra workers between 1960 and 1980 which was four times the number of immigrants—yet the baby boomers too are not blamed for unemployment. Rather immigrants are made the subject of resentment for what is in effect the boom-bust cycle of the capitalist system.

Nor is it the case that immigrants draw disproportionately from the welfare state. Studies have shown that in the case of Caribbean migration to Britain in the 1960s few of the immigrants drew retirement pensions—one of the largest items in the benefits system. Also their use of other provisions was less than those people born in Britain. Yet over the years the government has gone to extraordinary lengths to prevent immigrants and asylum seekers claiming benefits.

One of the most powerful images that the Tories conjure up is the idea that there are literally millions of people waiting to 'invade' this country if they were to relax the immigration laws. Part of this argument is shown to be ridiculous by the simple fact that the entire population of the EU is entitled to come to Britain yet they hardly feel the urge to pack their bags and flee here. The governor of Hong Kong, Chris Patten, let the cat out of the bag recently, when arguing for the right of all Hong Kong citizens to have the right of abode in Britain, by giving figures which show that the vast majority of Hong Kong citizens don't choose to come to Britain but prefer the US, Canada and Australia instead as a final destination.

But behind the hysteria it is worth reminding ourselves that Europe and the US still take only a very small percentage of the world's refugees—the vast majority of whom are forced to move because of war, poverty or persecution for which the Western powers are largely to blame. In the late 1980s there was a rapid increase in the number of people seeking asylum both from the world's trouble spots (such as Somalia, Ethiopia, Sudan or Sri Lanka) and also because of displacement within Europe (due largely to the East European revolutions and the removal of the Berlin Wall). As Nigel Harris states in his book *The New Untouchables*:

> In the eight years to 1991, the number of people applying for refugee status in Europe increased from 65,000 to half a million (the bulk of them entering Germany), and to nearly 700,000 in 1992. In the US over the same period, applications increased from 25,000 to 100,000. The press had a field day in highlighting this as a matter for panic... Yet even if we count all those applying to enter one or other of the 16 leading countries in Europe and North America (and this is far in excess of the numbers of those actually accepted) the total still reaches only about one fifth of the refugees received in Pakistan during the Afghan war, and three fifths of the numbers of Iranians taken in by Turkey (and well under 5 percent of the world's total refugees).

In Britain the stated intention of the 1993 Asylum and Immigration Appeals Act was to reduce the number of asylum seekers granted 'Exceptional Leave to Remain'—temporary permission to stay—which had been the surest method of getting the legal right to asylum in the 1980s. The result has been dramatic. In 1990 a full 83 percent of asylum seekers obtained permission to live in Britain either as refugees or on 'Exceptional Leave to Remain'. Last year only 21 percent were allowed to stay. There has been a dramatic increase in the number of people applying for asylum—in 1993 there were 24,604 applicants, in 1994 there were 32,830 and this year it is expected to be about 40,000. One of the main reasons for this is the increase in the number of places from which people are trying to flee—the war in Bosnia or instability in Africa for example. As the British Refugee Council confirms (*Exile*, April 1995), 'The increase in claims over the last year coincides with a marked increase in instability around the world and large increases in refugees and displaced people.'

But even then the government tries to stop the flow. In 1992, as the number of asylum seekers from former Yugoslavia rose sharply to over 5,000 a year, the government announced that no Bosnian could travel to Britain without a visa. This was 'catch 22'. There was and is no British embassy in Bosnia where Muslims could get a visa. If they left to get one in a neighbouring country, in Austria for example, they would be denied the ability to claim asylum in Britain. This is because the 'third country rule' requires refugees to claim asylum in the first safe country they reach. So the number of refugees from the former Yugoslavia collapsed.

Britain receives a lot fewer applications from asylum seekers than other European countries. Between 1992 and 1994 there were 887,000 applicants for asylum in Germany compared to 102,000 in Britain. A further result of the 1993 act has been a dramatic increase in the number of asylum seekers and immigrants being detained in detention centres like Campsfield House and prisons. Asylum seekers are never told the reasons for their detention or given any opportunity to defend themselves. In a 1994 study Amnesty International found that their detention was arbitrary, in that those detained were as likely to be granted asylum finally as those not detained. Over 11,000 people are detained under immigration powers every year, with deportation rates running at around 4,000 to 6,000 a year. These are often done in a most brutal way, as the murder of Joy Gardner by police and immigration officials graphically showed.

The Institute of Race Relations, in its report *Europe on Trial*, tells of a Somali refugee who, in April 1993, flew to Britain via Rome, collapsed on arrival and was found to have shrapnel lodged in his head and neck. The authorities gave him painkillers and sent him back to Rome the following day. It also tells of a Pakistani man the authorities wanted to deport in October 1994, who was so desperate not to go back he slashed himself in his stomach, wrists and legs, and needed 59 stitches.

The airline captain refused to take him and he was taken to prison, where the prison officers refused to detain him and sent him to hospital. He was deported the following day and a prison officer commented that the man's treatment was worse than inhuman.

Yet even those refugees lucky enough not to be held in detention centres are subject to racism. For example, North Middlesex Hospital was recently reported to the Commission for Racial Equality for not treating Kurds. Although entitled to treatment the refugees were refused appointments because of their need for interpreters.

But one of the most pernicious aspects of the proposed law is the claim by Amnesty International that the government intends to implement a 'white list' of countries (which are deemed safe and from which all applicants for asylum are refused). It is nothing new for the government to change its policies on other countries (and 'their' refugees) depending on its foreign policy needs—or rather the needs of British capitalism overseas. A good example of this was the case of the Tamil refugees. From 1983 a growing number of Tamils came to this country to escape communal violence. However, by 1985 the Home Office adopted a new policy which meant that those who had already been admitted were given 'Exceptional Leave to Remain', but those seeking asylum thereafter were to be treated on a case by case basis. In the late 1980s, when the Jaffna peninsula was being bombarded by shelling, Britain returned Tamil asylum seekers on the ground that the shelling was indiscriminate and did not therefore constitute persecution. As the Centre for Research and Ethnic Relations says:

> While there may be some evidence to suggest that part of the explanation of the Home Office's attitude towards Tamils was due to fear of 'bogus' refugee status being used to evade the strict immigration controls, an additional factor was the foreign office perception of the need to maintain good relations with the government of Sri Lanka, which holds a considerable strategic value in the Indian Ocean for the eastern Alliance.

One of the more brutal regimes to which people are deported is Nigeria. In the first three months of 1995 over 1,700 new asylum seekers arrived in Britain from Nigeria fleeing from a regime which according to the US government Department of State, has 'committed numerous, repeated human rights abuses in its efforts to prevent citizens opposing it by peaceful means'. Nigerians are now the largest group of asylum seekers arriving in Britain—in 1989 there were just 20 claims; in 1994 over 4,000. Yet since 1985 only three Nigerians have been awarded refugee status, and in the first three months of 1995 all decisions made on Nigerian applications were to refuse the right to asylum.

Sierra Leone is a country suggested for the white list. Its residents have been subjected to a brutal civil war and military regime, and over one million (out of a total population of four million) have been displaced, with over a quarter of a million fleeing to Guinea and over 120,000 to Liberia. In 1994 only 1,810 Sierra Leoneans applied for asylum in Britain. Of the 565 decisions, five were granted refugee status, ten were allowed 'Exceptional Leave to Remain' and 540 were refused. Many more still await a judgement. This is hardly surprising as there are still nearly 57,000 applications outstanding from all asylum seekers.

But despite all this the Tories' attempts to whip up racism have been met with enormous resistance. This has been seen in the numerous anti-deportation and anti-racist campaigns that have taken place over the last few years, which have involved thousands of working class people, both black and white. The murder of Joy Gardner was greeted with anger and outrage on the streets of London. And the recent TUC anti-racist demonstration saw numerous banners from various anti-deportation campaigns. Largely this is because in an integrated society—where black and white live, work and struggle together—the Tories' attempts to scapegoat black people or refugees for the appalling state of the economy just does not fit the reality of people's everyday lives.

The response of socialists to this is to recognise that all immigration controls are inherently racist. Capital is allowed to move unrestricted around the world in search of resources, markets and profits. Therefore we support those who are forced to follow this investment to improve their standard of living. Indeed this has been a feature of capitalism since its birth, which the ruling class recognises.

In times of boom they are intent on recruiting immigrant labour, as they were in Britain during the 1950s and 1960s with the recruitment of West Indians, or in the last century with the mass immigration of Irish workers. The US has been built on immigrant labour and today is still dependent on immigrants. Indeed in the early 1980s, when the Reagan administration arrested 6,000 illegal immigrants in nine cities during a clampdown on immigration to 'free' jobs for unemployed American citizens, they found that so few Americans applied for the work because of the appalling wages and conditions that the 'illegals' returned to take the jobs. Whole economies today are dependent on immigrant labour—the Middle

East is one of the largest importers of labour from South East Asia.

But as the economy moves into recession so the ruling class, which in the past welcomed the movement of labour, turns round and imposes restrictions to try and impose the burden of crisis onto 'foreign' workers—either by cracking down on their wages and benefits, or by imposing stringent and draconian controls on their movement. This is largely an attempt to divide worker against worker and deflect the blame for economic crises away from the ruling class.

As the Tories try to play the race card once again, they should be resisted every inch of the way. Those who have suffered most under their rule have a common cause with those who, in the most desperate of circumstances, go to extraordinary lengths to gain entry to this country. It is in the interests of all workers to welcome every immigrant and refugee, whatever their reasons, whatever their nationality.

Ireland

Chapter 25

A history of repression

Chris Bambery

The events in Northern Ireland last month prompted the following response from Margaret Thatcher: 'There seems to be no depths to which these people will not sink.' 'These people' she refers to are the population of West Belfast, the crucial Catholic working class ghetto.

Thatcher seeks to present the Northern Ireland troubles as some endless tribal conflict in which British troops are trapped in the middle.

The growth of the IRA since the troops went in in 1969, the fact that Sinn Fein wins the majority of votes in West Belfast, the continued opposition to the army and RUC, are all explained in terms of 'tribal loyalties'.

The truth is rather different. The reason Republicanism retains a following is that the Northern Ireland state created in 1921 remains fundamentally unchanged. Unionist control may have gone forever, destroyed by the upsurge in the Catholic ghettos, but the nature of the state remains the same.

What is the nature of that state?

Even before its inception it was clear that a sectarian and highly repressive state apparatus was being created in order to keep the Catholic population in its place. Take the following quote for example:

> No rebel who wishes to set up a republic can be regarded merely as a 'political opponent', but must be repressed. Consequently all officials

First published April 1988

who hold Republican views...should either be dismissed or given the opportunity of resigning or transfer... The new government officials and all new appointments to the constabulary etc should all be those who are prepared to accept this new form of government.

These words appeared in a memo handed over in 1920 to the British official responsible for drawing up plans for the creation of a Northern Ireland state. The memo was presented by the leadership of the Unionist Party and was drafted by Lieutenant Colonel Wilfrid Spender.

Spender became the first secretary to the Northern Ireland cabinet in 1921 and went on to become permanent secretary to the ministry of finance and head of the Northern Ireland civil service.

Spender was an Englishman, the son of a newspaper owner, who had joined the army and, after service in India, returned to become the youngest ever member of the Imperial General Staff with responsibility for home defence.

Spender was one of a generation of military men concerned with maintaining Britain's imperialist position who threw in their lot with the Unionists. They were therefore at one with the Tories who entered into alliance with the Unionists.

When Spender drafted the memo he was hastily reorganising the Ulster Volunteer Force (UVF) in order to counter the growing support across Ireland for Republicanism and the IRA's military campaign.

The Unionists' key demand was that the British government legitimise the Unionists' private army by incorporating them into a special, armed constabulary. They were pushing at an open door.

They were told that a special constabulary would be formed and in order to satisfy Unionist concerns were assured that 'the Special Constables will be selected by a committee of Loyalists'.

Thus were born the infamous B Specials. The UVF enlisted en masse. The officer corps mirrored the UVF command structure with the South Belfast commander being Colonel Fred Crawford who was the organiser of the Larne gun running of 1914 when Tory money helped arm the UVF with German rifles.

Initially 2,000 full time A Specials were recruited along with 19,500 B Specials, part timers who were allowed to keep their arms at home. Catholics were entirely excluded.

This force was to be the biggest single factor in copperfastening partition and terrorising the Catholic population of the new Northern state.

This state itself was carefully designed to ensure Unionist domination. Three counties of the historical province of Ulster were excluded thereby creating a six county state with a permanent majority of Protestants.

By April 1922 the Unionists had also abolished councils with Republican or Nationalist majorities. These included Fermanagh county council and councils in Newry, Armagh, Strabane and Downpatrick.

Boundaries were redrawn so that when new elections were held the Unionists took all but two of the 80 councils. These were the boundaries that ensured that Derry (with a Catholic population of 20,000 out of a total of 30,000) had a Unionist majority from 1924 until the beginning of the current troubles in 1968, which forced the state to remove some of the more blatant sectarian excesses.

Altogether there were 40,000 armed men at the service of that state when it was founded in June 1921. Facing them were at best 4,500 IRA volunteers who were badly armed and inexperienced.

Winston Churchill agreed to Britain paying half the costs of the Specials, to arm them, and to provide vehicles and radios and 250 ex-army officers.

In the first few weeks of the state's existence the Specials distinguished themselves by parading through Enniskillen singing Orange songs and shooting up a Catholic church. In Newry they burned down a Sinn Fein hall. A Catholic youth was shot down in cold blood by them in South Armagh, and in Clones in County Monaghan they became involved in a gun battle with the Royal Irish Constabulary following the looting of a pub.

In March 1922 the Special Powers Act was introduced. Aside from permitting internment without trial and the flogging of offenders, it also gave the Northern Ireland home affairs minister the power to take any measure 'he thinks necessary for the maintenance of order' with no reference to parliament.

It was to this clause that South Africa's prime minister, John Vorster, was referring when replying to critics of his Coercion Act. He said that he 'would be willing to exchange legislation of that sort for one clause of the Northern Ireland Special Powers Act'.

Such powers were accompanied by an orgy of state terror. Between July 1920 and July 1922, 453 people were killed in Belfast—37 members of the crown forces and 416 civilians, of whom 257 were Catholics and 157 Protestant.

Of the city's 93,000 Catholics, a quarter of the population, nearly 11,000, had been put out of their jobs and 23,000 driven from their homes. Over 500 Catholic owned shops and businesses were burned, looted and wrecked.

Outside Belfast at least 106 people died, 45 crown forces and 61 civilians, of whom 46 were Catholics and 15 Protestants.

This was no tribal conflict. The terror was state inspired and carried out by its own armed bodies of men.

On 22 March 1922 two Specials were shot in Belfast. The next night Specials burst into the home of a Catholic publican, Owen MacMahon—an opponent of Sinn Fein and a member of the moderate Nationalist Party. The male members of the family were lined up and shot. The father, three sons and a barman were killed and two other sons wounded.

On 1 April 1922 a policeman was shot by the IRA in central Belfast. In response uniformed police broke into nearby Catholic homes shooting three men dead, beating another to death with a sledgehammer and wounding three children, one of whom died.

Eyewitnesses, including Catholic policemen, identified the police inspector for the area, J W Nixon, as responsible. Nixon was proven to be running a death squad of police and Specials. The Unionist prime minister, James Craig, blocked any inquiry. Nixon became head of the Royal Ulster Constabulary's own Orange Lodge and was a Unionist MP for 20 years.

Craig, commenting on the pogrom sweeping Belfast, declared, 'The long and the short of it is that I will always say that the Protestants are not to blame.'

In May 1922 internment was introduced with 500 Republicans being held—this at a time when two Catholics were being killed for every Protestant and IRA activity was coming to a complete halt in Northern Ireland as its energies were directed to the civil war in the South.

May saw the peak of the killings. In Belfast and across the countryside the Specials spearheaded the terror. They were now joined by the Royal Ulster Constabulary (RUC).

From its inception the Unionists were determined to keep Catholics out, even those who had served with the old Royal Irish Constabulary. Preference was given to Specials. Spender listed the main qualifications for membership as 'Ulster birth, and a good record in the Special Constabulary'.

The first AGM of the RUC's own Orange Lodge reported 300 members, 10 percent of the force. The home affairs minister addressed it and the secretary of the Unionist Party with three of its MPs attended.

At its second AGM a Unionist MP declared that now they had a police force openly identified with the Orange Order. That year, 1924, saw 552 Catholics in the RUC, the highest figure. It has declined ever since.

It also saw the new Northern Ireland state with one policeman for every 160 inhabitants while the figure in England was one per 669.

Discrimination against Catholics was sanctioned from the top. No Catholic ever held a top post in the civil service. Northern Ireland's first prime minister, James Craig, summed up matters in April 1934 when he declared, 'All I boast is that we have a Protestant parliament and a Protestant state.'

The Catholic population was cowed into submission. For 50 years all but three cabinet ministers were Orangemen. Each decade saw internment without trial reintroduced and the B Specials unleashed on the Catholic community.

The reality of life for the Catholic population became one of discrimination, pogrom, repression and state terror, with no hope of change through the (rigged) parliamentary process.

It was against this background that the civil rights movement took to the streets in 1968 and began a process which would see the creation of Republican no-go areas, the arrival of British troops, internment (once more) and the fall of Stormont (the Northern Irish parliament). It is that process that leads us to where we are today.

Many argue that whatever else direct rule brought it rid the six counties of many of the uglier features of its past. 'We recognise Catholics suffered then,' they argue, 'but since Britain took over running things that's all changed.'

And at one level the changes are dramatic. Unionist government has gone forever, swept aside by the upheaval within the Catholic working class ghettos. Since 1972 every fundamental decision has been taken by Britain.

The old Unionist-Tory alliance is gone too with Thatcher scarcely concealing her distaste for the likes of Paisley.

Yet beneath this surface nothing fundamentally has changed. And there lies the root of the Northern Ireland troubles.

In 1969 we were told the old repressive practices would go.

But what's changed? The Hunt Committee (investigating policing in the North) at that time reported that just 11 percent of the RUC were Catholics. Since then that percentage has decreased while the RUC has increased in size by 268 percent. Hunt's proposals that the RUC should be disarmed and kitted out in uniforms the same colour as British bobbies are long forgotten.

In 1969 the Cameron Report into RUC attacks on Derry's Bogside and Belfast's Lower Falls admitted:

> A number of policemen were guilty of misconduct which involved assault and battery, malicious damage to property...and the use of provocative sectarian and political slogans.

Today, if anything, the situation is worse. The RUC has been given carte blanche to continue an official shoot to kill policy against unarmed Republican activists.

In 1979 the Bennett Report found the RUC guilty of practices amounting to torture. The chairman of the RUC Police Federation replied in *Police Beat*:

> The concentrated attack on the interrogation procedures which culminated in the Bennett Report will do nothing but hamper the defeat of terrorism.

Labour's Northern Ireland secretary, Roy Mason, addressing the annual passing out parade, announced, 'The RUC have come through with great courage and great integrity.'

Of course today the B Specials are gone. In their place is the part time Ulster Defence Regiment (UDR). But the Unionist government ensured former Specials were recruited. At its inception in 1970 the UDR was 18 percent Catholic. Two years later the figure was just 4 percent.

The UDR's involvement in sectarian attacks is well documented. In 1975 the Miami Showband were stopped at a UDR checkpoint on the main Belfast-Dublin road. As the UDR men tried to smuggle a bomb aboard the band's van it went off, killing two of them. The band were then gunned down.

Three UDR men were convicted. The two who died were members of the illegal Ulster Volunteer Force (UVF). Death notices for them appeared from UDR companies.

When interviewed at the time the commander of South Derry UDR said he'd be left without a regiment if every UDR soldier who was a member of the main Loyalist murder gang, the Ulster Defence Association, was dismissed.

In 1984 two journalists forced the RUC to act over the involvement of the UDR based at Drumadd Barracks, Armagh—13 UDR soldiers were charged with a string of sectarian attacks on Catholics.

In January 1985 one of them, Geoffrey Edwards, pleaded guilty to the murder of a Sinn Fein election agent, six attempted murders and a bombing. All had been claimed by the Protestant Action Force (a front for the legal UDA). Edwards had been in the UDR for seven years.

The *Observer* quoted a UDR officer as saying Edwards' actions were 'an act of war, a matter of pride' and that morale went up when it was realised UDR men were involved.

Today the UDR is in the forefront of policing the Northern Ireland crisis. That in itself is a reflection of the dominant view in British military and political circles that the Northern Ireland troubles will not go away and there is, in the words of the defence correspondent of the *Daily Telegraph* last month, 'no military solution'.

In a document drawn up in 1978 by Defence Intelligence Staff Brigadier James Glover and obtained by the Provisional IRA it is admitted, 'The Provisionals' campaign of violence is likely to continue while the British remain in Northern Ireland.'

Whatever Thatcher's rhetoric the aim now is one of containment or in the words of a General Officer in Command in Northern Ireland, Sir John Hackett, maintaining 'a hard military casing' with which to contain an 'explosive military mixture within, a mixture which will continue to exist into the foreseeable future more or less as before'.

British intelligence can digest statistics. And statistics point to the fact that to be born a Catholic means you are two and a half times more likely to be unemployed and that that position has deteriorated each year that the British troops have been there.

Unemployment rates currently run at 50.8 percent in inner West Belfast and 39.6 percent in outer. In comparison in Protestant East Belfast the figures are 32.7 percent in inner East Belfast and 12.1 in outer.

Discrimination remains too. Shorts Engineering, Northern Ireland's biggest employer, has a 95 percent Protestant workforce. Shorts is owned by the British government. The picture is the same at the Harland and Wolff shipyard, also government owned.

In the civil service just 12 percent of the highest grade are Catholics. In the state run electricity industry just 15 percent of the male workforce is Catholic, falling to 3.5 percent in management posts.

In simple terms that is why ordinary Catholic working class people support the IRA.

British finance maintains this setup, arming the UDR and RUC while British troops operate the daily grind of repression in the Falls Road.

The Anglo-Irish Agreement does not represent any attempt at a political solution to these problems. Its central concern is, as the defence correspondent of the *Daily Telegraph* wrote, 'to tighten the screw on the IRA'.

Socialists have to be very clear that, in what the *Sun* termed 'the Scarlet Isle', responsibility for the carnage lies full square with the British state.

Chapter 26

Easter 1916

Pat Stack

On Monday 24 April 1916, at a few minutes past noon, the centre of Dublin was taken over by anti-British forces. Standing on the steps of the General Post Office, a group of men and women listened while Padraic Pearse proclaimed the birth of an Irish Republic to a crowd of bemused onlookers.

In total perhaps three or four thousand people were to be involved in the insurrection. Desperately short of arms and unable to spread beyond Dublin, it was crushed within six days by British troops who outnumbered them 20 to one. The suppression of the rising was bloody and brutal. About 1,300 people, including civilians, were murdered or injured by the British army and an iron terror descended on Ireland. The leaders of the rising were court-martialled and executed by firing squad.

It might seem that the 'Easter Rising' had failed, but within five years the survivors of those isolated rebels would be part of an organisation with members in practically every town in Ireland and mass popular support. The movement which seemed laughably small in 1916 would force the mighty British Empire to the negotiating table to sign a treaty.

The reverberation of those days still echoes. The Provisional IRA can, with justification, claim to be the direct descendants of the Republican wing of the 1916 rebels. The terms of the Treaty of 1921 remain too: it led directly to the partition of Ireland and the creation of a sectarian Orange statelet in the North of Ireland.

The immediate origins of the rising lay in 1914. Nationalist politics in Ireland were then dominated by constitutional parliamentarians.

First published April 1982

On the outbreak of the First World War they urged the Irish to join the British army and fight 'to defend small nations' against the Germans. They hoped that their Liberal friends in parliament would reward them at the end of the war with Home Rule for their own small nation.

There was another, much smaller, group within nationalist circles who believed that the outbreak of war presented Ireland with an opportunity to rid itself of British domination. These people were the secret Irish Republican Brotherhood.

Its leader was a teacher and poet, Padraic Pearse. He took his inspiration from the 1798 rebellion led by Wolfe Tone. His first reaction to the war was that it was 'the greatest blood sacrifice given by man to good'. Yet the IRB decided almost from the outbreak of the war that an anti-British rising must take place.

Pearse and his supporters wanted a free Ireland, and they were prepared to fight and die for it. But for them a free Ireland was also one in which people would be free to own private property. In their Ireland there would be Irish bosses free to exploit Irish workers.

There was another wing to the movement present at Easter. It was called the Irish Citizens' Army and it was a revolutionary socialist organisation. Its best known figure was one of the finest Marxists and political agitators in working class history—James Connolly.

Connolly could not have been more different from Pearse. He had begun his political life in Edinburgh as a trade unionist and socialist militant. He had worked as an organiser for the Irish Socialist Republican Party, he played a leading role as a trade union organiser in America, and then returned to Ireland to work with James Larkin in unionising the workers of Dublin and Belfast.

Two aspects of Connolly's politics stand out: his 'syndicalist' ideas and his views on national liberation.

Before 1913 Connolly believed that, if workers took control of the factories, then the state would be powerless and would have to capitulate to the working class. This 'syndicalist' view was proved wrong in the Dublin Lockout of 1913. Connolly played a leading role in this struggle to gain union recognition which brought most of Dublin to a standstill. The unity of the bosses, the role of the government and the police, the activities of the church and the inactivity of British trade union leaders, all proved too much for the workers, who were starved back to work.

Connolly learned from this defeat that the struggle for workers' power meant a struggle against the state as well as against the bosses. As a direct result of this experience he founded the Irish Citizens' Army—the force he was to lead in 1916.

Connolly believed that the struggle for Irish freedom was intimately linked to the struggle for socialism. In this his view was very close to that of Lenin. It was this idea which led him to play a key role in the Easter Rising.

In fact, the rising was not the signal for a mass movement throughout Ireland and there was marked indifference amongst the workers of Dublin whom Connolly had led in mass struggle just three years before. The fact that Connolly found himself in this position, and that the socialist movement collapsed after his murder, can be explained by a key weakness in his politics. He never really understood the need for a revolutionary party which could lead the workers' movement not only in the upturns of the great strikes, but also in the years of downturn.

Connolly had not abandoned his socialism: just as his men were preparing to march on the Post Office, he told them to hang on to their guns even if the rising were to succeed, 'for they [the IRB] may stop at the minimum—for us only a socialist republic is acceptable.' During the rising he sent a detachment of men to raise the Starry Plough (the socialist republican flag) over the premises of one of the most savage employers of 1913 as a symbolic gesture of the meaning of the rising. But that fine socialist tradition depended entirely on one man, and failed with his death.

Connolly, along with the other leaders of the rising, was shot. His case was particularly horrible because he had been wounded in the rising. He was taken in an ambulance from the hospital to Kilmainham Jail on 12 May 1916. He was lifted from his stretcher, tied to a chair and carried in front of the firing squad. He died in that chair.

The rising had failed in its immediate objectives. It was disowned by the reformists in the labour movement and welcomed by Lenin. Within a year the savagery of British repression and talk of introducing conscription to Ireland led to the birth of mass resistance. The dead of Easter 1916 were about to be avenged.

Chapter 27

Bloody Sunday

Eamonn McCann

When the Paras began shooting on Bloody Sunday the main reaction among the thousands in Rossville Street—after terror—was bewilderment. Why were they shooting?

Everybody had known from the outset that a clash between some of the marchers and the British army was on the cards at some point during the day. The march was illegal, and there had been speculation all week about how the authorities would react if it went ahead. Loyalist leaders like Ian Paisley and William Craig had been shouting the odds about law and order and promising all manner of mayhem if British soldiers didn't make the civil rights marchers rue the day they defied Stormont.

But the day when Bogsiders could be put easily in their place was long gone. The young people of the area were well used to aggro. Hundreds of them had taken a hammering from the British soldiers at Magilligan prison camp the previous weekend. Here they were on home ground. Some of them were certain to have a go. You could sense that from the nonchalant way they'd ignored the instructions of stewards all the way along the march.

So an outbreak of some sort was more than half expected. But not this. Nobody had expected soldiers with self loading rifles steadying themselves to take aim and shooting ordinary people in the back as they fled in terrified disarray. Even as it was happening, people squirming for safety into the gutters were asking one another, 'Why?'

Just before it started people had been assuring one another that the violence was over, for today anyway, and that the march had been a tremendous success despite the bit of bother earlier. Indeed,

First published January 1992

the reason the march had ended in Rossville Street—there was a savage irony about this now—was to keep away from violence, to avoid confrontation.

The original plan had been to go to Guildhall Square in the city centre. There was a symbolic importance about that in Derry. Although Catholics were in a big majority in the town and were all anti-Unionist—and there were Protestant anti-Unionists too—the city centre for generations had been out of bounds to non-Unionist demonstrations. This reflected the fact that politically the Unionists had 'owned' Derry by dint of discrimination and gerrymandered boundaries.

The right to parade in the city centre had become a big issue in the heady early days of the civil rights movement. Then the age old unwritten law had been gleefully flouted, sometimes on a daily basis, and Guildhall Square and the Diamond deluged with civil rights demonstrators, giving local anti-Unionists their first taste of triumph in a lifetime.

So when it came to deciding the route of the 30 January march there had been no question of staying within the Creggan-Bogside 'ghetto'. The intention had been to assemble at Central Drive in the Creggan, a big postwar estate which spilled across a bleak hill overlooking the Bogside, and to wind down through the Bogside and then along the edge of the Bogside, down Creggan Street and William Street, and out into Waterloo Place and the city centre. There, it was planned, an impressive array of prominent speakers would rehearse the reasons for fighting on to end internment without trial.

The intended presence of Labour peer Fenner Brockway had enraged Unionists more than somewhat—a lord lending his prestige to civil rights law breaking! There had been sour remarks, too, about Presbyterian minister Terence McCaughey agreeing to speak. Others scheduled to appear on the platform included Bernadette Devlin and Frank McManus, the Independent MP for Fermanagh-South Tyrone.

However, even before the march left Creggan it was known that the mouth of William Street had been shut off with a barbed wire barricade and British army vehicles, and that there were scores, even hundreds, of British soldiers and RUC men behind the barrier. There was word, too, that the march organisers had spoken with RUC chiefs earlier in the day and had agreed to divert the march before it reached the barricade and to go to Free Derry Corner instead for the meeting.

There was some comment on this as the crowd assembled, and a degree of resentment. Then again, those who had been down to William Street and seen what a formidable obstacle the British had erected, advised that it would be pointless trying to force a way through.

The march formed up in high good humour anyway, behind a Derry Civil Rights Association banner on the lorry which was later to serve as a platform for the meeting. Members of a distinctive fraternity which had flourished in recent years, the Civil Rights Stewards, flapped and hassled around the fringe of the crowd trying to cajole the marchers into orderly array—'Four abreast, please!'—to little avail.

The march left late. Civil rights marches always did. It was 2.50pm when a cheer went up and the procession, maybe 5,000 strong, swung out and headed for Southway, to go down towards the Brandywell area. It was a lovely, bright winter's day and, walking down Southway, marchers took pleasure in the great view along the perfect sweep of the Foyle.

Southway snakes down a steep embankment in a series of loops designed to ease a giddy gradient. However, hundreds of mainly young marchers preferred the direct route to the winding road, and slithered and tumbled down the greenery to reach the bottom before the head of the march. There was now a sizeable contingent in front of the lorry.

Cheering and chanting and essaying the occasional ragged chorus of civil rights standards such as 'We Shall Overcome' and 'We Shall Not Be Moved', the march swelled in size as it passed through Brandywell and along the Lecky Road towards the Bogside. Sedate sorts who had decided not to trek up to the Creggan in order to trek back down again joined in at every corner.

The parade was perhaps 10,000 strong by the time it reached the Bogside Inn in the heart of Free Derry at about 3.25pm. There were crowds lining the pavements here two and three deep who had perhaps come for the spectacle but who, seeing the scale of the march, now began to merge in with it, keeping pace on the pavement. The march was thickly packed and filled the street wall to wall as it struggled up Westland Street.

Continuing on a circuitous route, the marchers turned right along the Lone Moor Road, right again into Creggan Street and then down William Street. At the junction with Rossville Street march organisers started shouting through public address equipment mounted on the lorry that everybody was to turn right into Rossville Street and go along as far as Free Derry Corner, where the meeting would now be held. The lorry swung right, and most of the crowd behind it followed.

But there was confusion. Not everyone had known about the changed arrangement. There was uncertainty about the status of the new instructions. And—of more practical importance—the numbers marching ahead of the lorry had by now reached 1,000 or so, and had already reached the British army barricade by the time the 'front' of the march turned into Rossville Street. Demands across the barricade to 'let us through. It's our town' and so forth soon gave way to exchanges of insults and then missiles. The marchers threw stones and bottles. Soldiers responded with rubber bullets. A run of the mill riot developed.

The rioters pulled back in face of the rubber bullet onslaught, then advanced again behind 'shields' fashioned from corrugated iron sheets purloined from an adjacent building site. The British retaliated by bringing up water cannon, which hosed the crowd with purple dyed water at high pressure.

The barricade was out of sight of the Rossville Street junction, past a dog leg bend in lower William Street. Rioters who withdrew from the fray mingled with the crowds milling around the junction, then perhaps returned to battle. As commonly happened, there wasn't a clear distinction between rioters, marchers and onlookers.

That was the situation when, at 3.55pm, the British fired their first shots, hitting John Johnston and Damien Donaghy, about halfway back along William Street, out of sight both of Free Derry Corner—where the lorry was now in position and the speakers were making ready for the meeting—and of the confrontation at the barricade.

At the time, amid the hubbub and chaos, the majority of demonstrators didn't realise that there had been gunfire and casualties. Stewards were attempting to summon and shepherd the crowd up towards the meeting, pleading with young people to resist the attraction of the aggro.

When an ambulance arrived to take away the two wounded, hundreds poured back down Rossville Street to investigate what was afoot. Meanwhile, the exchanges across the barricade had reached a fitful sort of stalemate: the water cannon had proven fairly effective in dousing combativity. From Free Derry Corner came the distinctive singsong soprano of Bernadette Devlin repeatedly announcing that the meeting was about to begin. There was an ebbing and flowing all round. But a drift back up towards the meeting was gathering momentum and the numbers in lower William Street and around the Rossville Street junction began to thin out. A local journalist standing at the corner shrugged her shoulders: 'Ah well. Another friendly wee Derry riot...'

People asked one another as they moved up the street what had happened, what they'd seen. Different accounts of how badly the two men had been hurt, and of how it had happened were in circulation.

Some said they'd heard five bullets had been used. But most took it for granted that, for practical purposes, whatever the exact details would eventually turn out to be, the violence was now over.

People on the march would have had a pattern in mind of the way these occasions would tend to work out. The British army and/or the RUC blocking the path of a civil rights march; the march leaders voicing protest but accepting the edict; the more pugnacious and energetic elements scorning this timidity and making some show of defiance; defiance developing into riot which might last late into the night or just as easily peter out quickly, depending on all manner of factors, from weather conditions to the standing of the march leaders with the rioting element.

The marchers on Bloody Sunday would have been connoisseurs of this sort of thing. As the drift up along Rossville Street gathered momentum towards the meeting, people said sagely to one another that it could have been worse, all things considered. It seemed obvious at this point that the march could be marked down as a significant triumph for the pro civil rights, anti-internment side.

It was then, in an instant, with no warning or preliminary indication, that there was an inrush of terror as the Paras erupted into Rossville Street and the slaughter began.

They killed Jack Duddy, 17, with a single bullet as he ran across the courtyard of the Rossville Street flats.

Michael Kelly, also 17, was shot in the stomach as he stood on a pile of rubble near the entrance to Glenfada Park, off Rossville Street, and died within minutes.

James Wray, 22, was shot and wounded as he ran through an alleyway from Glenfada Park to Abbey Park, then shot again and killed.

Gerald McKinney, 35, was shot and killed by a bullet which hit him in the chest as he ran with his hands raised towards soldiers in Glenfada Park.

Gerald Donaghy, 17, was shot in the abdomen as he ran up steps towards a flat in Abbey Park and died before reaching hospital.

William McKinney, 26, was shot and killed as he bent over Gerald McKinney on the ground in Glenfada Park.

John Young, 17, was hit in the head and killed as he stood beside a rubble barricade stretched across Rossville Street.

Michael McDaid, 20, was standing beside the same barricade when he was shot in the face and fell dead.

William Nash, 19, was in the same group at the barricade when shot in the chest and killed.

Patrick Doherty, 31, was crawling towards Rossville Flats when a bullet hit him in the buttock and travelled upwards through his body before exiting from his chest, killing him instantly.

Bernard McGuigan, 41, was killed instantly by a bullet which hit him in the back of the head as he crawled towards the body of Pat Doherty beside the Rossville Flats.

Hugh Gilmore, 17, was killed by a bullet which passed through his elbow and then horizontally through his body as he ran up Rossville Street.

Kevin McElhinney, 17, was killed as he crawled towards a doorway in Rossville Street, the bullet entering his buttock an inch from the anus and travelling up through his body to exit near his shoulder.

Patrick O'Donnell, Patrick McDaid, Alex Nash, Patrick Campbell, Peggy Deery, Daniel McGowan, Michael Bridge, Michael Quinn, Joseph Mahon, Joseph Friel and Michael Bradley were wounded by gunfire. Alana Burke was injured when crushed against a wall by an armoured personnel carrier.

But in the moments before all that started it was the size of the march which had excited most comment. It was the huge turnout which had made the day seem a triumph. It had been the key question in the Bogside and Creggan and in 'civil rights circles' across the North in the week leading up to the march: how many would show? It had been the constant topic of conversation even as the march wound its way down from Creggan—'What do you think of the turnout?'—it being clear from the inflection that this was not intended as a question but as an exultant observation. At the top of Westland Street it was possible to look back down the hill about 300 yards to the Lecky Road and see the entire stretch thronged solid with marchers. Everybody told everyone else to look back: 'Look at that!' A great cheer went rolling down through the march.

The way they saw it, the question which had been asked of the people of the Bogside and Creggan was whether, in all the circumstances, in view of dire warnings and threat, they would still push on forward with the fight against internment.

Thus the exhilaration of the marchers at their own numbers as they surged through the Bogside, and the sense of triumph as they gathered in towards Free Derry Corner, at about 4.15pm, just before the crack-crack of the rifles came from the bottom of the street.

Two days after Bloody Sunday, on 1 February, the Conservative prime minister, Edward Heath, announced in the House of Commons that the Lord Chief Justice, Lord Widgery, had been appointed to inquire into the deaths in Derry. Widgery, 60, from a landed background in Devonshire, had served in the Royal Artillery and risen to the rank of Lieutenant Colonel. Afterwards, he held Brigadier rank in the Territorial Army.

The appointment was welcomed by the opposition Labour and Liberal parties and by many British media commentators who argued that Lord Widgery's eminence was a measure of how seriously the authorities were taking the task of establishing the truth. The reaction in Derry was different.

In the Bogside and Creggan there was discussion and even disagreement about the details of how things had happened. But as to the question which loomed over all others—had the Paras opened fire in response to an IRA attack or had they engaged in an unprovoked massacre of unarmed civilians?—there was no argument. A large percentage of the local population had been in the vicinity of the shooting. Hundreds had actually witnessed killings happen. Local people knew the truth of it. The question was not what truth would Widgery find but whether, in the light of that, local people should give evidence to his inquiry.

Scarcely anyone in the area had confidence in Widgery. Republicans and leftists were instinctively scornful of the notion that a man of his background would or could show objectivity in such a matter. And the major parties of 'moderation', the SDLP and the Nationalist Party, initially urged a boycott of the inquiry as well.

John Hume (SDLP) said that he was surprised that Widgery had regarded himself as suitable for the role, and added, 'We shall have nothing to do with this inquiry and that is our advice to the people.' Eddie McAteer (Nationalist) pronounced himself 'stone-cold on this question of British inquiries' and hoped that Widgery's hearings would be 'completely ignored'.

Widgery arrived in Coleraine, a mainly Loyalist town 30 miles from Derry, for a preliminary sitting of the inquiry in the County Hall on Monday 14 February. He came in a British army helicopter. Travelling with him were Mr E B Gibbons and Mr Michael Underhill, who were to represent the British army at the inquiry. Widgery opened proceedings by assuring all concerned of his independence. He then outlined the scope of the inquiry:

> The limits of the inquiry in space are the streets of Londonderry where the disturbances and the ultimate shootings took place, an area of perhaps one mile in radius. The time within which the inquiry is concerned to make investigation can be expressed as the period beginning with the moment when the march taking place in Londonderry on the day first became involved in violence of one kind or another, and ending with the conclusion of the affair and the deaths.

Thus Widgery's original intention was to exclude investigation of whether the Paras had been following any pre-arranged plan. This drew such intense and broadly based protest that for a few days it seemed possible that the inquiry would hear evidence from no one other than British security force personnel, which would have drained the proceedings of all residual credibility. In response, at the first 'proper' sitting a week later, Widgery outlined slightly extended terms of reference. He would now investigate 'the orders given to the army, and especially the paratroopers'— but not 'the political or military thinking behind those orders'.

This was hardly satisfactory either. As far as people in the Bogside were concerned, the 'political and military thinking behind those orders' was precisely what needed to be exposed. Nevertheless, local people did, in the end, take part in the inquiry.

A joint statement from nine priests who had been in the Bogside during the killings that—despite reservations—they would be giving evidence was important in bringing about this change of mind. There was influential advice, too, from the National Council for Civil Liberties and the International League for the Rights of Man. Lawyers from the two organisations—including Professor Sam Dash, who was shortly to achieve a certain fame as counsel to the US Senate Committee investigating the Watergate cover up—told relatives of the dead at a private meeting in Derry on 21 February that the tribunal 'would provide...a fair opportunity to present their own testimony in an open hearing attended by the press of the world, and...permit their counsel to fully cross-examine the army witnesses.'

Additionally, constitutional politicians, on reflection, became somewhat alarmed at their own rejection of the only constitutional mechanism on offer for dealing with the fraught aftermath of the massacre.

More significant than any of this, however, was a feeling which gradually hardened in the area in the days after the killings that the truth was so obvious and the issues so clear cut that no fudging or cover up would prove plausible. Even before Widgery's appointment the British army's story had begun to come apart.

On the evening of Bloody Sunday a British army spokesman had claimed that two of the wounded had confessed to using firearms: it was rapidly and easily established that none of the wounded had made any statement at all. At the same time, a British army source had alleged that four of the dead had been on a 'wanted list' of IRA activists: almost immediately it was shown that 12 of the 13 then dead had either worked full time or had regularly 'signed on' outside the no-go area and would have been available for arrest at any time in the previous period.

Eddie McAteer summed up the developing consensus: 'The British army is obviously terrified of this inquiry and it is hardly for us to ease their pain by staying away.'

The tribunal held 17 sessions between 21 February and 14 March—114 witnesses gave evidence and were cross-examined. These comprised: 37 people, including seven priests, from Derry; 21 journalists/photographers; five named and 35 unnamed British soldiers; eight police officers; six doctors and forensic experts; and two other civilians, including Lord Fenner Brockway. The public gallery was packed for all of these sessions by relatives and political activists who travelled from Derry. The local press carried verbatim accounts. Each day's evidence was analysed in detail in Bogside conversation, the patent falsity of British army evidence occasioning bitter derision.

Three further sessions were held at the Royal Courts of Justice in London on 16, 17 and 20 March, at which counsel made their closing arguments. Widgery submitted his report to home secretary Reginald Maudling on 10 April. It was leaked to right wing London newspapers on 16 April and published on 18 April. The *Derry Journal* of 18 April described its findings as 'simply incredible' and 20 years later fierce anger against it is still felt in Derry.

The United States

Chapter 28

The American working class

Duncan Hallas

The central question in discussing the American working class is why there is not, and has not been, a political labour movement of any significance in the United States. This is in spite of the fact that the US is today the major capitalist power in the world and has been, since the turn of the century, one of the two or three major capitalist powers.

There are a number of explanations put forward. The first set of arguments are what you might call the 'sociological' arguments. They can all be found in letters which Engels wrote to various people in America in the 1880s.

They are important because they have been recycled and refurbished, time and again, by various American liberals. They come down in essence to three propositions.

The first proposition concerns the unique character of land settlement in the US. In the post civil war period, the victorious radical wing of the American bourgeoisie carried out their pledge to give most of the land formally in the hands of the state—the land in the West— to anyone who would actually agree to settle and improve it.

Consequently it is argued—and with some substance in that period—that this seriously delayed the formation of a permanent working class.

The second proposition is a connected one. American industry developed on an enormous scale in the post civil war decades. The

First published June 1986

extent of this development can be seen by one statistic. In 1860, the year the war broke out, American iron and steel production (mostly iron) was one fifth of the British output. By the turn of the century US output—now mostly steel—had completely outstripped the British and was the largest in the world.

This development was based on immigrant labour. But—and this is where it fits in with the land settlement question—this immigrant labour itself rapidly became assimilated into society.

The pattern went like this. Wave after wave of immigrants were brought in from Europe. They became, if you like, a temporary proletariat, because large sections of them moved on and up.

The important thing about this temporary proletariat, as Engels and others argued, is that it did not become stabilised and acclimatised in the cities—it was being drained at the top and the sides all the time.

The stockyards and steel mills were manned, so far as the mass of the workforce was concerned, by relatively recent, ever changing waves of immigrant labour.

This had a further consequence—the ghettoisation of the developing industrial cities, of which Chicago is the most famous example. So the picture developed: rapidly expanding industry—murderously efficient by world standards, and brutally managed; a way out—the new frontier—and therefore extreme difficulty in developing permanent organisation; and the ghettoisation of the cities.

Out of these conditions arose the third of the effective 'sociological' arguments. It is something which developed quite early on. The immigrant workforce would arrive poor, in trouble, in a strange land, with no social security and no social services. Who did they look to for help?

Here we come to the final peculiarity about the development of the working class in the US: democracy.

Democracy matters to the argument in two senses. Firstly, it is a fact that—long before it existed in Europe—there was effective universal suffrage for white males almost everywhere in the US.

Secondly, however, the system was democratic in another way— states with rights, and local government with powers, vastly greater than they have ever been in Britain.

What did this mean for the immigrant worker? There were people who, for a consideration, would do something for them or their children—in terms of jobs, or education, or talking to the precinct police captain. What was that consideration?

In short, that the immigrant workers had to learn enough English to pass the citizenship test, and then had to *turn out and vote*. The city machines, then, served in a sense as a substitute for a reformist labour movement. That is not so true now, but it certainly was in the 19th century.

For all these reasons, therefore, a political labour movement did not develop. At this point, however, we need to make a very important qualification. It is not true that in the period there was a low level of class struggle. In the 1870s and again in the late 1880s to early 1890s there were massive strikes, often very violently fought, involving large numbers of workers.

Typically, however, they did not lead to permanent trade union organisation or to a real alteration in the process whereby the workforce was being constantly renewed. This was because the wage rise and the improvement of conditions—assuming that you could get them—were still a lesser attraction than moving out.

All this seems to add up to a plausible sounding explanation, except for one obvious fact. The 'new frontier' was effectively finished by the 1890s.

True, immigration did not slow down. On the contrary, it continued to accelerate. The peak year for immigration into the US was 1914, when five million plus entered the country in one year. But that was on the basis of *intensive* growth of American industry, not *extensive* growth. The proletariat had become permanent, in the ordinary sense, by the turn of the century. And by the 1920s immigration had become much more difficult.

Consequently, you then got a certain development of a politicised labour movement, albeit of a rather peculiar sort. Roughly between 1900 and 1914 stable trade union organisation was largely confined to skilled workers. It was very patchy, geographically, and did not significantly affect mass production industry.

One partial exception to this was coal. But in steel and the developing automobile industry, the only people who held union cards were members of skilled craft societies.

The Socialist Party founded in 1901, which enjoyed a fair degree of support, was not therefore based on the trade union bureaucracy, nor was it at all closely associated with trade union organisation.

This is confirmed by the pattern of its electoral success. By 1912 the American Socialist Party had 100,000 members. Its strongest vote, however, was not in the eastern seaboard, which was still the major industrial area, but in the West—an area only recently settled.

All the special factors which can be shown to have operated in the US until 1900 or 1920 were now of steadily diminishing importance.

So the presence or absence of a political labour movement has to be judged in terms of certain specific events and struggles.

To understand this better, it is worth looking back at the British labour movement. From the 1830s onwards there were a number of massive struggles, leading by and large to defeat. By 1850 the big struggles were in the past, and stable mass union organisation did not exist, except in a few cases.

Then came the development of the craft societies, and 50 years of 'Lib-Labism'. This was due to two factors: the defeats, without which Lib-Labism could not have survived, and the increasing world dominance of British capitalism in the second half of the century.

It was only at the end of the century, which saw the relative decline of British capitalism, that a political labour movement in Britain was born.

How does that model compare to the US? The First World War produced an upsurge in attempts at union organisation, many of which were temporarily successful. This culminated in 1919 with an employers' offensive.

This offensive took a number of forms. There was a massive anti-red, anti-immigrant campaign. A number of important strikes—the packing house strike, the steel strike—were defeated. The unions, where they existed, were effectively driven out of large scale production. Consequently, the right wing inside the American Federation of Labour was reinforced, sitting on top of little craft societies.

This was combined with, from 1924, a period of very rapid economic growth. In spite of everything, real wages were rising. This, and the ideology that went with the boom, had a deadening effect.

What was the state of the significant political tendencies? The Socialist Party basically never recovered from the splits in the postwar period. All the guts were torn out of it. The party's better activists went to the Communist Party and the worst jumped on the bandwagon—share promotion schemes, the trade union bureaucracy and so on.

The Communist Party, on the other hand—the product of a fusion in 1919-20—was essentially a federation of factions. It must have been one of the very worst parties in the Comintern—and that's really saying something. It was internalised, fraught with problems and ineffective until two events coincided. One was the onset of the world slump. The impact of the slump in the US was enormous. In the years 1929-32 there was a catastrophic drop in industrial output of 40 percent. Secondly, by 1929 the American Communist Party had been effectively Stalinised—all the warring factions were done away with.

This combination of things meant that the development of a

political labour movement—which looked on the cards—was aborted.

So what happened? The Communist Party was initially tiny. In 1932 when it ran William Z Foster for president, it had 12,000 members. By 1938 it had 100,000 members. This growth was against a background of whatever the current line was that was coming from the Stalinist centre.

That meant until 1934 wildly ultra-left policies, and after 1935 policies based on the policies of the popular front. However, the growth could not have occurred but for what was happening industrially.

The initial impact of the slump was to destroy utterly even those vestiges of struggle which had existed in the 1920s. But following a marginal economic upturn in 1934, the accumulation of bitterness led to a series of disputes.

After a brief check in 1935, there was a real explosion, mainly around the question of union organisation. It was really spectacular. In the short period of time from the sit-in at Flint in 1936 to the unionisation of Fords in 1941, the basic industries were organised—even in the South.

Given this mass industrial upheaval, the breakthrough to political consciousness would most certainly have taken place but for one factor: the people who were most influential in these terms were opposed to it.

They were on the one hand the newly emerging labour bureaucracies, and on the other the Communist Party—which played a central role industrially.

There was a contradiction in the period. The explosion of union organisation radicalised large numbers of workers—no question about it. But the bureaucracies themselves were largely happy with the Roosevelt administration and its New Deal. They were willing to enter into what amounted to a coalition with one wing of the government.

The New Deal, despite its restrictive elements, entitled workers to a legally binding ballot on the question of a union. It was this side of it, under conditions where people were unorganised, that helped to spark the upsurges and consequently strengthen the bureaucracies.

But the bureaucracies couldn't go into this coalition with sections of government without the support of the Communist Party. Others on the left—the remnants of the Socialist Party, the Trotskyists and all sorts of independents—were calling for the formation of a labour party. In order to contain this process, the bureaucracy sometimes resorted to setting up labour parties in order to get a working class vote for Roosevelt.

In New York State the union bureaucracies set up an American Labour Party, which of course ran candidates of its own, but whose presidential candidate was Roosevelt.

In Michigan the auto union set up the Michigan Cooperative Federation which was a similar operation. There were many others, but in all cases the union leaders sought to tie them to the Democratic Party.

They could do so, from 1935 onwards, because the Communist Party was concerned above all else to promote the Roosevelt administration, and to prevent the development of any independent reformist working class organisation.

This analysis stops at 1940. But subsequent events can be summarised very simply by another comparison to Britain in the latter half of the last century with its massive expansion, world dominance and so on.

A single statistic will do to draw a comparison. In the late 1940s one half of the world total of industrial output—excluding the USSR—was produced in the US. For a period of two or three decades this was the objective factor. There was also the subjective factor.

The real function of the Cold War in America was to eliminate the substantial Communist Party influence, especially in the unions. It was to consolidate a labour bureaucracy that owed its allegiance, in the last analysis, to the US state. It was, over time, successful. By the 1950s the right wing was in control everywhere. Since then union organisation has dropped from 40 percent to 20 percent in 1986.

Under these circumstances, the development of political class consciousness was out of the question. But, just as in the British case, changing objective circumstances change the nature of the arena. This doesn't mean we'll see an automatic rerun of the British experience.

But it does mean that new possibilities will be—and are being—created by the relative decline of American capitalism today.

Chapter 29

The Great Crash of 1929

Alex Callinicos

On 29 October 1929 the bottom fell out of American capitalism. That was the day—Black Tuesday—that the New York stock market collapsed, dragging down with it first the US economy and then the world economy. There followed more than a decade of slump, which ended only with the Second World War.

The year 1929 has entered popular mythology particularly in the United States. Some of the stories associated with it (including, unfortunately, the legend that the streets of New York were bombarded with the bodies of ruined millionaires flinging themselves out of skyscrapers) are untrue. But the image of 1929 has stuck firmly in people's minds as the ultimate economic catastrophe.

During the boom of the 1950s and 1960s it was popular to dismiss the idea that there could be another such collapse as absurd. Thanks to Keynes, economic depression had become, we were told, impossible.

Today such arguments carry much less weight.

As if to celebrate the fiftieth anniversary of the crash, Wall Street suffered what the *Economist* called 'its worst day for more than five years' on 9 October 1979 (also a Tuesday). The Dow Jones industrial average (the equivalent of the *Financial Times* index) fell 26.45 points. The next day 82 million shares changed hands—an all time record.

Perhaps the idea of another crash is not quite so ridiculous after all.

First published December 1979

In this article I shall look at the causes of the 1929 crash, and its consequences, in order to weigh up the chances of a similar catastrophe.

American capitalism in the Jazz Age

The roots of the crash, and the Great Depression which followed it, lay in the First World War and the drastic rearrangement of relationships between the main capitalist countries which it involved. As the economist Lionel Robbins put it, writing in 1933, 'We live, not in the fourth, but in the 19th year of the world crisis.'

The war reversed the relation between Europe and America. To Trotsky must go much of the credit for grasping the significance of this reversal:

> Before the war, America was Europe's debtor. The latter served as the principal factory and the principal depot for world commodities. Moreover Europe, above all England, was the central banker. All these leading roles now belong to the United States. Europe has been relegated to the background. The United States is the principal factory, the principal depot and the central bank of the world.

The war drained the blood from Britain, hitherto the chief capitalist power. The war effort was financed by printing money and selling off foreign investments. The US, insulated from the main impact of the war, profited from it magnificently. American industry provided the combatants with goods.

Capital from all over the world sought the safety of New York. As Robbins put it, 'The gold supplies of the world tended more and more to be concentrated in the vaults of the Federal Reserve Banks.' By 1926, 60 percent of world gold reserves were in the US.

Finance capital—the big banks and industrial trusts—emerged from the war economically and politically dominant within the US. Both Britain and France were heavily in its debt.

American loans were essential to shore up the shattered financial structure of European capitalism. This was especially so in the case of Germany, whose economy, shaken by war, defeat, revolution and hyperinflation, burdened by the war reparations imposed by the victorious Allies at the 1919 Versailles peace conference, was desperately short of capital.

These loans were part of a huge increase in US foreign investment after 1918. In 1900 America had $500 million invested abroad (compared to $20 billion's worth of British overseas investment). By 1913 US foreign investment had reached $2.5 billion. In 1932 it was nearly $18 billion.

This drastically changed financial position was underpinned by the enormous superiority of American industry over its competitors. Trotsky gave the details in 1924:

> The United States produces one-fourth of the world grain crop; more than one-third of the oats; approximately three-fourths of the world corn crop; one-half of the world's coal output; about half of the world's iron ore; about 60 percent of its pig iron; 60 percent of the steel; 60 percent of the copper; 47 percent of the zinc.
>
> American railways constitute 36 percent of the world railway network: its merchant marine now comprises more than 25 percent of the world tonnage; and, finally, the number of automobiles operating in the trans-Atlantic republic amounts to 84.4 percent of the world total!... These figures decide everything. They will cut a road for themselves on land, on sea, and in the air.

And in the 1920s this massive industrial machine was booming. With interruptions (1920-22, 1924, 1926-27) the US economy expanded rapidly.

Growth was especially concentrated in those industries manufacturing consumer durables — radios, domestic appliances, cars. Output per worker in manufacturing industries rose by 43 percent between 1919 and 1929. The index of industrial production went up from 67 in 1921 (1923-25=100) to 126 in July 1929. Unemployment fell to 0.9 percent in 1929. And, as we shall see, stock market prices climbed to dizzy heights.

The pundits of the day claimed that capitalism had entered a 'new era' in which slumps had become a thing of the past. In June 1929 the financier Bernard Baruch told an interviewer that the 'economic condition of the world seems on the verge of a great forward movement'.

Prosperity and a booming stock market created in the US among the middle classes a unique sense of confidence and abandonment to the pursuit of pleasure. F Scott Fitzgerald, whose novels captured the ephemeral brilliance of the 'Jazz Age', called it 'the most expensive orgy in history':

> ...the whole upper tenth of a nation living with the insouciance of grand dukes and the casualness of chorus girls.
>
> We were the most powerful nation. Who could tell us any longer what was fashionable and what was fun?

Even J K Galbraith, a sceptical historian of the crash, could write:

> 1929 was the last year in which Americans were buoyant, uninhibited and utterly happy.

The crash

But the boom rested on foundations of sand. Although, as we have seen, labour productivity rose sharply during the 1920s, wages and prices remained stable. In other words, profits alone benefited from the increase in productivity: the share of capital in the national income rose. This encouraged a high rate of investment, principally in those industries producing plant and equipment. During the 1920s production of these capital goods increased at an annual rate of 6.4 percent; by contrast, production of non-durable consumer goods rose by only 2.8 percent.

In other words, the boom was top heavy, concentrated in sectors producing, not for mass consumption, but for capital itself, expanding the already massive industrial apparatus of American capitalism as if it were an end in itself. The purchasing power of the mass of the population—workers and small farmers — remained as yet a limited market for goods. The top 5 percent of household heads disposed of one third of total consumer purchasing power.

Under these conditions, the boom could only be kept going through a constant infusion of capital into the industries producing plant and equipment, enabling them to expand their investments further. The source of this capital was the stock market.

Stock markets occupy a peculiar position within the capitalist economy. On the one hand, they are an important source of the funds necessary for investment in industry. As such, the stocks and shares purchased and sold represent claims to a portion of the surplus value produced in industry. The dividend paid out to an investor is his share of the profits of that company, in exchange for the money he had advanced to that company when he bought his stocks. Ultimately, therefore, the stock market is governed by the movements or the 'real economy'—the production and sale of commodities.

On the other hand, the stock market has a life of its own, determined by factors quite independent of industrial production. The rate of interest is one such factor—if it rises too high it will attract some investors away from the stock market because interest bearing bonds have become a more attractive investment, while others will find it too expensive to borrow money with which to speculate on the stock market.

In 1927 the Federal Reserve Board (the American equivalent of the Bank of England) reduced its discount rate from 4 to 3.5 percent, in order to discourage the flow of funds from Europe to America. According to Lionel Robbins, it was this cheap money policy which fuelled the stock market boom:

From that date, according to all the evidence, the situation got completely out of control. By 1928 the authorities were thoroughly frightened. But now the forces they had released were too strong for them. In vain they issued secret warnings. In vain they pushed up their own rate of discount. Velocity of circulation, the frenzied anticipation of speculators and company promoters, had now taken control.

But cheap money alone cannot give rise to a stock market boom. Crucial to such a state of affairs is the belief that share prices will continue to rise. For this belief has a self fulfilling dynamic: investors, expecting a rise in prices, will buy shares and the increased demand will push up prices. Those already holding stocks enjoy a capital gain as the value of these stocks increases with the rise in share prices.

The late 1920s saw a veritable orgy of stock market speculation. Prices rose and rose and rose. Investment trusts sprang up overnight to organise complicated operations often involving buying their own shares to boost the price and thus attract other buyers. Many shares were held 'on margin'—in other words, you didn't actually have to have the purchase price of a block of shares in order to buy them. Your broker bought them for you. You deposited them with him for security along with a certain amount of cash (the margin).

By the end of 1928 brokers' loans—loans secured by shares bought on margin—totalled $6.4 billion. The generous interest rates on these loans (12 percent at their height) sucked in money from all over the world. After June 1928 American foreign lending fell drastically: the returns on brokers' loans had become more attractive than those on any overseas investment.

The stock market seemed the ideal way to get rich quick. There was much talk of 'economic democracy'. One financier, John J Raskob, published a scheme which would enable the poor man to increase his capital as quickly as the rich man. It was proclaimed a 'practical Utopia'. The only trouble was that the rich man had rather more capital to start with.

In reality, of course, it was the rich who got richer. Often this was through straightforward theft. There were, for example, the officers of the Union Industrial Bank of Flint, Michigan, who made off with $3,592,000 of the bank's funds and invested in the New York call market—the market for brokers' loans.

Galbraith tells their story:

In the beginning this embezzlement was a matter of individual initiative. Unknown to each other, a number of the bank's officers began making away with funds. Gradually they became aware of each other's activities, and since they could scarcely expose each other, they cooperated. The enterprise eventually embraced about a dozen people, including virtually all the principal officers of the bank.

This was an extreme case perhaps. But then there was Charles Mitchell, chairman of the huge National City Bank. When the crash came he borrowed heavily from J P Morgan and Company to buy National City shares to prevent too drastic a fall in their price. This operation failed and Mitchell was left with a huge debt to Morgan's, secured by his own holdings in National City stock. He then sold these holdings to his wife at a loss of $2,872,305.50 without telling Morgan's, thus wiping out all his tax liabilities. When this transaction came to light he was prosecuted for tax fraud.

The boom, people believed, would never come to an end. The Dow Jones industrial average rose from 191 in early 1928 to a peak of 381 in September 1929. One economist, Irving Fisher, declared, 'Stock prices have reached what looks like a permanently high plateau.'

But even before prices fell from their 'plateau', the real economy was slowing down. Industrial production fell at an annual rate of 20 percent between August and October 1929. One factor behind this was surely the credit squeeze imposed by an increasingly worried Federal Reserve Board. The Federal Reserve Bank of New York increased its re-discount rate to 6 percent on 9 August.

The stock market ignored these warning signs. On 20 September it was, however, shaken by the news of the collapse of the empire of Clarence Hatry, a British conman who made a fortune out of slot machines.

It does not require any earth shattering event to end a stock market boom. As Galbraith puts it:

> It is in the nature of a speculative boom that almost anything can collapse it. Any serious shock to confidence can cause sales by those speculators who have always hoped to get out before the final collapse, but after all possible gains from rising prices have been reached. Their pessimism will infect those simple souls who had thought the market might go up forever but who will now change their minds and sell.

So it was in September and October 1929. Confidence seeped away, first gradually, and then a panic gripped the stock exchange, catastrophically. As investors began to sell and prices began to fall, brokers issued margin calls to their clients, demanding more cash as surety for their loans. This process encouraged further sales of stocks.

Two days are particularly identified with the crash. On 24 October

1929—Black Thursday—panic first really caught the market in its grip. The tide of selling was stemmed temporarily by 'organised support'— the big banks buying shares to prevent too drastic a fall in prices (for example, the activities of Charles Mitchell referred to above).

These activities only delayed the final disaster. 'Tuesday 29 October', writes Galbraith, 'was the most devastating in the history of the New York stock market': 16,400,000 shares changed hands—a record for nearly 40 years. Persistent selling virtually wiped out the quoted value of many companies. By 13 November, the low point of the year, the Dow Jones industrial average had fallen to 198.

Into slump

The collapse of the stock market was rapidly translated into general economic collapse. As we have seen, the industrial boom depended on the constant expansion of investment. Even the consumer durable industries depended heavily on credit, in the form of hire purchase. A major source of the funds necessary for the growth of investment was the stock market. Its collapse led to a general 'race for liquidity': those who had lent money now called in their loans. The fragile structure on which the boom had been founded collapsed.

Between 1929 and 1931 industrial production in the US fell by 28 percent. The number of unemployed rose in the same period from 129,000 to seven million, 16 percent of the working population. The wages of those still in employment fell by 39 percent. Prices fell by a little less (33 percent) so real wages were pushed down.

American capitalism soon pulled down the rest of the world in its wake. The Wall Street Crash forced American investors to recall their loans in Europe, especially Germany. The German economy was already slowing down before the crash, with nearly two million on the dole in the summer of 1929. Complete catastrophe was temporarily deferred, especially thanks to short term loans from Britain.

The slump was worsened, however, by US policies. The fall in foreign lending particularly affected agricultural countries which were already suffering from falling prices in their products before the slump. Now a vital lifeline—American credit—was cut off. In 1930 the US Congress increased its tariffs upon imported goods (the Smoot-Hawley Act). The American market was firmly closed to outsiders.

Moreover, President Hoover and his advisers, after initial hesitation, adopted a policy of strict laissez-faire. They believed that if they left the economy to its own devices it would, sooner or later, revive. In the short term, this meant drastic deflation—only through a series of bankruptcies and sackings could the economy right itself. So the administration balanced the budget, and refused to undertake public works designed to stimulate the economy. Their slogan as coined by treasury secretary Andrew Mellon was, 'Liquidate labour, liquidate stocks, liquidate the farmers, liquidate real estate.'

By 1931 this policy had come near to liquidating the American economy entirely. When Franklin Roosevelt replaced Hoover as president there were nearly 14 million unemployed in the US. All the banks in the country were closed to prevent people from withdrawing their deposits and thus destroying the financial system. Roosevelt's reaction was to take the dollar off the gold standard, permitting the value of the currency to fall, and thus rendering American exports more competitive.

By this time Europe had caught up with America. The Austrian bank Kredit-Anstalt, which had accumulated a large number of bad debts, filed for bankruptcy on 6 May 1931. The close links between Austrian and German banks led the ensuing withdrawal of funds by foreign investors (especially the French, who wanted to sabotage plans for an Austro-German common market) rapidly to spread to Germany. Soon the attack shifted to London in the light of large scale British lending to Germany.

Deflation spread across Europe. Heinrich Brüning, German chancellor from 1930, had already increased taxes and cut wages and public spending in an effort to satisfy his foreign creditors. By March 1931 there were 2.8 million more unemployed than there had been two years before.

The run on sterling in the summer of 1931 increased the demand for the British government to adopt similar policies. The recommendation of the May committee that the budget be balanced by cutting unemployment insurance (which had risen sharply after 1929 with the increase in the jobless) lent further force to this demand.

In August 1931 the Labour prime minister, Ramsay MacDonald, formed a coalition government with the Tories and introduced a budget which raised taxes and cut spending. Panic reaction to the news that sailors at Invergordon had mutinied against pay reductions forced sterling off the gold standard and led to a sharp devaluation of the pound.

Depression brought in its wake a surge in nationalism. Individual states attempted to close themselves off from the rest of the world economy. The American example led to an upsurge in protectionism as country after country imposed tighter import controls.

Nationalism was obviously greatly strengthened by the coming to power in Germany, in the wake of the slump, of the Nazis. Hitler introduced drastic state controls on the economy and launched an ambitious rearmament programme in order to lay the basis for the vast expansion of German imperialism of which he dreamed.

But liberals and 'democrats' added great force to the nationalist revival. President Roosevelt singlehandedly sabotaged the World Economic Conference of 1933 which was convened in the hope of stabilising currencies like sterling and the dollar.

'The sound economic situation of a nation is a greater factor in its well being than the price of its currency,' he told the conference. In other words, he was not prepared to abandon the competitive advantage offered American exports by a cheaper dollar if that was the price of world economic recovery.

J M Keynes, often regarded as the unheeded prophet whose policies could have prevented, or ended, the Great Depression, gave his full backing to these nationalist sentiments. He wrote an article entitled 'President Roosevelt is Magnificently Right' and lent his support to import controls.

He wrote in justification:

> I sympathise, therefore, with those who would minimise, rather than those who would maximise, economic entanglement between nations. Ideas, knowledge, art, hospitality, travel—those are things which should of their nature be international. But let goods be homespun whenever it is reasonably and conveniently possible, and, above all, let finance be primarily national.

'Let goods be homespun'. Such was the view, certainly, of the Tory dominated National government in Britain. From 1932 a policy of 'imperial preference' was adopted ie imports from Britain's colonies and the 'Dominions' (Australia, Canada, etc) were encouraged and the rest were kept out. In both Tory Britain and Democratic America the state intervened to restrict output, encourage monopoly and keep prices high.

The effect of this combination of deflation and protectionism upon the world economy was devastating. Between January 1929 and March 1933 the value of world trade fell from $2,998 billion to $999.2 million.

Recovery had to wait upon war. Roosevelt's New Deal policies of public spending helped stimulate a revival in the American economy. Slight at first, the revival led to a sharp increase in prices and production in 1936-37. The relapse into slump was equally sharp, as a drastic fall in government expenditure coincided with a decision by companies to run down the stocks of finished goods they had accumulated during the boom.

Between September 1937 and May 1938 industrial output in the US fell by 30 percent while unemployment rose by 22 percent. As Charles Kindleberger put it:

> The steepest economic descent in the history of the United States, which lost half the ground gained by many indexes since 1932, proved that the economic recovery in the United States had been built on illusion.

The spread of economic nationalism meant, however, that the main capitalist economies no longer moved in phase with each other. To quote Kindleberger again that, 'busy preparing for war, Europe and Japan suffered no more than a few sniffles' from the American recession of 1937-38.

The German and Japanese economies in particular, because of their rearmament programmes, continued to expand rapidly throughout the 1937-38 recession. British and American capitalism, however, returned to full employment only after the outbreak of the Second World War.

Could it happen again?

Both the boom of the 1920s and the slump which followed it were made possible by the development of the credit system. We have seen how easy credit—both via the stock market and in the form of hire purchase—made the top heavy expansion of American capitalism in the 1920s possible, and how US loans helped to prop up European capitalism.

Marx had shown many years before how credit makes the process of investment independent of the production and sale of commodities:

> Credit renders the reflux of the money form independent of the time of actual reflux both for the industrial capitalist and the merchant.

Firms can expand investment and production where they do not possess the internal resources for doing so by borrowing the necessary money. They use the money lent to them to purchase plant and equipment from other firms, thus promoting their expansion. The workers employed by the firms concerned spend their wages on consumer goods, adding to the social demand for these commodities. Hire purchase arrangements may enable them to borrow the money necessary to buy consumer durables, like cars.

Credit thus stimulates the overall growth of the economy. As such,

Marx argued that 'the credit system appears as the main lever of over-production and over-speculation in commerce'. The expansion of credit naturally gives rise to speculation quite unrelated to production of the sort characteristic of the stock market boom in the late 1920s.

Swindlers and crooks crawl out of the woodwork and are able to make fortunes thanks to the prevailing conditions of easy money and confidence. But the castles erected on the basis of this sort of specu-lation prove to be houses of cards. A crash is inevitable, sooner or later. Marx writes:

> In a system of production where the entire continuity of the repro-duction process rests upon credit, a crisis must obviously occur—a rush for the means of payment—when credit suddenly ceases and only cash payments have validity.

Such was 'the rush for liquidity' in October 1929 as creditors called in their loans and brokers increased their margins.

Marx's rounded judgement of the credit system was, therefore, as follows:

> The credit system accelerates the material development of the pro-ductive forces and the establishment of the world market... At the same time credit accelerates the violent eruption of...crises—and thereby the elements of disintegration of the old mode of production.

If the slump of the 1930s was precipitated by the credit system, its length is to be explained both by the disintegration of the world econ-omy and by what John Strachey called 'the dilemma of profits or plenty'.

The restoration of the rate of profit required wage cuts and cuts in government expenditure. Yet if this policy was pursued, as economists like Robbins proposed, demand for goods would be further depressed. The world economy stagnated on the horns of this dilemma. Only rearmament by guaranteeing profits on a 'cost-plus' basis and provid-ing firms with a safe market offered profitable avenues for investment.

The world economy in the late 1970s and early 1980s presents in many ways a different picture. Prices have continued to rise during the recession, rather than falling as was the case in the 1930s. At the same time, output and employment have not, as yet, fallen so drastically.

The principal reasons are twofold. First, arms expenditure remains at historically very high levels and is indeed rising. This prevents pro-duction falling too drastically. Second, the very close integration of the state and big capital today means that large scale bankruptcies tend to be prevented by government intervention.

At the same time the world monetary system is riddled with instability. Its most important source is the decline of American capitalism from the heights reached first in the 1920s and then again following the Second World War.

The weakened position of the American economy compared to its main competitors—notably Germany and Japan—underlies the decline of the dollar. Since the dollar is the world's main trading currency, and New York the chief financial centre, its gradual fall over the past two and a half years has sent ripples of fear throughout the rest of the world economy.

Huge American balance of payment deficits have pumped vast quantities of dollars into the world economy. Over $40 billion is held outside the US. The foreign holders of dollars have been led by its decline to move out of the currency. 'Diversification'—exchanging dollars for stronger currencies like the mark—helps to accelerate the decline of the dollar.

A further factor for instability is that many of the dollars held by interests outside the US have been lent, via the American banks, to various Third World countries. Worries about the dollar could mean an end to these loans, which have prevented economic collapse in many countries. And default by a major Third World debtor—say, Brazil—could bring the New York banks down with it.

The *Economist* commented recently:

> There has to be fear that on some black Tuesday the flight from the dollar
> could take wings, including maybe a flight by Americans out of their own
> currency. Heaven knows what would happen to world liquidity then.

Underlying the present recession is the low rate of return on capital throughout the main capitalist countries. As in the 1930s profitability is too low for capitalists to find it worth their while to invest.

Similar remedies are being touted. 'Monetarism', as practised by the Thatcher government, for example, is a modern version of deflation. Its effects are the same. The recent fall in Wall Street prices was occasioned by the decision of the Federal Reserve Board to impose a savage credit squeeze. Deeper recession is creeping throughout the Western economies as interest rates are forced up and government spending cut in an effort to restore the rate of profit.

The alternative offered by the left is too often also an echo of remedies which failed in the 1930s. The import controls advocated by Labour left wingers or Eurocommunists would, if implemented, simply lead to a further contraction of the world economy and further stimulate economic nationalism, fragmenting instead of uniting the world working class.

In the 1930s it was Nazi barbarism which profited from the failure of capitalism—and the failure of the workers' movement to provide an alternative. Barbarism in other guises lurks round the corner today—perhaps in the form of a renewed arms race with the threat of nuclear holocaust contained therein.

The task of socialists today is great—to encourage the resistance to capitalist attack in the here and now, while always recognising that only the world working class can offer a solution to the world crisis.

Chapter 30

The great Flint sit-in

Jim Scott

In February 1937 the United States working class won one of its decisive victories. The United Automobile Workers (UAW) forced the mighty General Motors (GM) to surrender and grant union recognition. The defeat of the biggest company in the massive motor industry was a breakthrough for trade union organisation among US workers.

Up to the 1930s the history of US unions was appalling. Despite the traditions of the International Workers of the World (the IWW, better known as 'the wobblies'), the major unions were concerned only to organise skilled workers.

Manufacturing plants, and indeed whole company towns, were run on the lines of police states. The bosses employed hordes of spies. They had their own private armies The local and state governments were theirs, bought and paid for. The penalty for organising was the sack and the blacklist—if you were lucky. If you weren't, you could be beaten up or even murdered by the company goons.

But all of these terror methods proved useless in the face of the new mood of anger and militancy which grew in the Great Depression. In industry after industry workers fought back and organised. The UAW was one of the new general unions which recruited all workers and which formed a new organisation—the Congress of Industrial Organisations (CIO).

There were no easy victories. Despite the pro-labour claims of the Roosevelt government, bosses and state machine went all out to stop the organising drive. Nowhere was the issue harder fought than at the heart of the GM empire, in the car plants in and around Detroit.

First published February 1982

On 3 January 1937, 200 delegates from all over GM met in Flint, near Detroit, to coordinate a campaign which had already got under way with a wave of sit-ins and disputes in Atlanta, Cleveland, Toledo, St Louis, Kansas City and Jamesville. They elected a 'board of strategy', including many left wing militants, among them Kermit Johnson, a leading militant at Flint. Their first action was to call a company wide strike and issue a series of demands, including union recognition, a signed contract, abolition of piecework, a 30 hour week, time and a half for overtime, the re-employment of victimised trade unionists, and control of the speed of the track.

The company was ready for them. The centre of the battle developed in Flint around the Fisher plants of GM. The rank and file workers were not content merely with striking. From the very start they struck and occupied the plants. The bosses responded by organising a vigilante force, the 'Flint Alliance', which was open to 'all citizens who wish to return to work and are against the strike'. The vigilantes, the police, and the company thugs dressed up as 'deputies' were quickly in action.

On 12 January the heat was turned off in Fisher Body No 2 plant and the cops attacked the pickets outside. They announced that no more food would be allowed into the plant. The intention was to let hunger and the bitter cold of the winter force the occupiers out. The workers responded by counter-attacking against the police and, in 12 hours of running battles, forced their way through with supplies of coffee and fresh bread. Casualties were high, with 14 strikers injured from gunshot wounds. But the sheriff lost his car and three police cruisers, and his men were finally driven off when high pressure fire hoses from inside the plant were turned on them.

The response to this great victory was a familiar one. The government acted quickly to bring together the employers and the union bureaucrats to hammer out a compromise.

The workers saw victory in their grasp. At the Fleetwood plant they marched out with bands playing and banners flying; at Fisher 1 and 2 they were halfway out of the plant when the news came that GM was also negotiating with the scab Flint Alliance. The victory demonstrations turned round and marched back into the plants, and rebuilt the barricades for a long fight.

By this time it was clear to the rank and file militants that they could not rely on the government or the trade union bureaucrats to win the fight. They needed to go on the offensive and close down more GM plants. But they had a problem. They knew by this time that the company had a spy in the local leadership and would thus be forewarned of any new move and deploy the cops to try to stop it. As a last resort, they organised a secret meeting to give the impression they were telling the 'most trusted' militants what their plans were.

The meeting took place by candlelight in the darkness of an occupied plant. Kermit Johnson recorded the scene:

> I laughed to myself and felt like a conspirator when I considered all the pretence we had gone through to organise a meeting for one despicable man, a stool pigeon. It seemed like a real dirty trick to dupe so many good men, but to make the big fish swallow the bait we had to have a lot of little fish nibbling. I was sure we had convinced the stool pigeon that at 3.30pm the workers at No 9 plant would stage a sit-in.

By the early afternoon of 1 February, Johnson knew the fish had bitten. The No 9 plant had been surrounded by police and deputies and several thousand workers were marching on the plant.

But it was all a diversion. The real plan was for other men to break into the unorganised No 4 plant, which was still working, link up with the hard core of union activists, stop the plant and occupy it. This the men inside the decoy plant did not know, and seeing thousands of workers fighting the cops outside, decided to try for an occupation anyway. The diversion grew in scale, with police firing teargas into the plant and the workers outside smashing windows to let in fresh air.

With the cops and the bosses fully occupied, the real fight started at Fisher No 4 plant. Johnson takes up the story:

> The door burst open and there was Ed! Great big Ed, his hairy chest bare to the belly, carrying a little American flag, and leading the most ferocious band of 20 men I have ever seen. He looked so funny with that tiny flag in comparison to his men who were armed to the teeth with lead pipes, metal bars and chunks of steel three foot long. It didn't take a mastermind to know that trying to strike a roaring plant of 3,000 men and machines with just 20 men was impossible. We huddled together and decided to send back for…reinforcements, and if that failed, to get the hell out of Chevrolet in a hurry. Luckily we were back with several hundred men in a short time.

The battle was not over; there would be two more weeks of confrontation and threats, but the heart of GM was stopped. With their major plants occupied and their workers in open revolt, they had to give way. And give way they did: on 11 February GM capitulated and signed a contract with the UAW. The victory echoed through the US. In the next month 193,000 workers were involved in sit-in strikes. By the end of 1937 one and a half million workers had struck for the right to organise. US unions were on their way.

Chapter 31

A dream distorted

Lee Sustar

With the passing of the 20th anniversary of the assassination of Martin Luther King Jr on 4 April, virtually every liberal Democratic Party politician in the US, black or white, will piously claim his legacy.

King's more patriotic speeches, particularly the 'I have a dream' speech at the 1963 march on Washington, have become part of American political mythology—even though two decades of recession, a sharp rise in black poverty and an upsurge in racist violence have turned the dream into a nightmare.

What nobody will mention is the fact that in the last few months before his assassination in 1968 King broke with Democratic president Lyndon Johnson over the Vietnam War and the administration's unwillingness to meet black demands in the North—a stand that few of today's black Democrats would be willing to take.

The reforms advocated by King were quite mild compared to the demands of radical black nationalists of the time. Nevertheless they were condemned by the Democrats who have since turned King into a symbol of black accommodation to the system.

In order to understand King's eventual shift to the left it is necessary to look at the class struggles that underpinned the civil rights movement and the nature of King's organisation, the Southern Christian Leadership Conference (SCLC).

When King emerged as leader of the Montgomery bus boycott of 1955-56 he was at the forefront of a local movement whose example was followed in dozens of other Southern cities in subsequent years. The SCLC was essentially made up of a group of professional middle

First published March 1988

class organisers who typically moved from city to city to lead struggles initiated by local black students, workers and farmers.

The SCLC's policy was not to help these activists develop independently, but rather to lead them into 'non-violent' confrontations with segregationists and the brutal cops who backed up the racist Jim Crow laws.

SCLC leaders such as Hosea Williams and Wyatt T Walker believed that the federal government would then be forced to intervene to stop the mayhem and to force the states into compliance with civil rights laws.

At first the strategy seemed to work. A Supreme Court decision supported the Montgomery boycott. President John F Kennedy introduced civil rights legislation after cops in Birmingham, Alabama, repeatedly attacked SCLC organised marches in 1963. Kennedy's bill became law a year later.

Bloody confrontations in St Augustine, Florida, and Selma, Alabama, prodded Kennedy's successor, Johnson, to push the Voting Rights Act of 1965 through Congress. Of course Kennedy and Johnson only supported civil rights when they believed it was necessary to stave off more militant black rebellion. They had no wish to alienate the powerful Southern 'Dixiecrat' senators.

King and the SCLC's protests could be tolerated as long as they remained 'non-violent' and were limited to fighting Southern legal segregation and did not address the discrimination against black workers in the North. Indeed, King constantly reaffirmed his faith in American 'democracy'.

By 1965 King's credibility among Southern activists was waning. The SCLC's habit of arriving in a town in the midst of a struggle, grabbing the media spotlight and negotiating a settlement irritated both local blacks and the increasingly radical Student Non-violent Coordinating Committee (SNCC), which was trying to help Southern blacks develop their own leadership.

Black nationalist Malcolm X mocked the idea of a 'civil rights revolution' and correctly argued that King's 'non-violence' needlessly exposed blacks to attacks by police and racist thugs.

While King did not join more conservative black civil rights leaders in attacking the 'Black Power' slogan as 'racist' he refused to support it on the grounds that it implied violence and would alienate potential white support. 'We've got to transform our movement into a positive and creative power,' he said when asked his opinion of Black Power advocate Stokely Carmichael.

To black militants King's stance was that of an 'Uncle Tom'; to

Democratic liberals, worried by the influence of black nationalist ideas and widespread black rebellions in Northern cities, King's position seemed a virtual endorsement of Black Power.

King realised he was trying to bridge an ever widening gap. 'The government has got to give me some victories if I'm going to keep people non-violent,' he said.

Since the Voting Rights Act of 1965 had abolished the last of the Southern Jim Crow segregation laws, King turned his attention to the North in 1966.

The SCLC was caught between big city Democratic machines and a growing number of black militants who demanded jobs and improvement to housing which, even without Jim Crow laws, was just as segregated as the South.

In Chicago King was outmanoeuvred by racist Mayor Richard Daley who extracted a promise from King to call off SCLC marches through all-white neighbourhoods. In return Daley promised only to pressure real estate developers to pursue open housing.

King was accused of selling out and black nationalist groups led the marches without him. King finally broke with the liberal establishment in April 1967 when he called on President Johnson to pull the US out of its 'colonial' war in Vietnam.

While a number of important Democratic senators had already turned against the war, most civil rights leaders admonished King and continued to support the administration. Liberal newspapers such as the *New York Times* and the *Washington Post*, which had been sympathetic to King, viciously attacked him for his anti-war stand.

In their view King's non-violent protest tactics and his support for the Democratic Party had been an important counterweight to the radicals in the Black Power revolt, his criticism of the war was therefore treachery.

Meanwhile a vengeful Johnson allowed the Federal Bureau of Investigation to step up its long term harassment of King and other SCLC leaders. The president was outraged at King's plans to lead a 'Poor People's March' on Washington to close down the capital.

While his influence had declined, King was often discussed as a potential third party protest candidate and would still have been popular enough to split the Democratic vote in the 1968 elections.

Yet King's break with the Democrats did not earn him the support of Northern blacks whose street rebellions swept every major city in the country. He was jeered by young black radicals when he lectured that the 'riots' of 1967 were a setback to the struggle.

The radicals correctly argued that King's criticism of the rebellions played into the hands of the cops and the racists who were the real source of inner city violence. Attacked from both left and right, King was forced to rethink his career and the SCLC. 'We must admit there was no limitation on our achievement' in the South, he told a meeting of the SCLC board in 1967. The SCLC would have to call for a 'radical redistribution of wealth and power', he said.

On several occasions King told his aides that the US needed 'democratic socialism' that would guarantee jobs and income for all. But SCLC staffers such as Andrew Young, Jesse Jackson and Ralph Abernathy, who spent a great deal of time squabbling among themselves, were hostile to the 'Poor People's March'.

Moreover, the SCLC's Southern field officers had been neglected during an ill fated attempt to organise in Chicago, and the group's Northern offices were even weaker. The SCLC's experience in using local activists to goad Southern cops into headline making melees did not prepare the group to organise the inter-racial 'poor people' and working class movement envisioned by King.

The plan also clashed with the 'black capitalist' orientation of the SCLC's Operation Breadbasket, directed by Jesse Jackson. 'If you are so interested in doing your own thing that you can't do what the organisation is structured to do, go ahead,' King said in response to Jackson's criticism of the march. 'If you want to carve out your own niche in society, go ahead, but for god's sake don't bother me!'

King's drift to the left was highly confused. While advocating 'democratic socialism', he also accepted Daniel P Moynihan's racist theory that a 'culture of poverty', rather than oppression, was the reason for much of black America's problems. And although women served on the SCLC staff, King ignored the growing women's liberation movement and believed that a woman's place was in the home.

Still, the far right asserted that King's Poor People's Campaign proved their long time claim that the SCLC leader was a 'Communist'. These elements, encouraged by the presidential campaign of segregationist Alabama Governor George Wallace, publicly threatened King's life.

Hostility from the Johnson administration, criticism from both black nationalists and the black establishment, and a divided staff had isolated King as never before when he was assassinated in Memphis on 4 April 1968—less than three weeks before the Poor People's Campaign was to begin.

King had travelled to Memphis to support a strike by black sanitation workers; he was the only national civil rights leader to do so. Yet it wasn't long after his death that the media hacks began to convert King into a harmless saint.

With the Black Panther Party emerging as a national force and the anti-war movement at high tide, King's reformism began to seem palatable to the employers. Since old guard civil rights groups such as the Urban League and the National Association for the Advancement of Colored People (NAACP) had lost credibility among black workers, the Democrats invoked King's activist, 'movement' image as it opened the doors to a new generation of black civil rights organisers who have since become elected officials in the nation's most important cities.

The success of the Democrats' strategy can be measured in the conservatism of former civil rights leaders such as Atlanta mayor Andrew Young and Washington DC mayor Marion Barry. Even as they administer austerity programmes and social service cutbacks, these black Democrats pose as the legitimate political successors to the movement led by King.

This claim is given a theoretical gloss by black sociologist Manning Marable, who calls the Jesse Jackson campaign a 'mass movement in electoral mode'—the continuation of the King movement. But that is sheer nonsense.

For all his vacillation King often did lead blacks into collective direct action in the 1950s and 1960s. This ultimately put him at odds with the state.

By contrast, the electoral strategy pursued by today's black Democrats actually demobilises black workers, fostering a political dependence on the same state machine that has presided over a massive decline in black living standards in the past 20 years.

While today's black politicians solemnly recall King, they make deals with the same Democrats who were happy to see him dead.

Chapter 32

Who was the real Malcolm X?

Gary McFarlane

The huge growth in interest about Malcolm X and his ideas reflects the fact that the racism which he confronted in his lifetime is still very much alive and prospering. The reality of everyday racism leads many blacks to look to him, and today Malcolm is held up as a hero of the struggle. But he is often praised by people Malcolm would have had great difficulty identifying as friends or allies. Indeed many of today's worshippers of Malcolm X played some part in 'contributing to the atmosphere' (in Louis Farrakhan's phrase) that led to his assassination.

In the 28 years since his death something of a consensus has emerged around Malcolm which seeks to canonise him as a role model for ghetto youth. The argument runs that his life shows how even the most downtrodden individuals can uplift themselves by their own strength of character and endeavour. For the *Wall Street Journal* he has become the 'conservative hero'. The *Guardian* in an editorial comment uses Malcolm's 'individual advancement' to make the case for the viability of reforming the system. Jesse Jackson headed up a meeting to commemorate the 25th anniversary of his assassination, hoping to bolster his credibility for his career with the US Democratic Party—the party Malcolm described as 'vultures sucking on our blood'.

Others like Douglas Wilder, governor of Virginia, are more honest: 'I think Thurgood Marshall was right when he said he never knew of anything Malcolm ever did and would not miss him if he had never lived.'

First published March 1993

But the bulk of the black establishment, represented by the moderates in the civil rights movement of the 1960s, now wish to appropriate Malcolm from a safe distance—to point to his transformation from petty criminal into the selfless leader of his people—but without mentioning the struggle of which he was a product.

This is possible only because of the collapse of the black movement in the 1970s, as the black middle class scooped up the fruits of the civil rights movement, leaving the mass of black people today as badly off as they were in the 1960s. The 'role model' view of Malcolm fits nicely for the black middle class that has been incorporated into running America's decaying cities, because it seems to justify the assertion that it's not social deprivation that is to blame for the hopelessness to be found in the ghettos, but instead the lack of 'moral rigour' among today's young black men.

Terry McMillan, a leading black writer in the US, says in the introduction to Spike Lee's book on the making of the film:

> I pray that when [my son] grows up he has a tenth of Malcolm's courage, insight and wisdom...he'll be interested in being a real man by making something out of himself and adding something to our community instead of being a burglar of black life.

Louis Farrakhan continues in a similar vein:

> The life of Malcolm is one of the most exemplary lives that shows the ability of our people to make the transition from ignorance to knowledge, aimlessness to purpose, in the span of one lifetime.

As part of the Nation of Islam's own attempt to attach themselves to Malcolm's legacy, Farrakhan hopes to bury the differences of the past with statements of affection. 'I loved Malcolm much more than words are able to describe... When Malcolm would be preaching, I would be scanning the rooftops.'

In the hands of both the black establishment and the Nation of Islam, Malcolm's ideals are being sanitised and much history is being rewritten. The truth is that when he lived Malcolm was a threat to the mainstream leaders of the civil rights movement because of his advocacy of self defence and black liberation by any means necessary, and to the leaders of the Black Muslims because of his advocacy of militant political activism.

Malcolm was attracted to the Nation of Islam because of its total rejection of 'white society'. The anger and disappointments that thousands of working class black people were beginning to feel with the 'non-violent' and moderate direction of the civil rights movement found a voice in Malcolm X. But the Muslims' rejection of whites was not the same as wanting to fight to rid the US of the system which bred racism.

The Black Muslims followed the well worn path of building towards economic independence and self reliance within the black community. The job of members was to convert more followers, not to engage in politics. Malcolm was in this organisation for 14 years and accepted the entirety of its very unorthodox approach to Islam. It was a very conservative organisation, insisting women were the property of men, and preaching a diet of hard work and clean living.

It was only when Malcolm broke with the Black Muslims, after his suspension for the speech which declared that 'the chickens have come home to roost' following the assassination of John Kennedy in 1963, that he began to really think for himself. Upon his return from pilgrimage to Mecca he revised many of his old ideas. Whites were now no longer all 'devils' from whom black people must separate. He began to see more clearly how the struggle of black Americans was part of a larger canvas in which other oppressed groups would also be fighting against the same enemy—the white capitalist ruling class. However, this did not mean that Malcolm was moving away from black nationalism. He was not, and he still saw the need for blacks to organise separately. Rather he was attempting to develop a more effective strategy.

The fact that Malcolm was responding to racism in his political development was deliberately blurred by people like Bayard Rustin (Martin Luther King's adviser) and Roy Wilkins (of the National Association for the Advancement of Colored People). Rustin wrote in March 1965, 'Malcolm is not a hero of the movement, he is a tragic victim of the ghetto.' Or again, 'Now that he is dead, we must resist the temptation to idealise Malcolm X, to elevate charisma to greatness.' Wilkins was scathing, insisting Malcolm was preaching 'a hate-white doctrine'. The NAACP's chief lawyer, Thurgood Marshall, said of the Muslims (while Malcolm was still a member) that they are 'run by a bunch of thugs organised from prisons and jails, and financed, I am sure, by Nasser or some Arab group.'

Nor did Malcolm get better treatment from the Nation of Islam. Elijah Mohammed, still the leader of the organisation in 1965, said of Malcolm's death, 'He seems to have taken weapons as his god. Therefore we couldn't tolerate a man like that. He preached war. We preach peace.' Before Malcolm was killed Louis Farrakhan's 'love' was expressed by the following threat:

Only those who wish to be led to hell or to their doom will follow Malcolm. The die is set, and Malcolm shall not escape... Such a man as Malcolm is worthy of death.

In later years, when the Black Panther Party explicitly took up Malcolm's ideas, it was the Nation of Islam, for example, that destroyed the Panthers' headquarters in Philadelphia.

The major reason for the competing claims to Malcolm's legacy is to be found within the core of his thought—namely his commitment to black nationalism. He still held to the notion that black unity and pride in our African descent were the most important precursors to struggle. As he put it himself:

In phase one, the whites led. We're going into phase two now. This place will be full of rebellion and hostility. Blacks will fight whites for the right to make decisions that affect the struggle in order to arrive at their *manhood and self respect*.

Many of his better speeches, which try to connect the struggle against racism with other oppressions, and which nail the capitalist system as the number one enemy, are more often than not in reply to interviewers from left wing organisations. This is not because Malcolm was dishonest but because his ideas were in a state of flux. They vacillated from the old Black Muslim beliefs to ones which were much more challenging to capitalist society. But he became a revolutionary in a very subjective fashion—events of the day and who he was talking to could pull him this way and that. This meant he never developed a clear or total understanding of how to fight the system.

The tragedy of Malcolm's life was that it was cut short as his ideas were developing. It is therefore much easier for all sorts of different people to claim him as their own. There are those today who praise Saint Malcolm but who did their utmost to isolate and vilify him in life. Following his death it wasn't a black newspaper or university that put Malcolm's speeches and writings into print, but Pathfinder Press, the publishing house of a small socialist organisation on whose platforms he had spoken in his last months.

A recent poll conducted for *Newsweek* magazine found that eight out of ten young black Americans consider Malcolm X a hero, and of those over 50, a third accord him hero status. Malcolm has not always been so regarded, especially in the years immediately after his death. Denzel Washington has admitted that he first heard of Malcolm X only 'ten or 11 years ago'. 'I grew up in Mount Vernon, New York [a middle class neighbourhood], and my father, Denzel, was a minister. I was in my 20s before I'd heard of Malcolm X.' There must have been many more like Denzel whose parents recoiled from Malcolm's message. And as Paul Gilroy (author of *Ain't no Black in the Union Jack*) has noted, in Britain young kids 'look back at Malcolm X from a position of absolutely stunning ignorance of the politics that spawned him.'

Millions of blacks and other oppressed look to Malcolm not out of clear identification with his politics but because he symbolises defiance and resistance to racism and white society.

Black and white socialists have to build on that defiance to develop revolutionary opposition to the system today. That doesn't mean pretending that Malcolm X's ideas were fully fledged socialist ideas. They were not. But nearly 30 years after his death, class divisions and the depth of the crisis are even more stark than in his lifetime.

Malcolm complained that black/white unity wasn't possible because whites wouldn't be welcomed 'uptown'. In Los Angeles in April 1992 they were!

The lesson of Malcolm's life, and even more of the great black struggles that followed his death, such as the Black Panthers and DRUM, is that black organisation alone can challenge and shake the system, but cannot win on its own. That requires unity of blacks and whites in a socialist organisation.

Chapter 33

The rebellion that rocked a superpower

Interview with Mike Davis, author of *City of Quartz*, after the LA uprising

How would you describe the uprising?

Even the *Los Angeles Times* editorially acknowledged the relationship between the globalisation of the LA economy, which has undermined employment structures in South Los Angeles, and the outbreak of the country's first modern multi-ethnic riot.

But I think there were, in a way, three separate kinds of social processes of revolt woven into the complex fabric of this riot.

First was Rodney King as a lightning rod for the accumulated grievances of youth in the streets in LA, who've only known a constant regime of brutality from the police, particularly from the mass sweeps, Operation Hammer, that have criminalised middle class black youth as well as street youth. Rodney King is the link in the consciousness of millions of people between the conditions in Los Angeles and the kind of crisis felt by African Americans everywhere in the United States, and even in Canada.

This crisis centres, as it has historically, on what is the meaning of black citizenship, given that the most ordinary democratic demands aren't addressed or provided by white society. It has that kind

First published June 1992

of revolutionary, democratic content.

Secondly, however, although the outburst began directed against whites and against the police, the brunt of the destruction, at least the property damage, and also some of the deaths from the riot, was directed towards the Korean community. The Korean community is the middleman community between people in the ghetto, black and Mexican, and big capital.

The name you heard most frequently on people's lips during the uprising was Latisha Harlins, the 15 year old black girl killed by a Korean shopowner over a $1.79 bottle of orange juice last March.

The shopkeeper was convicted, but let off with a $500 fine and some community service, a much lighter sentence than homeless people arrested for curfew violations, who have to spend ten days in jail, or somebody who looted some sunflower seeds, who may get two years in jail.

So Latisha Harlins was a kind of rallying cry, but Korean shopkeepers have come to represent everything the international Pacific Rim economy has done to South Central LA. The disappearance of local jobs under foreign competition, racist remarks by Japanese ministers— all of that has kind of coalesced together with the sense that black customers are usually treated either rudely or impolitely by Korean store owners.

Unlike the Jewish store owners that they replaced, they don't employ black youth. So the result has been a kind of catastrophic collapse of any relations between the black and Korean communities. Something like 2,000 Korean stores have been looted or destroyed.

The third aspect which is apparent to anyone looking at the images, but which never until the last moment did the news commentators grasp, is that from the beginning of the looting, it turned into a kind of postmodern equivalent to traditional bread riots—an uprising of the poor. In many places it was totally good humoured, indeed almost like a carnival.

People looted sometimes for luxury goods, but on the whole they were just looting the necessities of life. And to understand why this occurred on the scale that it did, involving as many poor Salvadorean and Mexican immigrants as African Americans, you need some understanding of the impact of two years of recession in Los Angeles, which has cut most deeply into the ranks of new immigrants.

Unemployment has tripled. People are homeless or crammed together, several families in a single house. It's a real crisis of life, probably the worst social emergency in the county of LA since the Depression. Last Christmas 20,000 Latina mothers and their kids stood around all night in the cold just to get a turkey and some blankets. County welfare loads have doubled and tripled over the last year.

But by and large the media as well as the political leadership has refused to talk about this as the crisis it really is, above all because these Mexican and Salvadorean immigrants—who, far more than aerospace engineers, represent the victims of the recession—don't have any political power. By and large, they don't tend to vote.

What you saw was this new immiseration translated into looting.

What about the truce that has emerged between the two major black gangs, the Crips and the Bloods?

The event here was really complex. Also, it involved something else which I think is enormously important and positive, the suspension of gang warfare. Something that a lot of people would have thought to have been impossible has occurred and it is deepening into processes of political discussion and mobilisation, into defining permanent truces, on a local level in Inglewood and Watts, and now spreading throughout the city.

The cultural transmission and impact of this, particularly through the hip hop rap scene, will be enormous. What it is doing is taking away a lot of the lustre of the tough street gangster and substituting an image of black unity, of black power.

A lot of the gangs are talking about not just Crips and Bloods, but Crips, Bloods plus Mexicans. You're seeing an enormous reassertion, no matter how temporary a truce this may be, of an identity of being black freedom fighters, or being a black liberation movement. Of course, its ideological horizons are Farrakhan and the Nation of Islam, Farrakhan being the one national political figure that any of the gang kids I've talked to or heard speak make any allusion to.

In Inglewood, under the auspices of a local mosque, all the local gangs, rival Crips and Bloods, spoke before the local media. In a sense, they were not speaking to the media, but using the white media to speak to the black community to transmit some of their hurt and anger about the fact that none of the elder leadership, with the possible exception of Representative Maxine Waters, had recognised the riot as the rebellion it was.

They said, 'Look, we're trying to be black men and do the things you accused us of not doing, struggling to defend the community and to take care of women and children and be freedom fighters. This is a slave rebellion like other slave rebellions in black history. We're proud of what we've done.'

The overall strategic purpose of the rebellion was to make not just the white power structure, but also the black leadership, hear the voices of criminalised black youth.

The other night there was a meeting of between 600 and 700 Crips and Bloods to make peace in Watts. The police came with SWAT teams and arrested 50 or 60 people, which normally would have been a provocation to riot. But people were extremely cool and basically said, 'We'll deal with the pigs later, but the key thing now is to establish peace between ourselves, to put the war on hold.'

This incident just proves that what has happened is not in any sense an aberration. It's a quite extraordinary thing. Even if for some reason the truce were to break and some gangs go back to fighting, the residue would be an awful lot of kids who I don't think would go back to the gang banging scene, but now see themselves, in some sense, as rebels or freedom fighters.

Can you explain more how the rebellion forged unity between blacks and Latinos?

Blacks in Los Angeles County are in the process of going from the largest minority to being the third largest. Eventually in all of California Latinos will be the largest group, although not a majority. Blacks, traditionally the second largest group in the state, will find themselves in the fourth position—Latinos first, then Anglos, then Asians, then blacks.

The black community is gripped with a sense of the possible decline of its political and economic gains so hard won over the last generation. The Latino community lag far behind everyone else in political representation and jobs in proportion to their numbers.

So there has been a lot of friction between blacks and Latinos. Particularly, there have been a lot of fights and riots between blacks and Latinos in prisons.

At the beginning of this uprising some Latinos were attacked and brutally beaten. But the major aspect of it, particularly on the east side of the ghetto, which is totally mixed—black and Latino—and where every Latino kid has a black friend and vice versa, was that the looting was totally bi-racial.

And there is a broad interface between black youth culture and Latin youth culture. Kid Frost, the leading Chicano rapper, has totally identified with the rebellion. A famous local group of Samoan rappers have said that the rebellion was great, but said it should have been directed from the Korean stores to the rich people in Beverly Hills.

This is very important, because this will transmit itself to inner city youth all over the country, with these new images of black power and militant unity of inner city kids. The celebrity of gangs is gone and the celebrity of rebellion is in.

I suppose in its most extreme form, which must be the nightmare of the LAPD, it is some version of a kind of urban black *intifada* in the United States, which is why right now there is tremendous repression going on.

How have the authorities responded?

About 17,000 people are in jail. Federal prosecutors have particularly targeted gang youth because they are most worried about their role and their potential politicisation in the uprising.

The mass arrests really began not at the height of the looting, but the day after, on Friday 1 May. People were arrested for scavenging in burnt ruins. Curfew violators were often homeless street people or Latino immigrants who don't speak English and didn't know of the curfew. Increasingly, they've been arresting people in their homes, for possession of loot or receiving stolen goods.

You've had this enormous military occupation, not just by the National Guard or police from all over California, but by rapid deployment infantry from Fort Ord and the marines who landed in Compton. The city has been subjected to regular mass sweeps through black and Latino neighbourhoods.

In the area in which I live on the edge of MacArthur Park, the largest Central American community in the country, you had the Border Patrol brought in from as far away as Texas. Possibly as many as 500 people have already been immediately deported to Mexico.

People who weren't charged, but who were picked up during the riot, were just deported. So people in the neighbourhood are talking about 'desaparecidos' [the disappeared], just like back home in El Salvador.

They're throwing the book at people, demanding maximum sentences. They're not plea bargaining—totally different from what they did in 1965 [during the Watts rebellion], making crimes which would normally be small misdemeanours into felonies.

It's clear now—and I don't think this is well understood across the country—that really the prosecution of all this is becoming federalised. The Bush administration has had a direct hand in it. The idea is to make an example of people here.

At the moment the single most important thing is to struggle against this repression. People who violated curfew should just be released immediately. People who looted or committed arson should be given some kind of community service like the grocer who killed Latisha Harlins, and their criminal records expunged. They shouldn't be put in jail.

So many of these people were mothers who were stealing milk and so on. In some parts of the community I talked to people who said, 'Look, I looted there because after all the stores were burned out, and the crowds were looting the grocery, I realised that if we were going to have any food for the next few days, I better go in and get some.'

These are the kind of people who are facing a maximum of two years in prison.

How have middle class organisations in the minority communities responded?

The mainstream Latino leadership barely said anything during the event. Now that Latino participation has been recognised and much commented on, you have Republicans talking about deportations and nativist politics have heated up. There have been two different reactions.

People like Antonio Rodriguez of MALDEF (Mexican American Legal Defence and Education Fund) have accepted that, 'Look, this was a Latino riot too. People did it because they were hungry,' and have taken a stance of defending people.

Some right wing Latino leadership like the group News of America, which is headed by Julian Nava, the former US ambassador to Mexico, tried to blame it on Central Americans. They weren't Mexicanos [immigrants from Mexico], and above all they weren't Chicanos [people of Mexican descent born in the US], but they were these *declassed* refugee Salvadoreans.

So there's a use of almost racist imagery against Salvadoreans. The single most depressed and powerless group in the city is the Central American community.

The black community's political leadership, unfortunately, have mostly embraced Pete Ueberroth, the Republican millionaire, as a white knight and a saviour. They think that Ueberroth alone, because of his role in the Olympics and so on, can generate the kind of confidence required for banks and insurance companies to allow reinvestment in the black community.

At the same time, some black leaders think there's a silver lining to all of this— that the burned out Korean stores could become black businesses, that maybe black business can replace ethnic Asian business in the community. To the extent that this became an explicit goal, it further outraged the Koreans, who are a very stereotyped community.

The Korean community has its ferociously right wing elements— there were former KCIA [Korean Central Intelligence Agency, the South Korean secret police] guys running around with AK47s shooting at crowds. But it also has a very democratic and progressive wing as well.

So the Korean community is stuck in this middleman position facing all the anger generated out of not only racism, but out of de-industrialisation and the new industrial peonage in South LA. It is the middleman community between that and Pacific Rim capital downtown, which wasn't touched at all.

How did race and class interact? What about whites who were involved in protesting at the King verdict and the looting?

The history of the 1960s was compressed into a few days. These events have produced an enormous manifestation of solidarity across the country.

In the Bay Area several thousand people have been arrested. But here it brought kids out of high schools. It brought an incredible mixed crowd laying siege to Parker Centre [the police headquarters]. We've had hundreds of demonstrators arrested totally illegally. They even had to dismiss the charges against them.

So another of the positive things has been the crystallisation of a much broader multi-ethnic left or progressive, anti-racist movement. There have been demonstrations on the West Side [mostly white, middle class areas near the University of California at Los Angeles].

It really has forced people to take a stand. It has really reinvigorated left and oppositional politics in the city. I think the point has been taken by some of the youths in black communities, who have seen this, and also by the fact that, like at Parker Centre, there was a tremendous outpouring of people from some of the Latino housing projects.

One housing project alone sent more than 50 people down to demonstrate. That was in sharp contrast to the failure of the Latino leadership even to speak out on Rodney King.

In terms of the relationship between race and class, it's complex. In this dynamic there are different kinds of ways to go. One dead end would just be to embrace the kind of black capitalist aspect of Farrakhan, which some of the gang youth have bought into temporarily, rather than seeing the enormous social power which resides in the unity of black, Latino and, indeed, Asian poor in the city.

This was a kind of experience of power. That of course cuts both ways. For a few days thousands of ordinary people here could feel the power of rage, could feel that they had some social power in the city.

On the other hand, in the re-establishment of so called order here, the LAPD has got its own back. At the top it remains totally demoralised and in chaos because of its failure to protect small businesses and the white community.

The white middle class is divided. A lot of people individually came out in support of the black community. But I think by and large you're going to see a huge backlash. The tentacles of this revolt penetrated such inner sanctums as the Beverly Centre, Westwood Village and so on. The crowd that looted in Beverly Hills was multi-racial.

The white middle class doesn't make any distinction. It just sees one demonic mob coming towards it and its property. People's reactions were hysterically far fetched. Thousands of people fled the county. They went into exile like the aristocrats leaving Paris during the revolution. They sat around the swimming pools in Palm Springs listening to the radio to find out if Beverly Hills had been burned down or not.

What does the LA rebellion mean for the future?

In 1965 LA prefigured the 100 rebellions in 1967 and 1968. A lot of us thought that by the 1970s the paramilitarisation of the police was so formidable that riots couldn't happen, that people would just be shot down. Well, one thing that this riot has proved, even with the enormous repression that's occurred, is that people can stand up and rebel, and did so to an extraordinary degree and gained control of the inner city.

You're getting a weird thing now of people who condemned the Rodney King decision acting as if the police should have shot looters.

Once the riot got started, it spread with great rapidity. By that time so many people were taking part in it and it was happening over such diverse terrain in so many different parts of the city—from gays in Hollywood to Latinos in MacArthur Park and so on—that it couldn't be controlled without militarisation, or by police firing into crowds.

On the other hand, you'll see now the lesson learned from this may be not to wait three or four days but to have the equivalent of rapid deployment forces in the US. You would have federal anti-riot, anti-insurgent stocks that could be moved in almost immediately into our cities. LA was a rehearsal.

What will be its impact around the country?

I think it spurs revolt. It emboldens people to rebel. It sharpens the sense of injustice. It presents people with the image of black and brown and other groups united with class and racial anger.

In LA itself the biggest contradiction of the revolt was the attack on the Korean community. You might be able to justify attacks on specific racist merchants and so on, but there is a kind of logic behind this, a kind of Farrakhan like logic, that I think a progressive or socialist would find totally unacceptable.

All unorganised rebellions tend to have their negative or contradictory elements. But the overwhelming thrust of this, which has been enormously positive, has been that a generation has found that it can fight back.

I think that's very exciting. But people have to understand, as Regis Debray once said, that the revolution revolutionises the counter-revolution. And I think, particularly on the national level, they're going to learn how to be more effective and immediate in responding to these.

How would you situate the LA uprising in the broader world political and economic context?

If *International Socialism* wrote about this in England, they would probably call attention to the kind of context in terms of the Pacific Rim economy. The recession in LA, in fact the recession internationally, is specifically focused on the West Coast and in Japan.

In larger terms, this outbreak is part of the structural crisis of the Pacific Rim oriented regime of accumulation. Connections should be made between the meltdown of the Japanese stock exchange and the uprising in LA and the kind of destabilisation of that sector of world capitalism that's been the main engine of growth for the last decade. These events in LA have many important contexts which need to be analysed, none of which should be overlooked when trying to assess their political meaning.

International

Chapter 34

The Jewish question

Ann Rogers

Bad history exists about every sphere of human experience. But more bad history has been written about the Jewish question than perhaps anything else.

Those who want to justify racism, or argue that there is an inherent 'religious spirit' in human beings; those who wish to say that ideas can remain unchanged even when material circumstances change have all used the persecution of Judaism as evidence.

Luckily for us this long tradition of mystification and misinformation produced a response which must stand as one of the best works of Marxist history written this century, Abram Leon's *The Jewish Question—A Marxist Interpretation*.

Leon was a Jewish Trotskyist who wrote his masterpiece at the age of 24. This would be astounding enough, but he also wrote it in Nazi occupied Belgium, where he was a leading member of an underground Trotskyist group. It was a dangerous life, which proved to be short. Leon died in Auschwitz in 1944.

He set out to prove that the continued existence of a Jewish culture had nothing whatsoever to do with religion, racial characteristics or any other 'idealist prejudices'. Instead it could be explained by the particular economic roles which the Jews had played first in the ancient world and then under feudalism.

His project was to make concrete Marx's proposition: 'We will not look for the secret of the Jew in his religion but we will look for the

First published February 1986

secret of the religion in the real Jew.' In carrying out this task Leon not only provides us with fascinating information about the Jews, he also gives us a practical lesson in the Marxist method. At every stage ideas, religious persecutions and pogroms are explained in terms of the economic development of society.

Leon argues that, back in ancient times, the geographical position of Palestine forced its inhabitants to become traders and merchants. Thus the fame of the Jewish trader was nothing to do with Jewish culture and everything to do with the material condition of Palestine in the ancient world.

In addition, the ancient slave economies such as Rome forbade whole layers of the population from engaging in trade. For example members of the Roman aristocracy were forbidden to own trading ships.

Thus the Jews occupied a position distinct from that of the indigenous population. In an agricultural society they were carrying out a separate and different economic activity—that of trade.

In a society based primarily on production for need, on use values, they were engaged in the marginal economic activity—the exchange of goods.

As the Roman Empire declined the dominant economic mode of society changed. Ancient slave society gave way to feudalism and production shifted to the great landed estates in the countryside:

> The great proprietors, more and more reduced to living on the products of their own lands, were interested in replacing slave labour with the colony system which resembled the system of serfdom in the Middle Ages.

But the beginnings of the feudal epoch had one important similarity with the Roman Empire as far as the role of the Jews was concerned.

Feudalism, like ancient slave society, was still a mode of production based on use values rather than exchange values. Indeed trade played an even more marginal role in early feudalism than in ancient society. Under the Roman Empire one million Jews lived in and largely ran the great trading port of Alexandria. Such great centres of trade simply ceased to exist under feudalism.

But the Jews prospered. They did so because they became, not just one of various groups to make their living by trade, but the only significant trading group in the whole feudal world. And the goods which Jewish merchants brought into the feudal west were of great importance to the feudal monarchs. Because of this, Jews occupied a privileged place in society.

For a long period they were the only economic link between the East and West. In a society dominated by agricultural production for immediate consumption Jews both brought luxury goods from the Orient and lent the money they made to the rulers of Europe.

This activity of moneylending, or usury, may have been marginal to the dominant mode of production, but it was indispensable. Leon says:

> Only the merchant has the necessary cash for the rich noble wastrel... When the king has to assemble an army immediately and the normal revenue from taxation is inadequate, he is compelled to go to the man with the cash. When the peasant...can no longer meet his obligations...he must borrow his requirements from the usurer. The treasury of the usurer is therefore indispensable to a society based on a natural economy.

Thus under early feudalism the Jews were different from the mass of Christian agricultural society. But they were not persecuted on any systematic scale. They were too important to society for society to risk their destruction.

But from within the bosom of feudal society, a new form of production began to appear. It was this economic form which was to deprive Jews of their economic importance to society.

Production for exchange grew up in a number of medieval cities during the 11th century. This development was eventually to undermine the whole of feudal production, for in it was the seed of the capitalist class. Unlike the Jewish traders before, these embryo capitalists did not just engage in commercial activity, they also began to take control of production. Leon says:

> The development of native production makes possible the rapid formation of a powerful class of native merchants. Emerging from the artisans, they gain control over them by taking over the distribution of raw materials. Contrary to trade as conducted by the Jews, which is clearly separate from production, native trade is based essentially on industry.

It was the growth of this merchant class, first in Venice and Flanders, then spreading throughout Europe, that led to the persecution of the Jews. The Jews' former role was usurped and the rising new class found itself in conflict with the Jews. Leon says:

> This native commercial class collided violently with the Jews, occupants of an outmoded economic position inherited from a previous period in historical evolution.

It is from this period that we begin to see pogroms and expulsions of Jews. Spain, France, Britain and many German states all engaged in large scale expulsions of Jews. The Jews' economic importance died with feudalism, but feudalism was a long time dying. Leon says:

> In the beginning the economic transformation reaches only important urban centres. The seignorial domains are affected very little by this change and the feudal system continues to function there. Consequently the career of Jewish wealth is still not ended.

Not ended, but different. Expelled from trade, the Jews turned wholly to moneylending. But this in its turn was undermined. For the great merchants, the Medicis in Florence or the Fuggers in Augsburg, began to set up their own banks, banks which did far more than mere money lending to overstretched aristocrats. The new banks poured money into the growing industry in the towns, and they reaped the profits. The Jewish moneylenders were pushed more and more to the margins: 'The Jew became a petty usurer who lends to the poor.'
As Leon puts it:

> Above all the Jews constitute historically a social group with a specific economic function. They are a class or more precisely a people-class.

Leon correctly points out there was nothing unusual about this in the ancient world, based as it was on a rigid division of labour which was written into law. It was common for groups of foreigners to perform economic functions forbidden to the local population.

When Jews dropped their special economic role they frequently dropped the Jewish religion and culture as well. Judaism held together as a distinct culture when the economic role of the Jews remained marginal to the dominant mode of production. Where the economic activity of the Jews was the same as that of the wider society, as in the Jewish farming communities of North Africa or the pastoral tribes of Arabia, they quickly became assimilated. As Leon says:

> Only the Jewish communities with a clearly defined commercial character...proved capable of resisting all attempts at assimilation.
>
> The law of assimilation might be formulated as follows: wherever the Jews cease to constitute a class they lose, more or less rapidly, their ethnical religious and linguistic characteristics; they become assimilated.

This degeneration of the Jews' role gave new reason for anti-Semitism. Anti-Jewish pogroms were frequently the attempt of desperate peasants to burn the moneylenders' letters of credit, the only evidence that the peasant owed money.

Pogroms were one outcome of the degeneration of the Jews' role; emigration and assimilation were others. Jews emigrated to the new world as plantation owners and farmers. They then became Christians. By the 19th century there were no longer more than a handful of Jews in South America, for example, where there had been large scale emigration a century before.

In Western Europe Jews began to assimilate. Having no distinct economic role any more the existence of the Jews as a distinct social group was gradually undermined. But in Eastern Europe, especially in Poland, a very different process took place. Long after industry began to develop in the West the societies of Eastern Europe remained based on a feudal economy. They represented an area in which Jews could continue to carry out their traditional economic role. Leon says:

> This situation lasted as long as the social and political organisation in Poland remained static. In the 18th century…Polish feudalism found itself fatally stricken. Along with it the secular position of the Jews in eastern Europe was shaken to its foundations. The Jewish problem, close to vanishing in the west, flared up violently in eastern Europe. The flame, close to extinction in the west, received renewed vitality from the conflagration which arose in the east.

Jews fleeing from persecution emigrated to western Europe and America. In the heartlands of capitalism they ceased to occupy a distinct role and were therefore under pressure to assimilate. But they were moving into a system which had discovered the usefulness of racism in dividing the working class.

It was from this tension that Zionism came. Leon makes light work of all those who argue that the idea of a Jewish state was always central to Judaism, saying, 'Why during those 2,000 years have not the Jews really tried to return to this country [Palestine]?' He points out that previous advocates of a return to Palestine had been fiercely persecuted by orthodox Judaism. The answer, says Leon, lies in the changed position of Jews within wider society:

> In reality just so long as Judaism was incorporated into the feudal system, the 'dream of Zion'…did not correspond to any real interest of Judaism. The Jews of 16th century Poland thought as little of returning to Palestine as does the Jewish millionaire in America today.

Leon argued that even if a Jewish state could be set up it would provide no solution to the Jewish question. He predicted:

> The formation of a Jewish state, that is to say a state placed under the

complete domination of English or American imperialism, cannot naturally be excluded... But in what way will the existence of a small Jewish state in Palestine change anything... Admitting even that all the Jews in the world were today Palestine citizens, would the policy of Hitler have been any different?

Leon argued that Zionism was an attempt to solve the Jewish question without getting rid of capitalism. This was to try and turn the clock of history backwards. For 'capitalism destroyed feudal society and with it the function of the Jewish people-class. History doomed this people-class to disappearance.'

By this process capitalism created the Jewish question, for, without their special economic role, Jews were subject to persecution and pogroms. But capitalism proved incapable of solving the Jewish problem. Indeed it made a virtue of its insolubility by using anti-Semitism as a weapon to weaken class struggle.

Capitalism lay at the heart of the persecution of the Jews. But it also laid the basis for their liberation. For as Jews ceased to occupy a distinct economic role in society their fate became bound up with others who were struggling against capitalism.

Leon argues that it is only by carrying that struggle through to its conclusion that the plight of Jews can be overcome:

When the people of the factories and the fields have finally thrown off the yoke of the capitalists, when a future of unlimited development opens up before liberated humanity, the Jewish masses will be able to make a far from unimportant contribution towards the building of a new world.

This is a conclusion which can apply not just to the Jews but to all the oppressed groups in the world. It sums up what we mean when we say that socialism means freedom.

Chapter 35

Under Stalin's shadow

Clare Fermont

Anyone with even the slightest interest in the Middle East and its political movements will be enthralled by *A Man Apart: the Life of Henri Curiel* by Gilles Perrault. Centred on the life and mysterious death of the Communist Henri Curiel, the book is a gripping journey through Egypt's history and its struggles in the decades up to independence.

Curiel was an Egyptian Jew, the son of a millionaire, who became an influential figure in both the Egyptian and Sudanese Communist movements. In 1978 he was assassinated in Paris, probably by the OAS [the extreme right wing terrorist organisation opposed to Algerian independence]. His life as an activist and the hunt for his killers are threaded through the real investigation — the complex story of Egypt's development and the problems facing Communists trying to organise in a colonised country under the shadow of Stalinism.

Through vivid descriptions, the harsh realities which drove thousands to rebel are brought to life. Cairo, its streets filled by the mass of humanity, its houses bursting at the seams, groans at the rapid influx of first generation workers who still have 'the red earth of the Delta clinging to their shoes'. The overcrowded slums spill over into the cemeteries:

> Each family vault squatted by a large family, huts flourishing between the tombs, washing on the line, cooking pots out in the open and chattering swarms of children playing knucklebones over the bones of the dead.

First published January 1988

Woven into this background is a fascinating account of the faltering attempts of the Egyptian left to influence history. Although it is distorted by the author's adoration of Curiel, whose Stalinism he reflects, the book is so rich in detail and conflicting views that it gives a valuable insight into a fledgling Communist movement trying to grapple with the popular fight for national liberation and the small but growing working class struggle.

In February 1946 Cairo flares up after an anti-British demonstration is fired on. Committees spring up to organise the fight. The Communists are at the helm—everyone agrees on that. A mass mobilisation and general strike are called:

> On the morning of 21 February, Egypt is completely paralysed by the strike. A lifeless country. Then, in the afternoon, the towns, like a heart coming back to life, begin to throb with the heavy, dull pulsation of the footsteps of hundreds of thousands of demonstrators.

Sadly, the leadership did not understand that the struggle had to be taken further. As Curiel admitted:

> At the time it could be said that the masses were still ready to follow us. But we no longer knew where to lead them: we were completely inexperienced.

But it wasn't just lack of cadre that led to defeat. Through all the twists and turns, the national question took priority over class conflict, constantly leading the movement into splits, confusion and humiliating defeats.

There are many examples: the tragedy of Communists wasting away in Nasser's prisons while supporting their gaoler as a national hero; the splits over the formation of Israel; the confusion over which side to take in the Second World War—all are clearly exposed by the telling of the story, rather than by the analysis. The same applies to the appalling record of advice given by the Moscow led Communist movement, particularly the French Communist Party's 'Colonial Office'.

In addition to these little recorded moments of Egyptian history, there are many bonuses. One is the description of the large Jewish community's experiences in Egypt. The book shows how anti-Semitism was unknown until Zionists imported it through propaganda and bombings to promote emigration to their newly won state. Egyptian Jews until then had felt not the slightest need of another home:

> We couldn't understand why oriental Jews of European origin, the

Ashkenazis, were making such a fuss about Palestine. For us, Jerusalem simply meant the 9.45 train from Cairo station.

There is much, much more packed into *A Man Apart* and it is all in a style that is at once accessible, informative and rich in colour. I highly recommend it.

Chapter 36

Forced to the front

John Rose

The cynical manipulation of Jews frightened of a growth of anti-Semitism in Europe by the leaders of the US and Israel could not have been more obvious than in recent months.

Jews from the USSR are being forced into the frontline of a new struggle to remove Palestinians from their homes.

Jews have long been persecuted in Eastern Europe and the USSR. Anti-Semitism was an unspoken policy of the old Stalinist rulers. Now the failure of Gorbachev's perestroika to deliver concrete improvements has led to a renewed rise in anti-Semitism in the shape of the fascist Pamyat organisation.

Increased numbers of Jews from the USSR therefore want to use the opportunity created by Gorbachev's relaxation of emigration controls in order to flee this threat.

This would create no problem, were it not for a change in US immigration rules designed specifically to frustrate their attempt to find a better life.

The vast majority of Jews leaving the USSR have no desire to go to Israel at all. Of the people who had visas in 1988 to go to Israel, 92 percent ended up in the US instead.

All this has been changed by a decision of US president Bush last September to redirect the flow of Jews away from the US. Strict limits were placed on the number of entrants.

This move was bound to increase the numbers forced to go to Israel and had long been urged by extreme right wing Zionists. The plan had originally been put to President Reagan by Israeli president Shamir in 1987.

First published July 1990

The restriction is a direct attack on the rights of Jews to a relatively safe home. It was also always bound to create an explosive new element in the Middle East. Bush understood this, and so tried to keep the decision under wraps.

The *New York Times* reported on 3 September:

> A State Department document says that the administration hopes to 'avoid Congressional hearings and legislation' on the issue [and that] the plan was developed secretly by a group of officials from the State Department, the FBI and the CIA.

Now the effect is being felt in the Occupied Territories, with a new push to force Palestinians out of their homes.

This push is being backed by the new Israeli government, formed out of the right wing Likud coalition and various small parties drawn from the extreme right wing.

The new government plans to 'transfer' hundreds of Palestinians out of the Occupied Territories in Gaza and the West Bank and set up settler camps for the influx of Soviet Jews. 'Transfer' inevitably means terrorising the Palestinians out of their homes.

At the time of this article's writing, Ariel Sharon, the man responsible for the massacres of Palestinians in Beirut in 1982, is being seriously considered as minister of housing.

The new government has put sufficient pressure on the US to force it to break off talks with the PLO for the time being. The US strategy of trying to talk to non-PLO Palestinians, and of roping in Arab regimes to some form of peace process, will continue, however.

Shamir's government has rejected all this and thrown the relationship between the US and Israel into crisis.

Yet, while the Israeli leaders are clearly capable of taking decisions which conflict with US interests, it is US sponsorship which lies behind the existence of Israel as its local watchdog.

Whatever the final effect on relations between the US and Israel, the whole episode is a cruel illustration of the way imperialism uses anti-Semitism to strengthen the hand of its Zionist agent in the Middle East.

The tragedy is that most of the Soviet Jews did not want to go to Israel. Now between 100,000 and 200,000 of the two to three million Jews in the USSR are expected to emigrate to Israel in the next three years. Obviously the numbers depend on the level of anti-Semitism in the USSR and the level of resistance.

We've heard a great deal about Pamyat recently. Dangerous as it is, its immediate threat should be kept in perspective: the candidates it supported only polled 5 percent in the recent local elections.

We've heard much less about the levels of resistance.

All Jewish publications report a tremendous outburst of Jewish cultural activities. The genuinely radical forces recognise this and want to relate to it. The Popular Fronts in Georgia, the Ukraine, and the Baltic states openly defend Jewish interests and have Jewish sections.

In the huge demonstration in Moscow earlier this year, there were explicit slogans against anti-Semitism. Pamyat named 5 May this year 'Pogrom Day', the day of Saint George, the hero of Russian Christians. Nothing happened. Certainly Boris Kagarlitsky and the New Socialists do not see Pamyat as a serious threat at present. Kagarlitsky—himself of Jewish origin—reports that when at a miners' meeting where he was speaking a Stalinist official hinted that a Jew was not welcome, the miners ignored him. Meanwhile in Moscow the most popular magazine among the intelligentsia, *Ogonyok*, continues to take a firm stand against anti-Semitism. Still, the fact that many of its issues contain articles refuting such allegations as the 'Jews killed the Tsar' and that Stalin's terror machine was 'dominated by the Jews' reflects just how seriously radical opinion takes at least the threat that anti-Semitism might spread.

Chapter 37

Prison to parliament

Charlie Kimber

When the ANC wins the South African elections at the end of this month it will be a victory for everyone who has fought against apartheid. The party which the ruling National Party vowed in 1985 would be 'crushed like the terrorists they are' will become the government. The defeat of the racists will be a cause for real celebration. But what sort of change will Nelson Mandela and the ANC bring to the black majority?

Founded in 1912, the ANC was dominated by traditional leaders—chiefs—and intellectuals outraged at the increasing racial domination of whites. In particular, they wanted to organise against the removal of the right of non-whites to sit in parliament, and the preparations for a Land Act which would restrict black ownership to 10 percent of the country.

For 35 years ANC leaders stressed 'Christian values', non-violence and violent anti-Communism. Their preferred method of resistance to racism was to petition the British government for equality. Predictably it brought no response.

But the ANC remained true to its principles. Timid and respectable, it turned its back on the growing labour unrest after the First World War. The mining houses and financiers repeatedly used ANC leaders to persuade workers to give up strikes in favour of negotiation and discipline.

Had it not been transformed, such an organisation would have died

First published April 1994

after the Second World War. Large numbers of black workers had been recruited into the factories and felt a new power. The miners' strike of 1946, although defeated, demonstrated a new mood among organised labour. In addition thousands of blacks had fought in a war which was supposed to be about freedom. Instead they returned to find preparations for the full implementation of an utterly rigid policy of racial segregation—apartheid.

A new generation of leaders demanded new methods of struggle and a new spirit of resistance. 'We are no longer going to beg, we are going to take,' said one speaker to an ANC conference in 1949. The shift in rhetoric enabled the ANC to remain a viable organisation. It launched a series of mass non-violent protests designed to attract blacks of all classes in the struggle for democracy.

During the 1960s and 1970s the ANC faced extreme state repression and was virtually annihilated in many parts of the country. It was revived only on the basis of the rising worker organisation of the early 1970s and the Soweto student revolt of 1976—even though it led neither the strikes nor the uprising. By the 1980s it was firmly established as the leading anti-apartheid force, both nationally and internationally. The heroic sacrifices of its militants—its leaders' refusal to bow down before imprisonment, torture and death—meant the large majority of black South Africans looked to it to bring democracy.

But it always remained a nationalist rather than a socialist movement, stressed negotiations rather than revolution as the way to bring freedom, insisted on the need to keep blacks of all classes in a single movement and for the working class to moderate its demands in order to maintain this alliance.

Throughout its history the ANC has walked a tightrope. In order to secure change from a brutal and determined government, it has been forced to mobilise at least something of the power of the masses and of workers. Without strikes, without huge demonstrations, without the threat to overthrow not only apartheid but capitalism as well, the National Party would never have come to the negotiating table.

But at the same time, ANC leaders have always feared that matters would get out of hand, that the masses would not heed their leaders when the time came to stop protesting and start voting for parliament working inside a black led capitalism.

Since his release in 1990, Nelson Mandela has walked this tightrope brilliantly. He has focused the ANC on talks with the government and allowed nothing to obstruct the path to compromise with de Klerk. But he has also used the pressure of mass action to improve the terms of that compromise and to act as a safety valve for the frustration and the fury of militants who have suffered too much for too long. Mandela has achieved the remarkable feat of remaining by far the most popular black leader and also being the presidential choice of an overwhelming majority of businessmen.

At key points Mandela's leadership has come under serious strain. After the Boipatong massacre in June 1992 which saw 41 people shot or hacked to death by Inkatha vigilantes backed by the security forces, all the impatience with the slow pace of change bubbled to the surface.

Mandela, criticised by the youth for acting 'like a lamb while the government butchers our people', called off the talks. The ANC supporters in the trade unions called for strikes. But as soon as the emergency was passed, the negotiations started again.

An even greater trial was the murder of ANC and Communist Party leader Chris Hani a year ago. Spontaneous strikes and monster demonstrations involved millions. The whole country was in ferment. The movement sent a shudder through the capitalists who had envisaged a relatively stable movement from apartheid capitalism to capitalism led by the ANC.

But, as the American *Business Week* wrote:

> The ANC passed a test of leadership... Amid the turbulence it was Nelson Mandela who played the role of statesman. In prime television time for three nights he appealed for calm. Business leaders are beginning to appreciate the ANC's role.
>
> Companies bankrolled many of the aspects of Chris Hani's funeral The big mining companies jointly paid more than £140,000 for this purpose while Coca-Cola donated soft drinks. 'Business has to strengthen the position of that section of the ANC leadership struggling to achieve a relatively stable transition,' explains one senior mining executive.

The ANC's election manifesto contains some quite radical promises. It pledges to launch a public works programme employing 2.5 million people over the next ten years to provide houses, water, electricity, clinics, schools and roads. It says there will be tax reductions for everyone earning less than £800 a month (the large majority of black people) and the removal of VAT from basic goods.

But at the same time, ANC leaders have made it quite clear there is not going to be any assault on capitalism. In a speech to white farmers Mandela insisted they had nothing to fear from ANC rule and that their land would not be nationalised. He told businessmen in London, 'We have issued an investment code which provides there will be no expropriation of property or investments. Foreign investors will be able to repatriate dividends and profits.' The ANC's mineral and energy policy coordinator, Pallo Jordan, said last month that nationalisation of mining companies or mineral rights was not under consideration. There is talk that Derek Keys, the present finance minister, and Chris Stals, the chairman of the reserve bank, will be asked to stay on after the elections.

These major concessions to capitalism and increasing unease about how much workers will get from the new government have led to several union conferences discussing the idea of a workers' party separate from the ANC. The 170,000 strong Southern African Clothing and Textile Workers Union called on the Cosatu trade union federation to break its links with the ANC after the elections. Against the advice of its leadership, the 220,000 strong National Union of Metalworkers voted to consider a workers' party and to sever ties with an ANC led government of national unity.

None of this means that workers will not vote ANC. Above all else there is no mass alternative. In addition many workers will want to see the ANC tested in practice before they think about abandoning it.

But it does mean that workers have already begun to move on from asking how to get rid of apartheid to questioning what sort of society will follow the elections. The ANC will remain what it has always been—a nationalist movement whose political direction is dominated by the people who want to see a black capitalism. Given the immense works required to improve black living standards, the ANC's policies are likely to come under strain in the relatively near future.

It may not be very long before we see the first strikes by workers demanding more than an ANC government is ready to deliver. When that happens the prospects for the emergence of a genuinely socialist current will be massively increased.

Nelson Mandela made a remarkable speech last September. Addressing the Cosatu conference he threw away his notes at the end of his address and declared:

> How many times has the liberation movement worked together with workers and then at the moment of victory betrayed the workers? There are many examples of that in the world. It is only if the workers strengthen their organisation before and after liberation that you can win. If you relax your vigilance you will find that your sacrifices have been in vain. You just support the African National Congress only so far as it delivers the goods. If the ANC government does not deliver the goods, you must do to it what you have done to the apartheid regime.

He is absolutely right to point to the failings of movements like the ANC. The task is to build a socialist organisation which can offer an alternative to it.

Chapter 38

'We have a world to win'

Interview with Tao Ye of the Beijing Workers' Autonomous Union, following the 4 June 1989 massacre in Tiananmen Square

What is the significance of the Beijing Workers' Autonomous Union (BWAU)?

If you look at the background to the Tiananmen Square massacre you can see the effect of the workers moving into action. The state was afraid of the workers throughout the country standing up in support of the students' hunger strikes or of the intellectuals. But when the BWAU threatened to intervene the Communist Party (CCP) panicked and reacted violently. The workers showed great bravery in the struggle, blocking the paths of tanks with their bodies and shielding the students from bullets.

The movement was different from those of 1976 or 1979, or the 4 May movement of 1919. The movement changed radically after 4 June. Before then everyone joined the demonstrations as the protests were peaceful and safe. After 4 June this changed. Those who joined the protests risked death, yet thousands continued to demonstrate.

How did the BWAU join the movement?

It was formed on 20 May shortly after the declaration of martial law. Our immediate aim was to stop 350,000 troops from entering Beijing.

First published November 1989

The troops came from all directions and we had to organise the people of Beijing to put up barricades to stop them.

We also aimed to guard Tiananmen Square and protect the students in the square. Our slogan was, 'Don't let a single soldier in.'

Our long term perspective was: in order to get democracy, freedom and civil rights we must overthrow the dictatorship of the CCP and take political power, and that we would have to be prepared for bloodshed to achieve this.

Do you feel then that the resistance movement of 4-6 June was led by the workers?

No. After the declaration of martial law the BWAU and the Students' Autonomous Union lost the leadership, and though the BWAU was fighting to try and lead the movement, it was suppressed before it could get a grip. So the people's reaction to the CCP's violence was largely spontaneous. We argued for the building of barricades against the troops but we had insufficient resources to lead the activity. Although our members were very active in the resistance it isn't true to say that we led it.

Before the BWAU was formed the workers were like bystanders listening to a conversation. At the end of April one group of workers put out a poster saying, 'We Beijing workers support the students. Your demands are democratic and right... However, at the moment we can't come out to help you, though we can give you financial support.' Without the BWAU, workers could only show their solidarity like this. But after it was formed, we stopped being bystanders, we stood side by side with the students—we were involved.

This provided the workers of Beijing with a direct channel of participation, and helped the student movement to develop into a democracy movement.

It is said that the BWAU did not have a mass base during the struggles. Is that true?

Essentially, yes. At the beginning, with a mass movement on such a big scale, the democracy movement existed without real organisations. But with the formation of the BWAU the workers created their vanguard. You were not a member of the vanguard simply by being involved in the spontaneous movement.

For example, I didn't join until 1 June. Before that there was no need to because we were all doing the same thing anyway—fighting for democracy. But from 1 June the numbers in Tiananmen Square shrank as the movement began to cool.

Troops in plain clothes were sent into the square by the CCP to infiltrate the crowds. It was then that the BWAU made a broadcast appealing for the formation of a counter-force to stop the troops spying. I joined up together with all my friends, including my best friend, Chen Jian, who was later executed, in order to fight the actions of the troops. Most BWAU members joined between 19 May and 3 June. If you wanted to join you simply told one of the leaders your name and the district you lived in, and you could then take on responsibilities like organising the barricades in your district.

The CCP allege that the whole movement was pre-planned by a counter-revolutionary gang. But when it started the movement was completely spontaneous and would have broken out without the existence of the BWAU, the Intellectuals Autonomous Organisation or any other organisation.

In May I read several impressive leaflets issued by the BWAU which contained very clear critiques of Chinese society. Were your arguments influenced by Wei Jingsheng?

In 1979 Wei Jingsheng started the 'Democracy Wall' movement at Xidan [a district in west Beijing] by putting up wall posters. Deng Xiaoping, who had returned to power by making use of the Tiananmen riots in April 1976, was forced to accept some of the principles of the 1979 movement.

From 1976 to 1979 we breathed the air of freedom. The Cultural Revolution was just over and people wanted to stretch out. At the Democracy Wall Wei Jingsheng was just a worker, he was not a great theorist. His theory had such a great influence because he based his arguments on his own personal experience.

It is not difficult to talk about real life experiences. I do not need to be a great theorist to talk about the events of Tiananmen Square. It is easy for me because I was there.

Wei Jingsheng was a youth of that generation whose ideas about democracy developed in counterposition to CCP dogmatism. The CCP claimed to be servants of the people. Some ordinary people therefore argued, 'It's better to be a public servant than a master.' People asked what kinds of cars do the servants drive? What sort of food do the servants eat compared to the kind of food we masters eat? The Chinese people invited the leaders to 'come down and taste what it's like to be a master'.

Would you say your principles don't come from books or academic theories?

Definitely. Every Chinese person is realistic. After living with the reality of our lives for several decades we understand what we really need.

Before 1949 people were poorer and worried much more about simply surviving. Later their demands were for better clothing. Now food and clothing matter less and our demands are for democracy and human rights, demands which directly threaten the dictatorial rule of the CCP.

People ask why it is that if we criticise the leaders we're labelled counter-revolutionaries and killed or tortured. They conclude that it is because there is no concept of human rights. Before we can criticise the leaders we must fight for our human rights, without which any criticism we make will result in persecution. However, even if we win human rights we may still be put to death. If all the workers see this they will stop working for the ruling class. Then their rule will be overthrown.

In May when workers were building barricades to stop the army, did they try to persuade the soldiers to turn the guns on their officers?

No. There were a number of reasons for setting up the barricades. One was to keep soldiers where they were and to let the students and workers appeal to them. But these appeals were not made as attacks on the CCP, because that would have been useless. The news of what was happening in Beijing had been hidden from the soldiers. They didn't know what it was they were supposed to be doing there. Most of them thought they were taking part in a film, while others just thought they were going sightseeing in Tiananmen.

Once the students had patiently explained what was going on, the soldiers could see the problem they faced and didn't know what to do. For a long while the troops and the people were on friendly terms, laughing and talking together and at ease with each other. This continued after the CCP had given orders to fire.

Deng Xiaoping succeeded in changing this by engineering a clash between the people and the soldiers to arouse the troops' anger [the night of 3 June]. The anger became worse when the troops found out that other soldiers had been attacked and killed by the people. At the same time the CCP sent spies into Tiananmen to stir up trouble.

Don't you think that the CCP was prevented from acting decisively in May by the sheer weight of numbers in Tiananmen, which was much bigger than in June?

No. In May the BWAU had only just been founded, and we couldn't organise anything on a large scale. By June this was no longer the case. We were organising for a ten million strong demonstration on 30 June. There was to be a mass hunger strike of 5,000 intellectuals starting on 5 June and a general strike on 6 June. These actions would have revived the movement. The CCP could not tolerate this. They risked everything on launching a wave of repression on 4 June to head this off.

What do you think of the Federation of Democracy in China [the umbrella group of exiles founded at a Paris conference in September 1989]?

It is a shame that some of the best activists have pulled out after the first conference. The Front appears to be less of a convention of overseas democracy activists, and more an organisation for reformists, more suitable for the CCP moderates who have been exiled from China. Its guiding principles don't seem to have been drawn from the recent protests and their drowning in blood. It lacks militancy and the power to mobilise.

As one who experienced the massacre in Tiananmen Square I can't accept this. The deaths of my friends are too fresh in my mind. The founding declaration is a long way from reflecting the realities of what happened on 4 June. Still, the conference has produced an agenda for democracy. It remains to be seen if real activists will be elected to leading positions. If this doesn't happen, I will withdraw from the Front.

How big a part did Marxism play in your thinking?

Marx's ideas are very influential since I have been educated along those lines. But the kind of education I got is far removed from the essence of Marxism. The socialism prescribed by Marx differs very much from any form of socialism practiced by the socialist countries.

Marx argued that socialism was the highest stage of development of human society. Capitalism creates a rich material basis on which socialism can be built. The question is, can it succeed?

The past 100 years has proved that it is not successful. Many countries have practised Marx's theories in a number of forms. The results are unsatisfactory, which makes me sceptical about Marxism. However, if you look at it another way, none of the forms of so called socialism which exist work according to the way Marx prescribed.

In my opinion, capitalism and socialism differ only in political opinions, in the jargon of different factions. Communism or socialism as Marx described them are too beautiful. When we strive for a faith, the road to the ultimate goal is far too long.

Does that mean you don't advocate socialism?

Yes, it does, because Marx's socialism is unrealisable. It is not necessary to have Marxism as the one theoretical basis for the workers' movement, because the movement changes. We need more tools. In essence, the workers in capitalist and socialist states are different. Workers in socialist states understand that their counterparts in capitalist countries are exploited. They believe there is no exploitation in socialist societies and that they are masters of the state. Yet their material conditions contradict this.

Chapter 39

Historic compromises

South Africa—Alex Callinicos

The world seemed to stand still when South Africa went to the polls in April. Tens of millions of black people voted for the first time in their country's history. Their action, and the victory of the African National Congress under Nelson Mandela to which it led, seemed to be the culmination of decades of bitter struggle against apartheid. It was all the more remarkable as Mandela himself had spent nearly 27 years languishing in jail, finally released by the apartheid regime in February 1990.

Voting for the ANC was far more than a symbolic act. For the black masses it was an affirmation of the demands that had driven forward the decisive battles of the 1980s—for jobs, housing, education, in sum, for a better life.

The most striking thing about the nine months since the election is how few and tiny the steps are that the new ANC government has taken towards realising these demands. ANC leaders seek to justify the slow pace of change by arguing that they came to power as a result of a compromise with the established order, and that consequently they have little room for manoeuvre.

It is true that, in line with the constitution agreed between the ANC and the apartheid regime, Mandela presides over a coalition government including representatives of the old order. One of his deputy presidents is F W de Klerk, leader of the National Party (NP), the party of apartheid. The home affairs minister is Chief Gatsha

First published December 1994

Buthelezi, leader of the tribalist Inkatha Freedom Party, who wants to stop democratic local elections taking place in his KwaZulu fiefdom.

But the restraints imposed by the coalition are not sufficient to explain the government's lacklustre performance. It was ANC MPs who voted huge salaries for themselves and even larger ones for government ministers. It was left to the Congress of South African Trade Unions (Cosatu) and Archbishop Desmond Tutu to denounce this 'gravy train'.

Meanwhile, down below, in the townships and squatter camps very little has changed. One of the most burning issues is housing. Yet the ANC dominated national and provincial governments have still to launch the massive house building programme promised at the election. One of the few concrete steps was taken recently by Joe Slovo, housing minister and leader of the South African Communist Party. He signed a deal with the banks and building societies designed to make it easier for blacks to obtain mortgages. In exchange he promised that the state would take responsibility for evicting mortgage defaulters.

This agreement is part of a government assault on what it calls the 'culture of boycotts'. During the 1980s massive boycotts of rates, rents, and electricity bills developed in the townships as part of the struggle against the regime. Far from attitudes changing under the new government, the number of boycotters has actually risen since April!

One of the most defiant groups are ex-combatants belonging to the ANC's military wing, Umkhonto weSizwe (MK). They are supposed to be integrated into the new South African National Defence Force. Recently the former commander of MK, Joe Modise, now minister of defence, dismissed 2,000 of his men and women for protesting against the conditions under which they are being integrated.

Meanwhile a series of investigations into government hit squads under de Klerk serve as a reminder that the security forces remain, despite a few ANC figures at the top, essentially those who so brutally defended apartheid.

Elsewhere in the government there are more dubious plans for South Africa's new international role. One NP minister, Dawie de Williers, wants to set aside a 'sub-region' where imported toxic waste can be dumped. The state weapons company Armscor has a similar plan to earn foreign exchange by offering a remote part of the Northern Cape as a bomb disposal site.

ANC supporters have attacked the proposals. But they follow from the logic of the general policy being pursued by the government—namely seeking to make South Africa a competitive unit of the world market. As the fine print on the much touted Reconstruction and Development

Programme—centrepiece of the ANC's promised reforms—begins to appear, the continuity between this government's economic thinking and that of its NP predecessor becomes more striking.

One of the best known socialists in the government, former trade union leader Alec Erwin, has struck a pose as deputy finance minister little different from a Tory chief secretary to the Treasury eager to cut public spending.

The biggest threat to these policies comes from the ANC's most important support base, the unions. The initial strike wave after the election was snuffed out eventually, thanks to the efforts of the Cosatu leadership. The federation's congress reaffirmed its commitment to a partnership with the government and big business. But more recently there have been some militant strikes, for example by bus drivers in Johannesburg and municipal workers in Cape Town.

These struggles serve as a reminder that the ANC came to office thanks to the emergence in the 1980s of a powerful independent workers' movement. That movement has, however, been held back by its commitment to the politics of negotiation and compromise. Those politics are, however, likely to come under increasing pressure as the ANC becomes subject to the test of government.

Those who want to realise the hopes raised in April will have to look elsewhere—to those who are seeking not a compromise with the old order, but its overthrow.

Palestine—Mike Simons

The killing of Islamic fundamentalist activists outside a mosque in Gaza by Yasser Arafat's Palestinian police brought home how much Arafat is being used to control his own people.

A year of peace in the Middle East has brought Nobel Peace Prizes for Israeli leaders Yitzhak Rabin and Shimon Peres. It has produced a spectacular economic boom in Israel. Israeli politicians and business leaders are now looking forward to a massive expansion of trade into previously closed Arab and African markets.

Arafat, leader of the Palestine Liberation Organisation, was also awarded a Nobel Peace Prize, but few ordinary Palestinians have seen any benefit from the autonomy treaty signed a year ago. Arafat's declaration that the agreements were the first step to the creation of a Palestinian state looks increasingly like a pipe dream.

The deal which Arafat signed created the grandly titled Palestine National Authority but more Palestinians live in territories policed by

Israel than in the areas of Palestinian autonomy. Israel has been slow to implement the limited transfer of power agreed with Arafat—effectively giving the PLO the powers of a local council in the Gaza Strip and West Bank town of Jericho.

Meanwhile the US, European Union, Japan and the oil rich Gulf states have been even slower in handing over aid. The Palestinian National Authority was promised £1,500 million aid over the next five years. In the first 'year of peace' just £140 million has been delivered. That is enough to pay the new PLO police and civil service but not to make any improvements to the appalling conditions.

Unemployment in Gaza, one of the most overcrowded and impoverished areas of the world, is running at 50 percent. Life is made worse because the Israeli authorities repeatedly seal off the strip, stopping thousands of Palestinian labourers earning their living in Israel.

Autonomy has failed to deliver material gains to the Palestinians and it has delivered little else either. Israel still holds 5,000 Palestinian prisoners, jailed during the Intifada uprising. The Israeli cabinet recently agreed to formally sanction the use of 'physical force'—torture—during the interrogation of suspects.

Rabin and Peres have not disarmed Israeli settlers in Gaza and the West Bank despite the horrific massacre in a Hebron mosque by settler Baruch Goldstein. There has been no move to dismantle settlements. Indeed, the two year old ban on building new homes for settlers on the West Bank has been quietly lifted.

Inevitably Palestinian doubts about the accord have turned into deep disillusion. This has found expression in growing support for the fundamentalist groups Hamas and the smaller Islamic Jihad.

During the 1980s the Israeli authorities actively promoted Hamas as an alternative to the 'terrorist' PLO. Now, stung by spectacular Hamas attacks, the Israelis are demanding that Yasser Arafat's PLO police destroy the organisation.

Contrary to the image portrayed by Israeli leaders and repeated by the world's media, Hamas members are not a bunch of mindless killers, nor are they or their supporters homogeneous. The organisation is split. Its more pragmatic leaders want influence within the Palestine National Authority. In effect, this means recognising Israel. They have been prepared to order military action to force the Israeli authorities and the PLO to give it a slice of power. However, each success by the military wing strengthens those within Hamas calling for total rejection of Arafat's deal with Israel.

The Israeli newspaper *Haretz* summed up the process:

Hamas terrorist activities contain two main political messages. The first—to Arafat and the PLO—is do not dare ignore us. The second—to the state of Israel—is that negotiations with the PLO do not constitute the final word and that Hamas must also be taken into account.

In the last year Hamas has killed the chief of Israel's undercover operations in Gaza and a military chief of the West Bank. It organised a series of bombings after the Hebron mosque massacre, forcing Arafat and the PLO to offer Hamas places on the Palestine National Authority. When the Israeli authorities banned Hamas from running in elections the response was October's massive bus bomb which killed 23 in the capital, Tel Aviv.

Each military success brings Hamas more support, but that support has little to do with a massive upsurge in religious sentiment. It is simply a comment on the fact that Arafat has conceded too much and delivered too little.

Arafat's response has been to bow to Israeli pressure and turn his police on Hamas supporters. It has hardly been a year of peace in Palestine and peace is unlikely to break out in the future.

Ireland—Judith Orr

Some of the most lasting images of 1994 will be of Gerry Adams being feted by the Irish government and being wined and dined by the rich and powerful of the United States. The man who was interned without trial by the British is now happy to sit at the negotiating table with representatives of Britain. The compromise that will result will almost certainly fall a long way short of the united Ireland that has been the goal of the IRA and Sinn Fein since partition.

Adams claims that the IRA ceasefire is a sign of the strength of their side, saying the struggle for civil rights had started with marches from Coalisland to Dungannon but now it was going to the gates of the White House in Washington.

Sinn Fein's shift is about more than dressing up in the now familiar expensive suits. It is a direct result of the realisation that the military struggle, on which Sinn Fein has based its strategy over 20 years, was going nowhere.

It is also significant that the past year has seen 7,000 people at a rally for peace called by the Irish Congress of Trade Unions in Belfast and, amongst other strikes, the walkout by 4,000 mostly Protestant shipyard workers in protest at the sectarian killing of a Catholic workmate. The prospect of still more years of the military struggle has clearly been increasingly rejected by the mass of ordinary people.

When the IRA ceasefire was announced, the celebrations showed that, for many working class Catholics also, the relief that their sacrifices seemed at an end overcame anxieties about how little, if anything, they had won.

Now—after the initial euphoria—there is more questioning of what Sinn Fein has actually gained. The answer is simple—not a lot.

There are still 30,000 armed men walking the streets, and though they have swapped their hard hats for berets and left their flak jackets at home, there can hardly be much comfort in that.

There is no amnesty for prisoners jailed for political offences and no sign of one in the near future. Attempts by the Irish government to release Republican prisoners were met with a barrage of Loyalist criticism and have been abandoned. The massive fortresses which loom over the Catholic ghettos in the North are still manned, with cameras spying into people's homes. Talk of a 'peace dividend', money saved on security going instead to creating much needed jobs, has not gone beyond vague assurances that both the US and Britain will help with investment.

The right of each community to police themselves is central to talks and is also claimed as a victory. Sinn Fein has proved its credentials in towns such as Derry where they have been happily working alongside the middle class SDLP for some time. Any attempt to uphold a radical face has long since been ditched in favour of being seen as fit to share power. Those looking forward to getting the hated RUC out of their areas should note that the IRA's punishment of drug takers and joy riders and the smashing up of raves shows that they have no qualms about being tough on their own community.

There is now no pretence from the Republicans that Protestant workers have any common cause with Catholics, as the idea of two separate communities with their own culture and different interests becomes common currency. But if Sinn Fein is happy to see ordinary Protestants being represented by a bunch of middle class reactionary bigots, not all Protestants are. When a community worker from the Shankill recently phoned a radio programme on Radio Ulster about the need for a Loyalist working class party, more people phoned in response than ever in the programme's history.

The new Unionist parties that now claim to talk for Protestant workers can offer nothing but a crude rehash of the sectarian policies that the main Unionist parties have been spouting for years. Major's plans to now talk to Loyalist gunmen as well as Sinn Fein only reinforce the idea of two tribes with different agendas.

Loyalism can offer nothing to workers. It is the politics of uniting across class—everyone from a shipyard fitter to his boss through even to the queen.

The crisis which blew up in the South last month demonstrates how fed up Southerners are with the corrupt Fianna Fail government and its friends in the Catholic church. The pan-nationalist politics of Gerry Adams have got nothing to say to these workers. In fact Adams rallied to support Albert Reynolds, the now departed Irish prime minister who was a main architect of the peace deal.

The calling of the ceasefires means that socialists have a unique opportunity in future months to point to an alternative tradition in the Irish working class, a socialist tradition with a long history ignored by both Republican and Protestant leaders. They appear content to accept sectarian divisions just at the time when it is possible to challenge them.

Chapter 40

I is for imperialism

Balwinder Singh Rana

Every European, from the Greeks to the British, went in search of the riches of the East. From the 17th century onwards there was a steady flow of precious metals and other foods from East to West.

Together with the slave trade profits, this wealth was necessary for the development of capitalism. Marx called the process the 'primitive accumulation of capital'. The process also required cheap raw materials and an ever expanding market, and to ensure these Britain colonised the East.

In India the process got under way after Clive's victory at Plassey in 1757. It led to a massive increase in the transfer of wealth from India to Britain. It is estimated that in the 1760s capital investment in Britain was about £6 million to £7 million a year. The tribute from India was at least £2 million.

India was one of the biggest producers of cotton. Indian weavers using handlooms produced the best textiles in the world. The British began shipping raw cotton from India to England and the cotton mills of Lancashire, which turned it into textiles, were the start of the Industrial Revolution.

The unwanted competition of Indian weavers was stopped by chopping off their hands. Handlooms, and other handicraft industry, were systematically destroyed. India became both the biggest provider of raw cotton and the biggest market for British manufactured textiles. In a House of Commons select committee report of 1840 Sir Charles Trevelyan said, 'We have finished the (Indian) entrepreneurs. Now all they have got left is the agriculture.'

But this too was transformed. Agricultural land which had provided

First published January 1980

food for the Indians was increasingly turned over to produce raw materials for the developing British industry or to the production of opium for sale in China. Tea, cotton, wheat, oil seeds and jute were shipped to Britain at an increasing rate. Nine million pounds weight of cotton went to Britain in 1813, 88 million pounds in 1844, 963 million pounds in 1914. Similarly wheat worth £8 million went to Britain in 1849, £9.3 million worth in 1901, £19.3 million worth in 1914.

This transformation of agriculture created massive famines. Between 1850 and 1900 there were 25 famines in India which killed more than 20 million people. Those who were lucky enough to survive faced increasing land taxes which had to be paid in cash rather than products. Many who were unable to pay became bankrupt and were shipped to the West Indies and the Americas as indentured labourers.

A good example of this systematic pillage was Punjab. After the British conquest in 1846, Britain began to dismantle the existing political and economic systems and to impose its own system of maximum exploitation. Punjab had a communal land system in which the whole village community owned the land. All the various castes, according to their craft, contributed to producing sufficient food for the whole community. Communally, they paid land taxes in kind to the Sikh rulers.

The British divided the land into small plots and gave it to the farming caste. No other caste was allowed to buy or sell land and thus the caste system was rigidly enforced. To raise cash to pay the massive new land taxes, farmers had to sell their farm produce on the markets. Thus food became a commodity to be bought and sold rather than fairly shared to feed the village community. In order to pay taxes in periods of bad weather the farmers began to accumulate, thus depriving the other castes of their share.

But despite this accumulation farmers still went bankrupt in times of bad weather and were forced to mortgage their lands to rich merchants, who had developed out of the new commodity markets. According to the Famine Commission report of 1860 there were 200,000 court cases each year concerning bankrupt farmers and mortgaged land. Twenty five million acres of land were mortgaged by farmers between 1901 and 1909.

Breaking up the village communities also threw up a layer of corrupt officials and middlemen like merchants, lawyers, court officials, petty civil servants and of course policemen. On top of this heap were the despotic Maharajas and Nawabs. The impoverished and bankrupt peasants who were the victims of this process were recruited into the army to fight new wars for the British Empire, from Indo-China to the Second World War.

All efforts by the Indians to win freedom were ruthlessly crushed. In 1857 the first Indian War of Independence—better known in Britain as the 'Indian Mutiny'—was crushed with the utmost barbarity. In 1919 the repressive Rowlatt Act was passed. This denied the Indians freedom of assembly and allowed imprisonment without trial. In protest against this act 20,000 people gathered in an enclosed park at Amritsar on 13 April 1919. The British troops opened fire on the peaceful and unarmed Indians killing more than 500 and wounding nearly 2,000. This act of cowardly brutality is known as the 'Amritsar Massacre'.

The whole of this process of exploitation and murder was carried out, with Bible in one hand and sword in the other, under the guise of 'civilising the black hordes'. At the same time, Britain played the game of 'divide and rule' resulting in the division of the country into three parts in 1947 and the death of 100,000 people in the communal riots which followed.

Although direct British rule was ended in 1947, economic imperialism still continues. A large part of the capital investment in India is British owned. Most of the tea plantations, for example, still have British owners.

Karl Marx wrote:

> The Indians will not reap the fruits of the new elements of society scattered among them by the British bourgeoisie till in Great Britain itself the now ruling class shall have been supplanted by the industrial proletariat or till the Hindus themselves shall have grown strong enough to throw off the English Yoke altogether.

The Indians have thrown off the English Yoke, but it has been replaced by the corrupt Indian ruling classes. So, to reap the 'fruits of the new elements of society' the industrial proletariat needs to triumph not only in Britain but also in India itself.

Women

Chapter 41

Babes, Barbie and the battle of the sexes

Lindsey German

'I like my hair like I like my men—great looking and easily changed', is the slogan on a current advert for shampoo. It's a slogan that advertisers think will click with many women. And they are probably right. It's now common to hear the same kind of attitudes expressed even by socialist women. Others in the same vein run along the lines, 'At least Madonna's a woman who's in control', 'If you push hard enough you can get your own way', 'If a bloke makes a joke about the way I look, I just make a joke about the size of his ass', 'I'm in control of my own sex life'.

A sexual revolution has taken place within the lifetime of most women. Images, attitudes and subjects of discussion that are commonplace today would have been unimaginable to people only 40 years ago.

Yet sometimes it seems that the demands for sexual liberation—which played such an important part in the radicalisation of the 1960s—have been turned upside down. It is as if sexism has made a comeback by masquerading as sexual liberation.

So sexual freedom is symbolised by the poster at every bus stop of Demi Moore on top of Michael Douglas. The demand for women's equality is supposed to be met by turning women *and* men into sex objects—

First published April 1995

Club 18 to 30 advertises its holidays with a picture of a man in bulging underpants while the Chippendales draw in huge crowds of women to their shows.

The slogan 'Burn your bra'—always more popular with the media than with ordinary women but nonetheless symbolic of a search for freedom from restrictive clothing designed to portray women's bodies in a particular way—has been superseded. Now we have the Wonderbra ads—thought up by a woman and supposedly a sign not of women's oppression but of assertiveness and control.

The subtext of all this is that women's oppression no longer need concern us. Women can compete on equal terms with men. They no longer have to be sexually submissive. Their aggression comes from their personal stance, lifestyle and job. Indeed, in many areas they are becoming so successful that it is the traditionally dominant sex—men—who are under threat. (Michael Douglas has cornered the market in films perpetuating this view.)

The idea that inequality can be overcome with the right mixture of confidence and assertiveness is strongly reinforced by some of the new young post-feminist writers. Katie Roiphe made her name with a book, *The Morning After*, which argued that date rape (rape between acquaintances) was a figment of feminists' imagination. Roiphe's view that 'there is a grey area in which someone's rape may be another person's bad night' is an assault on the whole attempt in the 1960s and 1970s to demand that women should not be treated as sex objects in rape cases.

Only after much argument and campaigning did it become unacceptable for the judges, the police and the media to condemn a woman victim because of her dress, social life or sexual history. The move towards anonymity in court cases was a recognition that women did not usually make false claims of rape but, on the contrary, were often too distressed to make any complaint at all.

Seeing women as victims is, however, definitely out of fashion for the post-feminists. Roiphe feels that the issue of rape is used as a 'call to arms' for feminists and that it, like sexual harassment, is much exaggerated. Buy a new dress, put on some lipstick and snap out of it, seems to be the general message.

Naomi Wolf—more of a feminist than Katie Roiphe—also believes that no one will help a woman who doesn't help herself. In *Fire into Fire* she argues that women need to show their power and if they are strong enough they can gain equality. She talks of the 'genderquake' in recent years and embraces 'power feminism'. To her this means, 'Learn from Madonna, Spike Lee and Bill Cosby: if you don't like

314

your group's image in the media, decide on another image and seize the means of producing it.'

Wolf feels that 'women deserve to feel that the qualities of stars and queens, of sensuality and beauty, can be theirs.' Perhaps unsurprisingly, one of her great heroines of power feminism is Princess Diana.

What sums up both the images of aggressive and sexually predatory women and the notion of women becoming empowered on the same basis as men is that collective struggle is a thing of the past. We no longer need social conflict. Just celebrate identity and difference—or, as it used to be called, 'do your own thing'.

This is women's liberation viewed from the privileged comfort of the upper middle classes: a world of elite schools and universities, access to the media and lecture tours commanding high fees. Missing from the analysis is any real assessment of the world as it confronts millions of women. But many socialists and feminists who do not come from privileged backgrounds have accepted some of these attitudes, and prefer to see women's liberation as about changing lifestyles and confidence in a world where greater social change seems a long way off.

Sexuality here becomes detached from wider society. The sexual revolution is not then about a more equal and fairer society, or about a complete transformation of social attitudes and values. It is about women becoming more like men, accepting all the inequalities there are in sexual relationships, but this time making sure that women come out on top.

In sexual attitudes, as in so much else, we see the limits of women's liberation which will not challenge the fundamental inequalities of a society whose major division is that of class.

And, of course, this sort of power feminism cannot really challenge any of the attacks on women's rights which have come from right wingers over the 1980s and early 1990s. Instead, their answer to the 'backlash' they see against women's rights is to get more women in positions of power.

Yet to pose power dressing strong women as the only possible opposition to a backward looking and male chauvinist reaction is to misinterpret both the real position of women today and any strategy for liberation. It also leads to an overestimation of the backlash and therefore a tendency towards stressing the individual solutions to women's oppression so beloved of the post-feminists.

There has been an attack on some of the gains of women's liberation inside the US in recent years. The general climate which has led to real wages being cut, massive public spending on new prisons, and millions of people being denied any real welfare benefits, has had its impact on the position of women. Single parents—especially young black women—have been scapegoated as 'welfare queens'.

The vicious onslaught against 'political correctness' and the movement against affirmative action (positive discrimination) reflect the attempts of white middle class men—often given cover by career women who claim they can 'make it on their own'—to claw back the very limited concessions which blacks and women won in the 1960s and 1970s. In many recent rape cases it seems there are now two equally suffering victims: the accuser and the accused.

But we are not about to return to the 1950s. It may be fashionable to call women 'babes' and Barbie may have made an astonishing comeback as a role model for some women. But that is not how most women are, not how they see themselves. The behaviour of the 'new lads' may be one of the less savoury aspects of the 1990s (old fashioned sexism dressed up as detached irony) but it does not result in women being pushed into the home in a way that the worst sorts of bigots would like.

Instead women are on the labour market in unprecedented numbers, making up nearly half the workforce in Britain and over half in the US. They are the new flexible workers eulogised in the press. The unemployment rate for women in Britain is half what it is for men—showing that capitalism may be an exploitative system but it doesn't necessarily always favour men for exploitation.

Although women's wages are substantially lower than those of men taken overall, there has been a narrowing of the gap in some areas and, for a layer of managerial and professional women, there has been a fairly dramatic increase in earnings.

Indeed the growth of that layer of women has been one of the most notable social developments of the 1980s and 1990s. In 1991 in the US there were 2.3 million women with personal incomes over $50,000 a year. Around 7 percent of Hispanic, 7 percent of black and 11.9 percent of white women were executives or managers. Whereas in the early 1970s less than 5 percent of business masters' degrees went to women, by the mid-1980s that had risen to 40 percent.

The change in women's role—at work with access to new careers and in higher education—has altered social attitudes. Most noticeably this is true of abortion, where a large majority of women favour the right to choose. Even right wing Republicans are reluctant to launch a frontal attack on abortion rights because they fear it is electorally unpopular. The 'Contract with America' on which the Republicans fought last year's mid-term elections was conspicuously silent on abortion.

Attempts to roll back the clock for women always meet with spirited opposition because of women's changed political role. Even the much maligned single parents have refused to accept attacks on welfare without a fight. Most women do not see why they should have to put up with unequal treatment or sexist remarks, or have to choose whether they work or have children.

Even film and television programmes now reflect the change. Whether it is the distasteful *Disclosure* or the invigorating *Thelma and Louise*, women are much more likely to be given a role as independent beings. The material conditions in which women find themselves have incomparably more impact than the reactionary attitudes surrounding home and family which right wingers constantly reiterate.

But what the 'backlash' is able to do is create a more unfavourable ideological climate. Women's problems become their own fault. If the burden of the family is too great then there are only individual solutions. If welfare is under attack then women just have to accept more responsibilities in the home as well as going out to work.

There is therefore in the 1990s a strange combination of assertion of equality and a more egalitarian reality for millions of women, coupled with a shift to the right by those in government, media and other positions of power to blame the victims and put more pressure on individuals.

So what is really happening? Over the last 20 to 30 years more real women's equality has developed—whether in pay, in jobs or in reforms of the law. There has been much greater general acceptance of women's equality over the same period.

But there has been an ideological backlash over the last ten to 15 years. This has often been supported by middle class feminists and post-feminists keen to show that they can succeed in a 'man's world'. The backlash has only been partially successful, but does have resonance among some on the left. There has over the same ten to 15 year period been an increasing attack on welfare. This is an attack on us all, although it does affect women, in particular, in some areas.

Some on the left have the attitude that we should adopt personal and sexual assertiveness in the here and now—while also arguing the need to go further in the transformation of society. But there is a difference between assertiveness which develops from political awareness and collective struggle, and assertiveness which is simply about 'getting ahead' of everyone else. The individual attitude puts a barrier between socialists and the majority of women who have little illusion that merely asserting themselves can reverse the disaster afflicting their society. In fact, it can prevent unity of working class women and working class men by creating the impression that individual men are in reality the problem.

A theory of women's liberation based on class is more essential than ever: oppression is part of a wider system which exploits and oppresses nearly everyone, which divides and rules on the basis of sex or race, which tries to turn everything—even human beings—into commodities to be bought and sold.

The post-feminists are ill equipped to develop or to understand such a theory. Their ideas represent the thin layer of managerial and professional women who have done so well out of the 1980s and who see their role as playing a part in the exploitation of the rest of us or, at best, trying to run the system in a slightly more humane way.

The aspiring Labour MPs around Emily's List—the campaign to get more women into parliament—do not challenge the stereotypes of women's oppression with their identical suits and neat haircuts. Rather they mimic their male middle class counterparts and have a simple demand: more jobs for the girls.

Most importantly, they have no way of really challenging those who have done even better out of the advances women have made in the past decades. Capitalism has an amazing ability to use the changes in society to its own advantage, even if the capitalists and their supporters have done little or nothing to bring these changes about.

The capitalists are quite happy to use greater sexual openness where once they counselled repression—so long as they can make a profit. The more sex becomes a commodity, the more everything connected with it—and even the sex act itself—becomes for sale on the open market. Hence the Chippendales, the lacy bras, *Disclosure*, *Cosmopolitan* and page three of the *Sun*.

Having sexual matters openly discussed and advertised is a step forward. It makes it very difficult for the church or reactionary governments to keep the wraps on sexuality and relationships, as they did in Portugal and Spain right up to the mid-1970s, or in Ireland till even more recently. It makes people more aware about aspects of sex and sexuality than they might otherwise have been. It makes society more open.

But treating sex—and people's bodies—as objects to be bought and sold does not and cannot in itself lead to sexual liberation. That is why socialists have to go beyond the sexual stereotypes and beyond simply a post-feminist response to the question. Most socialist feminists don't like the post-feminists. But because they too stress that individual men are the problem, they are incapable of developing a strategy for ending women's oppression. Their main answer during the 1980s was to join the Labour Party—no wonder they now see individual solutions as the way forward.

The answer to women's oppression is not ogling at the Chippendales or picking up a different man every night. However enjoyable or otherwise these occupations might be, making men into sex objects or admiring their penises—as Camille Paglia urges us to do—does not negate or abolish the inequality which women suffer.

A socialist response to sexual liberation should be one which recognises the stultifying and destructive effect that class society has on social and sexual relationships, and which understands that only a society where there is no competition, inequality or alienation can truly produce sexual freedom and liberation—not just for women but for all humanity.

When we stress the importance of a class analysis of women's oppression therefore, it is not simply about our criticisms of middle class women. It is about developing a strategy which can end class society and the many inequalities—not least those of gender and sexuality—which it produces.

Chapter 42

Heading for divorce?

Goretti Horgan

The fall of the Irish government as the result of a scandal about the cover up of a priest's sexual abuse of children brought to the surface many of the stereotypes about Irish people—priest ridden and sexually repressed, the lot of us!

The power of the Catholic church in Ireland and in particular its success in repressing sex and sexuality is indeed peculiar to Ireland. But this has nothing to do with 'the Irish psyche' or anything particularly religious about Irish people.

Up to the 16th century one of the complaints made by English commentators about the Irish was their 'licentiousness' and the lack of stigma which they attached to children born outside marriage. In the 6th century, when Ireland was supposed to be the 'island of saints and scholars', every heterosexual liaison was recognised as a type of marriage—even one night stands! Homosexual liaisons were seen as a problem only if they led to the men involved neglecting the sexual needs of their wives. The concept of illegitimacy simply did not exist.

The power of the Catholic church over sexual matters in Ireland has nothing to do with the peculiarities of Irish people. That power has material roots which lie in the role played by the church's teachings on sexual matters in the development of capitalism in Ireland.

For centuries colonialism ensured that the Catholic church was identified with the oppressed in Ireland. Britain had introduced penal laws in the mid-17th century, making Catholics second class citizens

First published January 1995

unable to rent, still less own, any sizeable tracts of land and unable to enter the professions. It was illegal to celebrate or attend mass.

This attempt at suppressing Catholicism didn't work. As Wolfe Tone, the Protestant leader of the unsuccessful rebellion in 1798, wrote, 'Persecution will keep alive the foolish bigotry and superstition of any sect.'

In the last half of the 18th century, and particularly in the wake of the French Revolution, the British government decided to change tactics and to try to build an alliance with the Catholic bishops. In 1795 it subsidised Maynooth College as a national seminary for Catholic priests. The Vatican was unsure about the usefulness of such an alliance but in any case it was never developed.

Instead the Catholic church was to move towards an alliance with the emerging Catholic bourgeoisie. In the wake of the Great Famine of the mid-1840s sexual repression by the church was to play an important role in promoting capital accumulation by this class, allowing it to become the new Irish ruling class. This role first gave the Catholic church's view of sexuality the kind of power it has traditionally had in Ireland.

The famine had decimated the rural poor, several millions of whom either died of starvation or were forced to emigrate. The tiny plots of land they had worked were taken over by the larger tenant farmers (holding over 15 acres). This tenant farmer class survived the famine intact and emerged as the strongest class in Catholic Ireland.

In 1841 only 18 percent of land holdings on the island of Ireland were of more than 15 acres. By 1851, 51 percent of holdings were over 15 acres. By 1891 this had risen to 58 percent. At the same time the numbers of holdings had fallen from 691,000 in 1841 to 570,000 in 1851 and 517,000 in 1891.

The large tenant farmer class was determined that the fate that had befallen the smaller tenant farmers during the famine was never going to happen to their class. In order to ensure this two things were necessary. First, the custom of dividing the land between all the sons in a family would have to be discontinued and the holdings passed on to one son only. Second, the number of children born to families would have to be limited.

It was here that the Catholic church was to prove an important ally. The church was, anyway, a natural ally to the large tenant farmer class. Most priests came from this class, which was the only Catholic class which could afford to educate its children. In 1808, of the 205 students in Maynooth, 78 percent were the sons of farmers. Only the larger farmers could afford to send their sons into the priesthood.

The large farmers, together with the urban merchant class, provided much of the money and personnel to run the churches, convents, schools and hospitals which sprang up all over Ireland following the end of the persecution of Catholicism.

The church was crucial in providing the ideological basis for the sexual repression which ensured the pattern of late marriages and permanent celibacy which was to become the norm in Ireland.

Of course, the church could become far more strict about sexual matters, preaching hell fire and damnation from the pulpits, and it still need not have made much difference in the privacy of the bedroom had it not been for the third element in all this—the role of women.

Before the famine women had made an essential contribution to the family economy and as late as 1841 women accounted for more than half the non-agricultural labour force. Most of this economic independence was based on spinning wool, cotton and linen.

But the number of spinners fell by about 75 percent between 1841 and 1851. Only in the Belfast region, where linen became a factory industry, did this work survive the combination of Industrial Revolution and famine.

Women no longer had a clear economic role in the family. At this point the church became involved in Irish family life, preaching the centrality of the family, the evils of all sexual activity not aimed at the procreation of children, and holding up the Virgin Mary as the model for women. Women, domesticated, became transmitters of Catholic ideology—a role they have played right up to the present. In most countries of the world the religious head of the household is the man; in Ireland it is generally the woman. Women in the post-famine period were offered a role said to be the most important within society—bringing up children in the Catholic faith, with Catholic sexual morals, Catholic fear and Catholic guilt. The church did not have to police the family—the Irish mother did it for them.

To some extent the women had little choice. There was nothing else on offer and, in return for embracing the new morality, they received a level of respect, of status, even of authority which they could not have expected given their changed economic role.

This period also saw a tremendous explosion in devotion to the Madonna, to the Rosary—which is a prayer to the Virgin—and all over the country shrines of devotion to Mary sprang up. The Virgin Mother was the model for Irish women who wanted to be accepted in society; the alternative was to emigrate.

About one third of emigrants from Europe as a whole between 1850 and 1950 were women, but from Ireland the proportion reached more than half. Most of the women who emigrated from Europe went as part of a family unit; well over half of Irish women emigrants were single and travelled alone.

For the women who remained the role of Virgin Mother was not always on offer. By 1926 about 25 percent of women remained unmarried at the age of 45, compared with about 10 percent before the famine. Late arranged marriages meant that women, if they married at all, married men considerably older than themselves. Before the famine about 20 percent of husbands were ten years older than their wives. By the early 20th century the proportion had risen to about 50 percent.

Things weren't exactly a bed of roses for the men either. Told that women were an 'occasion of sin' since the time of Eve, separated from them in school, church and social occasions, they were often frightened silly of their wives when their parents finally arranged a marriage— usually after the 'boy' had passed 45. The quadrupling of the official lunacy rate in Ireland between 1841 and 1901 probably says it all.

Emigration, late marriage and permanent celibacy did, however, stem the growth in population. The land *was* held together and the material and cultural level of Irish society rose. The Land Acts of the late 19th century allowed tenant farmers to buy their land and the conditions for the basic accumulation of capital necessary for the development of indigenous capitalism were all in place.

The strong tenant farmer class became the emerging capitalist class— with the tiny urban bourgeoisie they were the ones in a position to accumulate. They were fed up of being the middleman between Britain and the exploited classes in Ireland. They wanted to be bosses in their own country, so they joined in the nationalist cause.

Despite Republican mythology to the contrary, the Catholic church was quite supportive of the nationalist cause in Ireland. Of course, the church condemned people like Fintan Lalor and James Connolly who meant it when they said they wanted the land of Ireland for the people of Ireland. But when it came to the people who constituted their traditional social base—the large farmers and their children who had since become lawyers, teachers, doctors, civil servants and joined with the urban bourgeoisie—the Catholic church was fully in support.

As it became clear to this group that independence was needed to advance their interests as a class, the church moved with them. By the 1918 general election, when Sinn Fein swept the board, Catholic bishops publicly endorsed them.

After independence the church moved to protect the interests of its long time class allies and to legitimise the new 'Free State' as the South was then known. This legitimacy was vital in a country which had come to the brink of revolution in 1919-21.

In return, the new state made divorce illegal, banned even information about contraception, gave the chair of the Censorship of Films and Publications Committee to clerics and maintained the church's grip on education and the hospitals. In 1937 the constitution gave a special place to the Catholic church and ensured the ban on divorce would never be lifted except by referendum.

Up to the 1970s the church maintained its control, but changes in material conditions started to challenge that power.

Industrialisation in the 1970s produced job opportunities for women on a scale not seen in the lifetime of the state. The number of economically active women in the Republic increased by 50 percent between 1971 and 1991, while the number of active men increased by only 10 percent.

Right up to the 1970s it was assumed that once a woman got married she would give up her job (even before children arrived). In 1961 only 5 percent of married women were in paid employment. Today almost a third of married women work outside the home.

Economic changes gave women in Ireland an alternative to the role of domestic religious educator and moral police force. As women started to go out to work, they started to opt for the alternative. That meant a different attitude to sexual matters, more equal marriage relationships and a completely different view of sex outside marriage.

As early as 1979 surveys found that 75 percent of married couples used a form of contraception not approved of by the Catholic church at some time in their marriage. The average family size has halved over a single generation. Women are no longer being forced into marriage because they find themselves pregnant; the number of 'shotgun' weddings of teenagers has fallen from 2,400 in 1971 to 600 in 1991.

Despite the ban on abortion, Irish women in their early 20s are as likely to have an abortion as women in Britain, and more likely than women in Holland. Single women who decide to continue their pregnancies usually opt to bring the child up themselves, rather than give it up for adoption.

Of course, the church has fought back. The abortion referendum of 1983 gave women equal status under the constitution with a newly fertilised egg. In the divorce referendum of 1987, 60 percent of voters opted to maintain the ban on divorce. Both of these showed that the church could mobilise a backlash.

But the church and its allies in the ruling class could not turn the clock back. When in February 1992 a 14 year old rape victim was prevented from travelling to England for an abortion, all the contradictions within the Catholic position on abortion came to the fore. Over 10,000 people—mainly young men and women—took to the streets of Dublin demanding, 'Let her go!'

People who had voted in favour of the anti-abortion amendment to the constitution phoned radio talk shows to say they never meant *this* to happen. The supreme court read the anger of the streets and, fearing riots if they did otherwise, announced their decision to allow her abortion. The decision was a political, not a legal one.

This became known as the X case and was the first of a series of events that have seriously eroded the power of the Catholic church, particularly regarding sexual matters. Since the X case, Bishop Eamonn Casey—one of the most populist of preachers against pre- and extra- marital sex—was discovered to have a teenage son by an American woman.

The horrible truth about the abuse and degradation to which Catholic sexual morality subjected women and children has been slowly but relentlessly exposed. Institutions known as Magdalen Laundries, where unmarried mothers were locked up for their entire lives and forced to work in slave labour conditions, were a subject for hushed conversation only. Then, when the land one of them was on was sold by the church to property developers for several million pounds, there was an explosion of anger from relatives of women who had been incarcerated and tortured there.

Stories of physical, emotional and sexual abuse in church run homes all over the island have become the regular diet of newspaper investigation. Journalists who expose one horror report that they are inundated afterwards with details of other more horrific stories of abuse.

The Father Brendan Smyth case, which led to the fall of the Reynolds government, was not unusual in any way in terms of his sexual assaults on children. What was different was the way in which the case exposed the frantic attempts by the church and its allies in the ruling class to cover up what was yet another blow to church authority.

The result of the attempted cover up has been the opening of the floodgates as generations of adults who had been abused by priests and nuns start to talk openly about it. And the present generation of children have also started to talk about the abuse that is still happening.

Every new allegation, every new conviction of a paedophile priest, exposes the hypocrisy of the church. Women with eight or ten children who have been told that they cannot use contraception and must either stop having sex or continue having children are confused and angry.

There are clearly more changes and more revelations to come.

Chapter 43

Skewered in the Senate

Sharon Smith

First there was Watergate, when the president was caught burgling Democratic Party headquarters. Then there was Contragate, when top government officials were caught running guns for the Contras in Nicaragua.

Now there's Thomasgate, when a nominee for the highest court in the land was caught referring to himself as 'Long Dong Silver'.

In early October, Clarence Thomas appeared to be a certainty for confirmation to the US Supreme Court. His appointment was viewed by everyone as a major victory for George Bush because, although Thomas is black, his attitudes mirror those of arch right winger Jesse Helms or George Bush himself.

His anti-abortion, anti affirmative action stands had inspired only feeble opposition from feminist and civil rights organisations.

Then, only days before the US Senate was due to confirm Thomas as a Supreme Court Justice, a story was leaked to the press that one of Thomas's former employees, Anita Hill, had come forward to complain that he had sexually harassed her on the job. The harassment had taken place, ironically, when Thomas was head of the Equal Employment Opportunity Commission (EEOC), the very programme set up to enforce laws against racial discrimination and against sexual harassment at work. Moreover, Anita Hill had come forward weeks earlier to file the complaint and had been ignored by the all white, all male Senate Judicial Committee.

First published November 1991

According to Hill, now a law professor, during the years 1981-83, when she worked as Thomas's personal assistant first at the Department of Education and then at the EEOC, Thomas repeatedly pressured her to date him. When she refused, he spoke graphically about pornographic materials describing people with large penises or large breasts involved in various sexual acts—including bestiality and rape.

Referring to his own sexual prowess, he claimed that his nickname was 'Long Dong Silver'.

With these revelations, years of accumulated anger about sexual harassment burst into the open. The day the vote was supposed to take place, furious women lobbyists crowded into the Capitol Room while feminists demonstrated outside. Politicians' phone lines were jammed with calls, all demanding that the vote be postponed and the charges be investigated.

With an election year looming ahead, the Senate quickly moved to postpone the vote until a hearing could be held. 'The thing everyone miscalculated was the reaction of the women, the girls' vote,' admitted a Bush adviser.

But when the hearing actually took place days later, all it did was highlight the corruption and the hypocrisy rampant in Congress. Just as nationwide polls revealed that nearly four in ten women have experienced sexual harassment at work, the media disclosed that Congress exempts itself from the laws it passes for others, including sexual harassment guidelines and civil rights legislation.

During the hearings, Democrats fell over each other trying to prove their new found sensitivity toward sexual harassment, but the case only drew attention to their own sexual misconduct. As one Bush administration official noted, 'Half the guys up there, now lamenting what a serious charge this is, had their hands on some underpaid female aide last week.'

Edward Kennedy, whose own career is riddled with sex scandals, was visibly shaken during the entire three days of hearings. With his own involvement in a well publicised rape case still filling the media, he could barely muster the courage to ask a question.

Eighty eight year old Strom Thurmond is apparently known as 'a groper' for his behaviour toward young females in Senate elevators. Brock Adams was accused in 1987 of drugging and fondling the daughter of a friend.

Bush's strategy was standard in cases of this kind: Anita Hill, not Clarence Thomas, was put on trial. Republicans flung a barrage of accusations at Hill, that she was a scorned woman seeking revenge against Thomas because he wasn't interested in her romantically, that she was working on behalf of liberals in an eleventh hour attempt to stop Thomas, that she was suffering from psychological 'delusions' and 'fantasies' about men's sexual interest in her.

To top it off, the Republicans claimed that Clarence Thomas was being attacked because he is black. Thomas himself was brought out to make a tearful speech in which he claimed the hearing was a 'high tech lynching' and he was being victimised by white liberals' stereotypes of black men. Little did it matter that Anita Hill is a black woman.

It quickly became apparent that for the Democrats the hearings were nothing more than a way to dodge charges of sexism. Having pushed Anita Hill out onto the Senate floor, they sat back and watched while she was skewered. They listened silently while the segregationist Strom Thurmond and the open racist Orin Hatch claimed themselves as defenders against Thomas's 'lynching'.

When the vote actually took place a week late, Thomas skated through by a margin of 52 to 48—the narrowest ever for a successful nominee to the Supreme Court. And the kangaroo court which conducted the Thomas hearings left the public with a sense of disgust at Congress itself. Nearly half the respondents in a poll conducted after the hearings say they have less confidence in Congress than before.

This is a point which hasn't been lost on sections of the ruling class. For example, Roger Smith, former chairman of General Motors, said:

> Stuff like this makes people feel bad—feel bad about themselves and about their country. That affects consumer confidence. Bush needs something, though I'm not for another Desert Storm.

The news media has made much of the fact that, when all was said and done, a clear majority of the US population was not convinced by Anita Hill's testimony.

But, as Nan Aron of the Alliance for Justice said in the *New York Times*, Thomas won 'because the Democrats were wimps'. They let the Republicans destroy Anita Hill. The only 'delusion' Anita Hill had was her belief that she would receive anything resembling justice at the end of this ordeal.

Fascism

Chapter 44

Masses against Mosley

Colin Sparks

[This was a review of *Out of the Ghetto* by Joe Jacobs, *Our Flag Stays Red* by Phil Piratin and *The Struggle against Fascism and War in Britain, 1931-1939* by Mike Power—Ed]

One of the few good results of the rise of the National Front in the last few years is that it has riveted the eyes of the left upon the experiences of the fight against the British Union of Fascists in the 1930s. All three of these books are concerned to describe and analyse that victorious battle.

It must be said at once that they are of very uneven quality. Mike Power's pamphlet is a worthless piece of writing which contains so many evasions, misrepresentations, and occasional downright lies that it succeeds in illuminating one thing only: despite its claims to recent conversion, the Communist Party is still committed to the same sort of intellectual honesty that made it famous in the days when it claimed that Trotsky was a Gestapo agent.

Joe Jacobs' book is a different matter as it is nothing if not honest. Unfortunately the author died before completing his work and, out of respect for his memory, his daughter has chosen, wrongly in my opinion, to publish his manuscript virtually without editing. This leads to a rather difficult book about which I will have to express some reservations.

Piratin's book has been, for many years, an underground classic and its publication in a new edition is an event of considerable importance.

First published December 1978

Although it contains much of the same sort of dubious practice as does Power's effort, it also has a number of passages which should be required reading for every anti-fascist.

Both Piratin and Jacobs were leading figures in the Communist Party in Stepney during the 1930s. Piratin later became the Communist MP for Mile End between 1945 and 1950 while Jacobs was expelled from the party twice—once in 1938 and again in 1952. Both were deeply involved in the East End struggle against the fascists and the core of both books is devoted to that question.

They present rather different accounts of the period and, although Piratin does not mention Jacobs by name, both are writing directly about the events which led to Jacobs' expulsion.

The crux of the matter was an issue which is of great contemporary relevance: to what extent should the fight against the fascists be conducted by military means and to what extent should political work play a part?

Piratin's argument is this: the support for the BUF was made up largely of working class people who found in the fascists a distorted answer to the very real problems of housing, unemployment and poverty which they faced on a daily basis. In order to counter this, he argues, direct physical attacks are of little use.

Piratin recounts how he went to a Mosley meeting and observed the audience, who were made up of ordinary working class people. As he put it, 'Where did you get by fighting such people?'

In order to destroy the popular support for fascism, it was not good enough to simply expose the fascists with good propaganda. Rather it was essential to try to offer solutions to their real problems:

> We urged that the Communist Party should help the people to improve their conditions of life, in the course of which we could show them who was responsible for their conditions, and get them organised to fight against their real exploiters.

By far the best sections of this book are the passages where Piratin describes how the Communist Party set about doing this. In particular, he recounts the story of a number of major struggles over housing conditions, in the course of which the CP did manage to build up very considerable support.

His description of the battle against evictions at Paragon Mansions, during which the CP organised to prevent a *fascist* family being thrown into the streets is crucial to understanding his case: 'The kind of people who would never come to our meetings…learned the facts overnight and learned the real meaning of class struggle.'

The two chapters in which Piratin develops this theme, 'Masses against Mosley' and 'Tenants Fight Back', are the best part of the book. I do not know of any better account of the way in which people change their ideas in the course of the struggle and how revolutionary militants have to try to take up the minute issues which are of immense importance to ordinary people.

The reality of a small but victorious struggle over something as petty as stair lighting can be as valuable in the struggle for socialism as the finest presentation of the theory of surplus value.

Jacobs' case stands directly against this. He argues that Piratin and his faction were a right wing tendency in the Communist Party who were opposed to physical confrontation with the fascists and who thus allowed the British Union of Fascists to terrorise and demoralise the Jewish people of Stepney.

His implicit argument, although it is never spelt out, is that the popular front policies of the Communist Party led it to avoid even the defence of the Jewish immigrants and that this was part and parcel of a more general development of opportunist politics throughout the party.

The difficulty that I have is that it seems to me that both were right!

Piratin's argument that it is necessary to provide a genuine political alternative to the misery upon which the fascists seek to play is undoubtedly one of the most important lessons we need to absorb today.

But Jacobs, too, is right when he argues that this should not be done at the expense of the physical confrontation with the fascists. The two should not be contradictory, and both writers pretend that they accepted the need for the complementary form of action, but in practice the balance is a very difficult one to strike.

This problem is highlighted by the events surrounding the famous Battle of Cable Street in 1936. The common view of this is provided by Power, who argues that 'the Communist Party launched a massive campaign aimed at preventing the [fascist] marchers reaching their destination.' As anyone who has looked at the *Daily Worker* for the period will tell you, this is not true, and Piratin at least admits that the CP was very late in calling for a mobilisation against the BUF.

Jacobs provides the detail behind all of this. He shows that the CP initially refused to call off their mobilisation in Trafalgar Square, despite the fact that popular pressure to oppose Mosley was building up. He reproduces a directive from the district organiser Frank Lefitte, dated 29 September 1936 (the fascists were due to march on 4 October), telling Jacobs that the District Political Committee had decided that the policy was to 'avoid clashes' and that 'if Mosley decides to march, let him.'

He also details the struggle inside the CP to get this decision reversed, including the refusal of the Communist leader of the Ex-Servicemen's Anti-Fascist Association, Harold Cohen, to accept any other policy than to try and stop the fascists.

Eventually, the CP changed its line on the evening of the 30 September and joined the mass agitation which was to bring perhaps a quarter of a million workers onto the streets of Stepney and write a glorious page in working class history.

What none of the writers really answer is the question of why this all happened. In my opinion, the reason why the leadership of the CP was determined to press on with a jamboree in central London while the fascists marched into an immigrant area of east London had nothing to do with their claim that it would be difficult to 'organise' opposition.

As with all such claims, the real problem was political. The Labour Party conference was about to begin, and the CP hoped to win it to a formal popular front; to the end of that unity they were prepared to sacrifice the Jewish people of east London. It is to the credit of Jacobs, Cohen and other CP militants of the area that they had the political determination to fight this opportunist manouevre and were prepared to go ahead even in defiance of the party line.

This political problem is the key to why the problem of 'violence' *versus* 'politics' is misplaced. The question for a revolutionary party is rather, can it retain the political flexibility to do *both*? The whole development of the CP in the 1930s was away from independent action and towards a policy of unity at any price; it is that which lies behind the quarrel between Jacobs and Piratin, not the question of violence.

We can learn much from both of these positions because we should not accept either of them without reservation. From Piratin we can take the need for mass mobilisation and the political struggle against the fascists. From Jacobs we can take the refusal to subordinate the struggle for working class politics to a phoney unity with the leaders of reformism.

With the benefit of hindsight we can see the issues around which they quarrelled were not simply parochial squabbles limited to the East End 40 years ago. They were part and parcel of the death of the Communist Party and the Communist International as forces for world revolution. It is up to us today to do rather better.

The balance between a broad popular mobilisation and the political independence of a revolutionary party is a difficult one to find.

There is a constant pressure to copy the leaders of the CP and to sub-ordinate a militant and principled policy to the apparent gains to be had from a matey relationship with assorted reformist dignitaries. There is also a counter-pressure simply to repeat into empty air the elementary truth that the fight against fascism is a fight against capitalism and that fascist marches should be stopped, if need be by violence.

In Britain the fascist menace never reached the point at which the price of a political mistake by the left would be the extinction of all working class organisations. In Germany the Communist Party faced such a position and, along with the German working class, paid the price of the sectarian 'Third Period' followed by capitulation to a false unity. The arguments in these books were part of that massive tragedy.

In summary, I would say of the books under review that no one should bother with Power's, but the other two deserve reading. Jacobs' book has all the faults of a first draft and it is easy to get lost in the welter of details of his personal life; interesting though these are, they seem secondary to the political purpose of the book.

In general, his political line veers towards the ultra-left 'Third Period' politics he learned when he joined the Communist Party. It is a book which anyone who wants to learn the details of the struggle in the 1930s should buy and read.

Piratin, on the other hand, wrote a book which, despite its many faults, should be read by everybody who opposes Nazi organisations. Buy yourself two copies. Keep one for your own use and lend the other to people sympathetic to the fight against the Nazis. Get them to read it. But try to help them to read it through red spectacles.

Chapter 45

The threat of Le Pen

Gareth Jenkins

Is the French National Front a fascist organisation? Many on the French left would reply no, or not yet.

They would say that Le Pen's party is deeply reactionary, racist and xenophobic, but that it draws its inspiration mostly from a native right wing tradition.

This tradition is a ragbag of lost causes—monarchism, extreme Catholic bigotry, admiration for the wartime collaborationist Vichy regime, etc.

It would therefore be a mistake, so the argument continues, to exaggerate the lasting importance of the National Front. It is, they argue, part of the same spectrum as the other right wing parties, if nastier than the others. The chief evidence put forward to support this view is that unlike classical fascism Le Pen does not attack the system of bourgeois democracy, nor has he created the French equivalents of the SA or SS with the aim of physically smashing workers' organisations—trade unions and political parties.

But the truth is that there is an element in the make up of Le Pen's party qualitatively different to the traditional right which allows us to characterise it as fascist.

There is the social base of Le Pen's party. Like the Nazis in Germany it is overwhelmingly petty bourgeois, despite the fact that Le Pen himself and some of his closest cronies are extremely wealthy.

A sociological profile of a sample of his electorate in the presidential

First published June 1988

race shows that 31 percent of the artisan and small shopkeeper vote went to Le Pen—twice what he got in 1986. This is more than went to either of the two classic right wing parties.

He also took 16 percent of the junior management vote, and 16 percent and 11 percent among office and shop workers respectively (this includes supervisory and managerial grades).

In addition he took 18 percent of the small farmer vote, 14 percent of the senior management vote and 21 percent of the professional vote.

This massive shift of the petty bourgeoisie was also able to pull a small section of the working class and the unemployed (16 percent of his vote from the working class, 19 percent from the unemployed).

What we have, therefore, is a situation in which the traditional parties of the French ruling class are being squeezed, with a significant part of their base deserting to the fascists. The allegiance of the working class vote to the reformist parties has not changed much, except that the 'harder' Communist Party element has declined at the expense of the 'softer' Socialist Party element.

What of Le Pen's programme? The ideology is fascist; however, the dominant ideas are not the elitist ones of the lunatic right but populist ones.

Around the theme of anti-immigration he weaves a programme aimed at helping 'ordinary people' who feel under threat from big business and from socialism.

Le Pen is able to use the visibility of the North African immigrant in the same way Hitler used the Jew. He feeds the myths that immigrants have taken over all the small shops, that they outbreed the French to take the lion's share of social benefits, housing and local amenities, that they are the troublemakers in key sectors of the economy.

The petty bourgeoisie feels the pinch of the austerity programme introduced by the 'reds' but which their parties have failed to roll back. The failure to deal with the 'burden' of immigrants appears to explain every manifestation of crisis in French society—from lack of security to lack of national competitiveness.

This explanation, endlessly replayed and only challenged half heartedly if at all by other political leaders, can begin to impress workers who are losing confidence in the system—and the left parties—to deliver.

Le Pen can begin to appear like a national saviour, above the petty disputes of party politicians.

But where, it might be asked, are the anti-parliamentarism and its corresponding street fighting forces? This is important because it is this element—the ability to mould the petty bourgeoisie into a *fighting* rather than electoral force—which makes fascism so dangerous.

Admittedly, hitherto the shock troops have only played a relatively minor role in the evolution of the National Front, though there has always been a thuggish element—attacks on left wing paper sellers, on left wing meetings and on immigrants being their speciality.

For the moment Le Pen chooses to keep such people in the background because he is anxious to build up his constitutional image.

Le Pen knows that the paramilitary trappings of Nazism, such as the swastika image, would be of no help to him in building a movement. Too many French people remember the horrors of the occupation.

So he concentrates on identifying the immigrant as the enemy and using elections to make the idea an acceptable everyday one. Once the crisis becomes worse, or there is some excuse (an immigrant 'riot' for example), it is easy enough to make organised *physical* attacks on the enemy and the 'reds' who defend the enemy equally acceptable.

In this respect Le Pen is no different from John Tyndall of the British National Party, who has always tried to keep the Nazi hard core of his party out of the limelight and who has concentrated as much as possible on building electoral support.

But Le Pen is determined to avoid the mistake that Tyndall made of letting the hooligan element appear too dominant at times—and therefore giving anti-fascist forces the opportunity to expose the reality at the heart of his movement.

Being nailed as a fascist obviously worries Le Pen and it is worth noting his reaction after the outrage that greeted his notorious comment about the gas chambers being a mere 'detail of history' in the Second World War.

It was revealing, he said in an 'off the record' remark, that so few demonstrated. 'With that kind of to-do, there should have been millions in the street.'

But if Le Pen is today hiding his Nazi sympathies and concentrating on building his soft support, no one should imagine this is a permanent feature.

If the impending elections to the National Assembly decimate his parliamentary representation (which seems likely, because proportional representation has been abandoned), he may be forced to develop the violent side to his party sooner rather than later, particularly in places like Marseilles where he is assured of massive support.

Because his is a fascist party he can switch to extra-parliamentary methods of organising in a way that traditional right wing parties cannot.

But could France go fascist in the near future? There are two main factors that need to be kept in mind when answering this question.

First, society is not polarised in such a way that bourgeois democracy is no longer an option for the ruling class.

Secondly, the nature of the economic crisis has changed. Nowadays the crisis is much more drawn out. The economic role played by the state cushions the system from the kind of extreme effects witnessed after the 1929 Wall Street Crash—but at the cost of failing to resolve the crisis.

So the petty bourgeoisie is less likely to be subjected to the kinds of intense pressure that open it up to counter-revolutionary despair and the mass appeal of fascism. Nor are political institutions so vulnerable— at least in the short term.

These factors suggest that a fascist takeover is not on the immediate agenda. Nevertheless it would be wrong to say fascism is no longer a historical possibility just because social circumstances have changed since the 1930s.

Furthermore, the presence of a large fascist party, even if remote from seizing power, can act as a useful smokescreen for the ruling class. Immigrants can be scapegoated; the reformists can justify their pro-capitalist measures as the only things that stand between democracy and the abyss; the left and the trade unions can be ideologically and physically weakened.

The growth of a fascist party, like the National Front, poses very real dangers of a massive shift to the right in the political spectrum. Ex prime minister Chirac's neo-Gaullist party is haemorrhaging to the fascist right, and the other right wing party, the UDF, never very stable, is under pressure to split into its component elements.

Consequently the Socialist Party is already moving rapidly to the centre and looking for a coalition with the centre right. This is reminiscent of French politics in the days of the Fourth Republic (1946 to 1958), when the forerunner of the Socialist Party, the SFIO, played a very right wing role, including support for the war against Algerian independence and for de Gaulle's demands for dictatorial powers.

Such is the pull of Le Pen that we find not only a strong echo of his anti-immigrant propaganda in the speeches made by Chirac, the leader of the neo-Gaullist RPR, but an echo at one remove in what Mitterrand has had to say on the subject. Mitterrand has deplored racism in much stronger terms than anyone on the right, but he 'admits' that people's fears need dealing with.

Why is there such reluctance to see the National Front as fascist and the defeat of Le Pen as a priority?

The anti-racist organisation SOS Racisme, which is tied to Socialist Party politics, refuses to do so, arguing that racism is the real enemy and that the struggle must not be directed against the National Front but against the social conditions that lead people to vote for Le Pen.

This sounds fine, but under the present circumstances such a view is an excuse, under a left cover, for not fighting.

It is designed to divert struggle into parliamentary channels on the spurious grounds that the Socialist Party is the only force capable of tackling the roots of racism. It thus hides the responsibility of the Socialist Party, because of its austerity measures, for the rise of Le Pen.

The revolutionary left, with its lack of illusions in parliamentarism, its commitment to workers' struggles and adherence to the Trotskyist tradition, should have a better position. Regrettably, this is not always the case.

If we look at Lutte Ouvrière, the biggest and most serious of the French revolutionary left groups, we can see that it too refuses to categorise the National Front clearly and unequivocally as fascist. And it refuses to organise against the Front.

It says only struggle in the workplace can destroy the capitalist system which breeds the support for Le Pen. In the absence of that, campaigns would be a diversion and a cover for the Socialist Party. Starting from a very different perspective from SOS Racisme, Lutte Ouvrière finishes up in a similarly abstentionist position.

It fails to understand the differences between reformist and openly capitalist parties (which led to a scandalously abstentionist line in the second round of the presidential elections). Reformist leaders are treacherous agents of the bourgeoisie within the working class and are incapable of consistently defending the interests of the working class against reaction (including fascist reaction). But they nevertheless have an interest in defending themselves and their organisations, which fascism seeks to destroy.

So too have revolutionaries, because in the struggle to defend reformist workers' organisations they can show who are the best and most consistent fighters. A successful struggle is not only good in itself, it also enables revolutionaries to discredit reformist leaders and pull sections of reformist workers behind revolutionary leadership.

This is why Trotsky proposed the tactic of the united front in the fight against fascism.

The other major group on the French revolutionary left, the Ligue Communiste Révolutionnaire (French Section of the Fourth International), has much better instincts. It recognises the threat posed by the growth of fascism and to its credit was responsible for mobilising large numbers of demonstrators and trade unionists on 1 May to march in protest against Le Pen.

The problem is that the Ligue is not clear about how to proceed. Because it tends to act on the belief that the Socialist Party can break with capitalism, it also tends to avoid independent initiatives of its own (it was completely buried in the campaign of ex-Communist Pierre Juquin, who stood for president this year).

Consequently, though better than Lutte Ouvrière on the need to fight the fascists, it is hesitant and indecisive. It said Le Pen's troops should not occupy the streets of Paris on 1 May—but as far as we know did not argue for physical confrontation with Le Pen's demonstration. Perhaps the Ligue fears the problems that could follow for its base, principally in the Socialist Party trade union, the CFDT.

The Ligue does not grasp the fact that the condition for an effective united front is the complete political independence of revolutionaries. It cannot be ambiguous about the thoroughgoing reformist nature of the Socialist Party. Otherwise it abdicates responsibility for leading the anti-fascist struggle to those who are confused or treacherous, and thereby undermines the struggle itself.

The truth is that the revolutionary left is not so weak it is unable to do anything to stop Le Pen. It could mobilise its electoral support and sympathisers to initiate a fight against the National Front. It could use that to attempt to force sections of the reformist trade unions and the Socialist Party (perhaps even the Communist Party) into an active struggle against the National Front.

That is what was successfully done with the Anti Nazi League in Britain in the late 1970s. Once the Socialist Workers Party had shown that large numbers could be mobilised in active opposition to the fascists it was possible to force some sections of the left reformists in the Labour Party (including Neil Kinnock!) and in the unions into a united front.

Of course the success of the Anti Nazi League was due to the fact that revolutionaries did not rely on the politics of the reformists in the united front to build the opposition to the National Front. But without their support it would have been impossible to persuade people who looked to reformist leaders to come into joint activity against the Front.

Of course conditions in France are different, but the growth of fascism demands that the French revolutionary left applies this tactic. The key would be a strategy to split Le Pen's hard core of Nazis from the much softer support he has built up. This needs to be done by physical confrontation where possible to frighten away all but hardened

Nazis, and by consistent propaganda work designed to explain the threat that fascism poses as much for French workers as for immigrants.

Many who are not revolutionaries could be won to activity on such a platform—as was shown by the size of the unity demonstrations on 1 May called by the Ligue Communiste Révolutionnaire.

Le Pen's remark—that it was revealing that millions did not demonstrate against his Holocaust comment—shows that he understood the threat to his movement a combative anti-fascist movement could pose.

The need to confront and defeat Le Pen is urgent. Otherwise the cost to the French working class—and eventually the European working class—could be disastrous.

Chapter 46

The crisis of British politics

Lindsey German

Wherever you look in Britain today the air of crisis, decay and despair is greater than it has been for many years.

Contempt for mainstream politicians (a recent poll showed over 90 percent of people distrust them), erosion of support for institutions such as the police or monarchy, and the feeling that every area of British life is in decline have never been greater.

When nearly 1,500 people voted for the fascist British National Party in Millwall last month, giving them their first local councillor, the grim reality of the crisis of British politics hit home. The decay, the closure of industry, the rundown of public services, the feeling of paralysis about any political change, have become the dominant features in a society where only five years ago we were being told we had escaped economic crisis forever.

The magic of the market, the trickledown of wealth from the rich to the poor, the enterprise culture, have been exposed as a sham. Nowhere in Britain is this more the case than in the Isle of Dogs, site of the BNP victory, where the grotesque monolith of Canary Wharf stands as a monument to the values which are so detested by most people today.

All the evidence suggests that institutions which have traditionally been central to holding British society together and winning the adherence of the majority of the population—including a sizeable chunk of the working class—have been dramatically weakened in recent years.

First published October 1993

Even the police themselves now declare that they have no confidence in the criminal justice system. What hope can there be for the rest of us?

At the centre of so much of the contempt and unpopularity are the politicians from the main parties themselves. The Tories are of course the main recipients of this feeling. Partly, they have fallen out among themselves. John Major has, after all, been quoted by the press in recent months referring to other cabinet ministers as 'bastards' and Tory backbench critics as 'barmy'.

Local Tory activists are at their most demoralised for years. For example, the membership officer for the Western region, Dr Adrian Rogers, said on John Major's recent visit to his area:

> I wanted to know if he really appreciated how hard it was being a Conservative and I think he did. It's a very loyal party but it's had the worst year ever and I think that's got through to him.

Another Tory activist, the leader of the Tory opposition on Taunton Deane council, John Meikle, said:

> People are concerned about a number of things, including VAT on fuel and a whole lot of unpopular issues. I feel that probably the party has unnecessarily inflicted on people things to grumble about.

But rows between Tory politicians are only one sign of more widespread contempt. There is a *universal* feeling that politicians are all liars.

And the ideological crisis goes much deeper than merely superficial discontent with politicians. It has its roots in the complete failure of Thatcherism to deliver what was required for the British ruling class.

A recent opinion poll shows that 46 percent of people, including 24 percent of Tory voters, agree that 'more socialist planning would be the best way to solve Britain's economic problems'. This demonstrates how far the mood has swung against the 'free market' and its supposed benefits.

Recent surveys on taxation show a similar change in attitudes: 59 percent were in favour, in a recent ICM poll for the *Guardian*, of raising the higher rate of tax; only 14 percent were in favour of higher VAT. In response to the question of what public spending should be cut if it is necessary, 93 percent and 90 percent were against cutting health and education spending respectively. The only area where there was a clear majority for spending cuts was in defence, where 64 percent favoured cuts.

The imposition of VAT on fuel has led to further erosions in the government's already low popularity. Privatisation of rail, the closure of more and more mines despite popular opposition, the drying up of funds for NHS hospitals, have combined with uncertainty about jobs and low wages to increase the level of bitterness.

However, contempt for Tory politics also spreads to the other parties. Despite some success by the Liberal Democrats in winning disaffected Tory voters in rural constituencies, their policies are unlikely to provide an alternative to Tory cuts or unemployment, and they are now quite correctly tarred with the brush of right wing populism and racism, a tactic they have employed for years far wider than just in Tower Hamlets.

Labour is increasingly seen as the main alternative by the majority of working class people with its poll ratings suggesting a majority government, if there were an election. But there is little enthusiasm for—and much disillusion with—Labour.

There are two main reasons for this. One is the total failure of Labour to address the problems facing ordinary working people. On taxation, on social security, on education, it trails after the Tories, wanting to ameliorate the worst of their excesses, but accepting the ground on which they stand. Labour, backed up by its allies, the trade union leaders, has opposed or downplayed any idea of direct action by people themselves to present attacks.

The second reason for Labour's unpopularity is its own record in local government. Acceptance of government cuts, a refusal to fight for better provision, the erosion of council services and a tendency to do deals with businessmen and property developers at the expense of local people have increased. Disillusion with Labour is at its greatest on many of the declining council estates which, with their non-existent services, are often little better than prisons for many of their residents.

Attacks on council workforces through the cuts and areas such as competitive tendering have eroded much of the Labour councils' traditional support. So any positive endorsement of Labour almost always now hangs on what they would not do—they would not privatise rail, cut public spending as far as the Tories have or extend VAT. This lack of support and identification does not mean that Labour cannot grow or cannot win elections.

But it does mean that a polarisation has developed. The old consensus politics, which was the bedrock of postwar society, has disappeared. In its place have appeared apathy and cynicism, punctuated by huge explosions of anger, such as over the poll tax or the miners. The economic crisis has greatly increased this mood, which is why the fascists were able to win their vote in Milwall. But disillusion with the system also gives a new audience for socialist ideas as an alternative to the dead end of parliamentary politics.

The polarisation in politics, the vacuum created by Labour's decline and the inertia of the unions, and the terrible effects of the crisis on ordinary working people, all combine to create an atmosphere in which the fascists can gain some support. Why is this when the BNP represents race hatred, forced deportation of immigrants, destruction of any form of democracy, the smashing of trade unions and democratic political parties, and the silencing of any voice of protest?

Their appeal is not, of course, based on propagating these views. If they were to campaign on such a platform, their support would never get any bigger than the tiny number of boneheads and fanatics who comprise their inner core. That is why it is so important for them to gain respectability—something the fascists have so far been unable to do—and why they base their campaigning on identifying with some of the key areas of discontent which so worry working class people today.

The Isle of Dogs was fertile ground in this respect. The contrast between wealth and poverty is vast and dramatic. Promises of jobs and houses for local people with Docklands redevelopment have not materialised. There is a justifiable feeling that these people have been left to rot by national government and by the local council as well—both Liberal and Labour.

The BNP has a completely false, yet superficially plausible, argument: the neglect of local people and the lack of concern by big business mean that Asians and other 'foreigners' are taking the houses, jobs and schools which should by rights go to locals—ie whites. This argument alone would not perhaps be persuasive—after all, it has had little resonance in many other equally deprived parts of the country—were it not for the fanning of racism by the local Liberals, which has given these arguments wider purchase and a respectable face.

The fascists will use these and other populist arguments to try to tap into the mood of bitterness and anger which the mainstream politicians are shocked by but have no answer to.

At the same time, we should put into perspective what has actually happened in the Isle of Dogs and how weak the far right's prospects still are. They have one councillor elected on just over one third of the vote in the area. They will obviously try to use the result to build in other inner city areas with bad housing and services. But the scale of opposition to the BNP, and the horror felt by millions at the result, show that they will not get it all their own way.

It is still very easy to smash what little influence they have built. Compare the one seat with the 1,000 local government seats held by Jean-Marie Le Pen's National Front in France. Or compare the support the British National Front gained in the mid-1970s. Not only are the fascists much weaker today, there are far more people who understand the need to oppose the Nazis.

This would seem to be a universal feeling. Everyone from John Major to the editorials of the posh papers has condemned the election result. But although these people will recoil in liberal horror, they will do nothing to stop the Nazis. Indeed, they are already accepting the need to work with the fascist councillor, on the grounds of 'democracy', and condemn mobilisations against the fascists. As in the past, in the 1930s and 1970s, beating the Nazis will lie with rank and file activists on the ground who directly confront them.

Already there are many signs that this is happening, from the magnificent walkout of Isle of Dogs council workers who struck in protest at having to work with a fascist councillor, to the mobilisations in Brick Lane to drive off the Nazis and the demonstration this month to close down the BNP headquarters in Welling.

The success of the Anti Nazi League in the 1970s means that even now it is much harder for the fascists to gain a foothold or a respectable veneer. The mobilisation has to ensure that it stays that way.

However, mobilising against the Nazis alone will not destroy the threat. The scapegoating of blacks for bad housing and unemployment will continue unless there is an alternative put forward. That means fighting on the social issues whose failings give the fascists their chance. If this fight were taken up by the whole of the labour and trade union movement, it would soon be victorious. Unfortunately the Labour and union leaders are apathetic or indifferent—sometimes even hostile—to these struggles. Labour councils are often in the forefront of implementing policies which result in, at best, the sharing of the crumbs from the Tories' table.

In every locality there has to be a fight over these issues squatting empty luxury homes in Docklands, keeping hospitals open, opposing cuts in schools. Most Labour and trade union members will back such campaigns enthusiastically—and their leaders can be pushed into doing so. Success in these issues will undercut any potential base for the fascists, by providing real improvements in people's lives.

However, the crisis of politics in Britain today requires more than these small scale reforms, important though they are in building confidence rather than despair. It requires trying to build an alternative to a system increasingly in decay.

The ruling class crisis means that there are more and more attacks on workers coming from both employers and government. The Tory declaration of a wage freeze is one example which has already led to a greater degree of generalisation among many public sector workers than had previously been the case.

The main recipient of the anger and bitterness at these attacks is not, at present, black people, but the government itself. The wage freeze is likely to increase the fury already growing from worsening living standards and increased VAT on fuel.

Unfortunately there has not yet been a significant fight by large groups of workers against the government. The public anger over pit closures was not turned into industrial action, and the attitude of the trade union leaders can be summed up by the new head of the TUC:

> The job of unions is to avoid strikes, particularly ones of any duration. There is often an initial enthusiasm among workers when they embark on industrial action. But during strikes income is lost, job security threatened and people are vulnerable to victimisation. Strikes are a weapon of last resort.

Yet the more the union leaders counsel caution, the more they are likely to disillusion at least a section of their membership who look for more militant action. And the more likely it is that those who want to fight—and the scale of the crisis is leading tens of thousands in that direction—will look to socialist organisation to link up and give expression to a whole range of different struggles.

It is commonplace for most media commentators to believe that the crisis in politics today will easily be resolved. Maybe a new prime minster will do the trick, or maybe economic recovery will solve the political problems. It is not going to be like that. We have higher taxes or further spending cuts in store, whatever happens and whoever is in government. The 1980s, when many believed that everyone could just get better off, have now been revealed as a cruel joke.

Despite all the hype during that decade, there are no clear answers to economic crisis, to how schools can be improved, how we can house the homeless, how we can end unemployment. Even capitalism's most optimistic forecasts allow for millions on the dole and a huge 'underclass' in all the major capitalist countries.

In such a situation the political crisis may have its ups and downs, but it is here to stay. The best that most people can hope for is that their personal situation will not get worse, but few believe it. Most people accept that their children's lives will be worse than their own.

The polarisation which has opened up in politics will continue, and is already posing the urgent question about how society goes forward. In such circumstances, a revolutionary socialist organisation like the SWP can grow—if it understands it has to provide an answer to those tens of thousands looking to an alternative to this rotten system.

War

Chapter 47

Marxism and the missiles

Chris Harman

One of the major themes running through *Socialist Review* over the last nine months has been the drive towards a new Cold War. We have insisted that it is a prime duty of socialists to resist this, and we have attempted to provide the arguments they need.

Until recently, however, our assumption was that we would be very much on the defensive over the question. The media were putting out a deluge of Cold War propaganda. There seemed to be no wider movement of resistance from which we could get support.

Over the summer, however, things have begun to change. The anti-bomb movement has suddenly taken on a new lease of life. From many different parts of the country come reports of very large public meetings, and of sizeable demonstrations, leading up to what looks like being a very big protest in London on 26 October.

At the heart of the revived movement has been the historian E P Thompson. In articles in the *Guardian* and the *New Statesman*, in the pamphlet *Protest and Survive* and in scores of public meetings, he has polemicised brilliantly against the cruise missile.

He has not been alone in putting the arguments. But it has been Thompson more than anyone else who has brought the movement back to life. And all credit is due to him for doing so.

It has also been Thompson who has provided whatever analysis the new movement has of the drive towards missile madness and of a strategy for combating it.

First published October 1980

It is here that we in *Socialist Review* (and the SWP generally) have to dissent from what Thompson says.

Thompson's strategy is, quite simply, to arouse the largest possible numbers of people to protest at the decision to deploy the cruise missiles:

> We must generate an alternative logic, an opposition at every level of society. The opposition must be international and must win the support of multitudes. It must bring its influence to bear upon the rulers of the world (*Protest and Survive*).

Who is to make up this opposition?

The impression you get from reading *Protest and Survive* is that Thompson is looking essentially for the same sort of people who made up CND 20 years ago and who turned out in considerable numbers to the public meetings over the summer—the articulate middle classes, people with university degrees, or possibly studying for them:

> As it happens the major bases (for the cruise missiles) are to be placed in close proximity to the ancient universities of Oxford and Cambridge, and it seems to me that useful work can be done from these old bases of European civilisation. There will be work of research, of publication, and also work of conscience, all of which is very suitable for scholars... Oxford and Cambridge then are privileged to initiate this campaign.

But it can involve:

> Any existing institution or even individual, universities and colleges— or groups within them—trade unionists, women's organisations, members of professions, churches, practitioners of Esperanto or chess...
>
> [With these] before long we will be crossing frontiers...bursting open bureaucrats' doors, making the telephone tappers spin in their hideaways...and breaking up all the old stony Stalinist reflexes of the East by forcing open dialogue and debate...

If this were all that Thompson were arguing, we would be tempted to make a few words of protest. Even on the basis of purely arithmetic calculation it seems a bit strange to give no more prominence to 12 million trade unionists than to the half a million members of professions, the two million churchgoers or the 45,000 university dons—particularly when all the emphasis is on the dons.

But Thompson does not end his argument there. Underlying his comments in *Protest and Survive* is a wide reaching attempt at analysis of the new Cold War dedicated to refuting the notion that 'the bomb is a class issue'.

This is most openly argued by him in a recent issue of *New Left Review*.

The burden of Thompson's analysis is that society East and West has reached a new and terrifying stage in its development—'exterminism'.

> Exterminism designates those characteristics of a society which thrust it in the direction whose outcome must be the extermination of millions...
>
> [It results from] the accumulation and perfection of the means of extermination and the structuring of whole societies so that these will be directed towards that end.

The factors which gave rise to 'exterminism' may once have been imperialist interests or the pursuit of profit by military-industrial complexes. But the methods used initially by ruling classes in the rational pursuit of their interests have taken on an irrational life of their own and are no longer reducible to their original courses:

> What originated as reaction becomes direction. What is justified by rational self interest by one power or the other becomes, in the collision of the two, irrational. We are confronted with the accumulated logic of process.

To treat this outcome as the product of 'rational' choices by ruling classes is 'to impose a consequential rationality' upon an 'irrational' object.

Exterminism has to be challenged by the presentation of an 'alternative' logic, by:

> Initiating a counter-logic, a thrust of process leading towards the dissolution of both blocs, the demystification of exterminism's ideological mythology.

It is this which has to be achieved by the alliance of 'churches, Eurocommunists, Labourites, East European dissidents (and not only "dissidents")...trade unionists, ecologists...' As 'the blocs' swing 'off their collision course...the armourers and the police will lose their authority.'

Any talk of the bomb as a 'class issue' makes these tasks more difficult:

> Class struggle continues in many forms across the globe. But exterminism itself is not a 'class issue': it is a human issue.

'Revolutionary posturing', Thompson insists, can only:

> carry division into the necessary alliance of human resistance—indeed, worse than that, it can inflame exterminist ideology.
>
> It should go without saying that exterminism can only be confronted by the broadest popular alliance, that is, by every affirmative resource in our culture.

The analysis

Is 'exterminism' something so entirely new in its irrationality?

The picture Thompson paints of rival blocs, each ruled by elites imprisoned by the pressures of the military competition between them, is correct. But it is by no means something outside the scope of old Marxist methods of class analysis.

Back in 1844 when Marx began to develop his ideas, he took over the notion of 'alienation' from the philosophers Hegel and Feuerbach. He observed that in capitalist society the activity of people on the world becomes something separated from them, takes on a life of its own and comes to dominate them:

> The object which labour produces confronts it as something alien, as a power independent of the producer... The more the worker spends himself, the more powerful the alien world becomes which he creates over against himself... The worker puts his life into the object; but now his life no longer belongs to himself but to his object.

But for the young Marx it was not only the worker who became imprisoned in this 'alien' world beyond his or her control. So did the capitalist: he was alienated as well, even though he was 'happy in his alienation'.

The point of Marx's later work—especially *Capital*, was precisely to work out the way in which 'objective laws' came into existence that controlled this world of 'alienated labour'. Marx showed how the ability of the capitalist to extract surplus value from the workers at the point of production put a continual constraint on both the worker and the capitalist. The harder the worker works, the more wealth he creates for the capitalist. This wealth can then be used to expand the productive forces at the disposal of the capitalist, to employ more workers and to create still more wealth for capital. The very labour of the worker has created the chains (even if the worker is well paid and they are 'golden chains') which tie him or her to endless production.

But the capitalist too is a prisoner. The very fact that exploitation and accumulation are possible for one capitalist makes them obligatory for all capitalists. Any capitalist who does not exploit in order to accumulate and accumulate in order to exploit will be driven out of business.

Yet, Marx went on to argue, the capitalist is doomed by the very world of alienated labour in which he thrives. The compulsion to endless accumulation regardless of the consequence leads, in the short term, to repeated economic crises in which many capitalists go bankrupt. And in the long term it drives the whole capitalist system to economic stagnation, political chaos and social turmoil which in the end doom the capitalist class, facing it either with socialist revolution or 'the mutual destruction of the contending classes'.

This did not mean that capitalists individually or as a class could be made to see sense and behave differently by reading *Capital*. Any capitalist who tried to do so would be driven out of business by the others. And so the ruling class necessarily identified the continuation of society as they knew it, of what they saw as 'civilisation', with the enthusiastic imposition of measures that could only end by destroying that society. Only the violence of an insurgent working class could make them step aside and allow the reorganisation of society on a rational basis.

Marx's analysis of the effects of 'peaceful' competition for markets might seem a far cry from the world of cruise and Pershing. But in 1915 and 1916 the analysis was expanded to explain the bitter, bloody and apparently pointless war which had the great nations of Europe locked in combat, rapidly threatening to tear all of them apart.

Imperialism and 'exterminism'

There was already one attempt at explanation of the war—expounded chiefly by the German socialist Karl Kautsky—that went something like this.

The war was not at all in the interests of the great majority of capitalists on either side. They had been conned by a minority of arms manufacturers into believing that only through war could they defend their capitalist interests in the colonies. But in reality it would be the easiest thing in the world for the different capitalist powers to meet together and agree jointly to exploit the colonies. And so the war could be ended merely by bringing pressure to bear on capitalists to behave differently (or, as Thompson might have put it, to pursue 'an alternative logic').

This account of the war was challenged by the Bolshevik theorists Bukharin and Lenin. Some aspects of Lenin's analysis of imperialism may not have stood the test of time. But in it, and even more so in Bukharin's *Imperialism and the World Economy*, are accounts of the 'logic' that produced the First World War. And these can still throw much light on 'exterminism' today.

Lenin and Bukharin insisted that the development of capitalism leads to military competition complementing and even taking over from peaceful competition for markets.

For as capitalism grows older two apparently contradictory things happen. On the one hand, within each country there is a concentration of economic power into fewer and fewer giant firms, increasingly integrated into the state. Yet, at the same time, the growing scale of production means it can no longer be contained within the narrow boundaries within which existing states operate.

The only way the contradiction can be resolved is if the national state can extend its powers beyond the boundaries within which existing states operate. It has to build up its armies, its navies, its airforces, its weaponry, so as to be able to safeguard markets, production facilities and raw material resources that exist abroad. This means annexing some territories, establishing spheres of influence over others, forcibly pressurising the rulers of the rest to safeguard its interests.

'The struggle between state capitalist trusts is decided in the first place by the relation between their military forces, for the military power of the country is the last resort of the struggling "national" groups of capitalists,' wrote Bukharin in 1916. 'The capitalists partition the world, not out of personal malice, but because the degree of concentration which has been reached forces them to adopt this method in order to get profits,' Lenin insisted a year later. But any partition could only be agreed on by all of them for a short period of time, since as some of them grew economically more quickly than others the military balance between the powers would shift and the stronger ones would demand a larger share of the world.

Under such circumstances, periods of peace 'inevitably can only be "breathing spells" between wars. Peaceful alliances prepare the way for wars, and in their turn grow out of wars.' Bukharin spelt the argument out again in 1921 in his *Economics of the Transformation Period*:

> The anarchy of world capitalism—the opposition between social world labour and 'national' state appropriation—expresses itself in the collision of the state organisations and in capitalist wars...
>
> War is nothing other than the method of competition at a specific level of development...the method of competition between state capitalist trusts...

Just as economic competition has a logic of its own, so Lenin and Bukharin argued that military competition does. Lenin observed that imperialism was characterised not just by the seizure of areas necessary to the national economy but by the seizure of areas which might strengthen the rural power if it possessed them and which were of importance from the point of view of military strategy. And Bukharin noted that the militarist structure of the state arose from the 'economic base', but 'like every "superstructure" reacted back on the base and moulded it in a certain direction.'

The point of this discussion of Marx, Lenin and Bukharin is not to show that Thompson has infringed some 'orthodoxy'. It is rather to emphasise that what he sees as completely new developments, right outside the perspectives of classical Marxism, are exactly the sort of things that classical Marxism was trying to explain. Competition between manufactured products gave rise to competition between those fairly nasty classes of manufactured objects, Dreadnoughts, machine guns and poisonous gases, and that in turn gave rise to competition between the most horrendous of manufactured objects, intercontinental ballistic missiles and nuclear bombs. The level of alienation is raised to an incredible degree; the physical future of all members of all classes is put at risk—but all on the basis of the 'world of alienated labour', the capitalist relations of production.

The logic of the Cold War

Let's look briefly at what motivates the major protagonists of the Cold War.

The facts about the expansion of the interests of US capitalism beyond its national boundaries are well known: it controls about half the productive wealth of the world; firms like Ford or General Motors or the oil giants operate productive facilities in scores of countries; US investments overseas produce more output than any single country apart from the US itself and the USSR; the US banks receive the lion's share of the $88 billion a year which developing countries have to pay out on debt servicing each year. The point has been reached where the viability of almost all of the major US industrial corporations and banks depends upon maintaining intact integrated complexes of components operations throughout the 'free world': the great banks could be brought to their knees if one of the great debtor nations defaulted; even Ford would have gone bankrupt in the last couple of years but for its overseas operations.

Under such circumstances the rulers of the US see the frontiers of their vital interests as much wider than the frontiers of the US itself. They believe that they have to maintain the most powerful armed forces in the world so as to be able to ward off threats to these interests, whether from genuine national liberation movements, from Russian moves, or from the other Western capitalisms taking measures that would damage the functioning of the US multinationals and banks (for instance, through protectionist measures).

This basic military drive is reinforced by subordinate factors: by the way in which over 30 years the cost of maintaining this huge military apparatus has been partially offset by its effect of stabilising the civilian economy and lessening the severity of economic crises; and by the way in which key firms and powerful bureaucratic sectors within the armed forces and the Pentagon gain as against other parts of the ruling class from the scale of the arms effort.

But the US does not operate as the only force in world affairs. Thompson quite rightly dismisses those who would see US imperialism as the only cause of missile madness. But he does not comprehend how Russia has developed an imperialist drive of its own. And so he can conclude imperialism is not the cause of the arms race.

Yet if we look closely at the way in which Russian society has developed since the late 1920s it is easy to see how an imperialist drive has developed symmetrical to that of the Western powers. When the group around Stalin took complete control of Russia, they set themselves the task of defending that control by developing a military apparatus as powerful as that of any potential foe. But that was only possible on the basis of imitating in Russia much of the basis of the Western military potential—building up heavy industry through squeezing the living standards of workers and peasants and ploughing the excess value so obtained into accumulation. But once such methods were adopted, it was logical to copy the West in other ways as well—to reach out beyond the USSR's borders for further resources for accumulation. Hence the division of Poland with Hitler in 1939, the division of the whole of Europe with Churchill and Roosevelt in 1944-45, the move into Afghanistan last December.

Accumulation in order to match the arms potential of a rival is an endless process. Every success in expanding the industrial base or armaments only spurs the rival to do the same. The arms budget has to be increased in order to hold together a ramshackle empire already groaning under the consequences (the shortages of food and consumer goods) of the existing arms burden.

Yet to relax, to let the arms programme slow down, is to risk being humiliated by the opponent at one or other point of confrontation, and to see allies switch sides, clients regain their independence, semicolonies rebel.

And so the mere possibility that the opponent might develop some new form of weaponry compels one to do the same. Just as in economic competition as seen by Marx, the accumulation of means of production is necessary, regardless of the individual desires of capitalists, so in military competition, accumulation of arms—and the economic potential to make them—is necessary, even if both sides can see that ultimately it is going to destroy them. But, of course, the individual desires of capitalists do come to be identified with accumulation—the system provides the appropriate psychological and ideological mechanisms to keep itself functioning. The bureaucracies of the state and industry which participate in the accumulation of arms become so structured that the individuals in them see that as a good thing in itself. In both the Pentagon and in the great firm that is USSR Ltd powerfully placed bureaucrats see their own career prospects as identified in further enlarging the military-industrial structure.

The continual expansion of military might feeds back into each protagonist, just as 'pure economic competition' would, forcing each ruling class to tighten its grip over subordinate classes, forcing each to broaden still further the base of its arms potential by spreading still more beyond its borders, creating still more interests in each society intimately bound up with the pursuit of further military expansion, even to the point where the demand of the military on resources pushes society as a whole into the deepest instability.

Cold War and crisis

This leads to the final point of analysis where we part company with Thompson. His account of the new Cold War cut it right off from an important element determining its course—the existence or otherwise of economic crisis.

The point can be put like this. Until the mid-1940s it seemed that the Western imperialisms could not coexist on the face of the earth without continual recourse to war with each other. But the antagonisms that had produced the First and Second World Wars were soon forgotten in the boom conditions of the 1950s and 1960s. The whole world economy was expanding, and the different powers could share in the prosperity without stepping on each other's toes.

As between the various Western powers and Russia things were more difficult. Although the division of Europe was agreed in 1944-45 and adhered to, with respect to the rest of the world there were problems. It was by no means clear what the real balance of forces was because of the number of unknown factors (the effects of the colonial revolution, the Chinese Revolution, the then higher growth rate of the USSR, etc). However, by the early 1960s something like a stable balance of forces seemed to exist. The basis was laid for 'detente'.

One of the things that has reactivated the old antagonisms has been the effect of economic crisis in both 'camps'. Both great powers have been faced with an increased need to deploy resources outside their own national frontiers at the same time as there has been a destabilisation of the foreign countries in which these resources are located.

In the case of the West there has been the massive growth of the international credit system (eurodollars and petrodollars) and the increased pressure to internationalisation of production (the 'world car', for example). But this has been accompanied by increased tensions among the advanced powers (the continual pressures for import controls against each other's goods, the attempts of Germany and France to play an independent role in international affairs) and by the creation of whole zones of instability in the rest of the world (especially the Middle East, but also Central America and the Caribbean).

In the case of the Eastern bloc the Russians have found the Chinese openly aligned with the West, have lost Egypt to the US camp, see Iraq changing sides, are having difficulties consolidating their hold on Afghanistan and fear new rumblings in Eastern Europe—all at a time when they are more dependent than ever before on their economic ties with the West and the Third World.

Both sides find themselves with economic problems that create dissent among allies, clients and semi-colonies. Both fear the other will exploit these to its own advantage. And so both attempt to increase the number of their warheads, to raise the accuracy of their missiles, to prepare to threaten the other with 'limited' nuclear war if it intervenes in the wrong 'sphere of influence'.

Theory and practice

The analysis of the world put forward above does not contradict Thompson completely. On many points there is concurrence. But the practical conclusions that follow are very different.

For Thompson the struggle against the missiles is *the* struggle, the resolution of which must be achieved before we can deal with other issues (with taking on the 'armourers and the gaolers'). For us it is a struggle that intersects with many other struggles over many other issues.

This is fantastically important. CND last time round was very successful in mobilising numbers of people. But in the end it failed. It did not get rid of the bomb and most of the activists moved on to other things: Thompson himself, for example, stopped campaigning and started writing (very good) history.

Failure was not the result of lack of effort. It was because, essentially, CND did not gather behind it a social force that could break the grip of the bomb makers. And that was because it was cut off from the everyday preoccupations of the great majority of people. Trade union leaders like Frank Cousins of the TGWU could cast bloc votes for CND. A Labour Party conference could even pass a resolution against the bomb. But neither enough TGWU members nor sufficient Labour Party supporters cared about the issue to enforce implementation of the resolution or blacking of nuclear bases. When, later, we sat down in the streets in an effort to get our way through direct action, we soon learnt it was powerless, because we, by ourselves, were not a social force.

The impotence of CND was something that had been experienced by anti-war movements before. Take, for example, the experience of the First World War. Ultimately that war ended because first the Russian and then the German workers and soldiers would endure it no more. But for long years before that the anti-war movement was isolated, on the margins of society, unable to influence events. One of the most important worker leaders of the German Revolution, Richard Müller, later explained why. He tells how the most virulent opponents of the war (organised in the Internationale grouping) remained cut off from the workers in the big Berlin factories. These workers were fairly hostile to the war, but it seemed something remote from them until it led to direct attacks on their living standards and their trade union rights.

To build up a movement in the factories capable of action took four years of slow, relentless work by Müller and his comrades. By contrast the anti-war socialists outside the factories called repeatedly for demonstrative actions which could only appeal to small 'vanguard groups' of workers, easily dealt with by the military and the police. There had to be a unification of the anti-war sentiment and the struggle over material conditions before there could develop a force powerful enough to crack the regime and the war.

One of the problems for CND in the late 1950s and early 1960s was that the material conditions were not such as to make possible such a unification of the 'economic' and the 'political'. Most workers could still look forward to rising real living standards year after year; unemployment was less than 2 percent; the welfare state was still expanding.

Today things are different, precisely because the new surge of nuclear missiles is linked with the trend towards international crisis. The increase in arms spending takes place at the same time as the cuts in schools, hospitals and housing; the militarisation of society takes place as workers engaged in traditionally 'peaceful' trade union practices find themselves up against the forces of the state; the growth of the new anti-bomb movement takes place as the retiring head of the

Supplementary Benefits Commission warns of the 'danger' of the unemployed rioting in the streets.

Yet Thompson virtually ignores all this. For him the way forward is to repeat the movement the last time round, with bigger numbers of essentially the same sorts of people. It is a recipe for unnecessary failure.

Thompson is not clear on another thing of immense importance—whether we are going to have to seize the weapons of destruction from the hands of our rulers, or whether all we have to do is peacefully persuade them of the folly of their ways. At times his tone is one of confrontation. But at others it seems we only have to point to an 'alternative logic'.

This is not surprising, since the very sort of people he sees as constituting the core of the movement would run a hundred miles at the very thought of real confrontation. Just look at his proposed allies. 'The churches'—are the archbishops and cardinals en masse going to lead an assault on the missile bases? 'The Eurocommunists'—as Edward Thompson well knows, the Italian Communist Party leaders have argued against Italy leaving NATO, the Spanish Communists do not argue for an ending of Spain's alliance with the US, lest that should 'destabilise' the international situation, and the French Communist Party is the most enthusiastic supporter of the French nuclear Force de Frappe. The 'Labourites'—if by this Thompson means the leading Labour lefts, then it should be remembered that it was only two years ago that their star, Tony Benn, was threatening the use of troops to break a strike at Windscale. Even the category of 'trade unionists' is ambiguous: does it mean those at the base, or those leaders who spend much of their time trying to stop strikes in places like the naval dockyard where the nuclear submarines are fitted out?

Thompson has drawn up a list of people who might on occasions put their names to anti-missile petitions. He has not located a coherent force that will fight to dismantle the missiles regardless of the consequences.

The deployment of nuclear warheads is *integral* to the society in which we live, capitalism. The more people are enmeshed in the higher structures of that society, the more they resist anything which threatens to overturn that society—even if such an overturn is necessary to stop it leading humanity to annihilation. They might sign letters to the *Times*; they will run in fear of riot. They may clap politely at a public meeting; they will shudder at the thought of social upheaval. They may distribute the odd leaflet; they will hide if the leaflet leads to real conflict.

This is not an argument for putting up a sign at anti-nuclear meetings: 'Workers Only'. It is an argument for developing strategies aimed at sections of society who are not so tied to existing structures as those who have pride of place in Thompson's vision. The missiles do threaten the future of the individual members of all classes. But the question is, how many of them can be won to a strategy not just of token opposition, but of active struggle?

And here it has to be recognised that the stockbroker who wants to fight the bomb has to look to a movement that will destroy his profits, the priest to a break with his own church, the Eurocommunist to a fight against party leaders who tolerate the weaponry of destruction, the Labourite to a battle with left figures who oppose bombs in opposition only to preside over their construction when in office.

In this sense, the bomb is a class issue. There are those whose class interests lead them to accept the threat to humanity (including themselves). And there are those whose class interests point in the opposite direction, who even if they have been conned into accepting the bomb can find themselves bitterly fighting the bomb makers over other issues. A really successful movement can win individuals from the first group, but only if it makes them break with that group to build among the second. Thompson with his near mystical incantation of terms like 'exterminism' and his grandiose verbiage about 'broad movements' obscures this essential fact.

Bolshevism in the age of the Bomb

Politics is not just about theoretical analysis or even strategy. It is also about getting things done, about the organisational forms that can turn theory into practice. What should these be in the era of missile madness?

For Thompson—and no doubt for many other people in the new movement—the sheer horror of what the missiles can do means dropping the traditional forms of organisation adopted by Marxists, especially the notion of a disciplined revolutionary workers' party. All that is needed, it is argued, is the broadest possible alliance. But before anyone goes along with Thompson on this they should reflect on one thing: it was precisely the way in which capitalism produced an earlier version of militaristic horror (that of trench warfare and poisonous gas) that led the most consistently anti-war socialists to adopt a precise organisational form, that to be found in the notion of the 'Bolshevik Party'.

The idea of such a party certainly was not adopted because of any obsession with orthodoxy. When first broached it was a most unorthodox innovation. People found out the hard way it was what they needed as they struggled against what was (at that point) the most horrendous war in human history.

A Gramsci, a Big Bill Heywood, a Eugene Leviné, an Alfred Rosmer, a John MacLean, a John Reed, even, at the very end, a Rosa Luxemburg, came to see that the only way to cope with capitalism in the era of world wars was to build a party of the sort that had been pioneered in the struggle against tsarist despotism in Russia. Why did they come to this conclusion?

Until 1914 opposition to the different aspects of capitalist society tended to flow into different channels. There was a trade unionism that was concerned chiefly (when it even did that) with the wage rates and working conditions of workers with particular skills. There was a 'political' socialism that only concerned itself with making propaganda and collecting votes. There was a pacifism that only made ineffectual protests against participation in wars. There was a feminism which restricted itself to fighting the legal disabilities facing women.

The war threw each and everyone of these currents into disarray. Trade unionists turned against one another as the state offered privileges to those union leaders who would support its war effort and prison sentences to those militants who resisted. The 'political' socialists had the choice of acting as a left front for militarism or continuing in the most difficult conditions with propagandism that seemed ineffectual against searing bullets and burning flesh. The pacifists were either converted to instant patriotism, or made individual protests which eased consciences but could not stop the carnage. The feminists split between those who saw 'equality' as meaning an equal right to suffer in the trenches, and those who asserted that it meant an equal part in the fight to turn the guns against the generals.

What was different about the party that had grown up around Lenin in Russia was that it showed that impotence could be overcome by linking the different struggles. Trade unionism which cut itself off from the struggle against other aspects of capitalism (militarism, despotism, discrimination against minorities and women) left intact a system that would not only recoup any concessions it made over living standards but which would threaten life itself: this was the import of Lenin's famous attacks upon 'economism'. Socialism which put its faith in pamphlets and ballot boxes alone talked about a future that was already being destroyed in the present. Pacifism which preached peace without locating a force that could seize from the militarists control of the means of waging war merely created the illusion that the blood pouring from capitalism's every pore was an accident. By contrast a socialism that was rooted in the day to day struggle in the factories was wrestling for control of the future in the here and now; opposition to the war that based itself on strikes over living standards, work conditions and trade union rights did not merely pray for an end to bloodshed, but made it more difficult for the Haigs and the Hindenbergs to keep bloodletting going.

This did not mean barring from factory struggles those who did not believe in revolution, or from the anti-war demonstrations those who accepted private property. But it did mean creating a party which would educate, agitate and organise within each of these wide move-ments for the connections to be made, for the strikes against food shortages to become strikes against the militarists, for the demon-strations against the war to be demonstrations against the system that created the war.

The party had to be 'of a new sort', no longer concerned just with propaganda or vote catching, no longer delegating to 'trade unionists' alone responsibility for agitation in the factory, but itself obsessed with action, above all action in the workplaces, and structured in such a way as to make action effective.

The question of building such parties was absolutely central be-cause of the way 'peaceful' capitalist competition for markets had given way to war and the preparation for war. Ruling classes which hurled millions of armed men against each other would not recoil from murdering and imprisoning socialists who tried to stand in their path: the fates of Luxemburg, Liebknecht, Leviné, Joe Hill, Connolly, Gramsci and MacLean bear witness to that. Parties were needed that could operate as peaceful protest became civil war, as legality gave way to illegality. Those who had already presided over 20 million deaths were not going to be stopped unless for every bullet they fired bullets were fired back from a thousand factories. And that had to be organised.

It would be utter folly to believe that it needs a lesser social force, a lower level of organisation, to deal with those who are prepared to contemplate the destruction of humanity than those who 'merely' sent a generation of young men to die in the trenches.

Chapter 48

Socialism and war

Duncan Hallas

We are not pacifists, we detest the Galtieri dictatorship, we dismiss the notion that the Argentinian seizure of the Falklands is progressive on anti-colonialist grounds. Nevertheless we believe that, in a war between Britain and Argentina, the defeat of British imperialism is the lesser evil. The main enemy is at home.

None of these statements, perhaps, is so self evidently true as to pass by mere assertion. Let us therefore return to basics. What are the criteria by which socialists determine their attitude to war in general and to a given war? An excellent starting point is the opening passage of Lenin's *Socialism and War* written amidst the slaughter of 1915:

> Socialists have always condemned wars between nations as barbarous and brutal. Our attitude towards war, however, is fundamentally different to that of the bourgeois pacifists (supporters and advocates of peace) and of the anarchists. We differ from the former in that we understand the inevitable connection between wars and the class struggle within a country: we understand that wars cannot be abolished unless classes are abolished and socialism is created; we also differ in that we regard civil wars, ie wars waged by an oppressed class against the oppressor class, by slaves against slave-holders, by serfs against landlords and by wage workers against the bourgeoisie, as fully legitimate, progressive and necessary. We Marxists differ from both pacifists and anarchists in that we deem it necessary to study each war historically (from the standpoint of Marx's historical materialism) and separately.

War is always 'barbarous and brutal', often horribly so. Think of the bombing, the napalm, the defoliation, the atrocities perpetrated by US

First published May 1982

forces in Vietnam or by the Khmer Rouge. War is always an evil and it generates other evils too. Therefore, goes the 'anti-war in principle' argument, it should be rejected regardless of circumstances. No more war.

There is a healthy and progressive strand in this attitude and it is often connected with a rudimentary kind of class consciousness. 'It's a rich man's war but a poor man's fight,' went the slogan of the opponents of conscription in the American Civil War.

I remember seeing, in an ordinary commercial cinema in Manchester a year or two after the end of the Second World War, a showing of the classic anti-war film *All Quiet on the Western Front*. At the point where one German soldier says to another, 'We should make the generals and politicians fight it out with clubs,' the audience, a fair number of whom must have been ex-soldiers, burst into loud and spontaneous applause.

That was a good spirit, a thousand times better than the patriotic flag waving of the Labour Party leaders then and now.

But by itself it will not do. Marx and Engels and their followers supported the North in the American Civil War. Some of them, mostly German exiles, fought voluntarily for the Union. And they were right. For in spite of the horrors, the slaughter, the mutilations, frauds and the fortunes made out of war profiteering, the war for the destruction of slavery was a just and progressive one.

The judgement is political, which brings us to Clausewitz's classic definitions:

> The war of a community—of whole nations and particularly of civilised nations—always starts from a political condition and is called forth by a political motive. It is, therefore, a political act... War is not merely a political act, but also a real political instrument, a continuation of political commerce, a carrying out of the same by other means. All beyond this which is strictly peculiar to war relates merely to the peculiar nature of the means which it uses.

The peculiarity of the means is stated by Clausewitz with his characteristic brutal clarity and total lack of hypocrisy:

> War is therefore an act of violence intended to compel our opponent to fulfil our will.

All of which is incontestably true and fundamentally important. One thing follows immediately. For revolution is precisely 'an act of violence intended to compel our opponent to fulfil our will'. It is much more than that of course, but it is that or it is nothing.

But we cannot stop there. Since, in any class society, the ruling classes invariably resort to force to defend their rule—the rejection in princi-ple of the use of force for political ends (not always, not usually, but in appropriate circumstances) is tantamount to abandoning the struggle for fundamental social change, for a classless society, for socialism.

Further, because wars cannot be abolished unless classes are abolished and socialism is established, the 'anti-war in principle' position, if widely adopted by workers, guarantees the inevitability of future wars.

The pacifist position, notwithstanding its humane impulses, is deeply conservative. That is why we are not pacifists.

But nuclear war, the threat of the nuclear holocaust, does that not alter the position entirely? It alters it certainly, but it does not change the underlying realities. There have been 100 or so wars since the United States Air Force dropped the atom bombs on Hiroshima and Nagasaki, all non-nuclear (although some only just).

Nuclear war between the superpowers has not happened because it is not in the interests, rationally considered, of either of their ruling classes. That is not to say that it cannot happen, merely to say that the holocaust, an ever present danger, cannot be avoided by burying one's head in the pacifist sand. It can only be avoided, in the end, by striking the nuclear weapons out of the hands of the ruling classes—by revolution.

From these most serious and weighty matters we turn to an affair that would be farcical if it were not so squalid and potentially dangerous—the Falklands (or Malvinas, if you prefer) crisis.

Back in the 1730s a certain Captain Jenkins, a smuggler and a pirate according to the Spanish authorities who then ruled much of South America, a peaceful and eminently respectable merchant skip-per according to his friends, was arrested by the Spanish Guardia Costa and had his left ear lopped off in the scuffle. The then equiva-lent of the *Daily Mail* and the Tory backbenches went into paroxysms of hysterical rage.

The outcome, the 'War of Jenkins' Ear', had about as much to do with the matter as the 'right to self determination' of the Falkland Is-landers has today. It was a transparent pretext. What was at issue was the slave trade, a highly profitable business in which British slavers came out on top through various wars.

There is, however, a difference. There was then a serious issue in dispute between the two ruling classes. The British bourgeoisie was determined to break into the South American markets and the rulers of Spanish America in Madrid were equally determined to keep them out.

In the 'War of Jenkins' Ear', Jenkins was simply an excuse. Had he never been born, the outcome would have been the same, give or take a year or two. But now the excuse has become the reason. What we have now is the war, if it develops into a war, of Thatcher's face (in the Chinese sense) and of Galtieri's face too.

There is no longer a rational, if predatory, cause of dispute. The Falklands are of no great significance. Pure prestige and internal politics are the driving force on both sides.

True, there is talk of oil; but whether it exists or not is neither here nor there. After all, Thatcher's government is busy trying to 'privatise' the British National Oil Corporation, foreign oil companies hold a good deal of the North Sea and foreign multinationals operate freely in Galtieri's Argentina.

The claim on the British side that Thatcher is motivated by concern for the people of the islands, that 'the interests of the Falkland Islanders must be paramount', is a masterpiece of impudent hypocrisy.

Under British rule, the inhabitants of the Falklands have never even been allowed a freely elected local government with the powers of a town council, let alone 'self determination'. Many of them are not even allowed security of tenure of their houses but are forced to accept the tied cottage system operated by the British Falklands Company which owns most of the useful grazing land. No serious consideration to the interests of the Falklanders had been given by any British government until the Argentinian invasion. Moreover, both Thatcher's government and Callaghan's before it have had secret negotiations with successive Argentinian governments about the future of the islands without any reference to the inhabitants, let alone the referendum now bruited about.

In any case, the self determination argument is spurious to the core. A declining population of less than would make a respectable turnout at a fourth division football match on an off day, and lacking any social, ethnic, linguistic, cultural or historical features of its own, cannot be seriously regarded as a 'national' entity. A far more plausible case could be made for national self determination for the Western Isles or the Isle of Man. And these more plausible cases would also be absurd and reactionary. For, as Lenin wrote:

> If we want to understand the meaning of self determination of nations without juggling with legal definitions, without 'inventing' abstract definitions, but examining the historical and economic conditions of the national movements, we shall inevitably reach the conclusion that self determination of nations means the political separation of these nations from other national bodies, the formation of an independent national state.

In the present case there is neither a national movement nor any possibility of a national state. The self determination argument is a fraud perpetrated to put a 'democratic' gloss on support for Thatcher's military adventure.

So far as the Falklands are concerned that is all that there is to be said but, to avoid misunderstanding, it is as well to point out that, in any case, we do not unconditionally support the right of self determination. We do not, for example, concede it to the Ulster Protestants, although they are indisputably a historically formed self conscious group with quasi-national characteristics. We reject the two nations theory for Ireland and we do so because its effect is plainly reactionary and not at all on the basis of legalistic quibbling about whether or not the Protestants do or do not have this or that 'national' characteristic.

The 'anti-colonialist' pretensions of the Argentinian dictatorship are not much better than the fraud of self determination. True, Argentina has some sort of more or less plausible claim to the Falklands on historical and geographical grounds and, certainly, the islands are a British colony. But these are legal forms and abstract claims.

We support anti-colonial movements as movements of struggle by oppressed people against their oppressors and we support them because, as Marx said, 'no nation can be free if it oppresses other nations.'

None of this has much relevance to the Falklands. There is no Spanish speaking population struggling against British imperialism. For Galtieri, 'anti-colonialism' is a convenient pretext to divert Argentinian workers away from their struggle against the dictatorship. The timing of the Argentinian invasion was no doubt influenced by the rising tide of demonstrations and strikes in Argentina. 'National unity' in support of a foreign quarrel is Galtieri's aim as well as Thatcher's and 'national unity' means the subordinating of the workers to the bosses.

We are irreconcilably hostile to both governments and both regimes. But we are in Britain and not Argentina and therefore the British government, the British state, is the main enemy for us.

The Labour Party leaders, and even some Tories who enthusiastically supported the Pinochet coup in Chile, have discovered that the Argentinian regime is fascist. That, of course, changes everything! Strictly speaking, the Argentinian dictatorship is not real fascism but let that pass. Also leave aside the Tories. It is the 'left wing' variant of this argument that matters. In essence, it is a very old one.

In 1907 the Second International meeting in Stuttgart adopted the famous resolution on war which states:

The Congress confirms the resolutions of previous International Congresses against militarism and imperialism and declares anew that the fight against militarism cannot be separated from the socialist class war as a whole.

Wars between capitalist states are as a rule the result of their rivalry for world markets... Further, these wars arise out of the never-ending armament race of militarism, which is one of the chief implements of bourgeois class rule and of the economic and political enslavement of the working classes.

Wars are encouraged by the prejudices of one nation against another, systematically purveyed among the civilised nations in the interests of the ruling classes, so as to divert the mass of the proletariat from the tasks of its own class, as well as from the duty of international class solidarity.

Wars are therefore inherent in the nature of capitalism. They will only cease when the capitalist economy is abolished...

In the case of a threat of an outbreak of war, it is the duty of the working classes and their parliamentary representatives in the countries taking part, fortified by the unifying activity of the International Bureau, to do everything to prevent the outbreak of war by whatever means seems to them most effective, which naturally differ with the intensification of the class war and of the general political situation.

Should war break out in spite of all this, it is their duty to intervene for its speedy end, and to strive with all their power to make use of the violent economic and political crisis brought about by the war to rouse the people, and thereby to hasten the abolition of capitalist class rule.

Five years later, at the Basle International Congress, this was unanimously reaffirmed, the British Labour Party delegates voting with the rest.

Two years after that, in 1914, the majority of the Labour and Social Democratic leaders in nearly all the warring states swallowed their words, abandoned the class struggle in favour of 'national unity' and supported their 'own' governments.

How did they justify this? Why, by pointing to the evils of the enemy regimes, of course.

The German Social Democratic majority, the most apposite comparison for our purpose, pointed to Russia. The tsar rules over the 'prison house of peoples', they said. 'He has most bloodily suppressed the movements of Russian workers and peasants in 1905-07. His is the most brutal, backward and vicious state in Europe, the bulwark of European reaction for over 100 years.'

Of course all this was perfectly true. Tsarist Russia was every bit as vile, vicious and reactionary as Galtieri's Argentina and a great deal more powerful. Moreover it had a long common frontier with Germany and the tsar's armies were actually invading ethnic German territory in East Prussia.

What did Liebknecht and Luxemburg and Mehring and Zetkin say in reply? They said, 'You are scoundrels, you are traitors. You have betrayed the German workers' movement and the international workers' movement. Tsarism today is no different to what it was in 1907 and 1912 when you promised to oppose war. The war, for Germany, is a "real political instrument" of the German bourgeoisie. You have deserted to the enemy and this desertion will not stop at temporary support for the war'—as was indeed proved in 1918-19 when these same pro-war 'socialists' organised troops to shoot down German workers.

In Liebknecht's immortal words, 'The main enemy is at home.' Not the only enemy of course. 'The tsar is an enemy but support for the Kaiser actually weakens Russian workers' opposition to the tsar and since the struggle against militarism cannot be separated from the socialist class war as a whole', support for our 'own' government strengthens reaction everywhere.

Lenin and Trotsky and Rosmer and Connolly and MacLean and Debs all said, with appropriate national variations, exactly the same thing. All opposed their 'own' government and its war. And they were absolutely right. Support for 'one's own' ruling class in such a war is tantamount to abandoning the struggle for socialism. For their war is a continuation of their politics by other means. And so, exactly, with the War of Thatcher's Face.

One good thing, at any rate, has come out of the Falklands crisis. The reaction of the Labour Party leaders has proved decisively, conclusively and irrefutably that the illusions of so many left wingers that there has been, since 1979, a real swing to the left by the Labour Party have as much substance as fairy gold.

Michael Foot, wrapping himself in the Union Jack, and righteously denouncing the government's neglect of British interests (and outdoing Denis Healey in the process!) is one thing. The support and applause he got from the overwhelming majority of Labour MPs are quite another. Not just the right but most of the left MPs enthusiastically cheered him on. They collapsed into jingoism at the first test. It did not take the courage of a Liebknecht or a MacLean to speak out against the Falklands expedition. Merely a modicum of principle and backbone. That, in the vast majority of cases, was more than the left

MPs could muster. What really matters is the spectacular demonstration of the lack of elementary class hatred, the indispensable gut reaction against militarism and war, on the Labour benches.

Can any sane person now believe that this crew, even if reinforced by reselection and conference resolutions, could stand up to the bourgeoisie in a real crisis where bourgeois interests are at stake? If you can't stand out, loud, clear, firm and, from the beginning, against a comic opera war in the South Atlantic, you will never resist the immeasurably greater pressures of the boss class against any attempt to impose economic policies they don't want, let alone achieve socialism.

Nor can too much be said in favour of Benn and the handful of others (including that unreconstructed right winger, Tam Dalyell) who did not back Thatcher.

Benn's position is basically, 'Let the United Nations settle it.' The UN is a club of governments. We know some of them: Thatcher's and Galtieri's, Reagan's and Brezhnev's and so on, enemies of their own and every other working class. Benn's position, in fact, is not very different from such important organs of bourgeois opinion as the *Financial Times* and the *Guardian*. It may well gain him some credit, especially if the expedition proves a failure, but there is not a spark of socialist internationalism in it.

As to the Labour leaders as a whole, left, right and centre, we have been fortunate to have a foretaste of their conduct in any future Labour government—cowardly, mean, chauvinist, grovelling before the ruling class.

Chapter 49

'Send George Bush…'

Sharon Smith

No sooner had the bombs started to drop on Iraq on 16 January than the US news media rushed to report that public support for George Bush's war had jumped to 82 percent.

Since then there has been a virtual news blackout. All reports must pass US military censors.

In its effort to please the Pentagon, the US media has all but ignored domestic opposition to the war, which reached massive proportions in the week the bombings began.

Daily marches and rallies, often semi-spontaneous or organised only by word of mouth, took place in every major city.

Morning, noon and night, protesters filled city streets, pacifists obstructed federal buildings and thousands of angry protesters blocked major roadways.

Some demonstrations, like the 30,000 strong march held in Seattle, were larger than at the height of the anti Vietnam War movement.

Protests of between 5,000 and 10,000 took place in New York, Chicago, Boston, Minneapolis and Los Angeles, 4,500 marched in Austin, Texas, and 100,000 San Francisco demonstrators and 30,000 Washington marchers took part in a national mobilisation the Saturday after the bombing of Iraq began. A massive 300,000 marched in Washington on 26 January.

The larger the movement has grown, the younger it has become. In Boston, for example, a contingent of 1,500 high school students

First published February 1991

marched in an anti-war protest, while 1,000 students aged 11 to 18 marched to a rally in Union Square in New York City.

Students at Burroughs Junior High School in Los Angeles staged a walkout when war began.

University students have played a key role in building the anti-war movement. The student anti-war committee at Howard University called a student strike on 15 January, while students at the University of California at Santa Cruz boycotted classes the day after the war started.

About 4,000 students from the University of California at Los Angeles marched and several hundred occupied the administration building to demand the university cancel classes for one day to oppose the war.

Students from the newly formed National Network of Campuses Against the War (NNCAW), representing 85 campuses across the country, came together in Chicago on 19 January to plan for coordinated actions—including a possible student strike—and a national student conference is to be held in Chicago on the weekend of 1 March.

The outbreak of war coincided with Martin Luther King Day on 15 January. The irony was not lost on demonstrators, who used the King Day commemorations to read some of King's anti Vietnam War speeches and to speak out against the war in the Gulf.

Some 20,000 demonstrators, many of them carrying anti-war signs, marched in a Martin Luther King Day demonstration in Phoenix, Arizona—where racist authorities refuse to recognise King's birthday as a holiday.

The mainstream press has taken little notice of the many thousands of people who have taken to the streets across the US to oppose the war.

Even an incident in which a car ploughed into a peaceful anti-war protest on the Brooklyn Bridge in New York, killing one and throwing several demonstrators off the bridge, was apparently not newsworthy.

While the media's claims of overwhelming public support for Bush's war against Iraq are clearly exaggerated, pro-war sentiment strengthened immediately following the outbreak of war.

The Scud attacks on Tel Aviv, in particular, brought Zionists and others out by the hundreds to demonstrate in favour of escalating the war against Iraq.

One such demonstration outside of the United Nations drew 10,000 and was addressed by two Democrats, New York governor Mario Cuomo and New York City's black mayor, David Dinkins.

While various wings of the ruling class had been bitterly divided on whether to start a war in the Middle East, they closed ranks once the fighting began.

Congressional Democrats carefully sidestepped the issue of the war itself by debating only its timing—calling for prolonged sanctions rather than immediate military action.

But by postponing the debate until the weekend before the 15 January deadline Democratic leaders ensured Bush a victory. And once the war started, Democrats, including Jesse Jackson, have fallen into step behind the president.

Before the war was even a week old, the news media was preparing the public for what is now sure to be a much longer and bloodier war than they had led anyone to believe.

Once the ground war begins, the blood will be shed overwhelmingly by working class soldiers.

Blacks make up only 12.5 percent of the US population, yet they are nearly 35 percent of the troops fighting in the Gulf. The disproportion is even greater in urban areas. For example, 80 percent of the troops from the city of Chicago are black or Latino.

This perhaps explains the popularity of the chant, 'Send George Bush. Send Dan Quayle. Send Neil Bush when he gets out of jail.'

Already large numbers of working class people, especially blacks, Latinos and Arabs, have taken an anti-war stand. If the experience of the 10,000 strong anti-war march in Chicago's city centre is any indication, where bus drivers, cab drivers and office workers smiled and flashed peace signs at the passing demonstrators, the potential for building organised working class opposition is there.

Culture

Chapter 50

The myth of the modern

Alan Gibson

From the 1890s onwards architects designed some of the most beautiful and exciting buildings ever. There were several factors behind this.

First was the development of the productive forces, th....e materials and new technologies which capitalism generated during the second half of the 19th century.

Initially this development had little impact on architecture. Most public and commercial buildings were either designed in the classic style or, like the Houses of Parliament, in neo-gothic—a style which its exponents claimed truly reflected Britain's cultural roots.

It was engineers like Brunel and Eiffel who pioneered the use of steel to construct magnificent warehouses, bridges, railway termini and towers—structures which, more often than not, were hidden behind classical and neo-gothic facades.

But architects were gradually affected by colossal changes and their social, political and economic repercussions.

Large scale industry created working classes across Europe and the US. Trade unions and socialist parties followed. Political and industrial turmoil arose in the rapidly expanding towns and cities of what became called the 'Machine Age'.

Scientific breakthroughs brought the telegraph, cinema, the motor car, the streamlined ocean liner, the aeroplane and so on. Capitalism invaded every aspect of life, imposing a price on everything.

First published March 1991

Many artists rebelled against industrialisation. Some, like William Ruskin, idealised the craftsmanship of pre-industrial society. For others, however, rebellion took a different course. Many were influenced by socialism, excited by the 'Machine Age' and the new opportunities which the rise of mass culture offered them.

At a time when ruling classes were championing nationalism in one country after another, many scientists, intellectuals and artists were throwing off their cultural roots and contributing to a new internationalism in art and science.

The 'art for art's sake' movement, for example, brought together artists working in a host of countries in an outright rejection of the sterility which art in general and architecture in particular had fallen into.

Architects began to fundamentally change the way buildings were built and the way they looked. Steel framed skyscrapers in the US, reinforced concrete housing, rectangular windows and plain walls in Vienna, richly sculptured buildings in Barcelona, simplicity combined with craftsmanship in Glasgow—all these and much more were the result.

In art, two movements developed which were to have an enormous impact on architecture.

The first, of the cubists and the Russian-Dutch abstractivists, provided a new way of both seeing and portraying reality. Abstract models—the interplay of lines, rectangles, spheres and so on—provided architects with new ways of understanding space and light.

The second, of the Italian futurists, celebrated the dynamism of industry and everything it produced—the modern city, 'the house of cement, iron and glass', as one of their manifestos put it.

What brought these two movements together and gave modern architecture its single greatest boost was the 1917 Russian Revolution.

It provided architects with the first opportunity to apply abstract models and stunning projects to real life. The Russian constructivist movement was the result, producing a huge array of designs for mass housing, factories, social clubs and monuments.

The turmoil which followed the revolution, the huge scarcities of materials and resources and finally counter-revolution meant most of the projects were never built in Russia.

But those that were had a profound impact on architects across the world, and particularly in Weimar Germany.

Modern architecture was systematically applied to the design of offices, stores and factories. Social democratic councils throughout Germany employed architects to design huge workers' housing estates.

But though modern architecture received its greatest boost from the Russian Revolution, and though many of its earliest practitioners were socialists, it quickly became clear that modern architecture was much more the product of advanced capitalism.

The basic condition for its continuation was not socialist architects but industry and modern urban life.

Many of the Italian futurists who inspired the Russian constructivists ended up celebrating the rise of Mussolini. Some continued to practise modern architecture in Italy.

Revolution and political turmoil had also produced another response among architects, best expressed by the great Swiss architect Le Corbusier.

Like his German counterparts he was thrilled by the achievements of modern structural and mechanical engineers.

But far from placing his work at the service of the socialist revolution he believed modern architecture could provide ways of living which would iron out social differences and ensure against a socialist revolution ever happening.

In 1928 he and other architects formed the International Congress of Modern Architecture. Its Athens Charter laid down a set of guidelines which influenced architects across the world for the next five decades.

Modern town planning was the result. Sunlight, trees and space were the key factors. Corbusier's solution was apartment blocks, not the blocks which scar the inner cities today, but ones constructed from high quality materials and which contained nurseries, schools, shops, swimming pools, clinics, social clubs and so on.

These apartment blocks were to be set among parks and trees. Cars and industry were to be strictly segregated from them.

The rise of Stalin in Russia and Hitler in Germany plus depression across the developed world stopped any of the projects being built.

But the long postwar boom saw a rebirth of modern architecture, or International Style as it became known.

There were good reasons for this. It was cheap and quick to build, it was easily standardised, it fitted the zoning laws which town and city planners imposed and it could be applied to the huge postwar expansion of office work.

The US particularly benefited from the German architects who had emigrated there to escape fascism. New York's Seagram building and Chicago's Lakeside Apartments are some of the finest results.

But the rich materials these projects used were not available for the mass housing projects that sprang up across postwar Europe.

Social engineering, Le Corbusier's belief that people's lives could be improved through imposing new living conditions, became a guiding principle followed by architects across the industrial world.

In Britain the new towns such as Harlow and Stevenage were one result. The inner city tower blocks in every major city in the industrial world were the other.

Prefabrication became a common feature. Designs, often imported wholesale from other countries and not adapted to specific weather conditions, were thrown up by often untrained builders.

The era of high rise blocks came to a crashing end in 1968. A gas explosion on the second floor of Ronan Point in east London blew out a structural wall, causing every floor above to collapse and killing four people.

The inquiry blamed tall buildings. Rising vandalism was also blamed on high rise living. And high rise living was, in turn, blamed on modern architecture.

Modern architecture became a scapegoat for the then Labour government—a government confronted with the beginnings of the first postwar crisis of capitalism.

Behind the furore over architecture the government of the day, and every government since, began cutting back on all forms of public housing.

The cutbacks were part and parcel of the economic changes which saw the gradual decline of the state's control of large sectors of the economy towards the crisis ridden free market capitalism of today.

Architecture has reflected this change. So called postmodern architecture with its clutter of ornaments and architectural styles has been taken up by companies and property developers eager to present a particular corporate image in an increasingly competitive world.

The often sleek new office blocks and hotels of every major city standing amid the growing degradation of inner city suburbs have come to more and more express the increasing polarisation of rich and poor.

The fact that their facades are stuck on the basic framework of modern architecture is hidden by the claim that in some way they mark a clear break with International Style.

They do not, though the best of them—those that continue to apply the latest materials and technologies which capitalism still produces—do show the endless possibilities which good architecture can develop.

Not so with the other major change in architecture, that championed by Prince Charles and his supporters. These people want a return to the neo-classicism of Victorian England—a period when capitalists desired an architecture which hid the violent revolution which produced them behind the facades of Greece and Rome.

It was sterile then, and it's sterile now.

But its advocates not only claim modern architecture is the cause of all of today's rotten buildings, many have dressed their ideas in the pseudo-radical language of community architecture. This was based on encouraging people to do up their own slums and build their own homes.

Today such ideas are a sick joke for they come nowhere near confronting the massive crisis of housing in this and every other country.

Today over 500,000 people are homeless in Britain. There are four million homes unfit for human habitation.

The huge cuts in public housing started by Labour in 1968, and continued since, mean that last year only 125,400 homes were completed by *both the private and the public sector.*

Between 1948 and 1963 first Labour and then successive Tory governments built on average 220,000 homes a year. By the end of this era of public housing 3.3 million homes had been completed as well as a huge number of often well designed and well built hospitals, schools and other public buildings.

Council housing costs on average £30 per square foot to build.

Compare this to the £509 per square foot cost of one of the most famous of modern buildings today, the Lloyd's building.

Architecture, harnessed to providing buildings fit to live and work in and using the best materials and technologies available, has enormous potential.

To unleash it, however, means the overthrowing of a system which values the working conditions and corporate image of Lloyd's underwriters at 17 times that of housing the people who built it

Chapter 51

The glory of Goya

Dave Beecham

The storm that burst upon Europe with the French Revolution of 1789 wreaked most havoc on Spain, once the most powerful European nation, now among the most backward.

The year 1789 was also important for Francisco Goya. The son of an artisan, he had just been appointed official painter to the royal household at the age of 43. Under the patronage of the king and in the company of his liberal friends, such as the liberal reformer Jovellanos, he could look forward to a prosperous future. But 1789 was a turning point in his life just as it was in the development of Spanish society.

For years the weak Spanish monarchy, surrounded by a small class of enlightened intellectuals and bourgeois, had been attempting to modernise the country and drag it out from under the cloak of the Inquisition. Commerce and industry too were established in port cities such as Cadiz, Barcelona and Bilbao.

But the rising bourgeoisie was extremely thinly spread. The state intervened again and again but the backwardness of Spanish agriculture and the weakness of the state machine compared to the hold of the church and aristocracy led to a mounting crisis on the land.

At the end of the century only 25 percent of Spain's ten million people were economically active. The largest active class by far was the rural proletariat and peasantry, some 1,800,000 according to the census of 1797, most living in perpetual poverty and periodic famine.

Despite royal ordinances over the previous 25 years which reduced the ranks of the aristocracy by almost half and the clergy by a third, there were still 400,000 aristocrats, 170,000 clergy and 85,000 monks and nuns.

First published April 1989

Symbolically there were 280,000 domestic servants, almost as many as all the artisans put together and 150,000 officially registered beggars.

The uprising of the French nation against its old regime shattered the illusion that Spanish society could be reformed and began the chain of events which led to civil war.

The Inquisition and aristocracy led a furious campaign against all things French and especially liberal ideas.

As the power of the Inquisition grew in response to the threat of French republicanism, Goya and his friends found themselves under threat. In 1793 Spain launched a holy war against France. Goya fell seriously ill and (like his great contemporary Beethoven) went permanently deaf. As he recovered and as Spanish society disintegrated around him, he began to produce pictures quite unlike the brilliant but conventional portraits, pastoral scenes and religious subjects of his earlier career.

From 1796 he worked continuously on a series of 80 engravings he called *Caprichos*. They were published during a brief period of liberalisation in 1799 and almost immediately withdrawn under threat from the Inquisition.

These pictures were far from being 'caprices' in the usual sense of the word. They are a sustained attack on hypocrisy, the aristocracy, sexual mores, superstition, clerical reaction and the Inquisition. Each picture contains an ironic, bitter caption. One shows the artist asleep, assailed by nightmarish visions of owls and bats. The caption reads, 'The sleep of reason produces monsters'—the theme of the entire series is an indictment of the state of society.

Each image has extraordinary power, but two stand out, reflecting the terrible contradiction which faced the enlightened Spanish bourgeoisie in the period to come. One shows two miserable peasants ridden by donkeys: the people forced to carry parasites on their shoulders. The caption reads, '*Tu que no puedes*', the first part of a proverb—'Thou who canst not, lift me on thy shoulders.'

The second also shows two riders, but here the burdens have turned into evil witch-like creatures, caricatures of the church and state. Beneath them, the peasants are no longer human but are transformed into stupid donkeys. 'Look how solemn,' says the caption.

The tragedy of Spain was precisely that the peasantry was kept in ignorance and superstition by church and state. It bore the burden but could not shake it off and so became a tool of the most ghastly reaction.

By 1800 power had passed decisively to the reactionaries. In 1808 a paralysed regime appealed to Napoleon to intercede: instead he installed his brother Joseph as king. It was the trigger for six years of civil war, famine and butchery as reactionaries and progressives battled both with the French and with each other.

In 1812, at the height of the war against Napoleon, a democratic constitution was proclaimed in a besieged Cadiz. But the old reactionary order was restored, courtesy of the Duke of Wellington. Those who had fought for national liberation found themselves back with the Inquisition.

Still the spirit of revolution would not subside. From 1810 the Spanish colonies of South America began one by one to revolt. In 1820 troops on their way to the colonies mutinied, proclaiming the Constitution of 1812.

Once again civil war broke out. The new government was moderate but it was forced to attack clerical power and privilege and thus to create an urban militia and use Jacobin methods. On the other side the church looked to the most backward sections of the peasantry. Terror and counter-terror followed. The bourgeois regime was short lived.

Once again bloody reaction was restored, this time after French intervention on behalf of all the Allied powers. Backward Spain was locked into a cycle of alternate rebellions and restorations which would culminate a century later in another and even bloodier civil war.

Twenty years after the *Caprichos*, at the time of the 1820 revolution, a series of drawings by Goya capture the hope that must have leapt in his heart at the rising of the people. One shows the classical figure of a woman—Reason (no longer asleep)—flailing at a flock of crows. Underneath he wrote, 'Divine Reason—don't spare one of them.' In another, we see again the bent figure of a peasant with a hoe. On his back he carries a fat monk. This time the message is explicit: 'Will you never know what you're carrying on your back?'

This 'private' work shows him as a great revolutionary artist. In public most of his output was quite different. He went on working for commission right through the civil war, producing paintings for leading figures on both sides. His portrait of Wellington, for example, which today hangs in the National Gallery, was a particular bore to produce because the duke insisted on constant changes to show his latest crop of medals.

Another portrait of Wellington on horseback seems to have been painted hastily over an earlier commission depicting Napoleon's brother Joseph, the puppet king of Spain. Even more ludicrous, his painting *The Allegory of the City of Madrid* had to be reworked several times in succession to suit the tastes of the party in power: at one time it included the bust of Joseph Bonaparte but this was then painted over with the words '*Dos de Mayo*'—commemorating the insurrection of 2 May 1808 against the French.

Goya did produce revolutionary work for public display during this period—the most celebrated of all being his vast painting showing Spanish partisans in front of a French firing squad. But his real energies were spent on hundreds of drawings and engravings. These did not become known in Spain until the late 19th century (the first exhibition devoted to Goya's work alone was in 1900) and even today modern bourgeois art critics focus on Goya the portraitist and describe the vast bulk of his output as 'difficult' or incomprehensible.

There is no difficulty for socialists. Here is art which depicts all the contradictions of the most intense political and social conflict in history up to that time. Unlike Beethoven, whose work for the most part expresses the revolutionary hope and optimism of the period, Goya was faced with the horrific consequences of what Gwyn Williams, in his magnificent book on Goya, describes as 'the impossible revolution'.

The agony of a people which cannot break with an old order and therefore devours itself is symbolised in one of the great paintings of his last years—*Saturn*—one of a series of terrifying visions Goya painted on the walls of his home between 1820 and 1823 at the height of the second civil war. The picture shows a desperate and tortured old man devouring a child: in mythology Saturn ate his sons because he feared their power as grown men. For Goya at the age of 75, there was no doubt a personal poignancy in this vision. For us, it is a vision of our own times.

Chapter 52

A touch of magic

Mike Gonzalez

The writings of Gabriel García Márquez have been translated into every major language and have sold in their hundreds of thousands—particularly his great panoramic novel *One Hundred Years of Solitude*. Yet he insists that they are simply the stories his grandmother told him as a child in the provincial Colombian town of Aracataca.

It would be easy to see Márquez as a kind of folklorist trying to rediscover a lost world of rural innocence, some kind of 'dream time' long since lost. And it is true that his work is full of extraordinary events: beautiful girls with long green hair, others who levitate to their deaths amid clouds of butterflies, tattooed boys with enormous sexual longevity, doctors who eat grass. Perhaps they were all part of his grandmother's repertoire of legends, myths and magical recipes. Yet they are not simply nostalgic fantasies that belong to a distant past; they are responses to a reality which is also present in all of Márquez's work.

There is the reality of 'La Violencia', Colombia's 14 year long civil war that claimed 200,000 lives—a time when all forms of civic life were simply suspended, and the only form of politics was the agreed alternation of Liberals and Conservatives taking turns at the presidency. *In Evil Hour* records that endless 'state of siege' when the only change was the deterioration of a society symbolised by the rotting tooth of the town's mayor. The town dentist, whose son is a leader of the revolutionary forces, tries not to relieve the mayor's pain. When the truce is lifted, one character expresses relief that 'things are back to normal'.

The military dictators, from Stroessner of Paraguay to Somoza in Nicaragua, are represented in the central figure of *The Autumn of the Patriarch*. He tortures his opponents, murders the children who could expose

First published April 1997

his crooked lottery, sells bits of the harbour to American businessmen and employs a double to listen to the gossip in the streets. All of these things were reality. In such a world it was unwise to speak, except in metaphors; yet the people told stories, rewrote their history, and pictured a different world.

The setting for all Márquez's novels is a fictional community called Macondo. In a way it was a paradise where no one grew old or impotent. This was Latin America as the European colonists imagined it. But for the inhabitants of the place, there was no escape from utopia. Wherever they turned, there were impenetrable swamps and jungles, mountains or the sea. The world could invade—but no one could leave. *Leaf Storm* recounts the arrival of a US banana company. It enters like a whirlwind, builds a ghetto for the American personnel, prostitutes all the town's young women, exhausts the banana trees, then leaves as suddenly as it had arrived, leaving devastation in its wake. The banana workers who strike in *One Hundred Years of Solitude* are massacred and their bodies are 'disappeared'—a verb that is one of Latin America's few contributions to the universal language. Next day a plague of forgetfulness wipes their very existence away—like the 500 students killed in Mexico on the eve of the 1968 Olympic Games. But the popular memory is not so easily emptied—and their memory is preserved there and passed on from generation to generation.

Macondo's isolation is both real *and* metaphorical. New developments in technology and social life in the metropolitan centres arrive partially and illogically in the colonial world. At the beginning of *One Hundred Years of Solitude* a gipsy, Melquiades, arrives in Macondo. He brings extraordinary things on his annual visits—false teeth, ice, wonderful machines. Colonel Aureliano Buendia, patriarch of this curious utopia, watches his tricks with astonishment. He has spent years searching for the philosopher's stone that will turn lead to gold, and bring him the secret of life. When he sees the gipsy he knows that it has already been found—but has been kept from the inhabitants of Macondo.

Locked outside history, Macondo is condemned to be a kind of parody of another world which it can only imagine, but never reach. The false teeth, the ice, like the train that arrives unannounced one day, seem like miracles because the logic of social and economic development that has produced them is not visible from here. Progress itself never reaches Macondo, only the consumer goods that are the product of change. In the shanty towns around every Latin American city, the kids yearn for Nike Air shoes and a glimpse of Madonna. They all have televisions but millions are without clean water!

The community of Macondo is caught between a past it can't return to and a future that it cannot shape. It is also caught between two kinds of language and imagination. On the one hand, popular culture passes on the experience of the dispossessed through the myths and stories that preserve their history; on the other, the official history denies their experience. In *Chronicle of a Death Foretold* even the knowledge of a future event cannot help to avoid it. What the community sees as its fate is actually the consequence of material forces at work out of its sight. The church has no explanations to offer—the holy water is full of dead rats (*In Evil Hour*); the bureaucracy hides behind mounds of unread documents (in *Chronicle*); and political life is indefinitely suspended. So people wait—like the colonel waiting for his pension (in *Nobody Writes to the Colonel*).

Márquez's 'magical realism' testifies to the vitality of a popular consciousness that can see beyond an imprisoning reality and preserve a spirit of resistance in its songs, its jokes, its myths, which continually imagine a world turned upside down. That is the source of his colourful, extravagant and witty language. At the end of *One Hundred Years of Solitude* Macondo collapses and disappears; but its (hi)story is left behind, to inspire those who come after. Since Márquez always writes about history as it echoes in popular understanding, then it will, one day, provide the means not only to mock or parody the history of the powerful, but to place those who have been marginalised for so long back at its very heart.

Chapter 53

Taste of the blues

Pat Stack

The recent death of Rory Gallagher has robbed us of one of the finest bluesmen of the age. For many of us growing up in Ireland, Gallagher personified the moment when we first felt we were no longer living in some cultural backwater.

Like most of my friends I was infatuated by music from my early teens. The Beatles, the Stones and Dylan were our heroes, and we despised anything and everything connected with the Irish record industry.

The Irish scene was dominated by two strains: the showband, which was normally made up of ten to 15 young or not so young men dressed in identical suits who did murderous cover versions of British hit singles. And Country & Irish bands who would sing about geographical locations spanning from 'my old maw in Kentucky' to the closer to home 'road by the river that flows through Raheen'.

The only exception to all this was Them with Van Morrison, but they were from the North and that didn't really count, especially when one of the band was reported to have responded to a question about being Ireland's first rock group by saying, 'We're British.'

Rory was one of ours, born in Donegal, and brought up in our own home town, Cork.

When his first real band, Taste, burst onto the scene in the late 1960s we thought we'd died and gone to heaven. They were not some top ten bubblegum group, but were playing raw hard electric blues, the most hip music of the time.

Gallagher seemed capable of doing anything with a guitar, and with none of the accessories that many of his contemporaries began

First published July 1995

using. There were no wawa pedals or clever electronic gadgets to make the guitar produce unusual sounds, but still he produced them.

His trademark became a beaten up old Fender Stratocaster but he also played wonderful acoustic guitar, stunning bottleneck blues and—a highlight of most of his 1960s and 1970s concerts—an electric mandolin which he played on a song called 'Going to My Home Town' for which there was a clapping routine for his audience, all of whom seemed to know it instinctively.

Gallagher's recordings in that period were probably his best, and there is little doubt that his two finest albums were both live: *Live in Europe* and *Irish Tour 74*. This is because, in the great blues tradition, Gallagher was first and foremost a live performer.

His concerts were almost like family affairs, and we wouldn't dream of going to see him in anything other than check shirts, denim jackets and jeans, the uniform of the man himself. Gallagher was also a fine vocalist and a talented songwriter who eschewed the sort of gimmicks that helped bring fame to others. There was no setting fire to his guitar or smashing it against the amps.

Despite international success, there were none of the usual trappings of stardom. I had known him vaguely from childhood and I decided some years later, after a few pints at a concert in Brighton, that I would attempt to go backstage and remind him of our great friendship.

By the time I got past all the usual obstacles and got to the dressing room door I had sobered up considerably and realised that he probably wouldn't have a clue who I was. I was about to turn tail when the door opened and Gallagher was standing there. To my amazement he said, 'You're from Cork, aren't you? Come in.'

I stepped in to what I presumed was going to be a haven of sex, drugs and rock and roll to find four or five guys sitting around surrounded by vast quantities of bottled Guinness. He ended up giving me a lift to London, and an open invitation backstage if ever I was at his concerts.

For three or four years after that, whenever I saw him perform I would take him up on the offer. He could talk all day about music. We shared a passion for Dylan, but his real heroes were the great black blues men of the past. It was to them and their music that he remained loyal even when it became unfashionable to do so.

He never followed the path of Clapton, from blues master to middle of the road crooner, nor did he try to cash in on the loathsome heavy metal revival of his last years. He just carried on doing what he loved, and we loved him for it.

When Mick Taylor left the Rolling Stones, Gallagher was invited to join. He turned them down, and told me that he just couldn't see himself as a Stone, leading that sort of life, where the image and glamour become more important than the music. After a long gap I went to see him with a friend two or three years ago. The music was as good as ever. I don't know why, but I didn't go backstage and therefore never met him again.

I haven't a clue what politics Gallagher had, but his genius combined with his dedication to his art, his lack of airs, graces and pretensions, and his unwillingness to sink into the mire of showbiz, all rightly earned this exceedingly nice man the title 'The People's Guitarist'.

Chapter 54

The new opium?

Chris Harman

Every so often someone raises the question of why socialist papers like *Socialist Worker* and *Socialist Review* do not carry more on 'culture'. Unfortunately, it is often a misdirected question. For those who put it have rarely thought through what is meant by 'culture' and what socialist activity in this field can achieve.

What is culture?

There is a sense in which it is something which is not separable from life as a whole. For it is the totality of the ideas, language, attitudes and ways of seeing the world which guide people's behaviour in any society.

The criticism of culture is then the criticism of social life as a whole.

But there is also a narrower sense in which the word is used. In any society there are people who display an ability to tell stories, to make songs and poems, to create artefacts, which get a response from their fellows.

There is a close relation between culture in this narrow definition, meaning popular art, and culture in the wider sense. People listen to stories, like songs, admire paintings or laugh at jokes because these relate in some way or other to their everyday lives. The story holds their attention because its elements provide a heightened representation of their own fears and hopes; the poem or song expresses feelings which they cannot express themselves; the joke is funny because it pushes aspects of normal life to the point at which they appear ludicrous.

But popular art does not simply express people's wider experiences. It also influences how they react to these: stories, songs, poems or jokes help shape the frameworks through which they interpret their

First published April 1986

interaction with each other and with the natural world. It is a determinant of the 'common sense' which guides the behaviour of the mass of people in any society.

Control over this 'common sense' is a vital part of any ruling class defence. It has to attempt to find mechanisms which can incorporate certain elements in popular art and ban others. In feudal society the church hierarchy continually strove to integrate popular festivals into a religious framework which could control them. The rise of capitalism was accompanied by a conscious attempt by the puritan protagonists of the new social order to restructure, and if necessary to stamp out, old forms of popular entertainment. And in mature capitalism the control is pushed to its utmost limit, with a specialised sector of the economy producing 'popular culture' (radio, TV, film, newspapers and magazines, pop music, sport) in just the same way that other commodities are produced.

There is always some degree of contradiction involved in such attempts at control. You cannot shape people's experiences unless you relate to them. And in a class society some of those experiences are of greater or lesser degrees of class struggle. The medieval Catholic church had to relate to the feeling of impoverishment and oppression of the mass of peasants if it was to explain to them that such poverty and oppression were part of heaven's plan. The modern day popular newspaper has to talk about strikes and protests if it is to condemn them. Popular culture is always a combination of contradictory elements—of people's immediately lived experience of life in class society on the one hand, and of a general set of ideas which justify existing society on the other. The ablest practitioners of popular arts are those most able to deal with this contradictory situation.

It is not only the popular art of the masses that has to face up to such problems. So does that of the ruling class. Its members too need to be bolstered up by ideological certainty, by an account of society that justifies their role to themselves, by an art that soothes over the painful dilemmas they face.

Any successful ruling class attempts, by patronage, to draw to itself the ablest artists. This accomplishes three tasks for it: it provides itself with the best, most aesthetically satisfying or most entertaining art; it enables it to feel that it itself is the guardian of all civilised values; and it provides a mechanism for ensuring that the ablest practitioners of popular art see that their own advance depends upon not challenging the ruling ideology.

Ideology in general is always propagated by a hierarchy of practitioners. At the most popular level there are those who repeat as truisms isolated fragments of the ruling ideology ('there will always be rulers', 'human nature means things cannot be different', 'the wealthy provide work for the mass of us', and so on). Above those there are the low level professionals who are continually putting across such ideas in newspapers, on TV programmes or through the educational system. Finally, at the highest level there are the 'intellectuals' proper, whose 'learned' discussions in books, articles and lecture halls justify the arguments put across by those below.

The same hierarchy operates within the arts. There is 'high art', popular art and the culture of ordinary life.

The relationship between the three is not as simple as that in other areas of ideology.

On the one hand, the high degree of division of labour in an advanced capitalist society means that high art can become so specialised as hardly to relate at all to popular art: while the books of the right wing philosophy professor Roger Scruton can act as a reference point for the *Sun*'s most rabid political columnists, the works of a composer like Stockhausen hardly do the same for its popular music columnists.

On the other, the need of art to give expression to the contradictions within people's lives means that even art aimed mainly at the upper classes can challenge certain aspects of existing society.

There are important consequences for revolutionary socialists from this hierarchical structuring of art.

First, most of the time the sheer scale of resources at the disposal of the ruling class compared with those on our side means that the ruling class have no great difficulty in pulling the great majority of practitioners of popular culture into their orbit. Again and again young writers, musicians, playwrights or comedians emerge who put across a message of defiant hostility to the status quo, only to 'mature' into tame entertainers and artists for it.

This is not only because the ruling class controls the funds which alone can enable people to have the time to specialise in artistic production or because it controls the means by which they can find expression (the TV channels, film studios or publishing houses). It is also because in a society which is not in a state of pre-revolutionary ferment, most people take the main structures of ruling class power for granted and art which is going to be popular is art which does the same.

It is only when there is a great upsurge of class struggle that there is any great pull upon the mass of artists to move in a different direction—as was seen in 1917 and, on a much smaller scale, in 1968 in France or during the miners' strike.

It is complete voluntarist nonsense for socialists to imagine that on the terrain of a long drawn out defensive struggle by the working class (a war of attrition, or what Gramsci called 'a war of positions') we can somehow match the ruling class's resources by our own efforts and counter their domination in the field of popular culture.

Of course, particular socialist artists will do their best to wage their little bit of the struggle. They will try to attract other artists to what they are doing. But they will also have to recognise that, until the working class as a whole makes a massive move forward, their own efforts will hardly make more than a dent in the defences of the other side. And even the dent they make will reflect the limitations of the defensive war of attrition: they will find it much easier to give expression to the horrors of existing society than to the idea that working class self activity is the answer to those horrors.

Most of us are not artists. We are socialists who have to argue with people influenced by existing popular culture (and with the prejudices and stereotypes which it implants in our own consciousnesses). The best that *Socialist Worker* and *Socialist Review* can do is to help us in this task.

Here the most important thing will usually be stringent examination and criticism of things that popular culture expects us to take for granted. This means, for instance, looking at the covert assumptions that lie behind the representation of people's lives in soap operas, pointing out the hidden (often very reactionary) message of some of the most popular films or pop songs, being iconoclastic towards the most fashionable trends in comedy or music.

The point is not that we can win the battle against the mystifying effects of popular culture. Today it fulfils some of the tasks which religion played in the days of the young Marx. And, as he insisted, the only way to challenge such mystification completely was to challenge in practice the society that produced it. However, such considerations did not lead Marx to drop his atheism and join the church, nor should they lead socialists today to drop a critical attitude towards most of the products of popular culture and to join in its fan clubs.

The second consequence of the hierarchical structuring of art concerns our attitude to certain 'high art'.

This, by definition, is usually art which is well out of the reach of the great mass of workers. Bourgeois society provides them with neither the time nor the education to partake in it. From that it is easy to draw the conclusion that it is an elite product we should not have anything to do with.

Again and again people say the socialist press should not deal with films that are only shown at art cinemas, with serious novels or with Channel 4 programmes. Why talk about Tolstoy, the argument goes, when most people are watching Tottenham?

The argument is wrong—and not just because only 3 percent of adults go to football matches as opposed to more than 50 percent who read books (according to *Social Trends*, 1986). Much more importantly, the best of 'high art' attempts to provide an overall expression of the society in which we live. It can deepen your insight into that society and into the problems of people who live in it.

This by no means applies to all 'high art'. Much of it is self indulgent crap, expressing no more than a mystified view of bourgeois angst. But some of it is much more than this.

For instance, when the bourgeoisie was struggling against the old feudal order, much of the art provided an insight into the clash of great social forces which still remains fascinating today. This is true of the plays of Shakespeare, the novels of Walter Scott, Stendhal or Balzac, and the music of Beethoven.

Or again, look at some of the novels produced in the 1920s and 1930s when even whole sections of the bourgeoisie felt existing society was slipping into barbarism. The best writings of Dos Passos, of Dreisser, of Malraux, of Sartre, of Silone, of John Steinbeck, of James T Farrell, all attempted to come to terms with this state of affairs and in doing so provided insights which any socialist can still benefit from.

A rounded revolutionary socialist is not one who will simply dismiss out of hand such advances in understanding. He or she will, in principle, want to gain access to them, even if in practice time and other commitments do not make this possible.

This does not mean, let me hasten to add, that socialists adopt a school teacherish, superior attitude to other workers. We are not in the business of telling them they are ignorant because they have not read certain books. But it does mean that we encourage people to read rather than not to read, that we reject any form of workerist philistinism which rejoices in the denial to workers of the gains made by some bourgeois high art.

If we look at things in this way, we are in a position to see what publications like *Socialist Worker* and *Socialist Review* can and cannot do.

We can attempt to puncture the various cultural fads and fashions, showing how they encourage people to take for granted things that should be questioned.

We can direct people to the most relevant and accessible bits of 'high culture'. This, for instance, has been what *Socialist Review* has quite rightly done in the case of novelists with its 'Writers Reviewed' series. It is what *Socialist Worker* occasionally does when it reviews an art cinema film or a Channel 4 series.

Here very much the same considerations apply as in the putting across of socialist ideas. We have to begin, in *Socialist Worker*, with those things which are most accessible for people who are new to socialist discussion and argument, and then move on, in *Socialist Review*, to those that are more difficult.

Finally, we can give publicity to those few socialist artists who try to go further with some sort of artistic representation of the contradictions of existing society.

But in all this we have to understand our achievements will be modest. Our criticism will leave the bulk of culture, whether 'popular' or 'high', untouched. We will only have the most marginal of successes when it comes to overcoming the way in which capitalist society cuts the mass of people off from the advances of 'high culture'. Our socialist artists will only make small advances onto the vast terrain occupied by the bourgeoisie.

It is nonsense to talk of creating a 'counter-hegemonic' culture under capitalism. We will never have the resources to do that this side of the socialist revolution. What we can do is aim at a much more limited goal—to build on those experiences of struggle which lead people to begin to envisage a different sort of society. Such building involves challenging all the ideological presuppositions of existing society, including those embodied in both popular and high culture. But we cannot go beyond this to begin to create a socialist mass culture which will be a component in the 'common sense' of the mass of people until the bourgeoisie has been beaten in the economic and political struggle.

Let's do what we can do with our meagre resources, and not make the mistake of embarking upon grandiose schemes that lead nowhere.

Chapter 55

Violent disorder

Judith Orr

The tragic murder of toddler Jamie Bulger at the hands of two ten year old boys in February 1993 marked the beginning of the latest outcry about the dangers of screen violence. The effects of this case are still felt today in legislation and policy on film censorship. The scare began with the judge's summing up of the case which claimed the boys had been influenced by their viewing of violent videos, in particular the film *Child's Play 3*. These claims had a resonance largely as a result of an article by an eminent child psychologist, Elizabeth Newson. She claimed to have uncovered new evidence that kids could become violent after watching 'video nasties'.

Yet on closer examination this 'new' report was nothing more than a rehash of prejudice and subjective feelings which had been specially commissioned by the anti-abortionist Liberal MP David Alton as part of his campaign to create a new video classification: 'Not suitable for home consumption'. This would mean that hundreds of films would be banned from all homes, including the 70 percent which do not include children.

Even the police have dismissed any link between the Bulger murder and *Child's Play 3*, stating, 'If you are going to link this murder to a film, you might as well link it to *The Railway Children*.' But is there any evidence to support the now widely held view that some screen violence causes violence in society?

There is no evidence that films today are any more violent than in the past. Films like *Friday 13th* (1980), Stanley Kubrick's *Clockwork Orange* and Sam Peckinpah's *Straw Dogs* (both 1971) all included scenes of graphic violence which caused huge controversy on their release.

First published January 1996

Yet criticism normally hangs on the claim that the level of violence portrayed in entertainment is unprecedented. US presidential candidate Bob Dole has singled out gangsta rap and film directors Quentin Tarantino and Oliver Stone as particular culprits, while campaigning against the ban on assault weapons. As veteran Hollywood left winger Ed Asner has pointed out, 'Apparently Mr Dole thinks it's okay to carry a gun but not to write a song about it.' But it depends who's making the film or writing the song. Dole describes the Arnold Schwarzenegger blockbuster *True Lies* as 'family friendly', despite the fact that it has a higher body count in the first ten minutes than the whole of *Reservoir Dogs*. Schwarzenegger is a Republican supporter and his film is a patriotic homage to American world domination, with the slaughter of hundreds of Arabs played for laughs.

Recent films—coined 'kiss and kill' by the press—have created enormous debate about the roots of violence in society. The film makers themselves, whatever their motives, do not offer explanations that would satisfy many socialists. The analysis of *Natural Born Killers* director Oliver Stone reflects his film's title:

> I believe that all of us are born violent—we're natural born aggressors. We have a million year old reptilian brain with a neo-cortex of civilisation on top, but it's doing a bad job of concealing the aggression. Killing is a combination of genetics and environment. When I go to my son's school, I notice a lot of aggression in kids, a natural cruelty.

This idea that humans are nothing but animals with a thin veneer of civilisation on top feeds into the argument that screen violence causes real life violence. Both the *Guardian* and the *Independent* have parroted the claims that 50 to 100 'copycat' murders have been carried out as a result of people having watched *Natural Born Killers*. This is the sort of simplistic cause and effect explanation favoured by moral crusader Mary Whitehouse: 'Looking at the increase in crime figures before the advent of television and after it you will see evidence that television does have a direct effect.' This both feeds the common sense acceptance of a causal connection which has yet to be scientifically proven and encourages the view that violence in both art and life is a modern phenomenon.

The reality is that both are as old as society itself. A recent editorial in *Sight and Sound* magazine refers to the famous public readings that Charles Dickens gave in the 19th century, including:

> ...his rendition of *Oliver Twist* which lingered on the blood splattered weapon to which strands of Nancy's hair still clung. So powerful was

Dickens' performance that members of his audience regularly fainted and had to be carried out... [H]e became a target for the moralisers of the day, the art critic John Ruskin denouncing *Bleak House* for the number of deaths it flaunted and for its effect on readers.

Today there is replacement of scientific rigour with panic, exemplified by Elizabeth Newson: 'If we wait for the research to be 100 percent perfect it may be too late. It might already be too late.' Her abrupt about turn on her position on screen violence and willingness to throw science out of the window have shocked fellow professionals.

Much of the research does not stand up to close examination. A fascinating book by David Gauntlett, *Moving Experiences*, looks at the problems of many studies in the highly artificial situation of a laboratory. Here it is often obvious what the experimenter 'wants' to happen, so the subject's wish to be helpful can completely distort results. In one instance an experiment was set up which involved showing a short film to a child which portrayed someone hitting a plastic rocking doll. They were then shown an identical doll and watched to see if they would imitate the behaviour. On her first visit to the lab one four year old child commented, 'Look, mummy. There's the doll we have to hit.' As Gauntlett points out, this is the most obvious reaction to being shown into a room containing only a mallet and a rocking doll regardless of any other stimulus.

In one study, the amount of aggression displayed by subjects was significantly greater when someone who was apparently a karate enthusiast was watching than if they were being watched by someone who appeared to be in a pacifist group. People's assumptions and expectations affect their behaviour, which in itself undermines claims of simplistic cause and effect.

Gauntlett shows the variety of contexts in which violent acts can be portrayed—wife battering, revenge, riot, self defence, police violence against criminals—all of which give the violence a different significance and moral judgement. Thus any objective measurement is utterly futile. He also shows that 'anti-social acts with no point, no moral justification, are almost never portrayed as good, or their perpetrators left unpunished.' So far from violence being 'celebrated' or 'promoted' on our screens it is most often shown in a negative light.

Also screen violence is not particularly popular. Studies show that overall in the population only 3 percent of people list horror as their favourite film type. Young offenders have been shown to have the same viewing habits as non-offenders—putting soaps at the top of their television favourites.

Only one thing can be said for certain about violent films—no two people have the same reaction. None of us are blank pages waiting to be filled. We all have different sensitivities, social backgrounds, families and different experiences of discipline and violence in real life. It is impossible to make predictions about how different people from different cultures and in different situations will react to the same images.

Some like to make comparisons between advertising campaigns which purport to change viewers' buying habits and the cinema's influence. Yet advertisements are made with no other purpose than to attempt to change behaviour and still many people buy according to price, quality and personal preference. The idea that it might be easier to influence you to murder your parents than to persuade you to buy a soap powder deserves little serious attention.

Yet it has become the commonsense view that the 22 inch screen in the corner of the living room has more influence on people's lives than the real life experiences of unemployment, desperate poverty, abuse, the violence of the police and the state, religion or racism. That someone sits in front of a screen absorbing images like blotting paper and turns into a serial killer is, on the face of it, ridiculous. But this utterly reductionist approach characterises the debate and has resulted in a level of censorship in Britain which is greater than any other country in the Western world.

Censorship has always been stricter in cinema than in the theatre, though 'art house' and foreign films suffer the least restrictions. The violent *Man Bites Dog* was released on video uncut while *Reservoir Dogs* was held back. As the current censor explained, *Man Bites Dog* is not the same kind of issue because it will have a fairly narrow release, it's a subtitled film and I don't expect it to go very wide.' It is felt to be safe to allow the middle classes to watch any amount of violence, sex and subversion, but as soon as this is portrayed in a format that is seen to be accessible to the mass of the population it becomes dangerous.

So in the 1920s Eisenstein's great films of the Russian Revolution, *October* and *Battleship Potemkin*, were banned from general release. A special request from the London Film Society resulted in a private showing there but a similar request from the Workers' Stage and Film Guild was turned down.

Today videos are seen largely as entertainment for the working class and class bias seeps out of every attack on their availability. James Ferman, the chief censor, has talked of his big fear being the 'unclassified videos sold through car boot sales to council estates'. In the 1980s Britain had the biggest audience for videos in the world. The fear that the masses were gaining access to images they could not understand and would simply imitate was crystallised. Now films that have been shown uncut in the cinema are regularly banned from video release, cut or put on a higher rating.

After the passing of the Video Recordings Act in 1984 all videos had to be classified. All titles were removed from the shelves for classification and some like *The Exorcist*, *The Texas Chainsaw Massacre* and *Driller Killer* have simply never been returned. The current legislation covering newly released videos has been tightened up with an amendment agreed secretly between the home secretary, Michael Howard, and Labour leader Tony Blair.

Much as many of us abhor some of the images that are portrayed in some films, this sort of state censorship is not the answer. The state is never neutral. What David Alton thinks is perverted or unacceptable—an explicit guide to safe sex for gay men for example—may simply be educational or just fun. Any strengthening of state control of what we see, read or listen to should be resisted. The criterion will not be how violent are the images, but what's the moral, who is killing whom and why? It is at heart a deeply political judgement.

A recent book on censorship, *Censorship and the Permissive Society* by Anthony Aldgate, reveals how the strict controls over theatre and cinema of the 1950s was strained by the new wave of films produced in the early 1960s which looked at the reality of working class lives. Negotiations could go on for months over the use of words like 'bugger'. This word, the censor claimed, was 'freely used in such places as the public bars of provincial pubs' but not in front of men's wives. So even in the film *Saturday Night and Sunday Morning*, which was 'obviously designed for the factory worker section of society', it had to be cut.

Yet not all the cuts demanded were trivial. Of a gruelling portrayal of a backstreet abortion in *Alfie*, Trevelyan wrote, 'These are strong scenes, but they will probably be acceptable in the context, since they do make a valid point against abortion.' Abortion caused many problems for the censors in the period before legalisation. The abortion in *Saturday Night and Sunday Morning* caused concern precisely because it was successful. One of the BBFC script readers said, 'I have strong misgivings about the slap-happy and successful termination of pregnancy which seems to be very dangerous stuff for our younger X certificate customers.'

Homosexuality was also censored in the early 1960s. Of *Victim*, a film about the blackmail of a gay barrister played by Dirk Bogarde, Trevelyan requested cuts where the case for gay sex was 'too plausibly put and not sufficiently countered'.

Nowadays censors don't simply cut what they don't like. New

technology made it possible for Ferman to change the order of scenes in *Henry, Portrait of a Serial Killer*, giving a different understanding of the story in the video version. Such state interference in any film sets a dangerous precedent.

This is not because as socialists we in some way support violence, or that we think that anything the state wants to ban must be good. Nor do we think that all violent films are a valid reflection of and an insight into a violent society. A look along any video shop's shelves shows that many violent films are the most crudely produced films with little artistic merit and ultimately reactionary messages.

The portrayal of violence in itself is no way to judge the value of a film. More important are the artistic skills of the film makers and their motives. Does the film tell us anything about the human condition, does it shed light on the world we live in and its contradictions, does it do so convincingly, does it in any way challenge accepted values and notions, does it engage and stimulate you? A film need not have an overtly or consciously political agenda to be stimulating, inspiring or powerful, nor does it have to offer solutions or answers.

The psychology of a violent vigilante was the subject of both Michael Winner's *Deathwish* films and Scorsese's *Taxi Driver* yet the two films could hardly be more different. Winner executes a simplistic, voyeuristic and crude morality tale of righteous anger against criminals—usually hippies and blacks—and the liberals who are soft on them. In contrast Scorsese's film is a visually powerful look at the darker side of America distorted through the rear view mirror of De Niro's taxi and his alienated mind.

Socialists do not want to be a sort of left wing police—banning Michael Winner and *Rambo* instead of Tarantino. There is no abstract principle we can lay down about images that should be banned, even an image of something like a brutal gang rape. In the film *The Accused* the horrific scene of a gang rape shows the experience of rape from a woman's point of view and makes the subsequent attitude of the legal system to her ordeal all the more shocking.

We have nothing in common with those whose enthusiasm for censorship is rooted in a fear of what the mass of the population is capable of. John Major says, 'We should condemn a little bit more and understand a little bit less.' Far from worrying about the brutalisation of young children in society, many of those in the ruling class positively endorse it as a means of class rule. So while schools for children with behavioural difficulties close, money is poured into prisons. All society can offer are solutions which reflect the very values which are the root of the problems.

Love on the Dole, a film which looked at the hell of unemployment in the 1930s, was initially banned because it 'showed too much of the tragic and sordid side of poverty'. A closer look at the 'tragic and sordid side of poverty' might give some clues as to why children and adults sometimes have so little feeling of self worth, so little stake in society, that they carry out acts of violence against themselves and others. It is the barbarism of real life that is too much to bear.

However powerful, art, cinema and music are not the motors of society. The images of the horror of Auschwitz, Hiroshima and the charred bodies on the road to Basra were brought to our screens by 20th century capitalism, not 20th Century Fox. If we want to protect children from being the future victims or perpetrators of violence then, unlike those desperate for scapegoats, we will have to look beyond the television screen.

Science

Chapter 56

Where we came from

Chris Harman

[This was a review of *Origins Reconsidered: In Search of What Makes us Human* by Richard Leakey and Roger Lewin, and *Self Made Man and his Undoing* by Jonathan Kingdon.]

The question of human origins is of special interest to socialists. We are continually bombarded with two ideological approaches to the role of humanity in nature: the *idealist* views which see humans as semi-divine, completely separated from the animal world, whose duty is to purify our souls, and the *crude materialist* views which see humans as no more than machines or animals. One version of this latter view is sociobiology, which sees the horror of society encoded in the molecular make up of human genes; another is behaviourism, which sees humans as completely conditioned by the material environment.

Marx and Engels challenged both idealism and crude materialism, especially in *The German Ideology* and the *Theses on Feuerbach*. Their central point was that, although human beings are a material product of nature, through labour they react back upon it, changing both it and themselves.

Much later Engels extended the argument in *The Part Played by Labour in the Transition from Ape to Man*, combining it with Darwin's account of evolution to provide an explanation of how human beings evolved from ape like ancestors—and he did so in a way that even

First published June 1993

today is in some ways more satisfactory than Darwin's own account (published five years before Engels wrote).

Engels' argument was that there were four key stages in the development of humanity, each laying the ground for the next. For reasons we cannot know, certain ape like creatures began using two limbs only for walking, leaving their front paws free for other purposes. This allowed those paws to hold and shape things—to use tools—and so increasingly transform the natural world to their own needs through labour. Labour encouraged them to work together, to cooperate, and so to live in denser groups than previously. Finally, working and living in groups encouraged the development of language and, with it, consciousness.

Each of these stages fed back into the others—a growing reliance on labour made use of the hands ever more important and ruled out a return to four legged walking; living in dense groups demanded more successful food gathering and therefore more developed forms of tool making and labour; language and consciousness enabled social interaction to take place on a much wider scale and knowledge of different labouring techniques to spread. What is more, each stage transformed the biological animal itself, giving preferential chances of survival to those with certain physical features—a bone structure which made two legged walking easy, a forehand anatomy that made it easy to grasp and manipulate things, a jaw and mouth cavity shape which permitted the making of a large range of different sounds, and a large brain capable of processing much more information than before.

Labour was the key to explaining the interaction of the stages for Engels. Without it two legged walking may have been a passing phase, social interaction would have remained at a fairly low level, language would never have gone beyond a few grunts and gestures, and the brain would never have grown bigger than that of the chimpanzee. 'Labour is the prime basic condition for all human existence, and to such an extent that we have to say that labour created man himself.'

But how do Engels' ideas stand up today? After all, he wrote at a time when archaeological research into the physical make up and cultural artefacts of our ancestors was in its infancy. It would not be surprising if he was completely out of date. Neither of these books mentions Engels. Yet the material in both of them shows he was far from being off beam.

Richard Leakey is from a family that has been responsible for some of the most important East African discoveries of human remains from up to three million years ago. He wrote an excellent book 15 years ago with Roger Lewin, *Origins*, which drew together the then existing knowledge about our forebears. Its message, as he puts it, was that:

> Contrary to much popular wisdom, the human species is not driven to violence... Human behaviour is flexible in the extreme. Humans do not march in lockstep to the demands of aggressive genes... There is no evidence of frequent violence or warfare in human prehistory until after about 10,000 years ago, when humans began to practise food production—the leading edge of agriculture... Evolutionary history has endowed our species with an inclination to cooperate. Homo sapiens has a greater flexibility of behaviour, a broader range of choice—and therefore of responsibility—than any other species. Much of the conflict in the world can be traced to materialism and cultural misunderstanding, not to our biological nature.

This was not, of course, Marxism. Missing was the centrality of class struggle once there was full agricultural production. But it was a starting point for an account of humanity that no serious Marxist could dissent from.

The new book sets out to incorporate into the account of human origins some of the most recent archaeological discoveries (some by Leakey himself). These overthrow some of the contentions of the previous work, but leave its central message untouched. The result is a very useful and readable survey of what is known right across the field, and provides a useful introduction to all its controversies (such as when the human line separated from that of our ape cousins, the origins of language and culture, whether all preceding varieties of humans died out when anatomically modern humans spread across the globe, probably starting from Africa 150,000 years or so ago, or whether there was intermixing). In each case Leakey is careful not only to state his own view, but to present alternatives fairly.

For me there were only two faults with the book. First, a minor irritation: a certain 'journalistic slant' to some parts of it leads to too much on Leakey as an individual (as when he describes flying his plane to Lake Turkana in the first chapter). Secondly and much more seriously, when he attempts to account for the growth in the human brain and mental abilities, he shifts in part away from a stress on labour and tool making. He accepts a currently fashionable argument that the brain grew out of the need to cope with complex social interactions.

But this leaves aside the cause of the growth of such interactions themselves—which leads back to the question of labour. It also underestimates the degree of advance humans have made over all other mammals in their ability to cope with a vast range of different ecological circumstances. Our ancestors may have been able to sustain themselves in limited niches in East Africa on the basis of the tool making possible with a brain size and mental capacity much smaller than that of modern humans—indeed, there is evidence that some early hominids did survive like this for hundreds of thousands or even millions of years. But they would hardly have been able to move out to colonise most of the rest of the world, as they had by a quarter of a million years ago.

Jonathan Kingdon makes this point, and does so well. For him, labour and tool making are the key to human evolution. And he uses his enormous knowledge of the lives of the mammals who would have inhabited East Africa alongside our ancestors—and competed with them for resources—to back up his argument.

His book, however, is weaker than Leakey's in many other respects. He gives only his own view on most of the controversial subjects, and he sometimes treats what are no more than hypotheses—sometimes very doubtful ones—as truths. He projects back into prehistory forms of social behaviour typical of class societies, especially war. And he spends an inordinate amount of space developing a speculative theory about the origin of that most superficial difference between humans, skin colour.

Nevertheless, the two books together are very useful in helping us to challenge the confusions still engendered by religious hangovers and by talk of the 'selfish gene', the 'naked ape' and the 'territorial imperative'.

Chapter 57

Star wars

Paul McGarr

In 1543 a little book by Nicolaus Copernicus was published in Germany. A century and a half later, in 1687, Isaac Newton in England published his work *Principia*.

The period marked by these dates has been rightly termed 'the scientific revolution'. It saw the breakdown of the old view of the universe dominated by religious dogma and the birth of modern science.

There had been all sorts of theories and ideas about the universe in earlier times. For instance, in the 3rd century BC a Greek called Aristarchos had a theory in which the earth went round the sun. But given the level of observational technique and the nature of society at the time, it could not compete with the dominant theories which derived from the Greek philosopher Aristotle and later Ptolemy in Egypt.

Aristotle's science was in part a simple reflection of everyday experience. He argued that objects did not move unless acted on by some force.

He also claimed the earth was the unmoving centre of the universe and that things had a natural place to which they tended to move. So fire rises and stones fall. The approach is a crude reflection of everyday observation.

This picture only applied to the world below the orbit of the moon. Above that, in the realm of the planets, sun and stars, things were different. Here was the realm of divine harmony where the laws on earth did not apply. Everything was unchanging and perfect.

The problem was this theory didn't fit observed facts. For example, if you look at the path of Mars in the sky it doesn't move uniformly at all,

First published September 1988

even seeming to go into reverse at one point in the year. Such problems caused some to try and construct theories to 'save the appearances'.

The culmination of such efforts came in the 2nd century AD with Ptolemy in Egypt. He constructed a sophisticated mathematical model which did the job. The earth was at the centre and the planets and sun revolved around it in a complicated series of circles upon circles.

These theories were the orthodoxy in Europe in the time of Copernicus over 1,000 years later.

By then the Roman Empire had disintegrated into localised feudal statelets, based on the forced extraction of surplus from the peasantry. Within these societies, especially after the turn of the millennium, there were two important developments—the growth of towns and of revolts from below, both of which represented potential challenges to the existing structure of society.

In such circumstances ideological justification of the status quo was extremely important for the ruling class. The Catholic church, itself a key landowner and exploiter, was the vehicle for this. This is where astronomy came in.

Of course, peasants didn't need to understand astronomy. But they did need to know that the universe and their place in it were constructed according to a divine plan which couldn't be changed. To rebel would be pointless and indeed sinful.

The same applied to other challenges to the existing structure of society, such as from the new classes based on trade and commerce in the towns. And any ruling class needs an ideology which justifies its own position to itself. Thus Aristotle's theories, though banned by the church earlier, came to dovetail with what was needed.

Aristotle's distinction between the laws on earth and those in the heavens implied you could not infer from experience on earth general truths about the universe. Enquiry and real knowledge were denied. A number of factors contributed to the breakdown of this orthodoxy, and to the breakdown of feudal society generally.

First was the destabilising influence of the towns. New forms of wealth and new classes grew, accommodating to existing society at first but nevertheless undermining aspects of it. There was also the growth of absolutist centralised states which attempted to restabilise feudal society while adapting it to a different and changing world.

New ways of thinking became possible because new social structures were evolving, the Renaissance and the Reformation being reflections of this. At a more fundamental level there were also big changes in the forces of production.

It is worth emphasising this because most academic discussion of the 'scientific revolution' concentrates on ideas alone, omitting that those changing patterns of thought depended on changes in the way human beings interacted with and worked on nature.

In the period leading up to the scientific revolution, the padded collar and horseshoe transformed the horse into a useful beast. Increasing trade and commerce led to better navigation and time-keeping techniques. The blast furnace and printing were developed in the 15th century, the first improving the tools that could be made, the second having a fantastically subversive effect on a rigid feudal society.

Also 1608 saw the first use of the telescope—significantly, for military purposes.

It is in a society in which such changes are taking place, giving rise to tensions in the old social structures, that the 'scientific revolution' is located.

In 1514 Nicolaus Copernicus was invited by the church to give his opinion on the question of calendar reform since the old Ptolemaic system no longer fitted. He tried to develop a simpler, more accurate system putting the sun at its centre.

When he gave lectures on his theory in Rome in 1533, the pope approved of it as a calculating device.

In fact Copernicus's system was neither more accurate nor simpler than Ptolemy's, but it attracted support because it was a breach with the old orthodoxies.

Copernicus's system meant that Aristotle's explanation for falling bodies was no good and a new one would have to be found—the road to Newton's theory of gravity was opened. Also, if the earth was no longer special then the whole notion of the laws on earth and in the heavens being different was shaken.

The demolition of the old way of looking at the world took another century to complete. This was the period of the Reformation, Counter-Reformation, the Thirty Years War and bourgeois revolutions in Holland and England. The key figures, in the scientific revolution of this period, were Tycho Brahe, Johannes Kepler and Galileo Galilei.

Johannes Kepler was Brahe's assistant and successor, and the decisive figure in the 'scientific revolution'. A dislocated individual in a crisis torn society, he spent several years living in poverty, and in central Europe as it was being ravaged by religious struggles and the Thirty Years War.

His early ideas were characterised by wild speculative theories. One explained the layout of the planets in terms of musical notes.

But later he made a number of important breakthroughs towards a scientific approach.

Firstly, he was prepared to ditch theories if they didn't fit the facts. Secondly, he saw theories as explanations for the way things really were, not just as calculating devices. And third and most importantly, he looked for explanations of planetary motion in terms of the experience of moving bodies on earth.

This is the decisive step in the scientific revolution. Real knowledge becomes possible on the basis of generalising and abstracting from our immediate experience.

Kepler drew on work by a man called Gilbert on magnetism (itself connected with the need for better navigation to help trade and commerce), and tried to explain planetary motion as due to magnetic force. He was wrong but that is secondary. It is the method that is crucial. The attempt to generalise from experience involved in Kepler's approach lays the basis for Newton and his famous apple.

The final steps in the breakdown of the old dogmas were the work of Galileo Galilei.

He systematically used experiments to try and learn about the world. After learning of the telescope in 1609 he built one and turned it to the sky. What he saw was the final nail in the coffin of the old world view.

The heavens were far from perfect and unchanging. The surface of the moon was irregular, Jupiter had satellites, comets wandered irregularly through the solar system. And, worst of all, the sun had spots!

However, the acceptance and development of Kepler and Galileo's new ideas depended on two factors.

The first was whether they worked, whether the new theories of astronomy helped navigation, allowed better timekeeping and so on. This is the ultimate test of any ideas which claim to be scientific. But their acceptance also depended on the outcome of struggles over the structure of society—that is, the outcome of class struggles. This is illustrated by what happened to Kepler and Galileo.

The very crisis which allowed new ideas to be developed also produced a reaction among those concerned to defend the status quo. Copernicus had been well received by the pope in 1533. A year later the Jesuits and the Roman Inquisition were formed as the shock troops of the Counter-Reformation.

This reaction to the religious dissent unleashed by Martin Luther in 1517 had been slow in developing, but when it arrived it was vicious.

Religious conflicts, a reflection of the clash between the old feudal order and a new bourgeois society, turned Europe upside down. There were bloody civil wars like that in France in the late 16th century, and then from 1618 to 1648 the Thirty Years War which ravaged central Europe.

Kepler and Galileo were a product of this crisis, but also the victims of reaction trying to reimpose order and orthodoxy. Kepler's work was banned by the Catholic church in the 1620s and the Jesuits denounced Galileo's work as 'more dangerous than the teaching of Luther and Calvin put together', which is a bit like Reagan saying someone is worse than the Ayatollah and Colonel Gadaffi combined!

Galileo was particularly dangerous because he wrote in ordinary Italian, rather than the elitist Latin. He was convicted of heresy, forced to recant, and spent the last year of his life under house arrest. But though reaction tried to roll back new ideas in much of Europe, it did not succeed everywhere.

The invention of printing meant that ideas now had a far wider circulation than ever before. In the years that followed, in the mid-17th century, the scientific revolution was taken up and completed in two places in particular.

The first was in Holland, where the 'free' printing presses of the bourgeoisie were crucial in keeping ideas alive, and secondly in England by people such as Isaac Newton. In other words, in those countries where the crisis of the old order had not resulted in the victory of reaction.

Where bourgeois revolutions had taken place a new more dynamic society was being built, a society which would transform the world taking up and developing science as a key part of that process.

Chapter 58

Good breeding?

Phil Gasper

Eugenics—the idea that it is possible to use scientific knowledge to breed 'better' human beings—is back. Developments in technique over the past decade or so have given geneticists much greater knowledge of the specific genes—segments of the DNA in our cells—that are involved in the production of various biological effects. The successes of the new genetics have led to a revival of the idea that everything important about us is determined by our biological inheritance.

This ignores the fact that even most physical diseases are not genetically determined, and that there is not a shred of convincing evidence that any complex human behaviour is biologically hardwired. Indeed, quite the contrary is true.

Lack of evidence, however, has done nothing to stop researchers making a series of well publicised claims that everything from intelligence to alcoholism and from criminality to homosexuality is genetically determined.

One of the implications of such claims is that social problems are not due to the way that society is structured—the distribution of income and wealth, for example, or access to jobs, healthcare and education—but are the consequence of defective individuals. The solution is thus not to change society but to improve the population through biological manipulation. In a recent editorial in *Science Magazine* Daniel Koshland explicitly drew this conclusion, claiming that genetic research can help to eliminate problems such as drug abuse, homelessness and violent crime.

The term 'eugenics'—which literally means 'good birth'—was

First published September 1994

originally coined by Charles Darwin's cousin, Francis Galton. In his most famous book, *Hereditary Genius*, Galton attempted to demonstrate that intelligence is inherited by tracing the genealogies of well known English families and showing that, generation after generation, the members of such families tended to acquire prestigious social positions. The alternative explanation, that what is inherited is not intelligence but access to social power and influence, seems not to have occurred to him.

Since biological explanations assume that existing inequalities reflect fundamental facts about human nature, it is not surprising that Galton reached racist conclusions. He claimed that 'the average intellectual standard of the negro race is some two grades below our own.' A few years later he wrote that 'the Jews are specialised for a parasitical existence upon other nations.'

Eugenics was adopted most enthusiastically in the United States. One of the principal advocates was the Harvard biologist Charles Davenport, a serious scientist who demonstrated the heritability of eye, skin and hair colour. But he was obsessed by the idea that our destiny lies in our genes. He claimed, for example, that the capacity to be a naval officer is an inherited trait, composed of two subtraits: thalassophilia (love of the sea) and hyperkineticism (wanderlust). Because there were no women in the navy, Davenport concluded that the trait is unique to males.

Davenport's tendency to assume a genetic basis for nearly everything would be amusing if the consequences had not been so tragic. Against evidence that pellagra—an often deadly disease that was at epidemic proportions in the Southern US—was caused by dietary deficiencies, Davenport (who was also head of the US Pellagra Commission) argued that there was a genetic susceptibility to the disease. Successive administrations used Davenport's false claims to avoid spending money on nutritional programmes. As a result, hundreds of thousands died unnecessarily between 1915 and the mid-1930s.

Like other eugenicists, Davenport held that characteristics such as 'pauperism', 'criminality' and 'feeble mindedness' are biologically inherited. On this basis the eugenics movement encouraged nearly 30 states to enact laws permitting the forced sterilisation of thousands of people in prisons and mental hospitals who were judged to be defective.

Eugenicists in the US also urged the federal government to restrict the immigration of 'undesirable' races. Their arguments dovetailed with those of psychologists like H H Goddard and Lewis M Terman, who developed the first standardised intelligence tests. These tests reflected the racist and cultural biases of their designers. Even when testing led to the conclusion that half the US population—including most blacks and immigrants from Southern and Eastern Europe—were of sub standard intelligence, the results were taken seriously. Terman advocated vocational training and placement for such unfortunates, warning that they could 'drift easily into the ranks of the anti-social or join the army of Bolshevik discontents'.

Others went further. Carl Brigham of Princeton University testified to Congress that 'American intelligence is declining, and will proceed with an accelerating rate as the racial admixture becomes more and more extensive'. Politicians relied heavily on such pseudo-scientific nonsense to justify passage of the viciously racist Immigration Restriction Act of 1924.

By the early 1930s leading eugenicists were praising Nazi race laws. In fact the Nazis themselves based their laws on those already passed in the US. Frederick Osborn, secretary of the American Eugenics Society, wrote, 'The German sterilisation programme is apparently an excellent one. Taken altogether, recent developments in Germany constitute perhaps the most important social experiment which has ever been tried.'

In 1935 the American Eugenics Society argued that 'crime and dependency keep on increasing because new defectives are born, just as new cancer cells remorselessly penetrate into sound tissue.'

Two years later Charles R Stockard, president of the board of the Rockefeller Institute for Medical Research, warned that the human race faced 'ultimate extermination' unless 'low grade and defective stocks' could be 'absolutely prevented' from reproducing. Eugenicists in the US were advocating the sterilisation of millions of Americans right up until 1940.

The disgusting idea that society's problems are due to biologically inferior individuals played an important role in paving the way for the massive barbarism of the Nazi Holocaust. But, largely because the Nazis took these ideas to their logical extreme, the eugenics movement was discredited for a generation after the end of the Second World War.

Biological determinism first began to make a comeback in the late 1960s as part of the ruling class response to the movements for social change in the US and elsewhere. In 1969 Arthur Jensen, a professor at Stamford, published a paper arguing that blacks are innately less intelligent than whites. Jensen's article, however, was soon subjected to withering criticism. The most devastating blow came in the mid-1970s when it was shown that research by the British psychologist Sir Cyril Burt, purporting to demonstrate that intelligence has a high degree of heritability, had been faked.

A second wave of biological determinism was soon launched with the development of sociobiology. E O Wilson and others claimed that evolutionary theory provides the key to understanding human behaviour. They argued that certain patterns of behaviour—such as hostility to outsiders, competition and male domination—were advantageous in the past and were now coded into our genes.

Ideas like this were taken up by the mass media. *Business Week* published an article entitled 'A Genetic Defense of the Free Market' which claimed that 'self interest is the driving force in the economy because it is ingrained in each individual's genes'. Sociobiology was also enthusiastically embraced by far right and Nazi groups.

The claims of sociobiology are not only flawed, they are not consistent with the huge variability of human societies through history. Not every human society has exhibited the same sexual division of labour as our own, for example. Indeed, there has been tremendous cultural evolution in the past few thousand years which cannot be explained in biological terms.

We are now confronted by a third wave of revived biological determinism, a product of the new genetics and the continued need for the ruling class to search for explanations of social crisis that do not question the established order.

In the US, for example, the National Institute of Mental Health (NIMH) and the Centre for Disease Control have spent tens of millions of dollars on the 'Violence Initiative'. This project aims to study the biological roots of violence. Unsurprisingly, its subjects are not the Pentagon or the Los Angeles Police Department, but young blacks.

The claims of the genetic determinists are scientifically worthless, but politicians will use them in an effort to justify right wing policies on a whole range of social issues, from crime to education. The reemergence of such ideas at a time when fascists have entered a Western European government for the first time since 1945 is particularly ominous. For this reason, these ideas must not go unchallenged.

But the challenge to these ideas cannot simply be an intellectual one, because science itself does not develop in a vacuum. It is not simply that under capitalism the fruits of science are frequently used by the minority who run society to dominate and exploit, although this is certainly true. For example, the most likely outcome of recent genetic research will be new forms of discrimination in employment and insurance, not cures for debilitating diseases. Social and political forces directly or indirectly affect the kinds of questions that are asked, the presuppositions that guide research and the interpretation of experimental results. In capitalism, the forces which shape science predominantly represent the power and interests of the ruling class. Those interests include a need to mystify the way in which society really functions. That is why the ideas of biological determinism constantly reappear, despite their lack of intellectual merit.

If we want to defeat biological determinism and its offspring, eugenics, we have to argue against its ideas while simultaneously attacking its material roots.

Chapter 59

More than its parts

John Baxter

The Human Genome Project is the biggest scientific project since the space race. In the US its managers are planning a budget of $200 million a year for the next 15 years. The project is an attempt to chemically map a typical human's genes. Genes consist of DNA, a complex chemical that consists of a long series of chemical units called bases. The order of the bases specifies the composition of proteins in the body. A single gene contains the DNA specifying the composition of a single protein. The ultimate aim of the Human Genome Project is to define the order of the three billion bases contained in human DNA.

The project was launched almost simultaneously in two competing American institutions—in both cases for reasons of prestige and profit. In 1984 the University of Santa Cruz had just lost a bid to build a giant telescope. It was casting around for another big money, prestige project and it hit upon the Human Genome Project. The nuclear research laboratories of the American Department of Energy (DOE) were also looking for new work. The end of the Cold War meant that much of the money for nuclear weapons research was drying up. The DOE also had some experience of research in human genetics—it did the research into the effects of radiation on human genes.

Vast fortunes will be made, not least by the leading scientists who run the project. These are not disinterested searchers after truth. Biotechnology companies, the companies which exploit the new genetic technology, have developed directly out of university research labs. Almost without exception the leading molecular biologists have prominent positions in these companies, which stand to reap huge benefits.

First published September 1994

The project is the practical outcome of the idea that everything worth knowing about human beings is determined by, or at least limited by, the genes. Put at its simplest the idea is that the so called universal features of human nature—heterosexuality, selfishness, violence in men or submissiveness in women—are carved in our genes.

Medical conditions like cancer and heart disease are treated in the same way. It may well be that these diseases have a genetic component. But genes do not cause cancer or heart attacks. Cancer generally develops after exposure to triggers like radiation or certain chemicals. Heart disease is brought on by poor diet and stress.

The idea that the actions and biology of human beings can simply be reduced to the structure of their genes is an example of reductionism. This is a form of logic which says that to understand anything we have to break it down into its smallest parts. To understand the properties of matter we break it down into molecules and atoms.

We can trace the rise of reductionism to the bourgeois revolutions of the 17th and 18th centuries. Before this time the natural philosophers who looked at nature saw it as one mystical whole. Everything was ordained by god and the job of the natural philosopher was to try to understand the world god had created.

Under the emerging capitalist society a new view arose. The new factories needed individuals who were free to sell their labour. Society was seen as being made of atomised individuals free to move from role to role. The properties of society resulted from the sum of the properties of the individuals. The new science mirrored this view. Rather than seeing nature as a mystical whole, it saw nature as something which could be explained by breaking it down into its constituent parts. This way of thinking has to a large extent persisted to the present.

Explaining where reductionism comes from is not the same thing as proving that it is wrong. Indeed reductionism has proved tremendously powerful at tackling simple systems. But it falls down when dealing with complex systems.

An alternative way of approaching genetics has been outlined by Steven Rose, R C Lewontin and others in the dialectical biology group. Instead of making DNA the master molecule and describing genes as *making* proteins, they describe genes as simply a part of a complex biochemical system. By themselves genes make nothing. It is only by them interacting with the other chemicals inside the cell that proteins are produced. In turn, which proteins are synthesised and which are not is determined by a complex dialectical interaction between the cell and its environment.

The reductionist philosophy behind the Human Genome Project leads to a number of problems. The first is trying to sequence *the* human genome. But there is no one single genome. Every human being has a unique genetic constitution. If gene sequencing is to lead to detection of inherited conditions then it would have to compare the genomes of thousands of individuals before it could pick out which differences are significant and which are not—a waste of time and money.

More efficient, targeted techniques exist which have already pinpointed the genes for a number of simple inherited conditions like cystic fibrosis. Rather than wading through the billions of bases of DNA, targeted techniques start from the symptoms of the disease and work back to the genetic errors.

This type of research has already yielded valuable results. It has also demonstrated that reductionist logic in its simplest form is wrong. Haemophilia B is an inherited condition which can be traced to a single gene. So far the reductionist logic works. But if we follow the logic we would predict that there would be a single error on the gene. Not so. In fact research in Sweden has shown that in 216 individuals 115 different chemical errors lead to indistinguishable symptoms. If 115 different errors lead to the same disease, what hope is there of finding the relevant mistakes in the three billion bases of human DNA?

It is claimed that the Human Genome Project will lead to a greater understanding of inherited conditions and therefore to their treatment. But greater understanding doesn't necessarily lead to treatment. Fibrosis is a single gene inherited condition which is very well understood, but treatments are still far from satisfactory. In fact medical advances have often come without any great understanding. In the 1940s scientists found that certain chemicals killed bacteria but not human beings. Antibiotics were born. It was 40 years before they began to understand how they worked.

Eventually some treatments may emerge out of the project. But more efficient, targeted methods exist which could achieve the same results. The project receives backing because it reinforces ruling class ideas about the world, and because governments and big business are frightened of being left behind in the biotechnology race.

In a sane society genetic research would be carried out to help humanity, not to feed the coffers of huge institutions. Research would be carried out without a multitude of competing research groups ploughing through an unimaginable number of chemical bases, many of which are irrelevant.

Socialists don't oppose all genetic research. The work on cystic fibrosis means women can now make an informed choice about whether to continue with a pregnancy. However, under capitalism such choices are often not free.

Genetic engineering has allowed scientists to programme bacteria to produce vital human proteins like insulin, clotting factors and growth factors vital in the treatment of a number of diseases. The fact that they are produced by giant biotechnology companies means that exorbitant prices are charged.

Without the developments of science and technology socialism would be impossible. Genetic science can increase our understanding of the way our bodies work and can increase our ability to shape the world around us. But until science is controlled democratically, by the vast majority in the interests of the majority, much of our human ingenuity will be wasted.

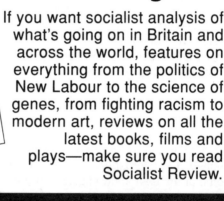